Annotations on
The Gospel According to St. John
The Lutheran Commentary Volume V

By Adolph Spaeth

Annotations on the Gospel According to St. John
The Lutheran Commentary Volume V

Though the original text is in the public domain, regarding this updated edition, no part of this publication may be reproduced, stored or transmitted in any form or by any means, electronic, mechanical, photocopying, recording, scanning, or otherwise without written permission from the publisher. It is illegal to copy this book, post it to a website, or distribute it by any other means without permission.

Paperback ISBN: 978-0-692-73003-4
Hardcover ISBN: 978-1-952295-78-2

Just & Sinner
Ithaca, NY 14850
JustandSinner.org

TABLE OF CONTENTS

Preface 7

Prolegomena 9

    I. Introductory Remarks 9

    II. The Life and Personal Character of the Apostle John 10

    III. The Gospel of St. John 14

First Part.—Chapters 1–4 43

The Beginning of Faith in the Incarnate Word, as the Absolute Revelation of God 43

John 1 44

    I. The Opening Section, 1:1–18 ("The Prologue") 44

    II. The Testimony of John the Baptist (1:19–34) 52

    III. The First Disciples of. the Lord (John 1:35–51) 59

John 2 63

    IV. The First Sign (John 2:1–11) 63

    V. The First Prophecy of the Lord Concerning His Death and Resurrection (John 2:12–25) 66

John 3 70

    VI. The Conversation with Nicodemus (3:1–21) 71

    VII. Jesus in Judæa and the Last Testimony of John the Baptist (3:22–36) 81

John 4 87

    VIII. Samaritan Faith (4:1–42) 87

    IX. Galilean Faith (4:43–54) 97

Second Part. Chapters 5-12. 102

John 5 103

I. The Beginning of the Conflict in Judæa (5:1–47) 103

John 6 113

II. The Crisis in Galilee 113

John 7 124

III. The Conflict in Jerusalem again taken up (ch. 7, 8) 124

1. Jesus the Fountain of Life (7:37–52) 129

John 8 133

2. Jesus the Light of the World (8:12–20) 134

3. The Lifting up of the Son of Man (8:21–30) 135

4. Last Words on and after the Feast of Tabernacles (8:31–59) 137

John 9 144

The Conflict with the Unbelieving Jews Reaching its Climax (Ch. 9 to 12) 144

I. The Healing of the Man Born Blind (Ch. 9) 144

John 10 151

II. The Discourses Following the Healing of the Man Born Blind (Ch. 10) 151

John 11 161

III. The Raising of Lazarus.—The Crisis in Judæa (ch. 11) 161

John 12 176

IV. The End of the Public Ministry of Christ (Ch. 12) 176

Third Part. Chapters 13–21 191

John 13 192

I. Historical Introduction to the Parting Discourses of the Lord (13:1–30) 192

II. First Parting Words Addressed to the Eleven (13:31–14:4) 198

John 14 201

III. Further Interruptions of the Disciples Answered by the Lord (14:5–11) 202

IV. The Parting Words Continued (14:12–31) 205

John 15 214

V. New Parting Discourse (Ch. 15 and 16) 214

John 16 226

John 17 242

VI. The High Priest's Prayer 242

John 18 258

The Triumph of Faith Continued in the History of the Passion and Resurrection of the Lord 258

I. The Capture of Jesus (18:1–11) 258

II. Jesus before the High Priest (18:12–27) 262

III. Jesus Before the Governor Pilate (18:28–19:16) 267

John 19 274

IV. The Execution (19:17–42) 278

John 20 290

V. The Resurrection of Jesus (Ch. 20) 290

John 21 311

VI. Appendix. The Appearance of Christ at the Lake of Galilee (21) 311

Synopsis of the Gospel of John 327

I. Introductory Remarks

PREFACE

The treatment of the Gospel of St. John as presented in this volume of the Lutheran Commentary is in some respects different from the volumes which have thus far appeared.

In the introduction the points referring to the Isagogics of this Gospel have received somewhat fuller consideration. The writer endeavored to give a brief survey of those features which are peculiarly characteristic of the fourth Gospel, and to show its relation to the other Gospels, the three Synoptists.

The question of authorship has also been taken up in a brief summary, furnishing the reader with the principal testimonies in favor of the Apostle St. John as the writer of this Gospel. This has been done without a full "review of the battle that may be raging" about this point, but in such a manner that the lay-members of the Church may have within easy reach, a short survey of the main question, and the leading arguments on the positive side. In view of the overtowering importance of the fourth Gospel for the faith of the Christian Church, we did not feel justified in passing this point in silence.

The exposition of the Gospel itself does not propose to give a detailed explanation of the words of the text, in a series of exegetical annotations from verse to verse. It rather aims to set forth the contents of this most organic of all the Gospels, in one continuous argument. Though the style and language of this exposition may sometimes approach that of the homily rather than that of a Commentary, the results here presented are based on careful and conscientious exegetical studies, covering the most prominent publications in the field of the exegesis of this Gospel, down to the exposition of the Gospel of St. John by Professor F. W. Bugge of Christiania, Norway. This last named work, which came into the author's hands after two-thirds of this exposition were written, has been a great encouragement to him. For what is offered in Bugge's

Preface

commentary, the writer had planned to present in a somewhat briefer and simpler form, "a psychological exposition, which, without learned discussions and excursus seeks to follow the one continuous thread which runs through the whole Gospel."

Some years ago the author delivered a course of seven lectures on the Gospel of St. John for the American Institute of Sacred Literature, in Philadelphia. Some of these "Studies" were published in the Lutheran Church Review and are substantially incorporated into this volume.

A. S.

PROLEGOMENA

I. Introductory Remarks

It has been well said by Dr. M. Luther: "Let every Christian exert himself to understand well the Gospel of John and to be posted in it; for John is the master-evangelist and his Gospel the one, true, tenderest chief Gospel, a commentary and exposition of the whole Bible."

Nor can we for a moment be in doubt concerning the influence and importance of this Gospel in the history of the Church. While it is true that Paul "labored more abundantly than they all" in the missionary field, gathering, organizing and building up the churches by his preaching and his epistles, it is equally true that John gave to the Church that clear consciousness of being a communion of believers, with one confession in which everything centres in the one mystery of God incarnate. Take away the Gospel of John and where is our Nicene Creed, with its ringing trumpet sounds: "God of God, Light of Light, Very God of Very God?" Julian the Apostate correctly saw the imprint of John in the whole theology of the fourth century: "He is the cause of all the mischief, for he declared that the Word was made flesh." In the Reformation era the paramount influence towards the restoration of sound Apostolic doctrine is usually ascribed to the Pauline epistles, especially those to the Romans and Galatians. While this was true concerning the doctrines of sin and grace, we must not forget that back of these doctrines, particularly in Luther's teaching, stands the great and fundamental doctrine of Christ's person, back of Paul stands John, with his testimony of the true God-man. And as for our present time, with its theological and religious conflicts, there can be no doubt that everything turns again on the great, old question: What think ye of Christ? Whose son is He? Transfer this question to the sphere of New Testament literature and it reads: What think ye of the Gospel of John? What is it to you?

II. The Life and Personal Character of the Apostle John

With the exception of Judas Iscariot, all the Apostles called by the Lord, during the three years of His public ministry, were Galileans. So also was John, the son of Zebedee and Salome. His mother was not, as has been supposed by some,[1] the sister of Mary the mother of Jesus. His home was in one of the towns along the lake of Galilee, probably, not certainly, in Bethsaida. His father, though a plain fisherman, seems to have been somewhat wealthy. He had his "hired servants" (Mark 1:20), and Salome was one of the women who ministered unto the Lord of their substance (Luke 8:2, 3). Her interest in the cause of Jesus also manifests itself in that ambitious petition, that her sons might sit, one on the right, the other on the left hand of the Lord in the kingdom of God; an ambition, though not altogether free from carnal zeal, yet showing an unlimited devotion to the Lord's cause. Under the training of this mother, the two sons, James and John, were led to join the disciples of John the Baptist as soon as he began to preach the kingdom of heaven. John the Baptist directed him to the Lord, probably with that striking testimony: "Behold the Lamb of God, which taketh away the sins of the world;" and John, in company with Andrew, the brother of Peter, followed the Lord, as one of His first adherents from the Jordan to Cana (John 1:35 ff). In Galilee he was formally called to the apostleship, together with his brother James (Matt. 4:21). Simon Peter and James and John, the sons of Zebedee, are represented in the Synoptical Gospels as standing in a more intimate relation to the Lord than the other nine apostles. At the raising of Jairus' daughter (Luke 8:51), on the mount of transfiguration (Matt. 17:1, and Mark 9:2) and in the garden of Gethsemane (Mark 14:33, Matt. 26:37), they form the select inner circle nearest to their Lord. And among these three there is one still nearer to the heart of the Lord than the other two—one that is anonymously spoken of as the disciple "whom Jesus loved." It is the fourth Gospel, which, while it never uses the name of the Apostle John, refers to this beloved disciple in John 13:23, 19:26, 20:2, 21:7, 20 ff. All

---

[1] In order to explain the intimate relation between John and Jesus.

II. The Life and Personal Character of the Apostle John

these passages belong to the last chapters in the life of the Lord, the history of His passion and glorification, as if only through the experience of those momentous hours of parting and meeting again the writer had come to a full consciousness of that special, personal affection of his Lord and Master. John's claim to the title "the beloved disciple" has been disputed by different writers in recent times. But the disciple "whom Jesus loved" was undoubtedly not only one of the twelve, but one of the seven mentioned in John 21:2; yea, one of the three—Peter, James and John. It was not Peter (see John 21:20), nor was it James whom Herod killed with the sword (Acts 12:2), about 44 A. D., and of whom the opinion could never have been entertained that "this disciple dieth not." It could only have been John. He was on the bosom of the Lord at the Last Supper; under the cross with Mary, who was committed to his care by her dying Son; at the grave with Peter, on Easter morning; and at the Lake of Galilee with the risen Lord.

After Pentecost, as we learn from the Acts and Galatians, John was one of the pillars of the Church in Jerusalem, but by far not so prominent as Peter, whose companion and assistant he seems to have been (Acts 3 and 8).[1] When Paul visited Jerusalem for the second time (Gal. 2) he met him there, about 50 or 51 A. D. After the Council in Jerusalem (Acts 15) we know nothing of John until, in later years, Ephesus is fixed by early tradition as the place of his abode. He probably left Jerusalem at the outbreak of the Jewish war, 67 A. D., when the Christian community withdrew to Pella. Asia Minor was then the most important and the most flourishing territory of the young Christian Church. Jerusalem had ceased to be the centre. Rome had not yet become the centre. Ephesus, the principal city of Asia Minor, formed a sort of half-way station between the two. There the Apostle Paul, on taking his leave from the elders of the Church, had foreseen and expected "grievous wolves to enter in not sparing the flock—men speaking perverse things, to draw away disciples after them" (Acts 20:29 ff). There we find false

---

[1] John is not mentioned as present in Jerusalem on the occasion of Paul's first visit to that city (Gal. 1:18). Possibly he may have taken the mother of the Lord, at that time, to his home on the Lake of Galilee.

apostles and Nicolaitans (Rev. 2:2, 6). There, above all other places, the presence of the only surviving Apostle was needed. To John was committed the task of continuing, defending and crowning the work of St. Paul in Asia Minor, building up and fully organizing in the unity of the faith the churches founded by the former. The testimonies of the fathers concerning John's sojourn in Ephesus are quite numerous and strong;[1] the principal witness being Irenæus, who still remembered Polycarp,[2] the disciple of John, speaking to his hearers of his beloved Master. At the time of the persecution under the Roman emperor Domitian, John was banished to the Isle of Patmos, and returned from there to Ephesus under Nerva. He lived, probably, to the year 100 or 101 A. D.

Compared with the other apostles, especially Peter, John was evidently of a quiet, reticent, meditative nature. There is in him a good deal of Mary, the mother of the Lord, who "kept all these sayings and pondered them in her heart." While Peter rushes into action with the question—What can I do? walk on the water? build tabernacles? smite with the sword? go into prison and to death?—John stands in the background watching his Lord with the one question: What is He doing? losing himself in the contemplation of His glory. Thus he was the man above all others not only to receive, but to reflect the glory of the Lord, and to reproduce it most fully in the presentation of his Gospel. What he observed and retained in his quiet receptivity, he afterwards testified most faithfully, without adorning or reconstructing it from his own imagination, simply being witness of what he had heard and seen, with a certain monotonous plainness.

This receptivity, however, is only one side in John's character, the one turned towards the Lord. But there is another side in him, turning towards the world and everything that is against his Lord. Here we find him a man of stern decision, and indomitable energy, admitting of no

---

[1] The various characteristic anecdotes or legends of the later life of the Apostle, such as meeting Cerinthus in the public bath, rescuing the lost youth, being carried into the assembly of the congregation, with his dying admonition: "Little children, love one another,"—all belong to Asia Minor.

[2] Born A. D. 70.

II. The Life and Personal Character of the Apostle John

compromises; the son of thunder, ready to call the fire from heaven upon the Samaritans, that would not receive Jesus; and forbidding the man whom he found casting out devils in the Master's name, because he followed not with them. The picture of John which we are accustomed to see, with the soft, dreamy, feminine features, is therefore a very incomplete and unsatisfactory representation of his true character. It may be said without hesitation that Paul, the fiery, zealous Paul, is milder and gentler in many respects than John, the "Apostle of love," who allows no middle ground, no putting off or considering, but insists on your prompt decision for or against, life or death, light or darkness, truth or lie, love or hatred, God or devil. Paul, from his own abundant experience, describes the *process of justification*, the *genesis and development* of Christian life, the *transition* from the old to the new, the *continued struggle* between the flesh and the spirit, the old man and the new. With John everything is *complete, settled*, decided; the battle is over, the victory won. His is the absolute, the ideal presentation, not only of Christ, but also of the Christian and of Christianity. He would never have gained the heathen for the gospel as Paul did, becoming all things to all men, that he might, by all means, save some. But John was the man to hold what Paul had gathered, and to guard it in its fulness and purity against every admixture and defilement which threatened the Church towards the close of the Apostolic era, when antichristian spirits were lifting up their heads, denying the very foundation, Christ the God-man. John, who had so little to say during the lifetime of the other apostles, had the last word for the Church in those days of imminent danger. Now he is right in sending the thunderbolts of the Spirit against those Christian Samaritans, the heretics, who strove to supplant the Gospel by a revised Judaism or a paganism in Christian garb. Now he is right in fighting those half-and-half men with his zealous, intolerant love for the whole undivided Lord. Now the dilemma is truth or lie, Christ or Antichrist.

III. THE GOSPEL OF ST. JOHN

i. *the relation between the fourth gospel and the three preceding ones, the synoptists*

The Church had no need to wait for the acuteness and learning of modern criticism to make the important discovery that between the first three Gospels, on the one hand, and the last Gospel on the other, there are marked differences, not simply as to form, style and manner of treatment, but also in matter and contents; which differences have been exaggerated by modern scientists into an irreconcilable antagonism, so that with their "synoptical Christ," whom alone they will admit as historical, they claim to be able to abolish and wipe out the Christ of the fourth Gospel,—"a purely visionary and ideal abstraction, without true historical foundation." Augustine pointed out the difference in this manner: "John has risen higher than the other three Evangelists. They walk with the Lord on earth as with a man, saying comparatively little of His divinity. But John soared above earth and heaven and all the hosts of angels, to come to Him through whom all things are made. He spoke of the Divinity of Christ as no other Evangelist has done. Drinking from the fountain at the very bosom of the Lord, he has proclaimed publicly what he drank in privately." Thus far Augustine, and it is only fair to say that the plainest Bible reader cannot fail to notice the important and striking differences between John and the Synoptists.

Let us try to look calmly but clearly into this whole matter, seeking for the truth, and nothing but the truth, and ready to accept it wherever it be found. First of all, we will try to array the principal points of difference against each other, and then we will consider the question, whether these differences really involve contradictions, or whether they do not rather serve as explanations, complements and solutions of problems otherwise mysterious and unsatisfactory, thus proving that the different accounts of the one Gospel of our Lord, presented by the four Evangelists, belong together, and conjointly furnish us that complete and

III. The Gospel of St. John

many-sided picture of the Lord and His work which the Church needs as the foundation for a pure faith.

1. *The Differences of a Chronological and Historical Nature.*—After the preliminary history of the birth and childhood of the Lord and the preparatory work of His forerunner, John the Baptist, the Synoptists, in narrating the public ministry of the Lord, take us at once into His Galilean ministrations; Matthew, after a sort of general description of the Galilean work (4:12–25), opening with the Sermon on the Mount; Mark, with the healing of the demoniac in the synagogue at Capernaum; Luke, with the discourse in the synagogue at Nazareth, all three showing a certain indifference as to the exact scene with which the public ministry of the Lord in Galilee was opened. But the fourth Gospel is very minute and careful in describing the first official beginnings of the Lord in Judaea, long before the Galilean work began: the first acquaintance of Jesus with His first disciples on the Jordan (1:35 ff), the beginning of their faith strengthened and developed by the first sign in Cana of Galilee, and the first public appearance of Jesus as the Messiah, not in Galilee, but in Jerusalem, in the sanctuary itself, the centre of Israel's faith and worship. The chronological arrangement of the life and work of Jesus, according to the Synoptists, seems clear and plain enough at first sight. It simply divides itself into two principal parts: first, the Lord's work in Galilee; secondly, His going up to Jerusalem to suffer and die, to rise from the dead and ascend into Heaven. It looks like one continued stay in Galilee, uninterrupted by any journeys to Judaea and Jerusalem, and finally one journey to Jerusalem to end His life on the cross. The natural impression from this account would be that the whole public ministry of the Lord occupied just one year, and this year, with the exception of the last week, spent in Galilee or outside of Jerusalem.

How different the perspective which the Gospel of John opens to our eyes! It speaks of three (or possibly four) distinct Easter seasons during the public life of the Lord, thereby extending it over a period of three years. It mentions five or (if His coming to Bethany after Lazarus' death be counted separately) six different journeys to Jerusalem, while it has very little to say of the works and discourses of Christ in Galilee, though the signs which He did there on them that were sick are referred to in a general way (John 6:2). After John the Baptist had prepared the way for the Lord by his powerful testimony *in Judæa* (not in Galilee), it would have been strange indeed if Christ Himself should have passed by this territory at the beginning of His public ministry. But the fourth Gospel tells us distinctly that He did make His official beginning in Judæa and Jerusalem, after His Baptism by John, on His first Easter visit to the city. After this beginning in Judæa, He came to Galilee[1] (John 4:3), where the preaching of the Baptist had not been heard. He therefore acts, so to speak, as His own forerunner in Galilee. He begins there with preaching exactly what the Baptist had been preaching in Judæa: "Repent, for the kingdom of heaven is at hand." After a few months He returns to Jerusalem for the next Passover, 4:45; 5:1 (supposing that ἡ ἑορτὴ refers to this festival). Then and there already His teaching becomes such an offence to the Jews that they seek to kill Him, "because He not only had broken the Sabbath, but said also that God was His Father, making Himself equal with God." At the time of the third passover mentioned in John, Jesus is in Galilee (6:4), the reason for his Galilean sojourn being again the enmity of the Jews: "He would not walk in Judæa, because the Jews sought to kill Him" (7:1). At the Feast of the Tabernacles He again goes up to Jerusalem, "not publicly, but as it were in secret" (7:2, 10). About two months afterwards we find Him in Jerusalem at the Festival of the Dedication (10:22). When they renewed their effort to take Him, He escaped out of their hand, and went away beyond Jordan, to Peræa, where John was first baptizing, and many believed on Him there (10:40–42). He returned to Bethany for the raising of Lazarus (ch. 11), which led to the final resolution of the chief priests and Pharisees "to put Him to death." He therefore departed once more into the country near to the wilderness, into a city called Ephraim, and there He tarried with His disciples. Then comes the last Passover, His royal entrance into Jerusalem for His passion and death.

---

[1] The increase in the number of His disciples had been a provocation and offence to the Pharisees. Hence His withdrawal into Gahilee (John 4:1 ff.).

III. The Gospel of St. John

This is in the main the order of events in the fourth Gospel; and while it opens many new aspects and clears up many obscure points, it is nowhere in conflict with the Synoptists, but presents the main pillars for a complete and clear chronology of the Lord's public life, affording ample space for all His work in Galilee and outside of Jerusalem, as detailed by the Synoptists. The intervals between the first Passover (John 2) and the last (John 12) of which the fourth Gospel has no special doings or sayings of the Lord to record, though it defines them very clearly, amount in all to about twenty-six months.[1] And this is certainly room enough to store away every item found in the Synoptical Gospels in distinction from John, particularly if we remember that all the events and discourses in the life of Christ which are given in the fourth Gospel actually cover only thirty single days out of about one thousand days of His public ministry! So far, then, the differences, however obvious, involve no contradictions. Frequently the new and additional information furnished in the fourth Gospel helps to clear up dark passages and to remove misunderstandings. The bright sunlight of ulterior harmony between John and the Synoptists breaks through the passing clouds which for a time threatened to overcast the sky.

It is admitted on all sides that the writer of the fourth Gospel was well acquainted with the record of the Synoptists, and that he takes it for granted that they are also well known to his readers. Neither the Synoptists, on the one hand, nor the fourth Gospel, on the other, claim completeness in their presentation of the life of Christ. The impossibility of furnishing an absolutely complete record of the many things He did is very forcibly set forth in John 21:25: "Even the world itself would not contain the books that should be written." The Synoptists evidently knew of certain movements and doings of the Lord which they, confining themselves to His Galilean ministry, did not enter into more fully. And so the writer of the fourth Gospel has a full knowledge of Galilean events and other facts which he passes by. He writes "as one who knows that

---

[1] There are several months between John 4 and 5; one month [possibly a whole year] between ch. 5 and 6; seven months between ch. 6 and 7; three months between ch. 7 and 10:22.

there are other books treating of the same subject, and who gives his own account rather unconcerned about his apparent agreement or disagreement" (Renan). His recognition of the first three Gospels does not mean dependence, much less antagonism, but confirmation. In 1:40 Andrew is introduced as the brother of Simon Peter, though the latter has not been mentioned before in this Gospel. The distinct statement, John 2:12, that at that time the Lord abode in Capernaum "not many days" is evidently made with a view to the longer sojourn of the Lord in Capernaum as His own city, of which the Synoptists have so much to say. In John 6:70 reference is made to the choosing of twelve apostles as a previous fact, though the fourth Gospel thus far has only narrated the calling of five (1:35 ff) disciples. Again, this first calling of the five as disciples of the Lord helps us to understand the readiness with which, at a later period, on the Lake of Galilee, they followed the call of the Lord, which made them fishers of men, apostles, as the Synoptists tell us. In John 11:1 Bethany is called the village of Mary and Martha, though those sisters have not been mentioned before in this Gospel. All these points, to which others might be added, are in reality so many references to things generally known from the previous record of the Synoptists.

On the other hand, the Synoptists contain certain passages which clearly demand or pre-suppose other and more extended periods in the life of the Lord than those belonging to His Galilean ministry. There is an extended section in the Gospel of St. Luke, forming more than one-third of the whole book, from 9:51 to the 18th chapter, which deals with journeyings of the Lord between Galilee and Jerusalem. At first sight they may impress us as being all in the South of Galilee and (towards the end) in Peræa. But if we come to Luke 10:38 and read: "As they went on their way, He entered into a certain village, and a certain woman named Martha received Him into her house, and she had a sister called Mary,"—it is certainly the most natural thing to think of Bethany, "the village of Mary and Martha," as the fourth Gospel calls it.

Again, the Synoptists tell us of certain people living in Jerusalem and the neighborhood who, at very short notice, were willing to grant to the Lord the use of their animals (at the entrance into Jerusalem) and

III. The Gospel of St. John

their house (at the preparation of the Supper). They must have become acquainted with Him on former occasions, so as to acknowledge Him as their Lord and Master. The same must be said of Joseph of Arimathea, who figures so conspicuously in the Synoptical Gospels as "a disciple of Jesus" (Matt. 27:57; Mark 15:43; Luke 23:50 ff). When and where did he become a disciple of the Lord if not on former visits of Jesus to Judæa and Jerusalem? But the most direct and conclusive proof in this direction is the well-known saying of the Lord (Luke 13:34 and Matt. 23:37): "O Jerusalem, Jerusalem! which killeth the prophets and stoneth them that are sent unto her! *How often* would I have gathered thy children together, even as a hen gathereth her own brood under her wings, and ye would not!" This "How often" is certainly not to be limited to the testimonies of the Lord during the six days *after* His final entrance to Jerusalem. Only six days, and all is over? Yea, only two days, and the figtree is cursed, and the rejection of Israel announced? Is it possible that on His first public appearance in Jerusalem the Lord should within two or three days have drawn upon Himself such an infernal hatred of the chiefs and Pharisees that His death was at once determined upon? On the other side, the Synoptists themselves testify to the exceedingly slow growth of the understanding and faith of the disciples and of the patience the Lord had to exercise in dealing with them as their teacher and pastor. It is safe to say that one year is entirely too short for their slow and gradual development. Both the hatred of His enemies and the faith of His disciples required such a period of time as is clearly and satisfactorily furnished in the fourth Gospel.

2. *Differences in the Form and Language of the Lord's Discourses.*—There is certainly a manifest difference in the form of the discourses of Christ contained in the fourth Gospel compared with those in the Synoptists. In John they are more *dramatic:* the form of the *dialogue* is far more frequent than in the other three. The utterances of the Lord consequently are more of a personal character from His first conversation with the disciples (John 1) to His dealings with the governor, Pilate. The *pastoral* element predominates in John, over against the *homiletical* in the Synoptists, who give us chiefly discourses addressed to

the multitudes. Closely connected with this is the use of the *parable* in the Synoptists as the favorite form of speaking to the masses, while in the fourth Gospel, at first sight, this use of the parable seems altogether wanting. In vain do we look in John for that familiar phrase: "The kingdom of heaven is likened unto—" And the difference in the surroundings, particularly the different character of the hearers of the Lord in the fourth Gospel, would sufficiently account for the change in the form of His addresses. But the parabolic, figurative form of teaching is by no means missing in the fourth Gospel. Only there is another theme to it. In the Synoptists it is the *"Kingdom of God,"* in John it is the *Head and King of that kingdom Himself,* who is likened to the things of this world: I am the Life, the Light, the Way, the Spring of living waters (4:14 and 7:37, 38), the Bread from heaven, the Door, the Good Shepherd, the Vine, the Grain of Wheat which in dying beareth much fruit (12:24). But we all feel these expressions go beyond the purely figurative or parabolic speech. The thing that signifies and He who is signified are one in these terms. He *is* the way, the light, the life, in the absolute sense. He is not simply *like unto a way*. The wonderful realism of the union between the Divine and the Human, the Logos and the flesh in which He appeared, reflects itself even in these simple, popular and yet most deep and comprehensive terms. In fact, the whole Gospel of John is thoroughly imbued with that heavenly symbolism and realism which reads the signs of divine manifestation everywhere in the universe, in all the processes of nature, the stages of human life, the events of sacred and profane history.[1] A few references may suffice to illustrate this: The Temple, 2:19; the Serpent in the wilderness, 3:14; the Manna, 6:31, 32; the Passover Lamb, 19:36; and again the wind, 3:8; the birth, 1:12, 13; 3:5; the marriage relation, 3:29; the harvest field, 4:35, 36; the day with its hours, 9:4; 11:9; the woman in the hour of giving birth to her child, 16:21. We may also point to Pilate, the representative of Pagan Rome, in its relation to the Gospel; the inscription on the cross in Hebrew, Latin and Greek, the first polyglot of the Gospel; the blood and water from the pierced side of the Lord, etc. In

---

[1] Cf. Goethe: "Alles Vergängliche ist nur ein Gleichniss."

III. The Gospel of St. John

all this, John is richer, deeper, fuller than the Synoptists,—nowhere in conflict with them, but towering high above them.

3. *The Tone and Spirit of the Lord's Language in His Conversations with the Jews in Jerusalem*, as has been justly observed, is quite different from what we are accustomed to in His Galilean addresses. On the Lake of Galilee, in the borderland of Paganism, in the midst of a despised population, among publicans and sinners, we find the Lord, on the whole, much more condescending, lenient and forbearing with the weak and lowly. But in Jerusalem, among the chiefs and rulers of the people, in the very centre of Israel's religious life, He was, even from the outset, more severe. In Galilee, as we said before, His own preaching was, on the whole, more of a preparatory, introductory character. In Jerusalem He at once came to the main point and centre of His testimony: His own person. Here the preaching of the Baptist had prepared the way for Him. Here the Law and the Prophets were known to all. But here the teachers and leaders of God's people had fortified themselves against the preaching of repentance. Being wise and learned in their own eyes, they would not listen to a Galilean as their teacher. Counting themselves among those "that are whole," they needed no physician, and least of all would they accept the Nazarene as the promised Messiah and the Son of God. The Lord, of necessity, was much severer with them from the beginning than with the Galileans. And the rejection of His testimony here would naturally lead to a crisis in a comparatively short time. Indeed, if the Lord had not, from time to time, withdrawn from Jerusalem to Galilee, the final catastrophe would have come much sooner.[1]

The *Galilean addresses* recorded by the Synoptists show us the Lord, so to speak, in his *every-day dress and walk*, away from the holy places and out of the festival seasons, moving among the fishermen and their nets and boats, tossed about on the very waves of that turbulent lake,— yea, among the herdsmen of Gadara and their swine. But the *conversations*

---

[1] The Synoptists, however, are not behind the fourth Gospel in some of their statements directed against the Pharisees. See the Baptist's preaching, Matt. 3 and the Lord's "Woe" to the Pharisees in Matt. 23.

and discourses of the fourth Gospel have a wonderful solemnity and dignity about them. They all belong to the great festival seasons of the Jewish year; here the Lord moves in the sanctuary itself, "His Father's house." He stands before us *in holiday attire*. He grants to the Holy City and to Mount Zion the most important and direct manifestation of His glory, that one ever-repeated testimony: I am He! I and the Father are one! But, strange to say, all those great, blessed festival days of Israel, which were thus hallowed by His presence,—the Passover, the Feast of the Tabernacles, the Feast of the Dedication,—were turned into days of awful responsibility, seasons of hardening the hearts of carnal Israel; they knew not the time of their visitation.

    4. *The Differences in Matter; the Doctrinal Aspect of the Utterances of the Lord in John, as compared with the Synoptists.*—The main point under this head has been referred to before. The principal theme in the synoptical discourses of the Lord is *the kingdom of God* and His righteousness, the members of this kingdom and their duties, and the growth and development of the kingdom. In the fourth Gospel the one main theme is the *Lord Himself*, His person as the God-man, the only-begotten Son of the Father. Our very salvation is bound up in this: "Except ye believe *that I am He*, ye shall die in your sins" (8:24). This is His solemn testimony to His enemies; and to His friends and disciples it is essentially the same, though in a less threatening, more positive form: "From henceforth I tell you before it come to pass, that when it is come to pass, ye may believe *that I am He*" (13:19).

    In the Synoptical Gospels the Lord has to answer all sorts of questions concerning the law and the way to eternal life. In the fourth Gospel the one great question with which He deals is: *Who art Thou?* (8:25). The synoptical discourses enter minutely into the description of the last things and the Lord's second coming to judge the quick and the dead. The fourth Gospel beautifully balances these statements by revealing the present judgment which is quietly going on in the hearts of men: "He that believeth not, being judged already, because he hath not believed on the name of the only-begotten Son of God" (3:17–19; comp. also 5:24, 45; 9:39,

III. The Gospel of St. John

41; 12:48).[1] And over against the second coming of the Lord in the far-off future, it emphasizes His continued presence with His own in mystical union through the Spirit. (See the parting discourses, John 14–17) The difference here again is one of mutual complement, not of exclusive antagonism; for John also knows of "the resurrection of judgment" (5:29), and the Synoptists are not ignorant of the promises of the Lord: "Where two or three are gathered together in My name, there am I in the midst of them," and "Lo, I am with you always, even unto the end of the world" (which might be fittingly called the theme of John 14–17).

Owing to the peculiar concentration which characterizes the fourth Gospel, the *range of subjects* treated in its discourses is naturally much *more limited* than in the Synoptists. We observe in John a constant recurrence to the one thing needful. It is the Lord! To believe in Him, to love Him, to have Him abiding in the heart, to be one with Him,—this is the one great subject. How different from this, for instance, the Sermon on the Mount! What a variety of references to the details of practical life with its cares, its struggles, its duties and dangers! Surely we would not like to miss those graphic details of Christian ethics, as they are set forth in Matt. 5–7. But much less can we afford to miss the solemn testimony of the fourth Gospel, setting forth the one source of this new ethical life with all its various fruitful branches: Christ believed in; Christ united with the believer by faith. Those are, indeed, glorious things which are said in Matthew of the disciples as the children of the heavenly Father, being free from care, happy, perfect, kind and merciful, being the salt and the light of the world, and of the beatitudes of the poor in spirit, the peacemakers, the pure in heart, etc. But, after all, the main question remains to be answered: How can those that are evil by nature ever attain to such a spiritual condition? How can they that are flesh, born of flesh, ever be truly children of the Father in heaven? And to this question the plain answer is returned in the fourth Gospel: "Ye must be born anew" (3:7).

---

[1] For judgment came I into this world, that they which see not may see, and that they which see may become blind.

We repeat once more: This is a variety of aspects, but no collision, no antagonism. The one blends most beautifully with the other. There is the *periphery* in the Synoptists,—the kingdom of God with the manifold and detailed duties of its citizens; and there is the *centre* in the fourth Gospel,—Christ the God-man Himself, the head and heart of all. No periphery without a centre, and no centre without a periphery. They belong together, and in their union round off the complete fulness of God's revelation in Christ. There are two sets of witnesses standing at that river of life, some looking downward, following with their eyes its ramifications and channels as it spreads itself over the meadows, carrying life and growth and quickening in every direction; the other looking upward, following its silver thread up to the lofty heights where the life-spring gushes forth from the everlasting rock. This is the difference in the view presented by the Synoptists and in the fourth Gospel. But it is one and the same river, one and the same water of life which they all describe.

It is, therefore, *one and the same Christ* whom we find in their different presentations. True, the divine majesty of Christ, His oneness with the Father, and consequently His existence co-equal with the Father before the world, is much more in the foreground in the fourth Gospel. It is the central, dominant idea in John. But it is not altogether lacking in the Synoptists; not even in those parts which are generally passed by when this topic is in question. Take, for instance, the Sermon on the Mount, and trace the evidences of the majesty and divine authority of Christ through that discourse, for which ancient and modern rationalists have always professed peculiar admiration, while shutting their eyes to its undeniable testimony on the Person of Christ.[1] The one sentence in the formal institution of baptism: "Into the name of the Father and the Son and the Holy Ghost," speaks volumes on that fundamental article of Christian faith, the divinity of Christ, and this is a synoptical passage (Matt. 28:19).

---

[1] Matt. 5:11, "For My sake;" 22, 28, 32, 34, 39, 44; "I say unto you," 6:2, 5; 7:24 ff.; comp. also Matt. 10:15, 16, 18, 22, 23, 32, 33, 37, 39, 40; Matt. 11:6, 10 ff., 20 ff.

III. The Gospel of St. John

One word yet on the identity of the synoptical Christ and that of the fourth Gospel, and we are done with this topic. Where in the synoptical Gospels the Lord enters most fully into the mystery of His own person as the God-man, He uses language which is so exactly like that of the fourth Gospel that even the most critical eye fails to discover a difference. "All things have been delivered unto Me of My Father; and no one knoweth the Son save the Father: neither doth any know the Father save the Son and he to whomsoever the Son willeth to reveal." Thus it is written, not in John, but in Matthew 11:27.

ii. the peculiar character of the fourth gospel

1. *The Language.*—No one, in reading even a few verses of this fourth Gospel, can fail to be deeply impressed with the childlike simplicity of its language. The essence of Christian truth has here been reduced to the briefest, plainest and most comprehensive expression. Its plainness, both as to the store of words used and the manner of their construction into sentences, is so obvious that it amounts even to a certain monotony. The same principal terms are constantly repeated; such as "believe" (98 times), "know" (55), "witness" (55), "glory" (55), "world" (78), "life and live" (over 50), "light" (23), "name" (25), "truth" (25), to "receive," "to take" λαμβάνειν, (44). But the profundity and comprehensiveness of these terms at once shows that the simplicity of this language is not that which we would choose for an elementary class of beginners in Christian knowledge, but rather that of a final *resumé*, in which the fundamental ideas of Christianity are set forth in pithy terms, full of meaning. If we take, for instance, those three ideas of light, life, love, so familiar to all the readers of John, and try to analyze them, we will at once perceive how difficult a task it is, how much is contained in these simple words; we will realize that it is impossible to say more in fewer words than is said in those simple statements: God is Spirit; God is Love; in Him was Life, and the Life was the Light of men.

This simplicity also extends, as before indicated, to the construction of sentences. They are short, crisp, concise and plain as plain can be. They have a decidedly Oriental, Hebrew cast, in the quiet, naive repetition of the same phrases and the circumstantiality of expression in minor details.

The Greek language is perhaps richer than any other in the means it affords to construct beautiful, complicated and yet well-rounded periods, and to set off one clause against another in minute and delicate shading with the help of its numerous particles. All this wealth is cast aside by the writer of the fourth Gospel. His sentences are short; and the more weighty and emphatic, the shorter they are. Clause is linked to clause on the principle not of subordination, but of co-ordination, so characteristic of the Hebrew language. Or, we should rather say, clause follows clause, because there is no effort made to link them together with conjunctions in the narrative. Wherever an intermediate, subordinate thought comes in, it is wedged in as a sort of parenthesis with the utmost indifference to the structure of the main sentence. (See 1:39, 44; 4:6; 5:9; 6:4; 9:14; 10:22; 19:29; 19:14)

This very absence of the refinements of artificial structure makes the language of John's Gospel so powerful and impressive. (See such passages as these: "Jesus wept." "And it was night." "Now Barabbas was a robber.") It is the language of assurance and determination, compelling its readers to yield to its weight and to believe. At the same time it is the language of strong, striking contrasts, frequently presenting them without a connecting particle, which would indicate the antithesis, but none the less emphatic for this. (See 1:17: "The law was given by Moses; grace and truth came by Jesus Christ.") It is, as Luthardt says, the utterance of "a man brought up in the holy language of Israel, but a strong mind, a full heart, an emotional soul, ready to burst out through the calm peace and even composure." Though there are not many direct outward Hebraisms to be discovered, it is undeniable that "a Hebrew soul lives in the speech of the Evangelist" (Luthardt).[1]

---

[1] "The original thought in the language of Palestine; the raiment of later making, Greek" (Credner, Ewald).

III. The Gospel of St. John

2. *The Historical Character of the Fourth Gospel.*—No other gospel has such *an array of chronological[2] and topographical statements*, telling us at what time, day, and even hour, and at what place the different events are to be located.[3] Moreover, the evidences of historical realism are exhibited not only in these minute details of dates, but also in the main lines of *true historical development* on which it moves. Let us recall once more the steady growth, the truly historic development of *the enmity* of the rulers *against Christ* as described in the fourth Gospel. We find an indication of its beginning in the very first chapter, in the uneasiness and the spirit of inquisition with which the forerunner of the Lord is looked upon by the Sanhedrim. This is followed by the indifference and even antagonism with which the first reformatory effort of the Lord is received (ch. 2). Nicodemus, a Pharisee and ruler of the Jews, dare not come to Jesus in open daylight,—a graphic testimony of the animus of that party (ch. 3). The manifestly unpleasant impression which the growing influence of the Lord had made upon the Pharisees moves Him to depart into Galilee (4:1–3). The first outburst of open hostility (5:16, 18). The sending out of officers on the part of the chief priests and Pharisees to take Him (7:32; cf. also ver. 1). First attempt to stone Him (8:59). Systematic persecution and excommunication of His adherents agreed upon (9:22), (see also ver. 34), and practised against the man born blind. Second attempt to stone Him (10:31). Formal council of the chief priests and Pharisees to put Him to death and commandment that if any man knew where He was, he should show it, that they might take Him (11:53, 57). Finally, the counsel to put Lazarus also to death, because that by reason of him many believed on Jesus (12:11). Herein culminates their enmity and hatred, and the final crisis follows promptly.

---

[2] See ch. 1:29, 35, 39, 43; 2:1; 2:2; 4:6, 43, 52; 6:16, 21; 7:14, 37; 11:6, 17; 12:1, 12; 13:1, 30; 18:28; 19:14; 20:1, 26.

[3] Another feature which ought to be pointed out in this connection is the frequent reference back to persons and events that have been mentioned before in the narrative of the Gospel: 4:46, Cana; 7:50; 19:3, Nicodemus; 18:14 to 11:50, Caiaphas. Also 11:2, pointing forward to Mary's anointing the Lord.

Parallel with this growing hostility against the Lord, there is, on the other hand, the *steady development of the faith of the disciples*. We can follow the different stages from the first interest taken in Christ by Andrew and his companions (1:35 ff), through Peter's confession (6:67–69), to the culmination in that outburst of Thomas: "My Lord and my God!" (20:28). A similar progress we notice in the three stages of the spiritual *development of Nicodemus*: first, the secret visit by night (ch. 3); next, the cautious and yet conscientious standing up against the chief priests and Pharisees (7:50 f); and finally, his coming out boldly as the friend and adherent of the Lord under the cross (19:39). Another striking illustration of the historical realism of the fourth Gospel may be found in that masterpiece of psychological delineation, the description of *Pilatê's conflict* between Jesus and the Jews (18–19). No other Gospel affords us such a key to the character of the Roman governor.

This leads us to another point of prominence among the historical features of this Gospel. It is the remarkable *clearness and sharpness with which the portraits of the different characters are drawn*. Those well-known figures, Andrew and Philip and Nathanael and Thomas and Peter, Nicodemus, the Samaritan woman, Judas and Caiaphas and Pilate; they are all life portraits, though the whole picture is done by a few touches. However typical some of them may be, they do not impress us as artificial studies, to embody certain abstract ideas, but as sketches from life, drawn in the most natural, unconscious manner by one who clearly remembered them as they stood and moved before his eyes.

Thus we come to the last point to be observed among the historical features of the fourth Gospel. It is the *personal interest* in the events narrated which the Evangelist manifests from beginning to end. These events form a part of his own life. He presents us with a sketch of autobiography as well as of Christ's public ministry. "We beheld His glory." The consciousness of this blessed privilege pervades the whole Gospel. The history proper of the fourth Gospel begins with the time when John, the son of Zebedee, was directed to the Messiah through the testimony of his first master, the Baptist. Those were the most memorable days and hours of his own life, and there his account of single

III. The Gospel of St. John

specified events in the life of the Lord sets in. In the passage John 19:35[1] this personal interest as an eye-witness culminates. As a circumstantial evidence of the personal interest of the writer in the facts narrated, we might perhaps also point to the strong antipathy which he exhibits against Judas Iscariot, whose name is never mentioned without reference to the betrayal of the Lord.

3. The Spiritual or Prophetical Aspect of the History presented in the Fourth Gospel.—This fourth Gospel, then, has throughout the marks of true historical realism. It is history. But it is more than that; it is history written with the spirit of prophecy. We say prophecy not in the narrow sense of looking forward into the future and foretelling it, but in its true, original sense of speaking out what is hidden, penetrating into the mysteries of God's counsel as well as into the secrets of the human heart,[2] and into the full and true, eternal significance of all the passing events of this present time. In fact, every true historian must have something of the prophet in him to see things in the true light, in the whole complex of God's counsel and government, in the light of eternity. Facts may be recorded as facts, and yet the historian may utterly fail to show their true character, their import and significance for the universe. One of the greatest historians of all times, the Roman Tacitus, gives his statement of the history of Christ after this manner: "At the time when Tiberius was Emperor, Christ was executed by the governor Pilate." All correct, true to the very word and syllable; and yet is this a history of Christ? Does this give to Christ and to the cross on Calvary their proper place in the history of the world?

Now, John is, in a peculiar sense, the prophet among the Evangelists and historians of the New Testament (as Isaiah was the Evangelist among the prophets of the Old Testament). John's Gospel, too, is a "Revelation" in the fullest and most comprehensive sense of the word.

---

[1] "He that hath seen hath borne witness, and his witness is true, and he knoweth that he saith true, that ye also may believe."

[2] "Sir, I perceive that Thou art a prophet," said the Samaritan woman to the Lord, not because He had foretold her future, but because He had penetrated into her past and told her "all things that ever she did" (John 4:19, 39).

With the very first words of his Gospel he takes his position on the heights of eternity, and from there, with the eye of the true Seer, he penetrates into the mystery of Christ's person, and into the true and eternal significance of all the historical facts he has to present. While he is an eyewitness to what he describes, and presents that which he has seen with his eyes, and which he has heard, and which he has looked upon, and his hands have handled (1 John 1:1), he, at the same time, witnesses and records things not less real, which no human eye could see, and no human hand could handle,—heavenly things, shown to him by the Spirit. This is true, not only of the opening of the Gospel (the "Prologue"), but, all through, the deeds and words of Jesus are presented in this spirit of prophecy. Everything becomes *a sign*, a manifestation of that eternal divine Love and Life and Light of which the Prologue spoke. Hence the symbolical and prophetical character of so many of the facts and sayings recorded in the fourth Gospel, such as the saying of Caiaphas, the anointment of the Lord by Mary in Bethany, and others. There are only a few of the miracles or signs of the Lord recorded in this Gospel, and these few were selected for the special reason that their significance was fully demonstrated by the Lord Himself in His accompanying utterances. The "signs" in John as a rule are the starting points for the most important discourses of Christ. The healing of the sick man in Bethesda on the Sabbath day brings out that full discourse on Christ's divine authority (ch. 5). The feeding of the five thousand in Galilee (ch. 6) becomes the occasion for that solemn talk in the synagogue at Capernaum on the Bread of Life that came down from heaven. The opening of the eyes of the man blind from his birth (ch. 9) suggests the fruitful theme: "I am the Light of the world." And in ch. 11 the conversation between the Lord and the sisters in Bethany at the raising of Lazarus brings out that glorious word: "I am the Resurrection and the Life. He that believeth on Me, though he die, yet shall he live." Those signs of Christ are not things of the past. There is in them a force, abiding, divine and constantly present. They are the acts of Christ, true God and true man, the same yesterday and to-day and forever, and this gives them their eternal and universal significance. Over the death chamber in Jairus' house and over the bier at

III. The Gospel of St. John

Nain's gate, as well as over all our Christian death-beds and tombs, we write the words: "Jesus Christ, the resurrection and the life." In the light of the fourth Gospel we now see more in those miracles than the eye-witnesses, including the Synoptists themselves, could see. We have learned to read and to preach John into the Synoptists.[1]

The very fact that John's Gospel is written in the fullness of this spirit of prophecy makes it sometimes rather difficult to decide whether we have the Lord's own words before us or those of the Evangelist. In the Synoptists such a difficulty is out of the question. There we can always clearly distinguish the writer from the Lord and His own words. But between the Lord and His beloved disciple there is such a mystic union that their very words and thoughts seem amalgamated.

4. *The Theological Character of the Fourth Gospel.*—In passing now to the special consideration of the theological or doctrinal character of the fourth Gospel, we have first of all to answer the question whether this Gospel was written with a direct and specific polemical or apologetical design, in opposition to certain dangerous errors and heresies by which the early Church was threatened. Such designs have been ascribed to this Gospel already by the Fathers. In fact, "there is scarcely a heresy which the ancients did not think this Gospel directed against." Irenæus found in it the refutation of the doctrines of Cerinthus and the Nicolaitans, the cotemporaries of John; others held that it was directed against those Judaizing errorists known in church history under the name of Ebionites; others, against the disciples of John the Baptist. The majority, however, of ancient and modern writers look upon it as an apostolic protest and

---

[1] This feature of the Gospel of St. John is beautifully brought out in the ancient Latin verse by Adam of St. Victor (died 1177)

Volat avis sine meta,
Quo nec vates nec propketa Evolavit altius.

Tam implenda quam impleta
Nunquam vidit tot secreta Purus homo purius.

defence against those powerful systems of theological or rather philosophical speculation, commonly called "Gnosticism," which attacked the very foundations of Christianity.

We willingly admit it as a historical fact, that Paul already in his late epistles had to combat new and dangerous forms of error which threatened the churches of Asia Minor, and which were most prolific in that hotbed of heresies, the City of Ephesus. (See Acts 20:29, 30; Rev. 2:2, the Nicolaitans.) It was no longer the setting up of the Law and its works against Faith and the Grace of the Gospel; but now it was knowledge against faith, claiming to be a higher stage of Christian development, a sort of philosophy of religion, as Paul describes it, 1 Tim. 6:20, 21, in his solemn warning to Timothy: "The oppositions of the knowledge (science), which is falsely so called, which some professing have erred concerning the faith." The representatives of this false science or knowledge (Gnosis, Gnostics, Gnosticism) most likely are the same men of whom the First Epistle of John speaks as "Antichrists" belonging to "the last times." The dangerous influence of these men manifested itself both in the sphere of doctrine and of life. In the former there was a tendency to slight and lose sight of, yea, an actual *denial* of the great *historical* facts, the concrete realities of Christianity, above all, the fundamental fact of incarnation,— "that Jesus Christ is come in the flesh,"[1] or "that Jesus is the Christ, the Son of God." In the latter, the sphere of practical Christian life, the one-sided pursuit of knowledge naturally resulted in a neglect of the duties and the spirit of Christian love. This cold intellectualism of the Gnostic had neither heart nor time for the brethren.

---

[1] 1 John 4:2: "Every spirit which confesseth that Jesus Christ is come in the flesh is of God;" ver. 15: "Whosoever shall confess that Jesus is the Son of God, God abideth in him, and he in God;" 2:22: "Who is the liar but he that denieth that Jesus is the Christ? This is the antichrist, even he that denieth the Father and the Son."

To the Gnostic the Divine can never become incarnate, because it is a mere thought, an abstract idea. Consequently, these systems are more or less characterized by a dualistic separation of the Ideal and the Historical, the Divine and the Human, the Christ of God and the Jesus of Nazareth.

III. The Gospel of St. John

Now it is evident that of all the books of the New Testament, there is none that could furnish such a powerful antidote to those erroneous tendencies as the fourth Gospel, which presents the central mystery of Christianity, the personal union of God and man in Jesus of Nazareth, in the most realistic language. Nowhere else in Scripture does the bridge between heaven and earth, between the Divine and the Human, between Spirit and flesh, stand out so firmly and conspicuously as in the Gospel of John. Those who saw and heard and touched the man Jesus, saw and heard and touched eternal life and light and glory,—Divinity itself. For the very reason that "the flesh (in itself) profiteth nothing," and because all "that is born of flesh is flesh," the Eternal Word became flesh, and His flesh and blood became meat and drink unto eternal life. Flesh and blood cannot enter into the kingdom of God; but the King of this kingdom, the only-begotten Son of the Father, can become flesh, to make us partakers of His own life and spirit. Thus this Gospel, the most spiritual of all, is at the same time the most material or realistic of all, and the eye of faith recognizes it and rejoices in it, knowing that what God has joined together, no man can put asunder!

And yet admitting all this, and knowing from the history of the Church what eminent service this Gospel did for her in later centuries, at the most critical times of conflict with deadly enemies; believing even that, in the providence of God, it was intended as the great storehouse and arsenal of the Church's heaviest ordinance for coming battles, we are not convinced, by all that has been written on this subject,[1] that in the composition of his book the author had special regard to various particular doctrines of Gnosticism or other "isms" of his time or of coming times. The character of the book is too grand and lofty for such details of controversy; it is preeminently *positive*. Its only antithesis is the unbelief of the world, which refuses to accept Jesus as the Christ; and against this the writer offers his *testimony* of Jesus the Christ, the Son of God, so that, believing in Him, men may have everlasting life. But let us

---

[1] Especially Grau goes entirely too far in his attempts to trace from chapter to chapter the "anti-ebionitic" and "anti-gnostic" features of the Gospel.

not forget that this fundamental error, the denial that Jesus is the Christ, the Son of God, is at the bottom of all deviations from the pure faith and common to all. And this is the reason why this fourth Gospel deals such vigorous and decisive blows to all forms of error, because it always strikes their very heart and head.

What, then, are the principal positive features in the theology of the fourth Gospel? We will let the author answer for himself; for there has never been a clearer and plainer statement of the real design and plan of a book than that presented in John 20:31: "These things or these signs are written, that ye may believe that Jesus is the Christ, the Son of God, and that, believing, ye may have life in His name." There are two things here: the one, the objective, the divine gift, Jesus the Christ; the other, the subjective, the human acceptance of that divine gift, believing in His name and living thereby. Exactly the same two principles we find in strikingly dramatic form presented in the preceding verses with which the Gospel narrative proper is concluded. The last word the apostles have to say is the confession of Thomas: "My Lord and my God!" The last word of the Lord, the beatitude of the believer: "Blessed are they that have not seen, and yet have believed." In another form yet, and in the most concise of all, these two fundamental ideas of the Gospel of John are found in the Lord's prayer of intercession, 17:23: "I in them, and Thou in Me." God in Christ, and Christ in the believer, everything centering in Him. Whatever is taught concerning God the Father, the Spirit, the world, the creation, sin and the Church, is presented in the light of Christ's historic manifestation. It is the absolute religion, the fulfilment of the Law, of Moses and the Prophets (1:17), as well as the answer to the pagan inquiry: "What is truth?" Let us sum it up once more:

The historical person of Jesus of Nazareth one with the Father; in this union His whole human nature, even His body truly and everlastingly participating. To this God-man the believers united (by faith in mystic union) as the branches are to the vine, and this union not simply an ideal one of thought, speculation or knowledge, nor a purely moral one of purpose and will, but an essential one, such as between the Head and the Body with its members,—such is the Christianity of the

III. THE GOSPEL OF ST. JOHN

fourth Gospel; neither an abstract theory nor a certain way of acting, but a *new life* through the God-man, whose wonderful love saves men from perishing, and whose Spirit makes them the children of God. This is, it cannot be denied, essentially a mystery, even as natural life with its beginnings is everywhere wrapped in mystery. But the anti-mysterious is the anti-christian. And those speculative or rationalistic views that would turn Christianity either into a philosophical system or into a new code of morals will forever find their invincible opponent in this Gospel of John, the Gospel of the union of God and man in Jesus Christ.

Considering this doctrinal character of the fourth Gospel, we may wonder that there is no reference found in it to the act of institution of Baptism and the Lord's Supper, the sacraments of the Church of Christ, those holy mysteries in which the union of the visible and invisible, the spiritual and material, the heavenly and earthly, is forever represented and continued. But here also John is the most fitting and beautiful complement to the Synoptists. After the latter have given us the exact circumstances and words of the institution of those ordinances, the fourth Gospel, more fully and clearly than any other part of Scripture, reveals the great principle that underlies those heavenly mysteries,—the union of the Divine and human in the God-man, and the mystic union between the believer and Christ,—a union not only with the Spirit of Christ, but with His very flesh and blood; it is accomplished and nourished and sustained by water and blood; for the Christ of the fourth Gospel (as well as of the First Epistle of John) comes not only by the witness of the *Spirit*, but also by water and blood (1 John 5:6–8). He cannot be detached from the reality of His sacraments.

iii. the question of authorship

1. *Negative Criticism.*—There was, in the second century of the Christian era, an insignificant sect, called Alogi, who rejected the doctrine of the Logos and of the Paraclete (Comforter), as contained in this Gospel, and attributed the Gospel to John's enemy, Cerinthus. But by their indirect testimony to the early date of its composition, they support rather than

weaken the authorship of John.[1] Since, then, there was essentially peace on this question down to the end of the eighteenth century, when an Englishman, Edward Evanson, in 1792, attacked the apostolic origin of the fourth Gospel, and ascribed it to a Platonic philosopher of the second century. Of a much more serious character were the objections raised twenty-two years afterwards by a German rationalist, Bretschneider, who, however, had the good sense to write his book in the Latin language for scholars only, and who formally withdrew his opposition a few years afterwards, saying that his object had been attained by calling forth more satisfactory proofs of the apostolic origin of this Gospel than had before been offered.

But the most powerful assaults were made against the authorship of John toward the middle of this century, when the speculative philosophy of Hegel had turned the heads of many learned theologians, especially in Germany, resurrecting in this nineteenth century the fundamental views of ancient Gnosticism, and particularly the principle that the "Jesus of history and the Christ of faith" are not and cannot be identical. Now this is the very position which in the Gospel and the Epistles of John is characterized as "anti-christian." We cannot, therefore, be in the least surprised to see that the fourth Gospel has become the main object of the most determined and cunning attacks on the part of modern speculation.[2]

We can readily see that the opposition to John, as the author of the fourth Gospel, is a life question for modern negative, theology which denies that Jesus is the Son of God in the sense in which the Church maintains this confession; that is, in the sense of the Gospel of John. The acceptance of the testimony of John, the son of Zebedee, the disciple whom the Lord loved, involves for a candid mind, in principle, the acceptance of Christ, the God-man, the incarnate Word, the Lord of glory.

---

[1] See Dr. Fisher's Remarks on the Alogi in "Papers of the American Society of Church History," Vol. II. 1.

[2] Moses in the beginning, Isaiah in the middle, and John at the end of the 1600 years of Bible literature are naturally the principal points on which the enemies of revelation concentrate their forces.

III. The Gospel of St. John

But very few are honest enough to confess that its antagonism to their philosophical standpoint is the first and principal cause of their opposition to this Gospel, while the "interests of unprejudiced science" and "historical criticism," of which we hear so much, are in reality a secondary consideration. The most systematic and learned effort to destroy the historical and canonical character of the fourth Gospel was made by Professor Baur in Tübingen (1844). He labored to prove that it was the most ingeniously planned and most successfully executed work of some "great unknown"[1] writer of the second half of the second century, designed to end the contests between Jewish and Gentile Christianity and to settle the controversies that had arisen in those days through different sectarian tendencies in the interest of one catholic church. According to this, the book would be all theory, theology, and partisan theology at that, while its artfully constructed historical form would be nothing but a sham. The followers and pupils of Professor Baur, though at first, as it seemed, zealously engaged to support and magnify their master's work, soon began to undermine it by new and conflicting theories, and ere long their own testimony had carried the date of the book back to the beginning of the second century; that is, close to the time of John's death. Unanimous only in the denial of the apostolic origin of the book, the members of this school vigorously demolished each other by their conflicting theories.[1] But all these attacks have, in the end, been of great service to the Church. This negative criticism has compelled the positive theologians of all creeds and nationalities to enter more fully than ever upon the investigation of this whole field, and the mature results they have obtained have established the fact, that "in order to combat with any show of success the authenticity of the Gospel of St. John, the whole history of the Church and its literature during the first

---

[1] Greater not only than the Epigones and literary pigmies of the second century whose names have all been preserved, but greater even than the Synoptists themselves! What a cruel freak of history!

[1] The revolting absurdity of these different attempts culminates in that blasphemous book of Noack, which undertook to prove that Judas was the disciple whom the Lord loved and the writer of this Gospel!

two centuries must be turned upside down and demolished" (Ebrard). For one thing particularly we have reason to be thankful to our negative critics. They have, with consummate skill and acumen, proved the organic unity of the fourth Gospel, and while in other fields of biblical criticism[2] the tendency has been to pick to pieces the books in question, and to show that they were composed on the principle of the "crazy quilt," they all agree that John's Gospel is one indivisible unit, "the seamless garment which cannot be rent" (D. Fr. Strauss).

2. *The Testimony of the Ancient Church.*—A few facts only under this head in the briefest summary. It is a fact that cannot be gainsaid that the fourth Gospel never appeared in the primitive Church under any other name but that of John. Through three centuries, beginning in the fourth after Christ, we can trace the testimonies of the fathers back to the very threshold of the Apostolic Era. *Eusebius* (A. D. 324), who certainly had the most comprehensive knowledge of the past history of the Church, as well as of its literature and tradition, mentions the fourth Gospel as one of the uncontradicted writings of the Apostle John, "unanimously acknowledged by all churches under heaven." *Origen* (185–254), the *Alexandrine*, the foremost scholar before Eusebius and the most critical mind of the patristic period, praises the fourth as *the* choice Gospel. *Tertullian* (160–220), the great representative of the *African Church*, who shows a deep insight into the whole organism of the Canon of sacred literature, has numerous quotations from John.[1] The *Canon of Muratori* (c. 170 A. D.) gives us the testimony of the Church of *Italy*. It has the fourth Gospel, and ascribes it to John, "one of the disciples." In the Syriac version of the Bible, called *Peshittho* (c. 170), the Church of *Syria* joins her testimony to that of the other lands. *Irenæus* (c. 130–202), uniting the testimony of Asia Minor and of the *Gallic* Church, is one of the principal witnesses, being the disciple of Polycarp (died 167, having been a Christian for eighty-six years), who told him of his intercourse with the

---

[2] Pentateuch, Isaiah, Synoptists.

[1] Clement of Alexandria, his contemporary, a very learned father, to whom we owe important statements concerning John's life in Asia Minor, speaks of John's Gospel as the last, and the spiritual Gospel over against the Synoptists.

III. The Gospel of St. John

Apostle John. Now, Irenæus gives it as a generally acknowledged, undisputed fact that John, the disciple who was on the bosom of the Lord, wrote his Gospel at Ephesus. *Justin, the Martyr* (100–166), the first Gentile scholar and philosopher within the Christian Church; who attempts to unite Christian thought with speculative elements foreign to Christianity, and has a peculiarly developed doctrine of the Logos, which is used by modern negative critics to prove his priority to John's Gospel, has been shown by the most recent and thorough investigations of Zahn to contain a number of unmistakable references to prominent passages in St. John. The *Epistles of Ignatius* (not later than 110 A. D.) and the *Epistle of Barnabas* (of the last decade of the first century) show traces of acquaintance with the Gospel of John. The recently discovered "*Doctrine of the Twelve*" (c. 90) reveals in the prayers of the Eucharist remarkable reminiscences of John 15 and 17.

3. *The Testimony of the Enemies in the Second Century.*—In addition to this testimony of friends, we also point to that of the enemies of Christianity in the second century. The first polemic treatise written against Christianity was the "True Logos" (161–180) of *Celsus*, who had evidently made a thorough study of his subject, going back to the first sources everywhere. His references are more frequently to Matthew; but he uses John more than either Mark or Luke, and the Christ whom he combats is mainly the Christ of the fourth Gospel, proving beyond dispute that even before the time of Celsus this Gospel was known and recognized by friend and foe as an authoritative record of Christianity. But the most remarkable testimony lies in the fact that not one of the *ancient Gnostics* ventured to deny that the fourth Gospel was written by St. John, though such a statement would have been the strongest testimony in their hands. Foremost among them stands *Marcion*, who came to Rome about 140 A. D., after having been at work for some time in Asia Minor. He was the most radical and consistent enemy of the Church, being convinced that it had degenerated under Judaizing influences, and resolved to form a new church on the ruins of the old. For this purpose he needed a new canon reconstructed on the idea that Paul was the one great authority over against the other apostles. His antagonism against the

Gospel of John is undeniable, and the attempts made by our modern critics to represent John in essential harmony with the ancient head of Gnosticism is a poor makeshift, the hollowness of which has been fully proved by the recent investigations of Luthardt, and particularly Zahn.

4. *The Testimony of the Gospel itself on the Question of Authorship.*—The last word we properly give to the Gospel itself. What does it say directly or indirectly on this point? The answer has really been given in the statements made on the relation of the fourth Gospel to the Synoptists, on the language and the historical features of the Gospel. Here it will be sufficient to recall the principal points, and sum them up briefly. The *language* of the book strongly indicates a Hebrew writer who continued to *think* in the language of his native country, though he wrote in Greek. The author is perfectly *at home in the ways and manners of Jewish life and belief*, and thoroughly rooted in the *Old Testament revelation*, which influences even his language, and suggests to him figures of speech altogether foreign to profane Greek. Of Old Testament books, the Pentateuch, the Psalms, the prophets, but particularly *Isaiah*, appear to be most familiar to the author (the last was also the favorite book of John the Baptist, the first teacher of John, the son of Zebedee). On Old Testament ground, not on Hellenic or Hellenistic, did this Gospel grow. The author knew the *Old Testament in the original*, not from the LXX. translation only. And as the Jews of the Diaspora in those days, as a rule, knew little Hebrew, this knowledge of the Old Testament language points to *Palestine* as the home of the writer. This is further demonstrated by his manifest familiarity with the different localities of Palestine, the scenes around the Lake of Galilee, the valley of Sychar, Jerusalem and its neighborhood he introduces in the narrative as only one well acquainted with all those places could do. It is an *eye-witness* who wrote this Gospel, manifesting from first to last the deepest personal interest in what he narrates. This is proven also by the great number of exact *chronological data* and the many *incidental little touches* which give to the whole account of this Gospel such a remarkable picturesqueness and realism. Moreover,

---

LXX. Septuagint

III. The Gospel of St. John

this eye-witness was one who moved in the circle of the Twelve, showing more familiarity with the conversations, and the intimate relation between the Lord and each member of this circle than any of the Synoptists.[1]

Finally, we make bold to say that the Gospel itself indicates one of the sons of Zebedee, John, as its author. The Synoptists tell us that James and John belonged to the inner circle of three who had special privileges in their intercourse with the Lord, and yet, in the fourth Gospel, those two and the other members of their family are never mentioned by name. This silence is certainly not due to an attempt to slight John or his family, but it is an indication of the modest reserve in which the writer kept himself, and from which he emerges only in the twenty-first chapter as the disciple whom the Lord loved, and whom the closing words of that chapter, added by another hand, designate as the author.

In addition to all this testimony, let us remember the manifest differences which have been pointed out, in the preceding pages, between the fourth Gospel and the Synoptic account, and to which we refer in this connection as one of the strongest evidences of the authorship of John. There is no rule of logic in the world that would compel us to believe that any record which adds certain essential features to another and previous account of the same history should in itself not be entitled to be credited. Why cannot both be true? Why cannot one witness or reporter notice and make prominent a feature which was not noticed or not marked in its full import by other witnesses or reporters? But more than that. In this case the very difference becomes an essential evidence of the originality and apostolic authority of the record, which, with all its palpable deviations from the earlier Synoptical accounts, quietly takes its place by their side, claiming, as a matter of course, fully the same authority and credence with the others. Who but an apostle, and, if an apostle, who but the last surviving apostle, dared to set before

---

[1] 1:38–50 4:31–38; 6:5–9, 70: 9:2; 11:16; 12:21; 13:6–9, 23–25, 27, 30; 14:5, 8, 22; 16:17 f., 29 f.; 18:16; 20:2, 3, 28.

the Church a record of the life of Christ so evidently at variance with the acknowledged gospel tradition of the Synoptists, which had taken such firm root throughout the Church? Would not an impostor, anxious to secure recognition for his new and original presentation of the life of Christ, have been very careful to preserve intact the whole historical frame of the Synoptists and to make the Lord Jesus speak as nearly as possible in the same style as the Sermon on the Mount and the Parables? How could such a writer, nearly a hundred years after the death of the last apostle, ever expect to find acceptance, instead of meeting with decided protest and being at once charged with intentional deception? But the writer of the fourth Gospel is utterly unconcerned about any such possibility. There is a grand indifference to it on every page of his book. He writes as one "having authority," being complete *master* of his subject, and ready to face the whole account of the Synoptists and the whole tradition of the Church concerning the life of Jesus Christ.

And thus this Gospel stands to-day, ready to face modern scientism, unshaken by its fierce attacks, the joy and the very jewel of Apostolic literature for all those who truly believe that Jesus is the Christ, the Son of God, and believing this have life in His name.

III. THE GOSPEL OF ST. JOHN

FIRST PART.—CHAPTERS 1–4

THE BEGINNING OF FAITH IN THE INCARNATE WORD, AS THE ABSOLUTE REVELATION OF GOD

JOHN 1

I. The Opening Section, 1:1–18 ("The Prologue")

1. Beginning and Theme of the Gospel

This opening or introductory passage is generally called the "Prologue," which, in the common understanding, means a sort of theological preface, wherein the writer is said to have set forth in an abstract, didactic form the fundamental ideas, by which he was guided in the presentation of his gospel. This view, which may suit well enough for the philosophical preface of a modern historical treatise, is altogether contrary to the spirit and conception of this fourth Gospel. It is, from the first word to the last, a *history*, a simple array of facts, told in the plainest manner by one who is called to *witness* these facts. The God-man is the subject of this Gospel. His history is to be presented. Accordingly the very first verse contains a statement of facts concerning the *beginnings* of this God-man, in the fullest and most exhaustive sense of the word. Far beyond the beginnings of Mark, Matthew and Luke—yea, back of the beginning of Genesis itself, into eternity we are carried by the opening words of John. He starts at the very gates of eternity and at once presents the theme of his Gospel in its full extent: *The incarnate Word [Logos], the absolute revelation of God; on the one side the faith that receives Him, and on the other side the unbelief that rejects Him*. The three principal parts of the Gospel are as follows: 1. The beginnings of faith, that receives Him, ch. 1–4; 2. The hostility of unbelief, that rejects Him, ch. 5–12; 3. The triumph of faith; the glorified Word among His own, ch. 13–21.

I. The Opening Section, 1:1–18 ("The Prologue")

2. The Word ("Logos")

Not before the 17th verse is the historic name of Jesus Christ introduced in this Gospel. In the beginning of the Prologue a peculiar name is used to designate Him. He is called "the Word" (Logos). John alone uses this term in speaking of the only begotten Son of the Father; and he uses it only in the Prologue, not in the other parts of the Gospel; in the first verse of the first epistle 1 John 1:1, "the Word of Life," and in the Book of Revelation 19:13, his name is called "the Word of God." We have the impression that this term "the Word," as used of the Son of God, was at once understood by the readers of the Gospel, as it was by the readers of the Epistle and of the Revelation. It is clearly used in a personal sense. It is not the impersonal word of God, the means of grace, which is being preached in the Law and the Gospel. This personal use of the term appears much more strange and uncommon to us than to the Greek readers, because the Greek word Logos is a masculine form. A great deal of learning has been expended by many writers in following up this term "Logos" through divers Jewish and pagan systems of philosophy and religious speculation. The names and writings of the great Greek philosopher Plato, and the Alexandrian Jew, Philo, are prominently brought forward in this connection, as if the writer of the fourth Gospel had been a pupil of Plato or Philo, receiving from them this peculiar term "Logos," to transplant it into the sphere of Christianity and to dress it up in a Christian garb!

But John uses the term "Logos" quite independently of Greek or Alexandrine scholars and their systems. He tells us himself in his prologue most plainly and directly what the name "Logos" means to him. We take the last verse of the Prologue (1:18) and compare it with the first and with all the others in which the term "Logos" is used. There he says: "No man hath seen God at any time; the only begotten Son, which is in the bosom of the Father, he hath *declared him*." He has become the exegete, the interpreter, of the Father. He reveals Him in such a manner as He has never before been revealed. "God, having of old time spoken unto the fathers in the prophets by divers portions and in divers manners, hath at the end of these days spoken unto us in his Son" (Hebr. 1:1). Even among men it is true, or it ought to be true, that the "word" is to be the full, adequate, honest representation of the "man." "Ein Mann ein Wort," says one of the most beautiful and significant German proverbs. The Word reveals and communicates to the outside world His innermost nature, His thoughts, feelings and volitions. The "Word" is therefore the most comprehensive and appropriate title for Him, in whom the final, essential and absolute revelation of the Father appeared in person. The "Logos" speaks out to the world whatever is in the bosom of the Father. He manifests His name to the men whom He gave Him out of the world. The words which the Father gave Him He hath given unto them. And the glory which the Father hath given Him, He hath given unto them (John 17:6, 8, 22). In His person we have the absolute, complete mediation and communication between the Father and the world. If anyone ask Him, as Philip did: "Shew us the Father," he will receive from the Logos that same old answer: "He that hath seen me, hath seen the Father."

3. The Eternal and Creative Word (1:1–3)

1–3. In the beginning was the Word, and the Word was with God, and the Word was God. The same was in the beginning with God. All things were made by him; and without him was not anything made that hath been made.

Of this Logos John says: "*In the beginning was the Word*," etc. (Ver. 1 and 2). It existed, or, speaking of the personal Logos, He had His being before anything had a beginning. He *was*—before time, before creation—He never was made, as all things were made; He simply *was* with God in close, loving communion with Him, co-equal, co-eternal with Him, Himself God. This uncreated Logos is Himself active in the creation. All things are made through Him. Creation itself is part of God's manifestation or revelation. In so far it comes into the sphere of the Logos. Without Him, the exegete, or interpreter, creation would not tell us anything of God, His nature and His thoughts. All the grandeur and beauty of nature would stare at us dumb and meaningless if the Logos had not given speech to it, and chosen it as an organ of revelation. From Him it is that "the heavens declare the glory of God and the firmament

I. The Opening Section, 1:1–18 ("The Prologue")

showeth His handiwork;" that "day unto day uttereth speech, and night unto night showeth knowledge;" from Him it is that "the invisible things of God, since the creation of the world, are clearly seen, being perceived through the things that are made, even His everlasting power and divinity" (Rom. 1:20).

4. The Word of Salvation (1:4–9)

4–9. *In him was life; and the life was the light of men. And the light shineth in the darkness; and the darkness apprehended it not. There came a man, sent from God, whose name was John. The same came for witness, that he might bear witness of the light, that all might believe through him. He was not the light, but came that he might bear witness of the light. There was the true light, even the light which lighteth every man, coming into the world.*

The Logos as the absolute revelation of God, does not simply reveal and communicate certain abstract *knowledge*. He is *Life and Light*, health and salvation in the midst of darkness. The Evangelist does not stop to answer the question, Whence the darkness? How did it enter this creation of the Logos, full of His life and His light? He simply states the fact that the light of the Logos is shining in the darkness. From the threshold of Paradise, lost ever since the fall of man, this light shineth in the darkness. The Spirit of Christ in the men of God, that prophesied of the grace that should come (1 Pet. 1:10, 11), testified beforehand of Christ. This testimony, coming from the Logos, extending through the whole Old Testament, and preparing the way for the personal appearance of the Logos in the flesh, culminated in the "man, sent from God, whose name was John, who came to bear witness of the Light." For this true light was on its way, coming into the world. How will it be received? It is coming, the way is well prepared for it by ample testimony. What kind of a welcome will the world give to it?

5. The Word Rejected by the World (1:10, 11)

10–11. *He was in the world, and the world was made by him, and the world knew him not. He came unto his own, and they that were his own received him not.*

Mark here the expression of sadness, the tragic character, which is one of the peculiar and prominent features of the fourth Gospel. Over against the flood of light and life and glory, offered to the world in the coming of the Logos, there is a complete indifference to Him on the part of the world. He was in the world, and the world was made by Him and the world knew Him not. He came unto His own, and they that were His own received Him not. Observe the climax in these two verses. It is bad enough that the world, which was made by Him, should not *know* Him. But it is much worse that His own—*Israel*, the members of the Old Testament Theocracy, the chosen people of God—should not *receive* Him. If the former is a lack of knowledge and recognition, the latter is a determined opposition, an unwillingness to give Him the place that properly belonged to Him, to submit to Him with grateful and believing hearts.

6. The Word Received by the Children of God (1:12–13)

12–13. *But as many as received him, to them gave he the right to become children of God, even to them that believe on his name: which were born, not of blood, nor of the will of the flesh, nor of the will of man, but of God.*

But after all, in spite of the enmity and indifference of the world, the old prophecy (Isaiah 55:10, 11) shall be fulfilled: "The word that goeth forth out of my mouth shall not return unto me void, but it shall accomplish that which I please, and it shall prosper in the thing whereto I send it." The Logos revelation is not altogether lost on the world. Not in vain has He been active from the beginning in the creation of the world. Not in vain has His testimony gone forth, shining through the darkness with light from above. There are in this world not only *creatures of God*, ignoring and rejecting the Logos; there are also *children of God*, receiving Him and believing on His name. Though "His own," as a whole, rejectt Him, there are *individuals* (ὅσοι), exceptions from the majority, counted by God and known to Him, however few or many, that receive Him. But to receive Him is to *believe on His name*. Here we meet for the first time this word, which is more frequent in the Gospel of John than in any of the Synoptists. It describes the proper attitude of men towards the light

I. The Opening Section, 1:1–18 ("The Prologue")

which appears in the Logos; not, however, as a work of man, of human strength, but simply as the receiving of what God works in man. It is believing on His *name*. He must be named and known in order to be believed in. (The words "name" and to "know" spring from the same root in the language of the New Testament.) There must be a making known, a revealing of His nature and character, giving light and knowledge concerning God and world and self. There is no faith without this knowledge, although this knowledge is not yet full, true, saving faith. Such faith is only where the heart accepts Him with the blessed assurance: Thou art mine! The fruit of such faith is the new creature. It may be of interest at this point to compare the different aspects under which the term "children of God" is presented by different writers of the New Testament. In the Synoptical Gospels (particularly in the sermon on the mount) the term designates the moral character of the Christian, being likeminded with God, Matt. 5:9 (the peacemakers); 5:16, by the good works of the children, the Father in heaven is to be glorified (5:45, 48); love to the enemies and moral perfection are to be the characteristic features of sons of God.[1] With St. Paul the state of adoption is contrasted with the state of bondage, it is the freedom of the Gospel over against the servitude of the Law. (Rom. 8:14, 15, ye have not received the spirit of bondage again to fear; but ye have received the spirit of adoption, whereby we cry, Abba Father.) With John the term "children of God" embodies the idea of being of the same nature with God—spiritual, begotten of God, born of the Spirit over against the natural birth of the flesh and that awful condition of being the children of the devil, as the Lord charged His stubborn, hardened adversaries: "Ye are not of God, ye are of your father, the devil, and the lusts of your father it is your will to do" (John 8:44, 47).

7. The Word Incarnate (1:14)

14. *And the Word became flesh, and dwelt among us (and we beheld his glory, glory as of the only begotten from the Father), full of grace and truth.*

---

[1] Cf. also Luke 6:36: "Be ye merciful, even as your Father in heaven is merciful."

This verse at last announces the cardinal fact of Christianity, the incarnation of the eternal Logos, in the same direct manner, which characterized the preceding statements concerning the Logos. The three words of the original introduce a simple historical fact; but it is the central fact in the history of mankind and in the history of God's kingdom, an everlasting offence to Jews and Gentiles, Rationalists and Pantheists. In its innermost nature it will always remain a mystery, an unfathomable wonder of divine love. To appreciate it we must not forget what had been said from the first verse concerning the Logos; nor what has been said, in the immediately preceding verses, concerning the flesh. What a contrast! But now the bold combination of the two—the Word and the flesh. The Word was in the beginning and never ceased to be what it had been from eternity. But now it became what it had not been before—it was made flesh. The term is stronger even than the well-known: "God manifested in the flesh" (1 Tim. 3:16), or the expression used by 1 John 4:2: "He came in the flesh." It is the fullest real communion of the Logos with us, which is emphasized by this expression. There is no change in the nature of the Logos Himself, but only in His mode of existence. The glory which belongs to the Logos from eternity is not lost through His incarnation. The divine nature, with its inherent glory, and the human nature, with its inherent weakness, are now inseparably united in the one person of the incarnate Logos, the God-man, of whom we say correctly: This man is God, and God is this man. Henceforth we cannot and dare not separate the eternal divinity of the Logos and the true humanity of the flesh which He assumed. Wherever we meet our Lord and Saviour, the incarnate Word, whether it be in the manger, or on the cross, or on the throne at the right hand of the Father, there the true God and the true man are inseparably united.[1]

---

[1] "Yea, if I should myself be lost (which God forbid!) I should still rejoice that Christ of my flesh and bone is sitting in heaven at the right hand of God. Such honor has been given to what is my bone, flesh and blood," says M. Luther.

I. The Opening Section, 1:1–18 ("The Prologue")

8. The Incarnate Word Dwelling among Us

He who, in the beginning, was with God, was now dwelling among men, a true Immanuel—God with us—a Shekinah, different from the passing manifestations of divine glory in the Old Testament called theophanies. He was at home with us men, says John, we have eaten with Him at the same table, slept with Him under the same roof: we have gone out and come in with Him; we had Him with us as our friend and brother—our fellow-citizen and companion of our pilgrimage. By this close fellowship we had an opportunity to behold His glory. We, says the Evangelist, including himself, and mentioning in particular, as the first one among these eye-witnesses, John the Baptist (in the 15th verse). To behold His glory eyes of faith were needed, then as well as now, as the Lord said to Martha: "If thou believedst, thou shouldest see the glory of God" (John 11:40). It is the "glory of the only begotten Son of the Father." Thus He is clearly distinguished from the many that received the right to become the children of God, through Him, the only begotten Son of the Father. His glory, as revealed by His incarnation, is characterized as the fulness of grace and truth: *Grace* that condescends to the sinner, reclaims the lost, invites the weary and heavy-laden, bears the weak in patience, makes intercession for His enemies on the cross—this is the true glory of the incarnate Word to which all the manifestations of His power, His signs and miracles are made subservient. And united to this grace is *truth*; the absolute revelation, as grace represents the absolute redemption; truth over against all darkening and misrepresentation, but also in antithesis to everything that is vain, unreal, passing, while the life and light, brought by the incarnate Word, are substantial realities of abiding value.

9. Receiving out of His Fulness (1:15–18)

15–18. *John beareth witness of him, and crieth, saying, This was he of whom I said, He that cometh after me is become before me: for he was before me. For of his fulness we all received, and grace for grace. For the law was given by Moses; grace and truth came by Jesus Christ. No man hath seen God at any time; the only begotten Son, which is in the bosom of the Father, he hath declared him.*

To the blessed experience of the 14th verse, "We beheld His Glory," a better one is added: "*Of His fulness we all received, and grace for grace.*" This actual receiving, taking from His fulness, is the one need for all. It is made possible through the testimony of the witnesses of the incarnate Word, such as John the Baptist. No matter what gifts men may have received already from the Creator's hands, their true and abiding treasures come only out of the fulness of grace and truth of the incarnate Word. Before Him all of us—the most learned and gifted, as well as the unwise and unlearned—must be simply receivers. But this very privilege of taking from His fulness is the glorious and distinctive mark of the New Testament revelation, of Christ over against Moses, the Gospel over against the Law. The Law demands, the grace of the Lord Jesus Christ freely gives. Here is the end of Moses. The absolute revelation came by the only begotten Son, who is in the bosom of the Father, who hath declared Him as the Word made flesh.

II. THE TESTIMONY OF JOHN THE BAPTIST (1:19–34)

1. *First Testimony before the Jewish Delegation (1:19–28)*

19–28. *And this is the witness of John, when the Jews sent unto him from Jerusalem priests and Levites to ask him, Who art thou? And he confessed, and denied not; and he confessed, I am not the Christ. And they asked him, What then? Art thou Elijah? And he saith, I am not. Art thou the prophet? And he answered, No. They said therefore unto him, Who art thou? that we might give an answer to them that sent us. What sayest thou of thyself? He said, I am the voice of one crying in the wilderness, Make straight the way of the Lord, as said Isaiah the prophet. And they had been sent from the Pharisees. And they asked him, and said unto him, Why then baptizest thou, if thou art not the Christ, neither Elijah, neither the prophet? John answered them, saying, I baptize with water: in the midst of you standeth one whom ye know not, even he that cometh after me, the latchet of whose shoe I am not worthy to unloose. These things were done in Bethany beyond Jordan, where John was baptizing.*

As in the other Evangelists, so also in John, the Gospel history proper begins with the testimony of the forerunner, John the Baptist,

II. The Testimony of John the Baptist (1:19–34)

whose surname "the Baptist," however, is not once mentioned in the fourth Gospel. He is simply "John," the writer of the Gospel finding it unnecessary to mark him more particularly in distinction from another John, the author himself. There is no doubt that the *writer* of the *fourth Gospel* stood in a peculiarly *intimate relation*, not only to the Lord Jesus Christ, but also to John the Baptist. We found already in two passages of the "Prologue," direct references to John the Baptist, the former master and teacher of the Evangelist. But now he leads us deeper into the very heart of the testimony of the Baptist concerning Christ. No other disciple so fully grasped the very centre of the Baptist's preaching. The fourth Gospel holds the same place in this respect as it does with its conception and presentation of the teachings of the Lord Himself. In the Synoptical Gospels the Baptist's preparatory preaching of repentance is the principal point. Only in a secondary and indirect manner do they refer to his testimony concerning the Person and work of the Lord. But in the fourth Gospel this latter is the main thing. Here we learn that the Baptist's preaching already gave forth such a full and clear sound concerning the Person of Christ, as the One that cometh after him, and yet is before him, the latchet of whose shoe he is not worthy to unloose, and concerning the work of Christ as the Lamb of God which taketh away the sins of the world. These were the principal features in the preaching of John the Baptist, and they are placed in the foreground in the fourth Gospel, in distinction from the Synoptists.[1]

At the time when the testimony recorded in these verses (1:19–28) was given by the Baptist, he must have already passed the height of his public ministry. He had made that deep impression which led many to ask whether he was not Christ (Luke 3:15). And under the pressure of the deep commotion created by his appearance and preaching, the Sanhedrim in Jerusalem at last finds itself compelled to take action with regard to this man. This Council, at the time of Christ, consisted of seventy-one members, including the president, high priests, elders and

---

[1] With them John the Baptist is pre-eminently the preacher of the Law. In the fourth Gospel he appears principally as the preacher of the Gospel.

scribes, among whose duties it was distinctly mentioned, that they should give their judgment concerning "false prophets."

The commission of Priests and Levites sent from Jerusalem to John the Baptist is represented as coming from *"the Jews."* This name "Jews" is one of the characteristic features of the fourth Gospel, in which it occurs about seventy times, whilst the Synoptical Gospels use it much less frequently. Here and there in the fourth Gospel it appears simply as an indifferent neutral term, to designate the nationality. But in most cases it has a specific meaning, referring to the religious attitude of the people, describing them as the enemies of the Messianic kingdom. In the Old Testament the original name of honor for God's chosen people is "Israel" (as the Lord speaks of Nathanael in this very chapter, ver. 47). The name "Jews" appears at a very late period, from the time that Israel was carried away into captivity (2 Kings 16:6; Jerem. 34:9), when the people as a whole had departed from the faith of their fathers. There can be no doubt that here also the animus of this delegation sent to John the Baptist was by no means friendly towards John and the kingdom he preached.

In the *three negative answers* which the Baptist returns to the questions of the ecclesiastical commission he clearly and decidedly refutes all the current ideas about his person and office. He is not the Messiah, not Elias, not the prophet. The first point is clear enough. But how about the other two? The very last prophetical statement of the Old Testament connected the appearance of Elijah with the coming of Messiah. (Mal. 4:5, 6), "Behold, I will send you *Elijah* the prophet, before the coming of the great and dreadful day of the Lord, and he shall turn the heart of the fathers to the children and the heart of the children to their fathers, lest I come and smite the earth with a curse." And the very first New Testament message of the angel to Zacharias, takes up that last word of the Old Testament at the threshold of the New, and applies it to John the Baptist, the forerunner of the Lord (Luke 1:17). And the Lord Himself leaves us not in doubt as to the meaning of that prophecy concerning Elias. (See Matt. 17:9–13) And yet in the face of all this John says to the inquiring Jews: "I am not Elias." In the sense in which the Jews expected the re-appearance of Elias, and which had been minutely

II. THE TESTIMONY OF JOHN THE BAPTIST (1:19–34)

detailed by their scribes,[1] in the gross material sense of a resurrection or soul-migration, he was not Elias, but an individuality of his own, distinct from Elias. It is a similar case with the *"Prophet."* Zacharias had said of the newborn John: "Thou child shalt be called the Prophet of the Highest: for thou shalt go before the face of the Lord to prepare His ways." And the Lord said distinctly: "What went ye out for to see? A prophet? Yea, I say unto you and more than a prophet." And yet again John answers in the negative: I am not the "prophet," in the sense of the Jews, after their construction of Deut. 18:15, or according to the expectation of the reappearance of the prophet Jeremiah.

At last, after all these negatives, John returns a *positive answer to* those inquiries concerning his person and work: "I am the *voice* of one crying in the wilderness," etc.—Of the two Old Testament passages (Mal. 3:1, and Isaiah 40:3) referring directly to himself he selects the one that speaks in the humblest terms of his position. "A voice," and nothing more; nothing in himself, no honor for his own person; merely an instrument of Him that crieth in the wilderness. "Wilderness!"—what a suggestion to Israel, and especially to the leaders of God's people who had come to interrogate John! The place of the darkest and saddest experiences of the Israelites before their entrance into the promised Canaan. Such was Israel's condition again at the time of John's preaching. Though in Canaan with their bodies, they were in the wilderness spiritually, in a state of utter desolation, like sheep without a shepherd, and the very men who stood before John as inquisitors, were responsible for this condition. Therefore the Evangelist significantly adds: The men that had been sent were *"from among the Pharisees."* The information which the Baptist gave concerning his person became a rebuke to the men that stood before him and those that had sent them. He had before this used the severest language against the Pharisees and Sadducees (Matt. 3:7; Luke 3:7). "But the Pharisees and the lawyers rejected for themselves the counsel of God, being not baptized of him" (Luke 7:30).

---

[1] They held that he would have to anoint the Messiah: that he should come three days before the coming of Christ, etc.

The Pharisees were the men of unyielding traditionalism, of the strictest ecclesiastical conservatism. Josephus mentions them first at the time of the high priest Jonathan, 145 before Christ. The exact time of their origin as a separate party is difficult to define. We can trace them back to the ancient "Chasidim," the pious, " 'the devout," from whom also came the Maccabean heroes. Gradually they developed into the "Perushim"—that is, the "separated ones," who held themselves to be purer and holier than others. But with their strict observance of outward forms and traditions they lost the spirit of true devotion and were henceforth characterized by their servitude to the letter, their self-righteousness and hypocrisy, and their readiness in raising questions of subtle casuistry. Ever since the time of the Maccabees, whenever those leaders began to favor an alliance with Rome, the Pharisees were also a political party, zealously contending for the national independence of Israel over against all foreign influence or interference.

Having received John's answer concerning his person, they add another question concerning his *authority to baptize*, being neither Christ nor Elias, nor the prophet. It appears, then, that they looked upon baptism as one of the signs and prerogatives of the Messianic Era.[1] John's answer characterizes his baptism simply as "baptizing with water;" as Matt. 3:11 has it: "I indeed baptize you with water unto repentance, but He that cometh after me is mightier than I. He shall baptize you with the Holy Ghost and with fire." His baptism symbolizes repentance on the part of those that receive it, and readiness for entrance into the kingdom of the Messiah. Here, then, is the justification of John's baptism: The kingdom of Christ is at hand. "He standeth in the midst of you!" But though the promised One has come, the leaders of Israel "know Him not."

So important seems this event to the Evangelist that he marks carefully the locality where it happened. It was at Bethany, not Bethabara,

---

[1] The practice of baptizing proselytes which is claimed by some writers as an ancient Jewish custom is very doubtful, at least as far as its date is concerned. Philo and Joseph us know nothing of it. Maimonides, in the 12th century, is the first to mention it directly, saying that it had been customary in the times of David and Solomon, whilst other rabbinical writers date it back to the time of the Patriarchs!

II. The Testimony of John the Baptist (1:19–34)

as Origen changed the text in the third century, because he was unable, more than two centuries afterward, to find a trace of such a village on the Jordan. As we have in the Scriptures two Canas, two Bethlehems, two Ramas, etc., so there were two Bethanys; the one "nigh unto Jerusalem, about fifteen furlongs off" (John 11:18), the other distinctly marked in this passage as "Bethany beyond Jordan."[1]

2. Second Testimony of John the Baptist Addressed to his Disciples (1:29–34)

29–34. *On the morrow he seeth Jesus coming unto him, and saith, Behold, the Lamb of God, which taketh away the sin of the world. This is he of whom I said, After me cometh a man which is become before me: for he was before me. And I knew him not; but that he should be made manifest to Israel, for this cause came I baptizing with water. And John bare witness, saying, I have beheld the Spirit descending as a dove out of heaven; and it abode upon him. And I knew him not: but he that sent me to baptize with water, he said unto me, Upon whomsoever thou shalt see the Spirit descending, and abiding upon him, the same is he that baptizeth with the Holy Spirit. And I have seen, and have borne witness that this is the Son of God.*

The solemn testimony of the Baptist before the commissioners from Jerusalem seems to have been lost on them. They departed without taking further notice of it. But the testimony given on the two following days, in the presence of the disciples of the Baptist and other hearers, had a different effect, as we shall presently see.

If the first testimony had spoken of the absent Christ, this second is given in His presence. The Baptist points to Him personally, bodily, as He is coming up from the Wilderness, probably after the temptation. "There He is Himself; behold the Lamb of God, which taketh away the sin of the world"—a brief and yet most comprehensive statement of the *work of Christ*. The "sins" of his hearers had been a constantly recurring theme

---

[1] The *distance* of the "Bethany beyond Jordan" is the point which the Evangelist intends to mark. John the Baptist "did not make things convenient for the Jews. He demanded that they should come clear over the Jordan to him."—Luthardt.

in the discourses of the Baptist. His preaching and baptizing were unto repentance and forgiveness of sins. But neither the personal repentance of the sinners, nor that symbolical baptism in itself, had the power of taking one sin really away and burying it out of sight. Here is the man to do this, and the true, divinely-appointed method of doing it: "The Lamb of God, which taketh away the sin of the world." It is *the* Lamb of God, provided by Him, appointed and chosen by God Himself; not altogether unknown in Israel, foreshadowed in the Passover-lamb, whose blood turned the avenging angel aside from the doors of God's people, directly prophesied in the well-known words of Isaiah 53, which were commonly accepted by the Jews as referring to the Messiah. Our English (Rev.) Version gives two readings of the verb in this sentence. In the text itself it is "taketh away;" on the margin it reads: "beareth." The two combined give the full meaning of this momentous term. The "taking away" of the world's sin is the principal idea, thus ridding the world of sin and all its consequences of guilt and judgment. But how can this terrible burden be lifted up and taken away if there is no one to put his hand to it, to take it up, burden himself with it, *bear* it on his own person and thus bring full deliverance from it? The question has been asked how far John the Baptist himself was fully conscious of the whole extent of this message, the mediatorial work of Christ, the meaning of His passion and death for the reconciliation of the world. We know how slow the disciples were to comprehend this. We know that John the Baptist himself, in his imprisonment, had his difficulties concerning the manner and method by which Christ carried on His work. But all this cannot affect the statement itself. It is, once for all, the briefest summary of Christ's whole work of redemption, and the Church could not but acknowledge its fulness and importance by incorporating it from the earliest time into her services, in the form of that beautiful prayer (the "Agnus Dei"): "O Christ, Thou Lamb of God, that takest away the sin of the world, have mercy upon us—grant us Thy peace."

    To this comprehensive testimony concerning the work of Christ, there is added a repetition and enlargement of his testimony concerning *the person* of Christ, emphasized by a direct pointing out of Him, who was

III. THE FIRST DISCIPLES OF. THE LORD (JOHN 1:35–51)

just coming to the speaker, and by a detailed reminiscence of what John had observed on the occasion of Christ's baptism. (Cf. Matt. 3:16, 17) The *Lamb of God* is identical with the *Son of God!* These are the culminating points in the testimony of the Baptist. Israel will find in the Messiah the *Son of God*, who makes His believers partakers of the glory of the children of God, only on condition that the Messiah must first be known as the *Lamb of God*.

III. THE FIRST DISCIPLES OF. THE LORD (JOHN 1:35–51)

35–51. *Again on the morrow John was standing, and two of his disciples; and he looked upon Jesus as he walked, and saith, Behold, the Lamb of God! And the two disciples heard him speak, and they followed Jesus. And Jesus turned, and beheld them following, and saith unto them, What seek ye? And they said unto him, Rabbi (which is to say, being interpreted, Master), where abidest thou? He saith unto them, Come, and ye shall see. They came therefore and saw where he abode; and they abode with him that day: it was about the tenth hour. One of the two that heard John speaks and followed him, was Andrew, Simon Peter's brother. He findeth first his own brother Simon, and saith unto him, We have found the Messiah (which is, being interpreted, Christ). He brought him unto Jesus. Jesus looked upon him, and said, Thou art Simon the son of John: thou shalt be called Cephas (which is by interpretation, Peter).*

On the morrow he was minded to go forth into Galilee, and he findeth Philip: and Jesus saith unto him, Follow me. Now Philip was from Bethsaida, of the city of Andrew and Peter. Philip findeth Nathanael, and saith unto him, We have found him, of whom Moses in the law, and the prophets, did write, Jesus of Nazareth, the son of Joseph. And Nathanael said unto him, Can any good thing come out of Nazareth? Philip saith unto him, Come and see. Jesus saw Nathanael coming to him, and saith of him, Behold, an Israelite indeed, in whom is no guile! Nathanael saith unto him, Whence knowest thou me? Jesus answered and said unto him, Before Philip called thee, when thou wast under the fig tree, I saw thee. Nathanael answered him, Rabbi, thou art the Son of God; thou art King of Israel. Jesus answered and said unto him, Because I said unto thee, I saw thee underneath the fig tree, believest thou? thou shalt see greater things than these. And he saith unto him, Verily, verily, I say unto you, Ye shall see the heaven opened, and the angels of God ascending and descending upon the Son of man.

The same impressive testimony of the "Lamb of God" is repeated by the Baptist on the following day in the presence of two of his disciples. They are moved thereby to leave John and to follow Jesus. *The transition from the Old to the New Testament is represented* in these disciples of the Baptist. There is no violent, revolutionary break. It is a matter of course, just as the natural falling of the ripened fruit, that these souls, so well prepared by the testimony of the Old Testament, and of their master, John, henceforth belong to Jesus. There is no outward constraining, no direct command of their former master, that sends them off to Jesus, but simply the testimony concerning Him which has convinced their hearts that in Him they have found the Messiah. Their question: Where abidest Thou? reminds us of the fact that the incarnate Word "dwelt among us." They have not far to go, and thus these first hearts come and see and receive from Him grace for grace. It is the beginning of the New Testament Church, after the definition of the Lord Himself: "Two or three gathered in His name," involving the principle also of constant growth, that the two—Andrew and his companion—increase to the number of five or six, and the six to twelve, to seventy, to 120, to 3000, and so on; one finding another, and brother leading the brother to Christ.

Andrew of Bethsaida, the man of prompt and quick decisions, is the first in the New Testament to call out that blessed Εὕρηκα in which the problem of life is solved. His companion is not named. No doubt it is the same anonymous one whom we can trace all through this Gospel, the eye-witness of the facts here recorded, who recalled so distinctly this memorable hour—the Evangelist himself. Having found the Lord, both go forth to bring their brothers also to the feet of Jesus. Andrew was the first to find his own brother Simon, whilst John the Evangelist went for his brother James.[1] There is a certain similarity of temper in the two brothers, Andrew and Simon; only what was promptness and readiness

---

[1] Clearly indicated in the original of the 41st verse οὗτος πρῶτος τὸν ἀδελφὸν ἴδιον.

III. THE FIRST DISCIPLES OF THE LORD (JOHN 1:35–51)

in Andrew frequently became rashness, impetuosity and hastiness with Peter. Looking to Simon's natural character, the wind or wave would appear to have furnished a more appropriate figure for a surname than the firm, immovable rock. But He who turned Saul the Pharisee into the herald of free grace and righteousness of faith, changed the excitable, hasty, denying Peter into the confessor who stood like a rock. But how often had sinking and vacillating Peter to be rescued by the Rock of Ages before he waxed strong enough to become a rock and a tower of strength to his brethren!

On the following day the Lord set out for Galilee, accompanied by those disciples. On the road he finds *Philip*, the townsman of Andrew and Peter. It is first said: "The Lord findeth Philip" (ver. 43), and afterwards Philip says: "We have found Him," etc. (ver. 45), even as Paul writes (Phil. 3:12): "That I may apprehend having been apprehended by Christ Jesus." This is in perfect accord with the peculiarity of Philip's character, which was marked by deliberation and slowness of decision.

Philip findeth *Nathanael*, who is generally regarded as identical with the Bartholomew of the other Evangelists, who all name him in connection with Philip. Possibly the name Nathanael (Theodore) might have been given to Bartholomew on this occasion. Philip evidently knows his friend Nathanael. He knows how well he is acquainted with Moses and the Prophets. The sober, devout study of the Old Testament and the earnest hope for the Messiah, who was to come, were prominent features of Nathanael's character. Therefore Philip announces the good news to him in these words: "We have found Him, of whom Moses in the Law and the Prophets did write, Jesus of Nazareth, the son of Joseph." In perfect harmony with this are the few directly personal words which the Lord addresses to Nathanael: "An Israelite indeed in whom is no guile." (See Psalm 32:2: "Blessed is the man unto whom the Lord imputeth not iniquity, in whose spirit there is no guile.") No wonder that he is completely overwhelmed as the Lord proceeds to remind him of those quiet, sacred hours of prayer and meditation spent under his fig tree! Straightway his heart leaps over the little stumbling-block—the lowly home of the Nazarene—and he bursts out in the fullest and most comprehensive confession of Christ: "Thou art the Son of God, Thou art the king of Israel," on which the Lord sets His own seal and approbation: "Thou believest," as He did on later occasions with Peter and Thomas.

And now with that solemn "Amen, Amen," "Verily, verily I say unto you," which is so frequent in John's Gospel, and which takes the place of the Old Testament "Thus saith the Lord," the last sentence of this wonderful first chapter is introduced, which pictures the beautiful union between heaven and earth since the appearance of the God-man—the heavens open, God's messengers active in lively intercourse between heaven and earth; another reminder of a well-known Old Testament passage, the ladder in Jacob's dream with that precious confession: "This is none other but the house of God, and this is the gate of heaven." But this experience, promised to Nathanael, is simply the reflex of what we read in the 14th verse of this chapter: Beholding "the glory of the only begotten from the Father, full of grace and truth."

One word yet demands a few remarks before we leave this chapter, *the Son of Man*. The whole chapter abounds in striking and glorious titles given to Jesus Christ our Saviour. The eternal Logos; the only begotten Son of the Father; the Lamb of God; the Son of God; the King of Israel; the Messiah. To these is now added this new and significant name: "The Son of Man," the Lord's favorite expression in speaking of Himself. Following, as it does, in this connection, so closely on the two names (used by Nathanael): "Son of God; King of Israel," the term "Son of Man" naturally seems to designate another important relation of Christ. If He is the Son of God in His relation to the Father, and the King of Israel in His relation to God's chosen people, He is the "Son of Man" in His relation to the human race as such. The Word incarnate is the seed of the woman, belonging to mankind, unfettered by any barriers of nationality. He is truly one of us. But He is at the same time above all men. With Him our history takes a new departure. He is "*the* Son of Man" (cf. Psalm 8), the second Adam, the new beginner. But this He can only be, because He is not flesh born of flesh, as other men, but the Word made flesh, true God, born of the Father from eternity and true man, born of the Virgin Mary.

IV. The First Sign (John 2:1–11)

JOHN 2

IV. The First Sign (John 2:1–11)

1–11. And the third day there was a marriage in Cana of Galilee; and the mother of Jesus was there: and Jesus also was bidden, and his disciples, to the marriage. And when the wine failed, the mother of Jesus saith unto him, They have no wine. And Jesus saith unto her, Woman, what have I to do with thee? mine hour is not yet come. His mother saith unto the servants, Whatsoever he saith unto you, do it. Now there were six waterpots of stone set there after the Jews' manner of purifying, containing two or three firkins apiece. Jesus saith unto them, Fill the waterpots with water. And they filled them up to the brim. And he saith unto them, Draw out now, and bear unto the ruler of the feast. And they bare it. And when the ruler of the feast tasted the water now become wine, and knew not whence it was (but the servants which had drawn the water knew), the ruler of the feast calleth the bridegroom, and saith unto him, Every man setteth on first the good wine; and when men have drunk freely, then that which is worse: thou hast kept the good wine until now. This beginning of his signs did Jesus in Cana of Galilee, and manifested his glory; and his disciples believed on him.

The first chapter closed with the promise of the Lord to Nathanael: "Thou shalt see greater things than these—the heavens opened and the angels of God ascending and descending upon the Son of Man." The beginning of the second chapter now brings the first sign of the Lord, of which the Evangelist says with special emphasis: "This beginning of His signs did Jesus in Cana of Galilee and manifested His glory and His disciples believed on Him." The word "sign" is one of the characteristic and favorite terms of the Gospel of John. The Synoptical Gospels use other words for the miracles of the Lord, which mainly embody the idea of stupendous deeds of superhuman power. With John they are "signs," to indicate, to show, to signify something. They demonstrate the divine glory of Christ and bring men to behold, to see the Lord. People believe in Him as they see the signs which He did (2:23).

On the third day after the Lord's departure from the valley of the Jordan, on the sixth after the delegation from Jerusalem to John the Baptist, the marriage in Cana took place. We hold the present village of Kefer Kenna—about six miles east of Nazareth—to be the site of ancient Kana (and not Robinson's "Kana el Djelil," which is too far off to the north, nearly ten miles N. N. E. of Nazareth). The presence of Mary, the mother of the Lord, and her probable connection with the family, secured the invitation to Jesus and His disciples—Andrew, John, Peter, Philip, Nathanael, and possibly James, the brother of John. It was something new in Mary's experience with her son, to find Him, who had heretofore led such a quiet, retired life, coming back from His visit to the Baptist at the head of a little band of followers, who looked up to Him not only as their teacher (Rabbi), but as the promised Messiah of Israel, in whom Moses and the Prophets were fulfilled. And it was a great change for the former disciples of the Baptist, to be led by their new Master straight up from the wilderness, from John's stern preaching of repentance, from his "food of locusts and wild honey," to the marriage feast in Kana! (See Matt. 11:18)

And now the significance of that first sign at Kana, which has been a stumbling-block to many, unbelievers and believers, though John and Andrew and all the disciples saw in it a manifestation of the glory of the Lord and a strengthening of their faith. In the first place there is a special *significance in the occasion* for this sign. It was done at a *marriage*. Within the four walls of the house, in the narrow precinct of the *family life* the first demonstration of New Testament blessings takes place, thereby recognizing the fundamental importance of the family as God's own sacred institution, also for the New Testament dispensation. In the family, first of all, the glory of the Lord is manifested. Out of the family His church is to be built.

Again, there is a great special *significance* in this sign affecting the *relation between Christ and His mother Mary*. Whatever may have been her intentions or expectations, when, the wine failing, she said to her Son: "They have no wine," it is manifest that the Lord will have no interference—not even intercession—on her part in matters that

IV. The First Sign (John 2:1–11)

concern His Messianic ministry, the revelation of His glory as the Godman. Eighteen years before this, Mary had gone through a similar experience, when the boy of twelve years defended Himself in the temple against the unmerited rebukes of His mother with those memorable words: "Wist ye not that I must be in my Father's house, about my Father's business?" Now, after His baptism and temptation, when He had formally entered upon His public ministry as the Messiah, He is more than ever "about His Father's business," and no human creature, not even the mother that bore Him, is allowed to interfere with that. However sharp the rebuke may appear to our modern way of feeling, it is evident that there was no resentment on Mary's part. Her word to the servants proves this: "Whatsoever He saith unto you, do it." This is Mary's last word recorded in Scripture, a word of quiet, humble, implicit obedience and submission to her Lord and Master: a last will and protest on her part against the unscriptural exaltation bestowed upon her by mediaeval Mariolatry, not only dishonoring her divine Lord, but robbing that humble handmaid of God herself of her brightest jewel.

Again, there is a significance in this sign, in that it sets forth the evangelical *freedom and joy* of the *New Testament dispensation* over against the *rigid legalism of the Old*. The contents of the six waterpots "set there after the Jews' manner of purifying," all changed into wine, form a striking illustration to John 1:17. The law was given by Moses, etc. At the opening of the New Testament era we see in the foreground not so much the serious task of the kingdom of heaven, its struggles and sacrifices, but rather its blessedness and comforts, even as the sermon on the mount opens not with the duties laid upon the citizen of God's kingdom, but with the beatitudes enjoyed by him. The Lamb of God which taketh away the sins of the world, certainly must go through a fight and bear a burden, at the sight of which we stand in awe; but here, at the beginning of His mediatorial work, He grants us an outlook into the very consummation of His kingdom, with its final victory, peace and glory; the marriage feast at Kana foreshadows the marriage of the Lamb, the tabernacle of God with men, He dwelling with them, every tear wiped away, and death no more, neither mourning, nor crying, nor pain any more, the first things passed away, all things made new (Rev. 21:3–6). And this is the last and highest significance of the sign in Kana, that it typifies the final transfiguration and glorification of *nature itself*, changing its imperfections, its woes and sorrows into the glorious liberty of the children of God.

V. The First Prophecy of the Lord Concerning His Death and Resurrection (John 2:12–25)

12–25. *After this he went down to Capernaum, he, and his mother, and his brethren, and his disciples: and there they abode not many days.*

And the Passover of the Jews was at hand, and Jesus went up to Jerusalem. And he found in the temple those that sold oxen and sheep and doves, and the changers of money sitting: and he made a scourge of cords, and cast all out of the temple, both the sheep and the oxen; and he poured out the changers' money, and overthrew their tables; and to them that sold the doves he said, Take these things hence; make not my Father's house a house of merchandise. His disciples remembered that it was written, The zeal of thine house shall eat me up. The Jews therefore answered and said unto him, What sign shewest thou unto us, seeing that thou doest these things? Jesus answered and said unto them, Destroy this temple, and in three days I will raise it up. The Jews therefore said, Forty and six years was this temple in building, and wilt thou raise it up in three days? But he spake of the temple of his body. When therefore he was raised from the dead, his disciples remembered that he spake this: and they believed the scripture, and the word which Jesus had said.

Now when he was in Jerusalem at the Passover, during the feast, many believed on his name, beholding the signs which he did. But Jesus did not trust himself unto them, for that he knew all men, and because he needed not that any one should bear witness concerning man; for he himself knew what was in man.

In the 12th verse there are two points of special importance. First the reference to the Lord's family: "He and His mother and His brothers." Were these brothers sons of Joseph by a first marriage? or of Joseph and Mary, born after Him? There is nothing in Scripture that would forbid this last and certainly most natural understanding of this term. (Cf. Matt. 12:46, 13:55; Mark 6:3; John 7:5; Gal. 1:19; 1 Cor. 9:5)

V. The First Prophecy of the Lord Concerning His Death and Resurrection (John 2:12–25)

The second point of importance is the statement that the Lord with His disciples abode at Capernaum "not many days." This is evidently said with a view to the Synoptical record of the longer and repeated abode in that place which had the honor of being called His own city. The writer of the fourth Gospel knows of those extended sojourns of Jesus in Galilee (see also John 6:2), though in his Gospel he has comparatively little to say about them. To him, the most important sphere of the Lord's public ministry was Jerusalem and Judaea. He pays special attention to the testimonies of the Lord given in the presence of the leaders of Israel in the holy city, at the temple and at the great festival seasons, especially Easter.

Here, then, the Messiah makes His first public appearance (with His fan in His hand), ready to cleanse His threshing-floor and to clear out the leaven from His Father's house. The sanctuary of the temple itself was surrounded by a number of courts; the outer court of the gentiles, that of the women, that of the men, that of the priests, each one on a higher elevation than the preceding one. In the outer court, with the silent approbation of the authorities, a sort of market and exchange had been established for the accommodation of visitors at festival seasons, who could there buy their beasts of sacrifice and exchange their Greek and Roman currency for temple money, in which the annual tax (a quarter dollar) had to be paid. It is easy to see that such a practice would, in the course of time, naturally lead to many disorders in the sanctuary. For eighteen years Jesus of Nazareth had been a witness to these things on His regular annual visits to Jerusalem. His heart was sore over the scandals dishonoring "His Father's house," which had been such an attraction to the boy of twelve. Here, then, the reformatory work and the official testimony of the Messiah had to begin. He opens and closes His public ministry with the symbolical act of purifying the temple. (Luke 19:45, 46, gives the account of the second act at the last Easter.) With flaming zeal the Lord attacks the profaners of the sanctuary; the scourge in His hand, though not as an instrument actually applied for punishment, but as a symbol of His authority to exercise discipline. For not to physical force did that crowd yield, but to the majesty of His person. The disciples themselves are so deeply impressed with these strange proceedings that, almost unconsciously, they turn into prophets, applying to their Lord the Old Testament prophecy: "The zeal of Thine house shall eat me up!" This was indeed the first divination of the passion of the Lord that passed through their souls. Yes, the zeal for His Father's house and business will eat Him up: will give him no rest until His life shall be spent and His blood shed!

On the other hand the Jews demand a sign in addition to the sign which had just been shown before their eyes. Such was the custom of their Pharisaic unbelief. The Lord answers them with a mysterious utterance, pointing indeed, as we will afterward see, to the greatest of all His signs (death and resurrection), but in the form of a parable, revealing and yet veiling a problem even to the disciples, who did not fathom its depth until after the death and resurrection of their Lord. The Jews also, after their manner, retained that remarkable word in their memory, using it as a testimony against the Lord before the high-priest (Matt. 26:61; Mark 14:57 f), and even afterwards in the tumultuous proceeding against the first martyr, Stephen (Acts 6:14). The difficulty of the Lord's statement lies in the double sense of the word "temple." The Jews limited its meaning to the visible sanctuary, built, or rather restored, especially through the efforts of Herod, during a period of forty-six years. The Lord, using the term in a much deeper and more comprehensive sense, referred ultimately to the temple of His body. "Go on," He says to the representatives of the Old Testament Theocracy, "break up, destroy everything here, as you are on the road to do: Ruin God's kingdom, God's people, God's house and Him, who is greater than the temple, God's Son, the divine Shekinah, dwelling among you." With the slaying of the Messiah this work of destruction is virtually accomplished. It is the death-knell of the Old Testament dispensation—its sacrifices, its priesthood, its temple itself—remember the veil rent in twain from top to bottom! But the slain Messiah rises from death, and the true kingdom of God, the spiritual Israel, the New Testament temple of the Lord is established! Thus the demand of the Jews for a sign is met by the Lord

V. The First Prophecy of the Lord Concerning His Death and Resurrection (John 2:12–25)

with a reference to the great central sign and miracle of His life—His resurrection from the dead. The same argument was employed by Him on other occasions (see Matt. 12:39): "This evil and adulterous generation seeketh after a sign, and there shall no sign be given to it but the sign of Jonah the prophet."

The chapter closes with a remarkable statement concerning the impression made by the Lord during His stay in Jerusalem. After all "Many believed on His name beholding His signs, which He did do." There is a certain play of words here in the original. The Lord did not quite believe in those believers. There was not in all cases a relation of personal communication and confidence established. Those that had been impressed to a certain extent by His signs had to draw nearer to be bound to Him in abiding, saving faith. Such a one was Nicodemus, of whom we are told in the next chapter.

JOHN 3

The connection between the 3rd and the 2nd chapter is obvious. At the close of the 2nd the impression had been recorded which the signs of the Lord made on many people. They "believed on His name, beholding His signs which He did." But at the same time the Evangelist indicates that this was in most cases not yet a full, clear, decided faith, but only a half belief which needed to be pruned and trained to a full, mature development.

We are also reminded at the beginning of this chapter, of the comprehensive and pathetic statement made in 1:11: He came unto His own, and they that were His own received Him not; but as many as received Him, to them gave He the right to become children of God, even to them that believe on His name. Though the great mass of the people are indifferent to the testimony of the Lord, still there are individuals emerging from the multitude of unbelievers and half-believers, who cast off the restraints of reigning prejudices and come to Jesus, to that same Jesus who said: No man can come unto Me except it be given unto him of the Father and all that which the Father giveth Me shall come unto Me; and him that cometh unto Me, I will in no wise cast out (John 6:65, 37). And we see them coming from very different, yea, opposite conditions and surroundings. It would hardly be possible to think of a more striking contrast than that presented by Nicodemus and the Samaritan woman, the highly respectable Pharisee, scholar, master in Israel and member of the Sanhedrim, and the poor ignorant woman of Samaria, under the cloud of her past life.

VI. THE CONVERSATION WITH NICODEMUS (3:1–21)

VI. THE CONVERSATION WITH NICODEMUS (3:1–21)

1. *Character of Nicodemus and his Motives in Coming to Jesus (3:1, 2)*

1–2. *Now there was a man of the Pharisees, named Nicodemus, a ruler of the Jews: the same came unto him by night, and said to him, Rabbi, we know that thou art a teacher come from God: for no man can do these signs that thou doest, except God be with him.*

We cannot fail to mark a certain reticence and reserve of the Evangelist concerning the character and intentions of Nicodemus on the occasion of his first appearance,—perhaps a hint to his readers not to judge the Old Pharisee prematurely. But knowing, as we do, the final outcome of the intercourse between Nicodemus and the Lord, we have a right even at this early point to consider the whole man, as he presents himself in the light of later developments with all his ups and downs, his advances and retreats on the way to Jesus. He was a Pharisee and a ruler of the Jews, a member of the Sanhedrim, belonging to the inner circle and the highest caste of unbelieving Judaism. Considering the animus of the leading class displayed towards the Lord on the occasion of the first purifying of the temple, we ought to give him much credit for venturing to Jesus, even stealthily and at night. But Nicodemus was "a man" before he was a Pharisee, and it was the *man* in him, the hungering and thirsting of a true human soul, which all his Pharisaism could not satisfy, that made him come to the fountain of truth. Without that direct, kind invitation, "Come and see," which had brought Andrew and John to the Master's room, Nicodemus found out where He abode and came and saw! Though late at night, Jesus is up and awake for him.

And now he is in, with Jesus and possibly a little group of attentive listeners, the disciples of whom we heard before, among them the writer of this Gospel. At the point of beginning the conversation we find Nicodemus all in ferment and conflict. On the one side a mighty drawing to Jesus, great reverence and admiration for Him,—an honest attempt to give Him His due honor; on the other side still a looking to men, a fear of losing his standing with them, a holding on to his former associations. "Rabbi, we know"—was this a greeting from a small circle of men disposed like Nicodemus and Joseph of Arimathaea, who had sent him as their commissioner to Jesus? We look upon it rather as a somewhat stiff and awkward way of introducing himself as a member of that privileged class, the rulers and Pharisees, an attempt to shelter himself in the perplexity of the moment behind the dignity of his august colleagues, the councilors. This "we know" was one of their characteristic phrases over against "the multitude which knoweth not the law."[1] And yet, what a remarkable concession and confession these words are in the mouth of Nicodemus! The words and the signs of the Lord then had been telling on them! Here is the testimony of their *conscience* uttered by honest Nicodemus, though he may stand alone in thus boldly expressing it: "We know that thou art come from God." This means a great deal in the language of Israel of that day. They did expect one that was to come in the name of the Lord. The *"coming one"* is the standing name of the *Messiah*. Nicodemus had certainly not forgotten the Baptist's answer to the delegation from the Sanhedrim: "In the midst of you standeth one whom ye know not, even *he that cometh* after me." The term "come from God," then, recognizes an immediate divine authority, distinguished from and above that of the regular official teachers and rulers; and even beyond that, it borders on the formal recognition of Jesus as the Messiah. But if this was a bold advance in the opening words of Nicodemus, it is quickly followed by a timid retreat in the cautious words "a teacher"—and "God with him;"—this is after all nothing beyond purely human possibilities! It represents essentially that Pharisaic position of common rationalism, that the people only need a teacher able to decide difficult theological questions and to interpret the law, so that, being properly informed, men may do the will of God according to their natural power and ability.

In all this Nicodemus has not yet asked a question. But the Lord who needed not that any one should bear witness concerning man, for He Himself "knew what was in man," took up the very things which Nicodemus needed most. He answered him. The salient points of the

---

[1] See also John 9:24–29 *We know* that this man is a sinner. *We know* that God hath spoken unto Moses, but, as for this man, *we know not* whence he is.

VI. The Conversation with Nicodemus (3:1–21)

whole dialogue are so many blows at the very heart of Pharisaism. It may not be improper to compare this first longer discourse in John with the Sermon on the Mount in Matthew. They are essentially directed against the same enemy, and the expositions made to Nicodemus throw a singular light on the central theme of the Sermon on the Mount: "Except your righteousness shall exceed the righteousness of the Scribes and Pharisees, ye shall in no wise enter into the kingdom of heaven."

2. The Necessity of a New Birth (3:3)

3. Jesus answered and said unto him, Verily, verily, I say unto thee, Except a man be born anew, he cannot see the kingdom of God.

The kingdom of heaven was in the mind of Nicodemus. On this subject turns the "answer" of the Lord. He meets the proud conceit of the Pharisaic "We know" with the solemn, positive assurance of the "teacher come from God:" "Verily, verily I say unto thee,"—No outward force or organization, no reconstruction of political relations or reformation of life can build up the kingdom of God or secure membership in it, but only a new birth, by which men become the children of God (1:12). Of course Nicodemus had never doubted up to this point that he himself was in the kingdom of God. Who in the world should be, if he was not? And now he is told that he, as well as every one else, must be born anew, before he can even see, have a clear conception of, much less a full participation in this kingdom! Whether we take it, to be born *anew*, or to be born from *above*, makes no difference in the end: the absolute necessity of a new beginning is the cardinal point in the Lord's answer. It is not a matter of teaching certain doctrines, but of having a new life; not of doing or leaving undone certain things, but of *being* a regenerate man; not of living differently, but of being born anew. Men will never get into the kingdom of God by reading, thinking, studying, inquiring, talking or fighting about it, they must be born into it. And this "new birth" is not, as it is far too commonly looked upon, a mere figure of speech. It expresses a divine act and human experience, the reality of which is in no wise behind that of the natural birth of man.

3. The Nature and Means of the New Birth (3:4–8)

4–8. *Nicodemus saith unto him, How can a man be born when he is old? can he enter a second time into his mother's womb, and be born? Jesus answered, Verily, verily, I say unto thee, Except a man be born of water and the Spirit, he cannot enter into the kingdom of God. That which is born of the flesh is flesh; and that which is born of the Spirit is spirit. Marvel not that I said unto thee, Ye must be born anew. The wind bloweth where it listeth, and thou hearest the voice thereof, but knowest not whence it cometh, and whither it goeth: so is every one that is born of the Spirit.*

The means or factors by which this new birth is to be accomplished are "water and Spirit," the earthly element and the power from on high, side by side joined together for this mysterious work, not the water without the Spirit, nor the Spirit without the water, not a water which is a figure of the Spirit, nor the Spirit as a spiritual water, but the one as objectively and really as the other; though the creative, life-giving power is of the Spirit. It is essentially a birth of the Spirit over against the birth of the flesh; which means the whole Adamitic nature of man, not simply his corporality, but his moral state in antagonism to the spirit of God (Gen. 6:3). In this bondage of natural corruption all that is born of flesh is involved. There is no getting out of it. It holds every one that comes into this world by natural birth (1:13), no matter how highly gifted, how well trained, how lofty his aspirations, he is flesh, born of flesh, and every new start in life, even if the impossible could happen and man could enter a second time into his mother's womb and be born (as Nicodemus said)—would still find him in the same hopeless condition. But depressing and desperate as this looks, the second clause of that verse has an assuring tone about it. "That which is born of the Spirit *is spirit.*" There is then such a thing in this world of flesh, as being born of the Spirit. It is a possibility and an actual reality in spite of its mysteriousness. This is further shown in the following verses (vers. 7, 8), in which the Lord so kindly points Nicodemus to an analogous every-day occurrence in nature. Remember the "We know," with which Nicodemus had introduced himself. With all his knowledge the learned doctor is unable to explain the whence and the whither of this natural process. It is the *mystery* in it which the Lord means to emphasize. "Thou knowest not," though there is no denying the fact, that the wind *is blowing*, for its voice is distinctly heard. With other processes of nature we are to some extent able to make out the whence and the whither. We can follow the river up to the tiny brooklet and to the spring where it bursts from the rock, and down to the mighty ocean in which it is received. We can dig up the root of the tree, we know the seed from which it grew, we can follow its fruits to all their different uses, we can even see the old barren tree cut down and cast into the fire—but the wind, that freest motion impelled by hidden power, is the most incalculable and mysterious of all. Surely "there are more things in heaven and earth than are dreamt of in our philosophy." And if, even in the sphere of nature we must a hundred times accept the verdict: "Thou knowest not,"—much more is this the case with the mysteries of spiritual life, those great central questions: Whence? Whither? The heart of man, more unfathomable than the deepest ocean! The fall of man, with its consequences, evil and death! The thoughts and ways of God for our salvation,—not as our ways and our thoughts! How can we *know* anything certain about all this? Who will tell us, when even the teachers of Israel do not understand these things?

4. *The Heavenly Witness (3:9–13)*

9–13. *Nicodemus answered and said unto him, How can these things be? Jesus answered and said unto him, Art thou the teacher of Israel, and understandest not these things? Verily, verily, I say unto thee, We speak that we do know, and bear witness of that we have seen; and ye receive not our witness. If I told you earthly things, and ye believe not, how shall ye believe, if I tell you heavenly things? And no man hath ascended into heaven, but he that descended out of heaven, even the Son of man, which is in heaven.*

Thus far the conversation was all on knowing and *knowledge*. Now it takes a new turn towards *faith*. He who speaks to Nicodemus is not a teacher, like other men, with wisdom gathered from the fathers, to be imparted to his pupils. He speaks as a heavenly *witness* who demands *faith*. He *does know* heavenly things from personal acquaintance, as the only begotten Son in the bosom of the Father, who has come to declare them. The glory of the Son of Man begins to beam in Nicodemus' eye. "In heaven," "out of heaven," "into heaven," that is His where? whence? whither? But the central and most important statement at this point is the *whence*, "descended out of heaven." Here is the Lord's answer to that hidden question of Nicodemus concerning His own person, which had been indicated in the words: "a teacher come from God." He reveals to him the mystery of His person, and insists on being accepted by him as a heavenly witness. At a later period the Lord once rebuked the colleagues of Nicodemus and his fellow—Pharisees: "Even if I bear witness of Myself, My witness is true; for I know whence I came and whither I go, but ye know not *whence I come* or *whither I go*" (ch. 8:14). If Nicodemus will now open his ears, this charge will not apply to him.

5. The Serpent in the Wilderness (3:14, 15)

14, 15. *And as Moses lifted up the serpent in the wilderness, even so must the Son of man be lifted up; that whosoever believeth may in him have eternal life.*

So far it was the testimony of the Lord concerning His person. Now for His testimony concerning His work. It is all told in the simple story of the brazen serpent. This was, no doubt, one of the most memorable of all the experiences during Israel's journey through the wilderness. Yea, the grateful remembrance of it, which they carried into the promised land, became a snare to the Israelites, who burned incense to it under the name Nehushtan, so that Hezekiah, in his work of reformation, had to break it in pieces (2 Kings 18:4). Was there a divination of the deeper, future significance of this figure in the inclination of Israel, to turn it into an idol? Here is the meaning of the type unfolded: It means the atoning and redeeming death of Christ on the cross.

The brazen serpent was the image of the fiery serpents which destroyed the people. But, however much alike, there was a great difference between them. The fiery serpents full of deadly poison for every one they reached. The brazen serpent without poison, harmless, wholesome and salutary to all that looked to it in faith. But as the serpent is the image of sin and its consequences, so Christ, exalted on the cross,

VI. The Conversation with Nicodemus (3:1–21)

is the representative of the sin of the world. "Him who knew no sin he made to be sin on our behalf, that we might become the righteousness of God in him" (2 Cor. 5:21). "God, sending his own Son in the likeness of sinful flesh, and as an offering for sin, condemned sin in the flesh" (Rom. 8:3). In Christ the sin of the world presented itself for judgment. Christ became a curse for us, as it is written: "Cursed is everyone that hangeth on a tree" (Gal. 3:13). The brazen serpent nailed to the pole is the picture of a conquered serpent, which is made harmless. This is what was done to the sin of the world in Christ on the cross. The fact that He was there made sin for us, and suffered the penalty of sin, has delivered us from the power of sin, death and the devil. He that hung on the cross in the likeness of the serpent, thereby bruised the head of the serpent. Again, the serpent in the wilderness was lifted up high above everything else, so that an unobstructed view of it could be obtained by all that were bitten. Thus God has openly set forth Christ crucified to be "a propitiation through faith by His blood." Christ, the crucified one, is to be known, to be seen from one end of this sin and death-stricken world to the other.

And lastly: Those that *looked* to the brazen serpent were saved. There is hardly, in all the Scriptures, a more expressive picture of faith than this looking to the serpent lifted up on the pole. How simple this means of salvation! However far off from the brazen serpent, however deeply wounded by the venomous bites, however weak and unable to move, to run away or keep off the destroyer,—a look to the pole, *that* was still possible to all. Such is God's way of faith. No effort of our own, no work, no struggle, no sacrifice of man, but a simple trusting, confident looking to Jesus, the Son of Man, lifted up on the cross—that is all! It is salvation for all.

6. The Father's Love the Headspring of Salvation (3:16)

16. *For God so loved the world, that he gave his only begotten Son, that whosoever believeth on him should not perish, but have eternal life.*

The following verses (16–21) have been considered by some (Erasmus, Tholuck and others) as not belonging to the dialogue between the Lord and Nicodemus, but simply as reflections or meditations of the

Evangelist on the subjects mentioned in that conversation. But we cannot share this theory. There is no break, but rather the closest connection between ver. 15 and 16; the conversation would be without a proper conclusion if it should stop at this point, and we are not willing to take that jewel of Scripture passages, the 16th verse, "the Bible in brief" (as Luther calls it), out of the Lord's own mouth. This revelation of the eternal counsel of salvation must be the direct word of the only begotten Son Himself, who is in the bosom of the Father (1:18). From the *Spirit*, who is the author of regeneration, to the *Son* who mediates and purchases our salvation with His atonement, we now come to the *Father*, whose love gave the Son for the life of the World. God loved, as the light must light, and the fire must burn, so God loves. This is His nature, for God is love. But: God loved the world! we have often read and passed and recited it thoughtlessly. It seems natural, as long as we do not realize what sin is, and a world in sin! But when this begins to dawn upon our mind there is nothing greater in heaven and upon earth than this: "God *so* loved the world!" Who will take the *measure* of this love, its breadth and length and height and depth? Who will realize the character and *manner* of this love? so that He gave His only begotten Son,—mark, the "Son of Man," of whom the Lord had spoken before, is identical with the Son of God. He was given by the Father, not simply *to* the world, but *for* the world, given into death! For this love of God is a *holy love*, and though it could command all the resources of God's omnipotence, wisdom and majesty, still it could not save the world without satisfying His justice by giving the Beloved into judgment and death for the sin of the world. Mark also the universality of this love. The *world is its object*. We dare not limit this to an "elect world." That would be the very opposite of what John means by the term "world." The Gospel of John repeatedly emphasizes the *world* as the object of God's gifts and God's plan of salvation. The Bread of God giveth life unto the world (6:33); the bread which I will give is My flesh, for the life of the world (6:51). There is only one limit to this salvation; it is the condition of *faith*. This love of God in Christ must be believed in, it must be accepted, appropriated by thankful and appreciative hearts. How many out of this perishing world will have their souls saved on this

VI. The Conversation with Nicodemus (3:1–21)

condition? How many in proportion to the multitude of Israelites who, in the wilderness, looked up to the serpent to save their *bodies*?

7. Salvation, not Judgment, the Mission of the Son of God (3:17)

17. For God sent not the Son into the world to judge the world; but that the world should be saved through him.

While we say in the creed that He shall come to judge the quick and the dead, we believe that He *was sent* to save, not to judge. So the Lord had once said to John and James, those fiery sons of thunder, in that Samaritan village, "The Son of Man came not to destroy men's lives, but to save them." All this was certainly in direct opposition to the Pharisaic program of the Messiah's kingdom. There the judgment of the Gentiles was one of the most glorious features in the coming of the Messiah; while the Jews would be heirs to that kingdom, as the descendants of Abraham and the keepers of the law of Moses. But there is no distinction made here in this "world" which the Son says, He was sent to save. Nicodemus is counted in, and all the Pharisees are counted in; and sinners down to the thief on the cross, together with all the Sadducees and publicans—only one way for all to be saved: ye must be born anew; ye must believe! Not what man is or does, but the labor, service and sacrifice of the true God Himself, in the person of Christ, is the salvation for Jews and Gentiles.

8. The Present Judgment incurred by Unbelievers (3:18, 19)

19. He that believeth on him is not judged: he that believeth not hath been judged already, because he hath not believed on the name of the only begotten Son of God. And this is the judgment, that the light is come into the world, and men loved the darkness rather than the light; for their works were evil.

But though this first advent of the Messiah is a time of *grace*, to save, not to destroy, there is at the same time a quiet inner judgment going on among men. Seasons of grace are critical times, when men must decide to accept or refuse what is offered by God's love. The refusal of him that believeth not, cuts him off from that love and its communion; it is suicidal, a judgment passed by himself. It comes with internal necessity upon every one that believeth not. It is no outward act, but an inward development. What can save a man if he will not admit the one physician and take his medicine? This certainly is a crisis, a decision, division and judgment: The light cometh into this world to dispel its darkness, to deliver men out of the power of darkness and translate them into the kingdom of God,—but men loved the darkness rather than the light. Such is man's love over against God's love. God so loved the world that He gave His only begotten Son—men so loved the darkness that they would not come to the light, yea, that they would hate the light.

9. The Climax and the Parting Word to Nicodemus (3:20, 21)

20, 21. For everyone that doeth ill hateth the light, and cometh not to the light, lest his works should be reproved. But he that doeth the truth cometh to the light, that his works may be made manifest, that they have been wrought in God.

It is a fearful climax with which the Lord unveils before Nicodemus the danger of holding back from the light. The light is come. Men love darkness rather than light. They do not come to the light. They hate the light! Nicodemus hears and shudders. Hating the light! Is it possible that it should ever come to that? No, not with him. He never had such an idea. And yet if he will not accept the testimony of this witness, if he will go on with his: But and How—if he will not decide to come out fully into the light, where will it end with him?

Mark also the reason of this aversion to the light which the Lord points out so emphatically. It is because men's *works are evil*, because they practice ill, because they will not have their works reproved! Here is the moral root of unbelief. These strong words of our Lord must not be limited to open and gross immoralities; they include all the respectability of a Phariseean life with its self-sufficiency and self-adoration, its desire to take honor and glory from men. These are among those besetting sins which become the habit and practice of an outwardly decent life, but they are φαῦλα, vile, rotten, good-for-nothing things, unable to bring forth abiding fruit for eternity. And they must be reproved. And men must humbly submit to such reproof. The way of faith leads through repentance.

VII. JESUS IN JUDÆA AND THE LAST TESTIMONY OF JOHN THE BAPTIST (3:22–36)

Severe as all this was for the ears of a Nicodemus—and it was all meant for him—the Lord after all gives him a parting word of encouragement (ver. 21) of "coming to the light, being made manifest, having works wrought in God." As the Lord spoke on, Nicodemus had not another word to say. He sat in silent submission under those heavy blows, which shattered to pieces his whole former life; he sat and wondered at the man before him, and the love of which He spoke and the power of darkness to resist such love. And yet he was not quite ready to surrender to it. It was a good thing to come to the Lord, to sit under His teaching. But he must not be ashamed to come to the Light, to submit to His reproof, to yield to His love. He must reach a decision! But the time has come for parting. John does not tell us how they parted, or what was the exact state of Nicodemus' mind in that hour. Did he come again? Were there more conversations between him and the Lord? Even to this there is no answer. Certainly the Lord could not tell him more than what he received on this first visit,—it was enough for a life-time to study out. But as he walked away through the lonely streets of the city, the Lord's "Peace be with thee" ringing in his ears, and the night wind fanning his burning head, two things were weighing heaviest of all upon his struggling soul, those two absolute "musts" in the discourse of the Lord: "Ye *must* be born again," and "The Son of Man *must* be lifted up."

VII. JESUS IN JUDÆA AND THE LAST TESTIMONY OF JOHN THE BAPTIST (3:22–36)

1. *Jesus in Judæa (3:22–24)*

22–24. *After these things came Jesus and his disciples into the land of Judæa; and there he tarried with them, and baptized. And John also was baptizing in Ænon near to Salim, because there was much water there; and they came and were baptized. For John was not yet cast into prison.*

After His first public appearance in Jerusalem and the conversation with Nicodemus, the Lord retires for a time from the city into the province of Judaea. And even in the character of His work there seems to be something like a retreat. He seems to step down to do the same work which His forerunner, John the Baptist, was called to do, and the result of the two men in the same region doing essentially the same work, is a collision in the mind of the disciples of John, which forms the occasion for their master's last testimony of Christ. The locality and the time are distinctly given in these verses. Ænon is probably the same as Ain in Jos. 15:32, in the south of the wilderness of Judah, on this side of the Jordan (while the former locality of John's baptizing was *beyond* the river). Concerning the time it is distinctly stated, that it was before John's imprisonment. This is evidently said with a view to the Synoptical account of the beginning of the Lord's public ministry in Galilee. It corrects not the statement itself, as found in the Synoptists (Matt. 4:12), but the possible misunderstanding that the Galilean work began immediately after the baptism and temptation of Christ.

2. *The Occasion for the Last Testimony of the Baptist (3:25, 26)*

25–26. There arose therefore a questioning on the part of John's disciples with a Jew about purifying. And they came unto John, and said to him, Rabbi, he that was with thee beyond Jordan, to whom thou hast borne witness, behold, the same baptizeth, and all men come to him.

There were men among the disciples of the Baptist unable and unwilling to see the difference between John and Christ, and, even now, not ready to believe their master and to follow Christ as Andrew and his companions had done. They were inclined to see the preparation for the kingdom of God in strict asceticism. They were in this respect more on the side of the Pharisees than of Jesus: "We and the Pharisees fast oft; but thy disciples fast not" (Matt. 9:14).[1] They would naturally look upon the work of Jesus so near the Baptist with jealousy and consider it unkind and an interference with the office of their master. This feeling of jealousy and irritation was further stirred up by a Jew or Jews, probably belonging to the ruling party, telling the disciples of John in a mischievous manner

---

[1] Even at the time of the writing of this Gospel there was a sect of "Disciples of John" extant in Asia Minor.

VII. Jesus in Judæa and the Last Testimony of John the Baptist (3:22–36)

of the remarkable success of Jesus. They come and complain to their Master, and without entering into the particular question which had arisen, he goes to the principles underlying their difficulty and shows them his true relation to Christ, with a severe rebuke to the unbelief of God's chosen people, including his own disciples.

3. The Last Testimony of the Baptist (3:27–36)
(a.) Christ and the Baptist (27–30)

27–30. John answered and said, A man can receive nothing, except it have been given him from heaven. Ye yourselves bear me witness, that I said, I am not the Christ, but, that I am sent before him. He that hath a bride is a bridegroom: but the friend of the bridegroom, which standeth and heareth him, rejoiceth greatly because of the bridegroom's voice: this my joy therefore is fulfilled. He must increase, but I must decrease.

He opens with a broad, general principle which must be recognized in the history of God's kingdom. Every man has his place and work assigned to him, whether it be Christ or John. From the beginning he had clearly told his disciples that he was not the Christ, that he held an inferior position. He is therefore not responsible for this petty jealousy of his followers. Instead of complaining, they should rather rejoice that the bridegroom has appeared, and that the bride, forsaking everything else, is looking to the Lord and husband. Thus even John the Baptist invites his sullen disciples to the marriage feast of the new covenant. And the sweetest and greatest name he bears, and of which he may be justly proud, is not "the prophet," or "the messenger" or "the voice crying in the wilderness "but "the friend of the Bridegroom." There is no jealousy between the two Johns, the Evangelist and the Baptist. The John who wrote this, the disciple whom the Lord loved, who was on the bosom of Jesus, rejoices in the name "friend of the Bridegroom," which the other John claims for himself. The Baptist sums up the relation between Christ and himself in another pointed, comprehensive sentence which not only describes most beautifully and truly the official relation between the Messiah and His forerunner, but again lays down a principle of far-reaching importance in God's kingdom. "He must increase, but I must decrease."[1] It rounds off and supplements most beautifully the sentence with which he had opened this explanation (ver. 27). It ought to be the motto of every true servant of Christ. It is the common human experience of all, that after a period of growth and increase we must make room for others that come after us. Nor will they stay forever. The same decrease must follow their increase. It is a bitter experience as long as man only looks to man, and the worn-out weary worker must yield his place to fresh and youthful forces. But it becomes sweet and blessed if our yielding is to Him, whose kingdom has no end, and for whom to lose and give up everything is gain.

(b.) Christ and the World (3:31–36)

31–36. He that cometh from above is above all; he that is of the earth is of the earth, and of the earth he speaketh: he that cometh from heaven is above all. What he hath seen and heard, of that he beareth witness; and no man receiveth his witness. He that hath received his witness hath set his seal to *this*, that God is true. For he whom God hath sent speaketh the words of God: for he giveth not the Spirit by measure. The Father loveth the Son, and hath given all things into his hand. He that believeth on the Son hath eternal life; but he that obeyeth not the Son shall not see life, but the wrath of God abideth on him.

At this point in the testimony of the Baptist a similar question is raised by a number of commentators (Bengel, Tholuck, Olshausen and others), to that in connection with the conversation with Nicodemus in the 16th verse of this chapter, viz., whether the following verses are to be regarded as a continuation of the words spoken by the Baptist, or as the statement of the Evangelist. We are decidedly in favor of the former view. It is the conclusion of the Baptist's testimony concerning Christ's position and reception in this world.

---

[1] Cf. the ancient and significant arrangement of the Church by which the birthday of the Baptist is celebrated in midsummer (June 24th), when the days begin to decrease; the birthday of Christ in midwinter, when they begin to increase.

VII. Jesus in Judæa and the Last Testimony of John the Baptist (3:22–36)

Let us mark the following prominent points in this section: (1.) The absolute dignity and majesty of Christ, whom John the Baptist has placed so high above himself. He cometh from above; He is above all, even all the prophets and servants of God sent before. (2.) Next: *The foundation and character of His testimony*; its directness and authority. He speaks as a witness, in the highest sense of the word, of that which He hath seen and heard as the Lord Himself had said to Nicodemus: "We speak that we do know and bear witness of what we have seen." (3.) Again: The *deep insight of the Baptist* into the reception with which this witness meets on the part of men. "No man receiveth His witness." This certainly is in direct opposition to what his disciples had just been telling him, "All men come to Him" (ver. 26). But their master is more sober and critical in his judgment of the popularity enjoyed by the Lord. He knows that it is one thing *"to come to Him"* outwardly, attracted by His word and signs, as the masses were at that time even in Judæa,—and another thing to *receive His testimony*, with a humble, believing heart. This bitter complaint is following us all through this Gospel: 1:5, the darkness apprehended not the Light; 1:10, the world knew Him not; 1:11, His own received Him not; 1:26, in the midst of you standeth One whom ye know not; 3:11, ye receive not our witness. (4.) Still the *Baptist must modify* his general sweeping statement, as the Evangelist did (1:12—as many as received Him, etc.); he testifies himself (ver. 33): He that hath *received this witness* hath set his seal to this, that God is true. While the New Testament otherwise speaks of God setting His seal upon His own people,[1] the Baptist here speaks of the believers as setting their seal upon their Saviour's testimony, that God is true! As Paul says: "I know in whom I have believed," and again: (2 Cor. 1:20)—"How many soever be the promises of God, in him is the yea: wherefore also through him is the Amen, unto the glory of God through us." The reverse of this is what John has written in his first Epistle (5:10), "He that believeth not God hath made Him a liar." (5.) But the *believer's*

---

[1] Cf. 2 Cor. 1:22, God, who also sealed us and gave us the earnest of the Spirit in our hearts.

trust in this testimony rests *on safe ground:* "For He whom God hath sent speaketh the words of God: for He giveth not the Spirit by measure." The speaker in this case is the Logos, who declareth the Father and speaketh the words of God, He to whom the Spirit is given without limitation, "not by measure," ever since the Baptist "beheld the Spirit descending as a dove out of heaven, and it *abode* upon Him." And still another reminiscence of the Lord's baptism follows in the next verse: "The Father loveth the Son." There John had heard the voice out of the heavens saying: "This is my beloved Son, in whom I am well pleased." He is sure to gain the victory, for "the Father hath given all things into his hand." (6.) And now the *last parting word* of the Baptist in this Gospel: (ver. 36,) He that believeth on the Son, hath eternal life; but he that obeyeth (believeth) not the Son shall not see life, but the wrath of God abideth on him. It is the same dilemma that we found in the conversation with Nicodemus, and in fact everywhere throughout the Scriptures, life or death, the love and grace of God or the wrath of God, salvation or perishing, and the decision altogether hanging on faith, either believing on the Son, or not believing, refusing obedience to Him, into whose hands the Father has given all things! Either eternal life for him who believes, or the wrath of God which abideth on him, not the manifestation of temporary and passing judgments, such as Israel had experienced time and again; but the final, irrevocable, abiding wrath, on him that rejects the Son. This is the last solemn warning and testimony of the Baptist to his people, reminding us strongly of that first preaching of his (Matt. 3:12), "He will gather his wheat into the garner; but the chaff he will burn up with unquenchable fire," and of the closing words of that Messianic Psalm,[1] "Kiss the Son, lest he be angry and ye perish from the way, when his wrath is kindled but a little. Blessed are all they that put their trust in him" (Ps. 2:12).

---

[1] The Christmas Psalm of the ancient Church.

VIII. SAMARITAN FAITH (4:1–42)

JOHN 4

This chapter also continues the history of the quiet and modest beginnings of faith here and there, which, as said before, form the theme of the first four chapters. After the Lord's beginnings in Jerusalem and Judea (ch. 1, 2, 3), it is now *Samaritan faith* and *Galilean faith* which the Evangelist describes in the direct continuation of his narrative.

VIII. SAMARITAN FAITH (4:1–42)

1. *Historical Introduction (4:1–6)*

1–6. *When therefore the Lord knew how that the Pharisees had heard that Jesus was making and baptizing more disciples than John (although Jesus himself baptized not, but his disciples), he left Judæa, and departed again into Galilee. And he must needs pass through Samaria. So he cometh to a city of Samaria, called Sychar, near to the parcel of ground that Jacob gave to his son Joseph: and Jacob's well was there. Jesus therefore, being wearied with his journey, sat thus by the well. It was about the sixth hour.*

The connection between this and the preceding chapter is close, though several months elapsed between the Lord's retirement from Jerusalem and His departure for Galilee. We saw how He withdrew from the capital into the province of Judæa. Now comes a further retreat from Judaea into Galilee. The reason for this is given in the first two verses of the chapter. The Lord (with emphasis this title, which is not frequently used in the Gospels; much more so in the Epistles) knew that the Pharisees had heard of the remarkable increase in the number of His disciples; He knew also the spirit with which they would notice it, the excitement and jealousy it would create. And as He was unwilling to provoke a conflict with them at this time, He left Judæa. This move then means a further retirement, a temporary suspension even, of His public work, which in Judæa had chiefly consisted in preaching. Jesus Himself baptized not, but His disciples. The reason for this was either because He

"Himself had to bring the Messianic baptism of the Spirit, which was only a fact of the future" (Luthardt), or for the simple, practical reason, that those who would have received baptism from Him in person should not be elated thereby as having received something more and better than the others. (For a similar reason even Paul says that he would rather not baptize but preach the Gospel, 1 Cor. 1:14)

On His way to Galilee He must needs pass through Samaria. The strictest Jews avoided the passage through that province, preferring the round-about way through Peræa, the country east of the river Jordan. And of the Lord Himself it is said (Luke 17:11), that on His way from Galilee to Jerusalem He was passing *between* Samaria and Galilee (probably the correct translation of διήρχετο). Compare His injunction to the Apostles on the first sending forth of the Twelve: "Go not into any way of the Gentiles, and enter not into any city of the Samaritans; but go rather to the lost sheep of the house of Israel." Remembering all this and the statement here, "He must needs go," it is fair to say, that Samaria was not on the program of His journey, not even as a way station. He had been forced to depart without loss of time. He had to take the shortest route and consequently "must needs pass through Samaria." The two days' sojourn in that country was, if we might say so, an unexpected episode.

For information about the history of the Samaritans we have to turn to 2 Kings 17:24–41. After the destruction of the Northern kingdom, the king of Assyria sent colonists from Babylon and other places, to possess the cities of Samaria. They were a mixture of nationalities and of religions. "They feared the Lord and served their own gods." After the return of the Jews from exile, the Samaritans offered their co-operation in the rebuilding of the temple,[1] and being refused they used every possible influence with the king of Persia to oppose the building of the temple in Jerusalem, while they built their own on Mount Gerizim. Manasse, their first high-priest, was the son-in-law of the Persian governor Sanballat. This temple was destroyed 200 years afterwards by Joannes Hyrkanus. The bitter hostility of the Jews against the Samaritans

---

[1] Ezra 4; Neh. 4; the scoffing Samaritans under Sanballat.

VIII. Samaritan Faith (4:1–42)

is chiefly due to this. Their character was a Paganism under the mask of Judaism. Therefore they were to the Jews a greater abomination even than the Gentiles. Robinson (Palest. III. 328), says that this relation continues essentially the same to the present day. The Samaritans will neither eat nor drink, nor intermarry, nor have any intercourse with the Jews, except for business or trade. (Cf. Ecclesiasticus 50:27, 28).

The place to which the Lord came was not the site of ancient Samaria itself, which was about 7 to 8 miles further north, but Shechem, with which Sychar is identical, the *m* and *n* frequently changing into *r* as in Achar, LXX., for Achan; Bar instead of Ben. (Others: Sychar, the town of *lying and intoxication*.) The present name of Shechem is Nablus, but the site of this place has moved somewhat to the west of ancient Shechem. Jacob's well is still found at the entrance into the narrow valley where Mt. Ebal (on the N. E.), and Mount Gerizim (S. W.), confront each other.

The Lord reached this place at noon-tide, and while the disciples, perhaps with the exception of John (Peter and James?) went to the city to buy food, He sat down by the well, weary and exhausted from the journey.

2. The Conversation with the Samaritan Woman (4:7–26)

(a.) The Living Water (4:7–15)

7–15. *There cometh a woman of Samaria to draw water: Jesus saith unto her, Give me to drink. For his disciples were gone away into the city to buy food. The Samaritan woman therefore saith unto him, How is it that thou, being a Jew, askest drink of me, which am a Samaritan woman? (For Jews have no dealings with Samaritans.) Jesus answered and said unto her, If thou knewest the gift of God, and who it is that saith to thee, Give me to drink; thou wouldest have asked of him, and he would have given thee living water. The woman saith unto him, Sir, thou hast nothing to draw with, and the well is deep: from whence then hast thou that living water? Art thou greater than our father Jacob, which gave us the well, and drank thereof himself, and his sons, and his cattle? Jesus answered and said unto her, Every one that drinketh of this water shall thirst again: but whosoever drinketh of the water that I shall give him shall never thirst; but the*

LXX. Septuagint

water that I shall give him shall become in him a well of water springing up unto eternal life. The woman saith unto him, Sir, give me this water, that I thirst not, neither come all the way hither to draw.

It was a region of holy and suggestive reminiscences on which the eye of the Lord rested as He sat there. Here the Patriarchs had waited for the promise; here Jacob had dug the well, a testimony of his firm, deep-rooted trust in his good title as possessor of the promised land; here Joseph was buried; here from these mountains of Ebal and Gerizim the solemn words of curse and blessing had been spoken over Israel;[1] but here also was the home of the dismemberment of the body of Israel,—what spiritual desolation and idolatry! The believing father's name used to hide the shame of strange children; and Israel itself, was it better than these mongrel Samaritans? Was not Jeremiah's word true even at that time: "They have forsaken me, the fountain of living waters, and hewed them out cisterns, broken cisterns, that can hold no water"? (Jer. 2:13).

Thus Jesus sat by the well and there cometh a woman of Samaria (a Samaritan woman) to draw water. Jesus saith unto her: "Give me to drink." The need of His true human body prompted this word; but in speaking it He was boldly reaching over the barrier which separated Jews and Samaritans;[1] He gave utterance to that deepest yearning of His heart, thirsting for the salvation of immortal souls, for which He would willingly give up His night's sleep to Nicodemus and His noonday rest to the Samaritan woman.

Ignoring her little way of tantalizing the Jew, who condescends to ask a Samaritan woman for a drink, the Lord at once proceeds to speak to her of something greater and better than this drink of water;—indeed it does not appear that the Lord ever got the drink He asked for, until the woman went away to the city, leaving her waterpot standing by the well.

"If thou knewest *the gift of God*." To know, to recognize the gift of God in the sphere of nature is one of the primary links to bind man to God, to

---

[1] Joshua 8:33.

[1] The Rabbis say: To eat the bread of a Samaritan is the same as eating pork. Unprepared food in its natural condition, however, was exempt; but to drink out of the same vessel was strictly prohibited.

VIII. Samaritan Faith (4:1–42)

remind him of his Maker, to lead him back to Him, when he has gone astray. The significance of all earthly gifts is to point to Him from whom every good and perfect gift cometh, and their very limitation is an impulse to seek something higher than what satisfies only the need of the body. "If thou knewest the gift of God and *who it is* that saith to thee: Give me to drink." There must be then a connection between "God's gift" and Him, that addresses her. It is through Him that even the natural gifts come to us and benefit us. What a "gift" again for the Samaritan woman, this opportunity to meet this "Jew," the man that addresses her. If thou knewest this! and knewest what God means to give thee through Him and *who it is* that speaks to thee! It is the same theme for the Samaritan woman, as well as for Nicodemus and the Jews, the central theme of the whole Gospel of John: Who is He? Who art Thou? "Living water!"—Here is a theme of a parable for her, to think about! But see how this child of nature pours out with unrestrained naïveté a very flood of words, to let this ignorant stranger know all about this interesting place, the excellency of its water, its historical reminiscences, etc. This is good enough for her! What more could this man offer to her? How cold, indifferent and even hostile is man's attitude towards God, wherever He offers him something more than what satisfies his body and "his sons and his cattle." Good provision for the necessities of this body; and for the ideal side of life, decent family and church connections, a touch of national pride with stirring historical reminiscences, this is all that this woman seems to care for in this life. Mark also the emphasis with which she dwells on "our father Jacob,"—not a whit less complacent than the Jews, when they spoke of "our father Abraham," nor does she fail to draw exactly the same conclusion as to the dignity of the Lord: "Art thou greater than our father Jacob?" (See 8:53: Art thou greater than our father Abraham?)

Now the Lord shows unto her directly the unsatisfactory character of the earthly gift: "Every one that drinketh of this water, shall thirst again." Though it be manna from heaven which the fathers did eat,—they die! Though it be water from Jacob's well they drink, they will thirst again and again, until at last they crave for Lazarus' finger to cool their tongue! The

Lord therefore offers something different: living water that shall become a well of water springing up unto eternal life! Spiritual water seeking its own level, just as natural water does. It springs from eternity. It rises to eternity! It is the spiritual life that leads to eternal life.

The woman's answer is not easy to understand. It is a strange mixture of conflicting possibilities. How well it sounds, that simple prayer in perfect accordance with the Lord's direction: "Lord, give me this water that I thirst not." Thus all souls may pray, that hunger and thirst after righteousness, and "they shall be filled," But what can we make of the second part of her response: "That I have not to come all the way hither to draw"? How far from all true, spiritual understanding of the Lord is this! How grossly material! Possibly there is a slight touch of skeptical irony in it. "If Thou canst do such wonderful things, I would like to see it." She would have no objection to be thus relieved from some of the burdens of the wearisome tread-mill of this life. It is evident that there is no consciousness yet of her inner spiritual need; she must first be made to *thirst*, before she will appreciate the "living water" which Jesus offers. To awaken that spiritual thirst, to convince her of her need and misery, the Lord in the following verse starts anew in His soul-dealing with this woman.

(b.) *The Prophet (4:16–26)*

16–26. Jesus saith unto her, Go, call thy husband, and come hither. The woman answered and said unto him, I have no husband. Jesus saith unto her, Thou saidst well, I have no husband: for thou hast had five husbands; and he whom thou now hast is not thy husband: this hast thou said truly. The woman saith unto him, Sir, I perceive that thou art a prophet. Our fathers worshipped in this mountain; and ye say, that in Jerusalem is the place where men ought to worship. Jesus saith unto her, Woman, believe me, the hour cometh, when neither in this mountain, nor in Jerusalem, shall ye worship the Father. Ye worship that which ye know not: we worship that which we know: for salvation is from the Jews. But the hour cometh, and now is, when the true worshippers shall worship the Father in spirit and truth: for such doth the father seek to be his worshippers. God is a Spirit: and they that worship him must worship in spirit and truth. The woman saith unto him, I

VIII. Samaritan Faith (4:1–42)

know that Messiah cometh (which is called Christ): when he is come, he will declare unto us all things. Jesus saith unto her, I that speak unto thee am he.

The Lord touches her conscience. He who knew Nathanael's sacred hours of longing and meditation under the fig tree, knew also the dark secrets in the life of the Samaritan woman. "Go call thy husband and come hither." It is as if He said: Go bring hither thy sin and shame! Gently but firmly He lays His hand upon the sore point of her life (ver. 18). Her prompt answer, "I have no husband," which seemed such a convenient escape from this demand of the stranger, is turned into a word of self-condemnation by Him with whom she has to do, and "before whose eyes all things are naked and laid open" (Heb. 4:13). She admits all that the Lord has charged her with. "Lord, I perceive that thou art a prophet,"—both a confession of her guilt and a recognition of the majesty of Christ. Indeed, here is a "greater" one than Jacob and Joseph and all the fathers. Her heart begins to thirst after the spring of living water. But where does it flow? Hardly here on Mount Gerizim, the place of worship of her fathers? Perhaps in Jerusalem? Let this great Jewish Prophet answer the question. We see how her Samaritanism, of which she made so much at the opening of the conversation, is dwindling away before the Lord. She is now perfectly ready to accept the teaching of the Jewish prophet. And what a new doctrine is this that He utters now! Would not His disciples have been amazed and shocked at this demonstration of "zeal for His father's house"? Would not His enemies who afterwards so bitterly denounced Him as a "Samaritan" (John 8:48), have found sufficient ground for their accusation in the first sentence of the answer of the Lord? "Woman, believe me, the hour cometh when neither in this mountain nor in Jerusalem shall ye worship the Father." The Jews then will have no preference before the Samaritans? The Father who is to be worshipped will have His children among them all without distinction? He will be Father to the Samaritans also! There will be an end to all these hostile barriers between Jews, Gentiles and Samaritans! This prophet will embrace them all in one fold, under one shepherd! What heresy this was to orthodox Jewish ears!

And yet, though soaring high to this ideal of the coming Church of God, the Lord does not mean to ignore the historical, providential position of Israel; the errors of Mount Gerizim, the truth of Jerusalem: Ye worship that which ye know not: we worship that which we know: for salvation is from the Jews. And the Jews are His kinsmen according to the flesh. Theirs are the adoption and the glory and the covenants, and the giving of the law and the service of God and the promises; theirs are the fathers and of them is Christ "as concerning the flesh" (Rom. 9:5).

There are two definitions of God in these words of Jesus: God the *Father*, that simple, most popular and practical one, which at once appeals to the human heart, particularly when we hear of a Father *seeking* lost children, that ought to return to Him and render Him the honor due Him by true spiritual worship; the other, which seems to be the most abstract, mysterious and difficult of all: God is *Spirit*. Even Fichte thought that for a *positive* definition of God this was utterly useless and unfitted. But even this definition has in this connection an eminently practical tendency. It is closely connected with the idea of worshipping God in spirit and in truth. The spirituality, the inner truthfulness, the life-reality in man's worship, is thereby emphasized over against outward forms, dead traditions, temporary limitations and the letter of the law. God, being Father and being Spirit, has children born of His Spirit, led by His Spirit, participating in divine spiritual life. And those only that are thus born of the Spirit are able to worship Him in spirit and in truth. But our true knowledge of God the Father-spirit, our partaking in His own spiritual nature in becoming His children, is only made possible through that mystery of divine love: The *Word* was *made flesh*. The God in the *flesh* reveals to us the God who is *spirit*, and there is no true spirituality in religion, either as knowledge of God, or as worship of God[1] outside of the incarnate Son of God. To be God's child through the Only Begotten, to say with truly childlike trust and obedience, Abba Father, this is to worship God in spirit and in truth.

---

[1] Both belong together: "Ye must know whom ye worship."

VIII. Samaritan Faith (4:1–42)

But what does the Samaritan woman do with all these revelations that open such a grand future before her? She seeks refuge in the one ray of hope for the realization of such great things,—that hope which found its way even to benighted Samaria, and was preserved there, though the Samaritans rejected the Prophets and clung to Moses alone,—the hope of the *Messiah*: "I know that Messiah cometh; when he is come he will declare unto us all things." But He *is* come: "I that speak unto thee am He." More plainly and directly than either to the seeking disciples, or to Nicodemus, or the Jews in Jerusalem, was this announcement made to the Samaritan woman! One of the most lofty and spiritual revelations concerning God and His kingdom made before a person whom no Jewish teacher would have deigned to address. For even the disciples, without knowing the full compass of this conversation, marveled that He was speaking with this woman (*a* woman).

3. *The Conversation with the Disciples (4:27–38)*

27–38. *And upon this came his disciples; and they marveled that he was speaking with a woman; yet no man said, What seekest thou? or, Why speakest thou with her? So the woman left her water pot, and went away into the city, and saith to the men, Come, see a man, which told me all things that ever I did: can this be the Christ? They went out of the city, and were coming to him. In the mean while the disciples prayed him, saying, Rabbi, eat. But he said unto them, I have meat to eat that ye know not. The disciples therefore said one to another, Hath any man brought him aught to eat? Jesus saith unto them, My meat is to do the will of him that sent me, and to accomplish his work. Say not ye, There are yet four months, and then cometh the harvest? behold, I say unto you, Lift up your eyes, and look on the fields, that they are white already unto harvest. He that reapeth receiveth wages, and gathereth fruit unto life eternal; that he that soweth and he that reapeth may rejoice together. For herein is the saying true, One soweth, and another reapeth. I sent you to reap that whereon ye have not laboured: others have laboured, and ye are entered into their labour.*

How different the manner in which this Samaritan woman left the Lord from the silent, meditative and undecided mood of Nicodemus! Leaving her water-pot, she runs back to the town, determined to bring all the people with her to the prophet, to see whether He be the Christ. Meanwhile the conversation between the disciples and the Master takes place, starting with their request to Jesus: "Rabbi, eat," just as the former conversation had opened with the Master's request: "Give Me to drink." And yet, the Lord did neither eat nor drink in that hour. He was above that; in a state of spiritual exultation similar to that on the return of the seventy (Luke 10:17–21) when He rejoiced in the Holy Spirit and said: "I thank Thee, O Father, Lord of heaven and earth, that Thou didst hide these things from the wise and understanding and didst reveal them unto babes: yea Father, for so it was well pleasing in Thy sight!" He had had His feast during the absence of the disciples, accomplishing His Father's work. "Four months yet and then harvest," said the disciples, as they came along through the sprouting fields, green with the fresh young wheat springing up. December was this time, as the harvest began in April. His sojourn in Judaea had therefore lasted eight months, from Easter till December. But the Lord turns their attention to another harvest field, the gathering in of immortal souls in the kingdom of God. Lift up your eyes! Look on the fields! White already unto harvest! There they are coming to Him (ver. 30), multitudes of Samaritans! His word to the woman has roused the whole place. After a short half hour of sower's work, such a plentiful harvest ready for the reaper! And this time the sower and the reapers (who are often so widely apart in the kingdom of God) so close together, united in one harvest-joy! It is the privilege and the joy of the disciples to reap, it was the labor of the Lord to sow. He had been at work. They enter into His labor.

4. Believing Samaritans (4:39–42)

39–42. And from that city many of the Samaritans believed on him because of the word of the woman, who testified, He told me all things that ever I did. So when the Samaritans came unto him, they besought him to abide with them; and he abode there two days. And many more believed because of his word; and they said to the woman, Now we believe, not because of thy speaking: for we have heard for ourselves, and know that this is indeed the Saviour of the world.

Here follows the description of the joyous harvest to which the Lord had just referred. What a result of this half-hour's sowing over against the eight months' work in barren Judaea! The personal contact with the Lord had a wonderful effect in developing the faith of the Samaritans, both extensively and intensively. Many more believed, now that they had an opportunity of hearing the Lord Himself. And they believe now because of His word, not because of the woman's speaking. They had tasted the fountain itself, that spring of living water. Whatever the service of men, parents, teachers, friends and fathers in the Church may have done for us in telling us of Jesus, our faith is fully and permanently established only when we rest on the word of the Lord Himself. These Samaritans, from their own hearing, have learned to know that this is indeed the *Saviour of the World!* (Only once more, 1 John 4:14, this beautiful name is given to the Lord.) Salvation is from the Jews. But the Saviour is the Saviour of the world, gathering the true worshippers of the Father from every kindred, every tongue.

IX. GALILEAN FAITH (4:43–54)

1. *Historical Introduction (4:43–45)*

43–45. *And after the two days he went forth from thence into Galilee. For Jesus himself testified, that a prophet hath no honour in his own country. So when he came into Galilee, the Galilæans received him, having seen all the things that he did in Jerusalem at the feast: for they also went unto the feast.*

The remark of the Evangelist (ver. 44): "*For Jesus Himself testified that a prophet hath no honor in his own country,*" is somewhat difficult to understand in this connection. How can this statement serve to *explain* the *return* of Jesus into Galilee at this time? The Lord went forth into Galilee, where He had indeed been before, without making an impression, without even a special attempt to draw public attention upon Himself, knowing that a prophet has no honor in his own country. In full accord with this principle was the reception which He now found among the Galileans. Having seen all the things that He did in *Jerusalem* at the feast, they received Him. His reputation, so to speak, was first made, not in His own country, but abroad, in the capital.

Galilee, originally the "region," "territory," "borders" (so in Josh. 13:2, the regions, that is, the Galilee of the Philistines), the name of the northern district of Palestine. Galilee (the borders), of the Gentiles (Isai. 9:1; Matt. 4:15), because the Jews (particularly the tribe of Asher) had failed to take full possession of it, leaving the important sea-towns in the hands of the Phoenicians. Under the reign of Solomon this district did not amount to much. King Hiram, of Tyrus, refused the twenty Galilean towns offered for his cedars as having no value whatever. At the time of Christ it was different. It was then a populous and most fertile district. Josephus speaks of 204 towns with more than 15,000 inhabitants, which would be equal to a population of over four millions, that is, as dense as in China of the present day. The inhabitants, ever since the return from the captivity, represented a mixture of Jewish and Pagan elements; despised by the Jews as ignorant, uncouth people, whose very language betrayed their lack of culture. They were brave warriors, but impulsive, passionate, unsteady, always ready for revolutionary movements.

2. *The Nobleman's Unbelief Rebuked (4:46–48)*

46–48. *He came therefore again unto Cana of Galilee, where he made the water wine. And there was a certain nobleman, whose son was sick at Capernaum. When he heard that Jesus was come out of Judaea into Galilee, he went unto him, and besought him that he would come down, and heal his son; for he was at the point of death. Jesus therefore said unto him, Except ye see signs and wonders, ye will in no wise believe.*

The history of Galilean faith in the Gospel of St. John begins with a very sharp rebuke of the unbelief which the Lord meets at first sight. The nobleman of Capernaum was not a relation of Herod's family, but an officer of the king's court,—possibly Chuza, the husband of Joanna (Luke 8:3), or Manaen (Acts 13:1), the foster-brother of Herod the Tetrarch. This man (emphatically said), from such surroundings and under such influences as that court would naturally exercise, came to Jesus and besought Him, that He would come down and heal his son—thus

IX. Galilean Faith (4:43–54)

conditioning the help he expected on the bodily presence of the Lord. This request (essentially the same as in the case of Jairus, and yet there was no reproof there) was answered by that severe rebuke: "Except ye see signs and wonders, ye will in no wise believe." It was the manifest aim of the Lord in all His pastoral dealings with individuals to bring them to that faith which rests on the *word* and is begotten of the *word*. All through the Gospel we observe the progress from the *sign* to the *word*, which follows or accompanies it, setting forth most fully its meaning. Here the Lord came from Samaria, where the faith which His presence created was altogether based on the *word*: "Now we believe—for we have *heard* for ourselves,"—no sign to be *seen* there, only the word to be heard. And this is the very thing in which the nobleman's faith was lacking.

3. The Nobleman's Faith Supported and Trained (4:49, 50)

49–50. The nobleman saith unto him, Sir, come down ere my child die. Jesus saith unto him, Go thy way; thy son liveth. The man believed the word that Jesus spake unto him, and he went his way.

The result shows that, however weak, there was in that man a beginning of faith which the severe trial to which it was subjected by the Lord could not extinguish, and which was consequently strengthened and quickened by that very trial. The father holds on to that one helper for whom he had come all the distance between Capernaum and Cana. He simply repeats his petition, with whatever defects and awkwardness it betrayed, emphasizing it with those touching words in which we see the father's heart trembling under the agony of that moment: Come down—"*ere my child die.*" Jesus saith unto him: "Go thy way, thy son liveth. The man believed the *word* that Jesus spake unto him and he went his way." The second word of the Lord was indeed another trial for the nobleman's faith. But of a much more positive character. If it required an unlimited, unreserved trust and surrender on the part of the nobleman, it furnished at the same time the means and support for such confidence in that simple word of Jesus: "Thy son liveth!" To accept the precious gift these words conveyed, and to follow the direction they implied, "go thy way,"—believing, rejoicing, never doubting, but obeying—this was the act of faith which filled the Evangelist's heart with wonder and gladness when he wrote, many years afterwards, "The man believed the word that Jesus spake." Thus far there was nothing for his eyes, no sign to be seen—only a word for his ear and his heart; but in this word, by the divine power it contained, a real act of deliverance at the very time when the word was spoken.

4. The Nobleman's Faith Crowned with Experience (4:51–54)

51–54. And as he was now going down, his servants met him, saying, that his son lived. So he inquired of them the hour when he began to amend. They said therefore unto him, Yesterday at the seventh hour the fever left him. So the father knew that it was at that hour in which Jesus said unto him, Thy son liveth: and himself believed, and his whole house. This is again the second sign that Jesus did, having come out of Judaea into Galilee.

The realities of the word, though invisible for a time, and objects of faith alone, become visible at last. The testimony of his servants meets the nobleman at the gate of the city with the very same word which Jesus had given him, and which had been his rod and his staff on his journey home: "Thy son liveth." He inquired of them the hour when he began to amend—surely not from any motive of doubt concerning the connection between this change and the word of Jesus, but to ascertain to his own fullest assurance and satisfaction that it was at the same hour. So the father *"knew"* and *"believed."* What a progress from that first stage of his coming to Jesus: "Except ye see signs and wonders ye will not believe."

5. The Nobleman's House Believing

Like the faith of the Samaritan woman, that of the nobleman also has a wonderful power of expansion. His whole house is brought to Jesus by the blessed experience of that day. The good news of the recovery of the sick child is far surpassed by the greater and better news: "My whole house liveth by faith in the Lord Jesus Christ!"

Thus far then the Evangelist has presented the beginnings of faith in the incarnate Word: in the *disciples*, through the testimony of the Baptist, their first personal acquaintance with the Lord and the manifestation of

IX. Galilean Faith (4:43–54)

His glory at the marriage of Cana; among the *inhabitants of Jerusalem* (2:23) during that first Passover; in *Nicodemus*, the learned Pharisee; in the *Samaritan woman* and the *people of Sychar*, and finally in Galilee, in the *nobleman's family* of Capernaum.

But now the curtain drops on these precious scenes, full of encouragement. We will see different things in the next eight chapters (ch. 5–12): The unbelief that rejects the Word; conflict after conflict against the faithful witness; an ever-growing hostility which culminates in the counsel to put Him to death.

SECOND PART. CHAPTERS 5-12.
THE HOSTILITY OF UNBELIEF THAT REJECTS THE INCARNATE WORD

The eight chapters from the fifth to the twelfth which form the central part of the Gospel of St. John, introduce the history of the great conflict between the Lord and His unbelieving adversaries, and the development of their opposition into that bitter hatred which finally resolved to put Him to death.

I. The Beginning of the Conflict in Judæa (5:1–47)

JOHN 5

I. The Beginning of the Conflict in Judæa (5:1–47)

1. *The Healing of the Sick Man in Bethesda (5:1–16)*

1–16. *After these things there was a feast of the Jews; and Jesus went up to Jerusalem. Now there is in Jerusalem by the sheep gate a pool, which is called in Hebrew Bethesda, having five porches. In these lay a multitude of them that were sick, blind, halt, withered. And a certain man was there, which had been thirty and eight years in his infirmity. When Jesus saw him lying, and knew that he had been now a long time in that case, he saith unto him, Wouldest thou be made whole? The sick man answered him, Sir, I have no man, when the water is troubled, to put me into the pool: but while I am coming, another steppeth down before me. Jesus saith unto him, Arise, take up thy bed, and walk. And straightway the man was made whole, and took up his bed and walked.*

Now it was the sabbath on that day. So the Jews said unto him that was cured, It is the sabbath, and it is not lawful for thee to take up thy bed. But he answered them, He that made me whole, the same said unto me, Take up thy bed, and walk. They asked him, Who is the man that said unto thee, Take up thy bed, and walk? But he that was healed wist not who it was: for Jesus had conveyed himself away, a multitude being in the place. Afterward Jesus findeth him in the temple, and said unto him, Behold, thou art made whole: sin no more, lest a worse thing befall thee. The man went away, and told the Jews that it was Jesus which had made him whole. And for this cause did the Jews persecute Jesus, because he did these things on the sabbath.

The first question which arises in connection with this miracle is one of considerable importance for the chronology of the public ministry of the Lord. What feast of the Jews was it that is mentioned in the first verse of the chapter? If we read "*the* feast,"[1] as the marginal note in the revised version indicates, the question is settled in favor of the Passover. In this

---

[1] Codd. ℵ, C. & E.; & Tischendorf.

case we have here the second Passover, during the public life of the Messiah, followed by the third in John 6 and the fourth and last in John 12, making in all about three and one-half years of Christ's public ministry. But if we read "*a* feast,"[2] it was most likely the festival of Purim (in March), and the Passover, spoken of in John 6, may have been in the same year, thus making the public life of the Lord only two and one-half years.

The site of the pool of Bethesda cannot satisfactorily be established in modern Jerusalem. The common tradition finds it in a large fosse "Birket Israil" 360 by 130 feet, north of the Temple mountain close to St. Stephen's Gate, on the eastern wall of the city, which, however, was most likely a part of the system of defense connected with the tower of Antonia. The revised version omits the last clause of the 3d and the whole of the 4th verse of the received text, and it must be admitted, on very strong authority. The periodical moving of the water, which occurs to the present day in a number of remitting and intermitting fountains throughout the country, could then have been the result of natural causes. The common superstition of the present inhabitants, which, as Thompson remarks (p. 459), ascribes this phenomenon to the agency of demons, believed to occupy all such places, seems rather to point to an original supernatural influence, as indicated in the 4th verse of the received text.

The miraculous healing of the sick man, in which Jesus had taken the initiative, without being asked, and during which He observed, as we would say, a strict incognito, provoked the conflict with His adversaries, because He did these things on the Sabbath day, the continual occasion for conflicts with His antagonists, also according to the Synoptical accounts. (Cf. Luke 6:1–11)

---

[2] Codd. A. B. & D.; Tregelles, Westcott & Hort, & Godet.

I. THE BEGINNING OF THE CONFLICT IN JUDÆA (5:1–47)

2. The Lord's Discourse Following the Miracle at the Pool of Bethesda (5:17–47)

(a.) The Personal Relation between the Father and the Son the Explanation of the Latter's Works (5:17–30)

17–30. *But Jesus answered them, My Father worketh even until now, and I work. For this cause therefore the Jews sought the more to kill him, because he not only brake the sabbath, but also called God his own Father, making himself equal with God.*

Jesus therefore answered and said unto them,

Verily, verily, I say unto you, The Son can do nothing of himself, but what he seeth the Father doing: for what things soever he doeth, these the Son also doeth in like manner. For the Father loveth the Son, and sheweth him all things that himself doeth: and greater works than these will he shew him, that ye may marvel. For as the Father raiseth the dead and quickeneth them, even so the Son also quickeneth whom he will. For neither doth the Father judge any man, but he hath given all judgement unto the Son; that all may honour the Son, even as they honour the Father. He that honoureth not the Son honoureth not the Father which sent him. Verily, verily, I say unto you, He that heareth my word, and believeth him that sent me, hath eternal life, and cometh not into judgement, but hath passed out of death into life. Verily, verily, I say unto you, The hour cometh, and now is, when the dead shall hear the voice of the Son of God; and they that hear shall live. For as the Father hath life in himself, even so gave he to the Son also to have life in himself: and he gave him authority to execute judgement, because he is the Son of man. Marvel not at this; for the hour cometh, in which all that are in the tombs shall hear his voice, and shall come forth; they that have done good, unto the resurrection of life; and they that have done ill, unto the resurrection of judgement.

I can of myself do nothing: as I hear, I judge: and my judgement is righteous; because I seek not mine own will, but the will of him that sent me.

In the plain opening words of the Lord we find both the foundation of the whole discourse which follows, and the occasion for the bitter attacks of His enemies. "My Father worketh even until now and I work." There are two points in this short sentence; and both were instinctively felt by the antagonists of the Lord. He is at *work*, in spite of the *Sabbath*, This is the one point. And He is in *union with the Father*, that is the other point. Or as the Jews express it without equivocation: "He not only brake the Sabbath but also called God His own Father, making Himself equal with God." The year before, when He appeared in the Temple with the scourge in His hand, they could not, however much embittered against Him, make out a case to prosecute Him. For the zeal He there displayed was for the sanctuary in Jerusalem. But now they find two charges at one time: breaking the Sabbath, and the blasphemy of making Himself equal with God. Mark the distinction, which His enemies made between what He actually *said*, when He called God His own Father; and the *claim* He thereby made, of being equal with God, which in their eyes was not a reality, and therefore nothing but a blasphemous assumption: "making Himself" what He was not—equal with God. (As in 8:53, Whom makest Thou Thyself?)

There is a heavenly peace, a truly Sabbatic restfulness, unruffled by the anger of His adversaries, in the answer of the Lord. Let your Rabbis discern the thirty kinds of work, forbidden on the Sabbath day, let them dispute that difficult question, whether it be lawful to heal, or even to comfort an afflicted fellow-man on that day. My Father worketh and so do I. And if He were not at work, preserving, keeping, blessing, protecting His people, laboring for their eternal welfare and salvation, where would our Sabbath be? With the mere ceasing from work nothing is gained on the Sabbath day. But to work with the Father, for the Father, in the spirit of the Father, this is a Sabbath, pleasing in His eyes. How natural it is for the Son to work as the Father worketh! He can do nothing of Himself, but that He seeth the Father doing. It is a moral impossibility for Him. Being one with the Father and fully conscious of His will and purpose, He cannot (as He was tempted to do, and as it would have been an easy thing for Him physically to do) change those stones into bread, or cast Himself down from the pinnacle of the temple. But He seeth the works of the Father; for the Father loveth the Son and showeth Him all things that Himself doeth. Love has no secrets. And the love of the Father and the Son is the basis of their full understanding and working together. We have

I. The Beginning of the Conflict in Judæa (5:1–47)

heard before that great word on God's relation to the world: God so loved the world! Here we have the still greater word on the relation between the Father and the Son, which grants us an insight into the eternal mysteries of the Holy Trinity. The father loved the Son. There has always been the Loving one and the Beloved one, independent of the created world. There has always been that communication and understanding between Father and Son, by which the Son becomes the interpreter, the executor of the Father's works. They are shown to Him, that is, in the end, they are committed to Him. They are all done through Him.

And now the two greatest works, which in their fulness are yet to be revealed through the Son, are set forth in vers. 21–29. The work of *raising the dead* or quickening, and the work of *judging*. In these two, the creative and the judicative, all that God does towards men is comprehended and consummated. And these two works are committed to the Son. He is henceforth exclusively the life-giver and the judge of the world. And the purpose for which these works are thus officially committed to the Son, is that all may honor the Son even as they honor the Father. Equal works, equal honor, this is the principle underlying this sentence. What a solemn warning to the enemies of the Lord who charged Him with blasphemy for "making Himself equal with God!"

But on the other hand what a kind invitation for all (in ver. 24) to share in those two blessed experiences, of having eternal life and not coming into judgment, by accomplishing that great step, passing "out of death into life." Observe here that humble, winning form in which the testimony of God, with all its inherent power of conviction is, so to speak, placed on the same level with ordinary, trustworthy, human evidence: "who believeth Him" the same as the Lord said to the Samaritan woman, "Believe Me"—just as man speaks to man and friend to friend.

The great work of life-giving, quickening, is first introduced (ver. 25 f.) as the spiritual raising of the spiritually dead. It is the present work of the Saviour, which goes on wherever His voice is heard, and brings divine life to the hearts of all that believe and obey. Afterwards the resurrection of the body and the future judgment are set forth as the crowning works of the Son. Life is given by Christ as the eternal Son of God, in whom, from the beginning, was the fountain of life for all creatures. Judgment is exercised by Christ as the Son of Man. Thus, by divine appointment, man is to be judged by his peer; by Him who is the most humble and the most loving of men, who has borne the sins of men. On the judgment seat sits grace itself in the person of Him who can be touched with the feeling of our infirmities, having been tempted in all points like as we are. Who then will complain of injustice, if judged and condemned by the Son of Man?

(b.) *The Testimony of the Father (5:31–40)*

31–40. *If I bear witness of myself, my witness is not true. It is another that beareth witness of me; and I know that the witness which he witnessed of me is true. Ye have sent unto John, and he hath borne witness unto the truth. But the witness which I receive is not from man: howbeit I say these things, that ye may be saved. He was the lamp that burneth and shineth; and ye were willing to rejoice for a season in his light. But the witness which I have is greater than that of John: for the works which the Father hath given me to accomplish, the very works that I do, bear witness of me, that the Father hath sent me. And the Father which sent me, he hath borne witness of me. Ye have neither heard his voice at any time, nor seen his form. And ye have not his word abiding in you: for whom he sent, him ye believe not. Ye search the scriptures, because ye think that in them ye have eternal life; and these are they which bear witness of me; and ye will not come to me, that ye may have life.*

In speaking of these great works, the Lord may well have read an expression of utter astonishment on the faces of His adversaries. Where is the authority for such great things on His part? To answer this the Lord sets forth the *testimony* which proves His authority and dignity; not His own personal testimony, nor even that of John the Baptist, but that of a greater One, the Father. The works (ver. 36) which the Father has given Him: the direct word of the Father Himself (ver. 37), and the scriptures (ver. 39), represent this testimony in its fulness.

The Lord accommodates Himself to His opponents to such an extent that, at this point, He admits that His own testimony in the sense of the Jews would not be conclusive and convincing evidence in His own case

I. THE BEGINNING OF THE CONFLICT IN JUDÆA (5:1–47)

(ver. 31)[1] He therefore appeals to other witnesses. But even John the Baptist's testimony He is willing to forego in this connection. He will not appeal to him and receive his testimony from him (ver. 34). Not from the human messenger as such, but from Him that sent him does the testimony for Christ derive its value and dignity. Most clearly and strikingly the transient character of John's office and testimony is described by the Lord: when He calls him a burning and shining lamp, and Israel "willing to rejoice for a season in this light." This "rejoicing" is rather a suspicious feature. Was that all? John's solemn preaching of repentance nothing but a passing sensation! If it had really taken hold of their hearts, would it not have caused them a deep godly sorrow rather than rejoicing? But they were not anxious to have their souls enlightened by that lamp. They rejoiced and were proud that their Judaism was shining once more in new lustre, through the appearance of this great prophet, after prophecy had been silent for four centuries.

Where the testimony of the Father Himself is to be found, is set forth directly in ver. 36–39. It is to be found in the *works* which the Father has given Him to accomplish, not simply the single miracles and signs, such as the healing of the sick man in Bethesda, but the whole great task of His life itself, the great double-work of life-giving and judging. Again: The testimony of the Father was the most direct one (ver. 37). "He hath borne witness of me," in the voice heard on the occasion of the Lord's baptism: "Him ye shall hear." Lastly: The testimony of the Father is to be found in the word of the Scriptures. The two different interpretations of ver. 39 are indicated in the Revised Version: "Ye search the scriptures," in the context, as accepted by the majority of modern commentators: and "Search the scriptures" on the margin and in the Authorized Version (the interpretation of the Peshitto, Chrysostom, Augustine, Luther, Calvin and others). Preferring the former, we find in these words both a concession and a warning to the Jews. They *have* the word, but have it not abiding in them (ver. 38). They have a knowledge of Scripture, based on

---

[1] Quite different in 8:14: "Even if I bear witness of myself, my witness is true," because in that connection He emphasizes His consciousness of His divine nature and origin: "I know whence I came."

thorough researches, on great familiarity with the contents of its letter. And even more than that. They have an idea (δοκεῖτε) of having eternal life in them. But what are all these researches in Scripture, what are all the minutia of rabbinical or theological interpretation, what is even the exalted idea of Scripture as a means and guarantee of eternal life, unless Christ be found in the Scriptures! "They bear witness of *Me*." This is the one main thing. Christ is the center and the sun of the Scriptures (here the O. T. Scriptures). No life in the Scriptures or through the Scriptures, except through Christ. But the testimony of Him is in all the Scriptures, this plural covering the whole of the O. T. Canon.

(c.) *Unbelief of the Jews, Lamented and Explained (5:41–47)*

41–47. *I receive not glory from men. But I know you, that ye have not the love of God in yourselves. I am come in my Father's name, and ye receive me not: if another shall come in his own name, him ye will receive. How can ye believe, which receive glory one of another, and the glory that cometh from the only God ye seek not? Think not that I will accuse you to the Father: there is one that accuseth you, even Moses, on whom ye have set your hope. For if ye believed Moses, ye would believe me; for he wrote of me. But if ye believe not his writings, how shall ye believe my words?*

With the 41st verse begins the third and last section of this discourse. The Lord shows the real and innermost cause of the unbelief of the Jews and the consequences of it. Their unbelief springs from their selfish pride, which craves honor from men, whilst it is indifferent to the glory coming from the only God. What else is faith, but to give ourselves up to God, fully, completely, in every sense of the word, so that we are no longer anything in ourselves, but God is everything in us, by His all-sufficient grace. This love of God towards men, appropriated by the believer, is not in the hearts of those men as something which they realize and experience. Therefore they receive not the greatest gift of that love, Him who came in His Father's name. Mark how directly and clearly the Lord here announces Himself as the one expected Messiah, come from God. We are not to look for another (Matt. 11:3). And if "another" cometh, it can only be a false Christ, or even an Antichrist.

I. The Beginning of the Conflict in Judæa (5:1–47)

The Lord having thus far defended Himself against the insinuations and accusations of His enemies, now proceeds to attack them most vigorously and with a weapon which they had looked upon as their greatest strength:—"There is one that accuseth you, even *Moses*, on whom ye have set your hope. For if ye believed Moses, ye would believe Me." Moses accuses them not only through the *law* which was given him as the mediator, but also through his whole testimony concerning the history of God's kingdom and particularly as the great prophet, who wrote of Christ and pointed to Him. If the Scriptures in general bear witness of Christ, the same is now said in particular of those Scriptures which were written by Moses, and written of Christ, bearing witness of Christ. Let our modern teachers and students of the Pentateuch remember these words of our Lord and Master.

It is a very severe charge against the Jews: "Ye believe not Moses," but true in every aspect. Did they believe what Moses said on fallen man, that he was flesh striving against the Spirit of God (Gen. 6:3), and that "every imagination of the thoughts of his heart was only evil continually" (Ibid. ver. 5)? Did they believe what Moses said of the hope and experience of the Patriarchs, especially of Abraham, how he believed in the Lord and how the Lord counted it to him for righteousness? Did they believe what Moses said of the Law and its curse upon every one "that will not do all these commandments"? Did they believe what was meant by all those Mosaic institutions of the sacrifices, and the tabernacle, and the priesthood, and by such types as the Passover and the serpent in the wilderness? Indeed, where did Moses not write of Christ? Accepting the writings of Moses, they must believe the words of Jesus. It is one testimony, an organic unity from the very beginning.

The tables are completely turned at the close of this discourse of the Lord; the two points of attack have been reversed against Christ's accusers themselves. They appeared in the beginning as the special advocates of Moses, defending his sabbath, protesting against its breaking. And now they stand here as the men who themselves, in their innermost heart, dishonor and disbelieve Moses, and are in turn accused by him. Again, they seemed at the outset most zealous for the honor of

God in persecuting Him who made Himself equal with God; but now they stand convicted as men anxious to receive glory from one another and utterly indifferent to the true glory of God! They are Jews only outwardly, in the flesh, and not inwardly, in the spirit, whose praise is not of men but of God (Rom. 2:28, 29. Jehudah, God's praise). Thus the great battle is opened between the Lord and His adversaries, and it is a conflict for life and death. But there is now a pause for a while, made by the Lord's retirement into Galilee.

II. The Crisis in Galilee

JOHN 6

II. The Crisis in Galilee

(A.) The Miraculous Feeding (6:1–15)
(B.) The Meeting with His Disciples on the Water (6:16–21)

1–21. *After these things Jesus went away to the other side of the sea of Galilee, which is the sea of Tiberias. And a great multitude followed him, because they beheld the signs which he did on them that were sick. And Jesus went up into the mountain, and there he sat with his disciples. Now the Passover, the feast of the Jews, was at hand. Jesus therefore lifting up his eyes, and seeing that a great multitude cometh unto him, saith unto Philip, Whence are we to buy bread, that these may eat? And this he said to prove him; for he himself knew what he would do. Philip answered him, Two hundred pennyworth of bread is not sufficient for them, that every one may take a little. One of his disciples, Andrew, Simon Peter's brother, saith unto him, There is a lad here, which hath five barley loaves, and two fishes: but what are these among so many? Jesus said, Make the people sit down. Now there was much grass in the place. So the men sat down, in number about five thousand. Jesus therefore took the loaves; and having given thanks, he distributed to them that were set down; likewise also of the fishes as much as they would. And when they were filled, he saith unto his disciples, Gather up the broken pieces which remain over, that nothing be lost. So they gathered them up, and filled twelve baskets with broken pieces from the five barley loaves, which remained over unto them that had eaten. When therefore the people saw the sign which he did, they said, This is of a truth the prophet that cometh into the world.*

Jesus therefore perceiving that they were about to come and take him by force, to make him king, withdrew again into the mountain himself alone.

And when evening came, his disciples went down unto the sea; and they entered into a boat, and were going over the sea unto Capernaum. And it was now dark, and Jesus had not yet come to them. And the sea was rising by reason of a great wind that blew. When therefore they had rowed about five and twenty or thirty furlongs, they behold Jesus walking on the sea, and drawing nigh unto the boat; and they were afraid. But he saith unto them, It is I; be not afraid. They were willing therefore to receive him into the boat: and straightway the boat was at the land whither they were going.

The healing of the nobleman's son in Capernaum had been the beginning of signs wrought in the public ministry of the Lord in Galilee. The miraculous feeding of the 5,000 is the culmination of the Galilean signs. All the four Gospels record it, but its fullest, deepest significance, both in point of history and of doctrine, has only been brought out in the fourth Gospel. Its date was about a year after the discourse in Jerusalem related in ch. 5. Here is the principal period of His Galilean activity, which is more fully described by the Synoptists.

The locality of the miraculous feeding is distinctly mentioned by St. Luke. It was Bethsaida; but not Bethsaida on the west side of the Lake of Galilee, the home of Andrew, Peter and Philip, but Bethsaida Julias, situated on the left bank of the river Jordan, a little to the north of the point where it enters the Lake of Galilee.

The Lord had intended to retire for a little season of rest, to the northeast shore of the lake, together with His disciples. But as the multitude pressed after Him, He forgot His need of rest and gave Himself up to their wants, just as we have seen it before in His dealings with Nicodemus and the Samaritan woman. It was the last Passover before His passion and death, and the Lord was willing to give to the Galilean multitude, in the miraculous feeding and the discourse connected with it, a sign and a word which should prepare them for the events of the following year, and reveal Him as the bread of Life, giving Himself for the life of the world. But what was the effect? The long suspended and frequently disappointed Messianic expectations of those passionate, warlike Galileans threatened to lead to a revolutionary outbreak. "They were about to come and take Him by force, to make Him king." But this attempt was promptly frustrated by the Lord; He withdrew again into the mountain Himself alone to pray, having constrained the disciples to enter into the boat and to go before Him unto the other side (Matt. 14:22). This separation even from the disciples in that hour naturally leads us to ask: Was there danger even in their midst? Had they also been tainted

II. The Crisis in Galilee

with this spirit of insurrection, with the desire after a Messiah-king of their own making? Or had the movement even been instigated by one of the twelve, the same who at the close of this chapter is so significantly called *a devil?* Even in the following event the scenes of next year's Passover are foreshadowed. A stormy night—the lonely disciples struggling helplessly on the raging sea—their Lord not among them, far away on the mountain to pray; but after the short separation a sudden reappearance of their blessed Lord with the sweet and comforting salutation: It is I; fear not!—Does not this change from the storm to the calm, from the separation to reunion, from fear and anxiety to joy and peace, suggest the great change from the darkness of Good Friday to the light of glorious Easter morning?

(C.) The Discourses Following these Miracles in Capernaum (6:22–59)

1. Historical Introduction (6:22–24)

22–24. On the morrow, the multitude which stood on the other side of the sea saw that there was none other boat there, save one, and that Jesus entered not with his disciples into the boat, but that his disciples went away alone (howbeit there came boats from Tiberias nigh unto the place where they ate the bread after the Lord had given thanks): when the multitude therefore saw that Jesus was not there, neither his disciples, they themselves got into the boats, and came to Capernaum, seeking Jesus.

After the miraculous feeding the people had remained on the other side (the N. E. shore) of the Lake of Galilee. Seeing that the Lord had sent off His disciples in the boat, whilst He remained on their side, they naturally expected to find Him again on the following day. In this they were disappointed, and consequently they used their first opportunity—some boats from Tiberias coming near the place where they ate the bread—to cross over to Capernaum. To their great surprise they find the Lord there, and at once the welcome thought of a new miracle suggests itself to their minds: How could He ever have come across the lake? They were sure that He had not crossed the lake in one of their boats. Therefore the question: Rabbi, when earnest Thou hither? And here is the starting-point for all the discourses that now follow. Not the enjoyment of miraculous signs, the satisfying of mere curiosity, the alleviation of temporary needs and distress is what they ought to seek from Him, but eternal life itself, which the Son of Man shall give them, if they will only believe in Him. This idea of apprehending the Lord Himself, appropriating and assimilating Him by personal faith, forms the principal subject of these discourses. They are narrated in that lively, graphic form of the dialogue, which is so characteristic of this Gospel, and presents most of its great facts and doctrines with truly dramatic realism.

2. The Jews Asking Questions (6:25–40)

25–40. *And when they found him on the other side of the sea, they said unto him, Rabbi, when camest thou hither? Jesus answered them and said, Verily, verily, I say unto you, ye seek me, not because ye saw signs, but because ye ate of the loaves and were filled. Work not for the meat which perisheth, but for the meat which abideth unto eternal life, which the Son of man shall give unto you: for him the Father, even God hath sealed. They said therefore unto him, What must we do, that we may work the works of God? Jesus answered and said unto them, This is the work of God, that ye believe on him whom he hath sent. They said therefore unto him, What then doest thou for a sign, that we may see, and believe thee? what workest thou? Our fathers ate the manna in the wilderness; as it is written, He gave them bread out of heaven to eat. Jesus therefore said unto them, Verily, verily, I say unto you, It was not Moses that gave you the bread out of heaven; but my Father giveth you the true bread out of heaven. For the bread of God is that which cometh down out of heaven, and giveth life unto the world. They said therefore unto him, Lord, evermore give us this bread. Jesus said unto them, I am the bread of life: he that cometh to me shall not hunger, and he that believeth on me shall never thirst. But I said unto you, that ye have seen me, and yet believe not. All that which the Father giveth me shall come unto me; and him that cometh to me I will in no wise cast out. For I am come down from heaven, not to do mine own will, but the will of him that sent me. And this is the will of him that sent me, that of all that which he hath given me I should lose nothing, but should raise it up at the last day. For this is the will of my Father, that every one that beholdeth the Son,*

II. The Crisis in Galilee

and believeth on him, should have eternal life; and I will raise him up at the last day.

There are four distinct questions or requests, with which the Jews approach the Lord. The first has been referred to already. Rabbi, when camest Thou hither? (ver. 25). The second is found in ver. 28: What must we do, that we may work the works of God? The third in ver. 30: What then doest Thou for a sign, that we may see and believe Thee? what workest Thou? The last is the direct petition of the Jews (ver. 34): "Lord, evermore give us this bread." The main points of this dialogue are as follows: Not for the meat which perisheth, but for the meat which abideth unto eternal life, they ought to work. But how can they work for this? Not by doing certain works prescribed by the law, but through that one work, which is God's work indeed, believing on Him, whom He hath sent. Faith, then, is not in this connection the work *wrought* by God (though other scripture passages undoubtedly describe it also in this light), but it is the one work *demanded by God*, the one thing pleasing to God, just as Luther used to say of the first commandment: "It is the intent of this commandment to require such true faith and trust of the heart as regards the only true God and rest in Him alone. So you have here the true honor and service of God which pleases God, and which He commands under penalty of eternal wrath, viz., that the heart knows no other trust or confidence than in Him" (Large Catech.).

Still the carnal mind of the Galileans unfolds itself more and more. If Christ be such a great messenger or commissioner from God, demanding such faith, where are His signs? That of yesterday was good enough as far as it went. But, after all, those barley loaves make rather a poor show, compared with the manna from heaven, on which the fathers were fed. If Jesus be greater than Moses, surely His gifts and signs ought to surpass those of Moses. This leads to the direct, positive statement of the Lord: I am the bread of life, given by the Father, out of heaven, and giving eternal life. Thus the attention of His hearers is concentrated upon Himself, His person. Instead of asking for gifts, however great and wonderful, from His hand, they ought to ask for Himself. Not: Give us such and such bread! But give us Thyself, thou heavenly Bread, that we may eat and live through Thee!

3. The Jews Murmuring (6:41–51)

41–51. *The Jews therefore murmured concerning him, because he said, I am the bread which came down out of heaven. And they said, Is not this Jesus, the son of Joseph, whose father and mother we know? how doth he now say, I am come down out of heaven? Jesus answered and said unto them, Murmur not among yourselves. No man can come to me, except the Father which sent me draw him: and I will raise him up in the last day. It is written in the prophets, And they shall all be taught of God. Every one that hath heard from the Father, and hath learned, cometh unto me. Not that any man hath seen the Father, save he which is from God, he hath seen the Father. Verily, verily, I say unto you, He that believeth hath eternal life. I am the bread of life. Your fathers did eat the manna in the wilderness, and they died. This is the bread which cometh down out of heaven, that a man may eat thereof and not die. I am the living bread which came down out of heaven: if any man eat of this bread, he shall life for ever: yea and the bread which I will give is my flesh, for the live of the world.*

We know, from the Synoptical Gospels, that a number of scribes and Pharisees had gone to Galilee, just about that time, to watch the Lord, and, if an occasion should offer itself, to stir up the people against Him (Matt. 15:1). Such men most likely were among this multitude. They would naturally be the first to point out the seeming presumptuousness in that claim of Christ, "that He came down out of heaven," whilst to them He was "this Jesus, the son of Joseph, whose father and mother we know." The Lord does not begin to reveal to them the mystery of His supernatural birth. An appeal to this will never create faith where there is none. It rather requires a believing heart to apprehend and appreciate that fact in all its bearings. Instead, therefore, of disputing with them on this holy mystery, He begs and warns them to submit to the drawing of the Father, and to come to Him. For the Father not only gives the Son, but also draws to the Son and gives Him all that come unto Him (see also ver. 37), and find everlasting life in Him. Do not, He says to His hearers, refuse to be taught of God, hear Him, learn from Him, come unto Me (ver. 45).

II. The Crisis in Galilee

From the statement made before, that He is the Bread of life, which came down out of heaven, He cannot retract anything. It is solemnly repeated, and He adds another important feature to it, which rather increases its weight, and is not calculated to make it more acceptable to the Jews. "Yea," He says, in a manifest climax: "and the bread which I will give is *My flesh for the life of the world*" (ver. 51 close). God is going to prepare a new Passover feast, to which not only His chosen people of old, but the whole world, is bidden. Christ is the Passover Lamb. His life is to be given on the cross for the life of the world. The Lamb of God, which taketh away the sin of the world, by His atoning death, redeems the world from the bondage of sin and death, and becomes the heavenly meat for a starving world hungering after eternal life.

4. The Jews Striving One with Another (6:52–59)

52–59. The Jews therefore strove one with another, saying, How can this man give us his flesh to eat? Jesus therefore said unto them, Verily, verily, I say unto you, except ye eat the flesh of the Son of man and drink his blood, ye have not life in yourselves. He that eateth my flesh and drinketh my blood hath eternal life; and I will raise him up at the last day. For my flesh is meat indeed, and my blood is drink indeed. He that eateth my flesh and drinketh my blood abideth in me, and I in him. As the living Father sent me, and I live because of the Father; so he that eateth me, he also shall live because of me. This is the bread which came down out of heaven: not as the fathers did eat, and died: he that eateth this bread shall live for ever. These things said he in the synagogue as he taught in Capernaum.

In this third and last section, the discourses of the Lord on the great theme: "The Bread of Life," culminate. In the first we had the simple statement: I am the Bread of Life, that came from heaven. In the second the important point is added: The bread spoken of is His flesh, given for the life of the world. In the third and last, the eating and drinking of His flesh and blood is the main point presented, as introduced by the question of the Jews: "How can this man give us his flesh to eat?" The language used by the Lord in this section is indeed strong meat, not only for the Jews of that time, but for Christians and believers of all times. This whole passage does not refer directly and specifically to the Lord's

Supper, or the sacramental eating and drinking of His body and blood. The ordinance of the Lord's table, by Christ's direct appointment, has its own earthly, visible elements of bread and wine. Without these, we have no sacramental partaking of Christ, however closely we may be united with the Lord by faith, however heavenly may be our enjoyment of His presence through the word and the Spirit. But there is not the slightest reference to either bread or wine, the elements in the Lord's Supper. The Lord speaks of Himself as the living bread, very much in the same manner as He spoke of the living water to the Samaritan woman. Moreover, we have such statements as those in the 53d and in the 56th and following verses. In the former we read: "Except ye eat the flesh of the Son of Man, and drink His blood, ye have not life in yourselves." Dare we limit this absolute rule, which allows of no exception, to the partaking of the Sacrament of the Lord's Supper? What becomes of those who (for very good reasons) live and die without ever having come to that sacrament? The children that have never been admitted to it? The adults who, for peculiar reasons, against their own will, have been prevented from receiving it? Shall it be said of them all: "Ye have not life in yourselves"? And in the 56th verse we read: "He that eateth My flesh and drinketh My blood abideth in Me and I in him." Accordingly, the relation to the Lord, and the connection with Him through the eating of His flesh and drinking of His blood, must be not of a temporary and periodical, but of an abiding character. So this statement also seems to preclude the specific reference of this passage to the sacrament.

The eating and drinking of the flesh and blood of the Son of Man is a description, in strongly figurative language, of the personal appropriation by faith of the blessings resulting from the atoning death of Christ. But more than this. It is not only the truths taught by the Lord, or the benefits purchased and conveyed by Him, that are to the believing Christian meat indeed, unto eternal life. It is the *Lord Himself*, Jesus Christ, not simply in His divine nature, dwelling in our hearts through the Spirit, but the whole, undivided Godman, with His human nature also, including His glorified body. This whole Christ must be ours, in order to have life everlasting. He must be appropriated, assimilated by

II. The Crisis in Galilee

true faith, and this mystic union with Him, the glorified Godman, is most beautifully and strikingly represented by this figure of eating His flesh and drinking His blood. It is undoubtedly the strongest, most realistic picture of faith, and its result the complete appropriation of Christ, His whole work and His whole person, divine and human; one of the principal characteristic features of the Gospel of John, with its wonderful heavenly realism.

(D.) The Wavering Disciples and the Crisis (6:60–71)
1. The Wavering Disciples (6:60–65)

60–65. Many therefore of his disciples, when they heard this, said, This is a hard saying; who can hear it? But Jesus knowing in himself that his disciples murmured at this, said unto them, Doth this cause you to stumble? What then if ye should behold the Son of man ascending where he was before? It is the spirit that quickeneth; the flesh profiteth nothing: the words that I have spoken unto you are spirit, and are life. But there are some of you that believe not. For Jesus knew from the beginning who they were that believed not, and who it was that should betray him. And he said, For this cause have I said unto you, that no man can come unto me, except it be given unto him of the Father.

These revelations of Christ concerning the mystery of His person, and the true, innermost nature of faith, that appropriates Him, became a stumbling block to all who looked upon Him simply with the eyes of human reason, considering Him merely as a great prophet, mighty in deed and word, or as the great organizer of an outward kingdom glorious before men. There came first the murmuring: This is a hard saying, who can hear it? and afterwards direct apostasy, "many of His disciples went back and walked no more with him." Even His attempt to give them a key for the correct understanding of those mysterious utterances concerning His own flesh and blood is of no avail. He points them to His coming ascension: "What, if you shall behold the Son of Man ascend to where He was before?" He tells them of His heavenly glory which He had before coming into this world, to which He expects to return by His ascension and in which even this flesh of His is going to participate. What He said of His flesh and blood was said of the glorified Christ. He spoke of the flesh united to the Godhead and glorified by the Spirit. The power of quickening, of giving life, which He ascribed to His flesh given for the life of the world, is not in the pure, earthly, human flesh as such, but in the Spirit. Without it the flesh profiteth nothing. But Christ is the incarnate Word: the God in the flesh; not flesh, born of the flesh as other men, but begotten of the Spirit as the Son of Mary, and glorified by the Spirit. Of Christ's flesh, therefore, we cannot say: it profiteth nothing. It is the flesh of the Godman and therefore giveth life to the world. Yea we are bold to say: God outside of the flesh profiteth nothing! We have no God that will save and give life to the perishing world except the God in the flesh, the incarnate Son of God, born of the Virgin Mary.

2. The Decision of the Twelve (6:66–69)

66–69. *Upon this many of his disciples went back, and walked no more with him. Jesus said therefore unto the twelve, Would ye also go away? Simon Peter answered him, Lord, to whom shall we go? thou hast the words of eternal life. And we have believed and know that thou art the Holy One of God.*

At this critical point in the midst of these wavering disciples the Lord demands a decision on the part of the twelve. (The twelve have never been named in this Gospel; but are spoken of as well known to the readers.) The question of the Lord: Would ye also go away? must not be understood as it is frequently taken, as a most pathetic lament, with a certain touch of sentimentality about it. It is in itself full of manly strength and resolution, insisting on an open, honest decision for or against Christ, on the principle announced by Him on another occasion: He that is not with Me, is against Me. He that gathereth not with Me scattereth. This is the dilemma. Now take your choice!

Peter, as on other occasions also, becomes the spokesman for the others. It must not be supposed that he or the others at that time were able to grasp the full meaning and import of the Lord's teaching on those weighty subjects. Nor does the Lord Himself expect or demand this on the part of the twelve, and much less from the great mass of the people. All that He asks is that implicit trust and confidence, which is so vigorously expressed in the words of Peter. "To whom shall we go? Thou hast [the] words of eternal life." Away from Thee—everything is empty, dark and dead. With Thee all is light, life and abundance. We have *believed* and know (observe the order of these two terms) that Thou art the Holy One of God,[1] guileless, undefiled, separated from sinners and higher than the heavens, sanctified, consecrated and sent into the world by the Father. See Heb. 7:26; John 10:36.—Also Peter's address in the temple (Acts 3:14, "Ye denied the Holy and Righteous One").

3. *The Devil among Them (6:70, 71)*

70–71. Jesus answered them, Did not I choose you the twelve, and one of you is a devil? Now he spake of Judas the son of Simon Iscariot, for he it was that should betray him, being one of the twelve.

A painful disharmony mars the beauty of that joyous accord which Peter had sounded. The Lord is ready and willing that the crisis, brought about in that hour, should go clear through the inner circle of the twelve. Twelve He has chosen and one of them is a devil! The preceding discourses of the Lord had had the effect upon Judas Iscariot, of bringing about the decision, in the depth of his heart, against Jesus. But he was not ready yet to break with Him outwardly. He held on to his connection with the disciples of the Lord. Jesus was to him a means to a selfish end, and his attachment to His cause a matter of business. He probably had his own ideas and plans to carry out, at a later period, with better success, what had been a failure in Galilee after the feeding of the 5,000: viz., to proclaim Jesus King of a new Jewish empire, with himself as the secretary of the treasury. He seems to have succeeded very well in hiding his true character from the disciples. Only the ever-watchful eye of the beloved disciple followed him with misgiving and suspicion. He clearly indicates this many years afterwards in the constant refrain, with which that name is mentioned in his Gospel: "he it was that should betray Him, being one of the twelve."

---

[1] The usual reading is: Christ, the son of the living God, as in Peter's confession, Matt. 16:16. But the best authorities have the reading of the Revised Version. It is evident, that, from a desire to make the two confessions of Peter as nearly alike as possible, the words used in Matt. 16 have been inserted here by some copyists.

JOHN 7

III. THE CONFLICT IN JERUSALEM AGAIN TAKEN UP (CH. 7, 8)

(A.) *Historical Introduction (7:1–13)*

1–13. And after these things Jesus walked in Galilee; for he would not walk in Judæa, because the Jews sought to kill him. Now the feast of the Jews, the feast of tabernacles, was at hand. His brethren therefore said unto him, Depart hence and go into Judaea, that thy disciples also may behold thy works which thou doest. For no man doeth anything in secret, and himself seeketh to be known openly. If thou doest these things, manifest thyself to the world. For even his brethren did not believe on him. Jesus therefore saith unto them, My time is not yet come; but your time is alway ready. The world cannot hate you; but me it hateth, because I testify of it, that its works are evil. Go ye up unto the feast: I go not up yet unto this feast; because my time is not yet fulfilled. And having said these things unto them, he abode still in Galilee.

But when his brethren were gone up unto the feast, then went he also up, not publicly, but as it were in secret. The Jews therefore sought him at the feast, and said, Where is he? And there was much murmuring among the multitudes concerning him: some said, He is a good man; others said, Not so, but he leadeth the multitude astray. Howbeit no man spake openly of him for fear of the Jews.

A period of six months intervenes between the events recorded in the preceding chapter and the Lord's visit to the festival of tabernacles, recorded in the seventh. This feast of tabernacles, one of the three great festivals of the Jews,—Passover and Pentecost being the other two—was the gayest and most joyous of all. It was celebrated in the month of October and lasted eight days; the Jews during this time dwelling in tents or huts built of green boughs on the streets or on the roofs of their houses. "Every morning, at the time of the morning sacrifice, a golden pitcher was filled with water from the fountain of Siloah and, with a song of thanksgiving, was poured out at the side of the altar in remembrance of

III. THE CONFLICT IN JERUSALEM AGAIN TAKEN UP (CH. 7, 8)

the miraculous supply of water in the wilderness. Every evening, at the time of the evening sacrifice, a brilliant light blazed forth from golden candlesticks in the court of the temple, in remembrance of the fiery pillar in the wilderness." As this festival drew nigh, the brothers of Jesus, who did not yet themselves believe in Him, urged Him to go up and manifest Himself as the Messiah in Jerusalem and Judæa, where He had formerly been, gathering a number of disciples (John 4:1) They could not understand, why the Lord should hide His Messianic authority and miraculous powers under the bushel, in obscure Galilee. They were anxious that He should show Himself in Judæa and make an impression there on the ruling classes. But they have no conception of the real attitude of the world towards Jesus; that it hates Him for His testimony, and that such a manifestation as His brothers urge Him to make, would necessarily lead to a fatal outburst of that hatred. But the time has not yet come for this. "This feast" (ver. 8, with special emphasis) is not the one to which He will go up as Messiah-King, to manifest Himself to His people. The Passover of the following year is appointed for that. And then the great crisis will come. But for the present, His Visit to this feast cannot be public, but must be, as it were, in secret.

(B.) Three Discourses during the Feast of Tabernacles (7:14–36)
1. Christ's Authority for Teaching (7:14–24)

14–24. *But when it was now the midst of the feast Jesus went up into the temple, and taught. The Jews therefore marveled, saying, How knoweth this man letters, having never learned? Jesus therefore answered them, and said, My teaching is not mine, but his that sent me. If any man willeth to do his will, he shall know of the teaching, whether it be of God, or whether I speak from myself. He that speaketh from himself seeketh his own glory: but he that seeketh the glory of him that sent him, the same is true, and no unrighteousness is in him. Did not Moses give you the law, and yet none of you doeth the law? Why seek ye to kill me? The multitude answered, Thou hast a devil: who seeketh to kill thee? Jesus answered and said unto them, I did one work, and ye all marvel. For this cause hath Moses given you circumcision (not that it is of Moses, but of the fathers); and on the sabbath ye circumcise a man. If a man receiveth circumcision on the sabbath, that the law of Moses may not be broken; are ye wroth with me, because I made a man every whit whole on the sabbath? Judge not according to appearance, but judge righteous judgement.*

It was undoubtedly owing to the special summons of the Father that Jesus went to the sanctuary and taught publicly. His sudden appearance, while causing great surprise and anger among His enemies, created a deep impression upon the multitude. He shows such a thorough knowledge of the Scriptures.[1] Who had been His teacher? Whence His theology? Surely not from the scribes and Pharisees. The doctrine proclaimed by Christ, and in so far His doctrine, is in reality the Father's that sent Him. What a humility on the part of "the only begotten Son, which is in the bosom of the Father and hath declared Him" (John 1:18). Both the origin and the contents of His doctrine are indicated in this paradox. He is the one whom the Father sent, so that in His person the law and the prophecy, and all the hopes and ideals of humanity should be fulfilled, He being the way and the truth and the life. And the evidence of the divine character and authority of His teaching is to be found by all those who honestly will to do the Father's will, wherever that will may be found, whether in the Law, or in the Prophets, or in the conscience of man. The moral character of Christianity is the testimony of its divine power and authority. It is the Old Testament principle: "The fear of the Lord—the beginning of wisdom," which is here by the Lord Himself applied to the New Testament revelation of the Gospel. The heart, the conscience, the will of man are involved in his search after truth. Wherever there is an honest will, an upright, sincere resolution, not the actual doing, or perfection in doing, the will of God (which is impossible), men will be drawn to Christ; they will appreciate the *gift* of God in the Gospel, having made an honest effort to do the *will* of God as they know it. The humility and unselfishness of Christ, who "seeketh not His own glory," will always be one of the most prominent features that impress the honest inquirer after truth.

---

[1] Not "letters," learning in general, but the Scriptures, as Luther translates. Comp. John 5:47, the writings of Moses.

III. THE CONFLICT IN JERUSALEM AGAIN TAKEN UP (CH. 7, 8)

But how about His adversaries and their character for uprightness and unselfishness? The Lord boldly and unsparingly uncovers their murderous designs, to the utter amazement of the people. To them it appears as sheer madness, owing to demoniac influences, that Christ should make such a statement. The leaders know better, and to them the Lord addresses the following argument, passing without notice the excited interruptions of the multitude. The Lord reminds His antagonists of that one work which at the very outset had provoked their deadly enmity, the healing of the sick man at the pool of Bethesda on the Sabbath day (John 5:1–18). He takes up the question of the authority of the Sabbatic law of Moses and beats the Jews on their own ground, showing that the law of the Sabbath is made to yield to the law of circumcision, wherever the eighth day after the birth of a son happens to be a Sabbath day. And however important circumcision may have been under the old covenant, Christ's act of healing and saving the whole man, body and soul, in time and eternity is far greater. If it be right and lawful to apply circumcision, the sign of the old covenant, to the newly-born Israelite on the Sabbath day, who will deny the full New Testament salvation offered and conveyed by Christ on the day of Sabbath, to a son of Abraham?

2. Whence is Christ? (7:25–32)

25–32. Some therefore of them of Jerusalem said, Is not this he whom they seek to kill? And lo, he speaketh openly, and they say nothing unto him. Can it be that the rulers indeed know that this is the Christ? Howbeit we know this man whence he is: but when the Christ cometh, no one knoweth whence he is. Jesus therefore cried in the temple, teaching and saying, Ye both know me, and know whence I am; and I am not come of myself, but he that sent me is true, whom ye know not. I know him; because I am from him, and he sent me. They sought therefore to take him: and no man laid his hand on him, because his hour was not yet come. But of the multitude many believed on him; and they said, When the Christ shall come, will he do more signs than those which this man hath done? The Pharisees heard the multitude murmuring these things concerning him; and the chief priests and the Pharisees sent officers to take him.

As the Lord in the preceding section had proclaimed the divine origin and authority of His doctrine, He now takes occasion to proclaim the divine authority and origin of His person. The boldness of His utterances, and the hesitation of His antagonists to say anything against Him, made a deep impression upon the people. The thought even suggested itself, that He might possibly be the Messiah. But it is promptly dismissed by those men who are unable or unwilling to "judge righteous judgment," who will always "judge according to appearance." The Messiah's origin is to be wrapped in mystery, but the pedigree of this "carpenter's son" is well known to them! But now the Lord emphatically and solemnly, with a loud voice, testifies, that He is sent by the true God whom they do not know. No wonder therefore that they also fail to know Him and the mystery of His person. For it is in bitter irony that He says: "Ye both know Me and know whence I am." The wavering multitude is again deeply affected by this declaration of Jesus. Could He not, after all, be the Messiah? Could any more signs be expected of the Messiah? These ominous murmurings lead to a meeting of the Sanhedrim, where it was resolved that He should at once be arrested and tried. But the fear of the multitude, especially of the pugnacious Galileans, puts off the execution of this plan, and for the present the Lord remains unmolested.

3. *His Approaching Departure (7:33–36)*

33–36. *Jesus therefore said, Yet a little while am I with you, and I go unto him that sent me. Ye shall seek me, and shall not find me: and where I am, ye cannot come. The Jews therefore said among themselves Whither will this man go that we shall not find him? will he go unto the Dispersion among the Greeks, and teach the Greeks? What is this word that he said, Ye shall seek me, and shall not find me: and where I am, ye cannot come?*

A solemn testimony intended for the leaders who had just sent their officers to seek and to apprehend Him. What Jesus here says is the warning of an impending judgment on them. He who had so often invited all inquirers to come unto Him, who had given His assurance, "Seek and ye shall find," now speaks of a time when they shall seek Him but not find Him,—a righteous judgment upon those who are planning

1. Jesus the Fountain of Life (7:37–52)

the murder of the Messiah. The delegate of the Father returns to Him who sent Him, to report on the result of His mission. (Compare Luke 14:21.) But His menace is met with sneers and derision. He will depart to the Gentiles, seeing that He can do nothing with Israel, the people of God! To appreciate the true meaning of these words we must remember the unspeakable contempt with which these children of Abraham looked down upon the heathen. And yet with all their abuse and mockery they become true prophets of the time when Christ's Gospel of salvation turns from them to the Gentiles. (See Acts 13:46.)

(C.) The Discourses on the Last Day of the Feast

1. Jesus the Fountain of Life (7:37–52)

(a.) The Words of the Lord (7:37–39)

37–39. Now on the last day, the great day of the feast, Jesus stood and cried, saying, If any man thirst, let him come unto me, and drink. He that believeth on me, as the scripture hath said, out of his belly shall flow rivers of living water. But this spake he of the Spirit, which they that believed on him were to receive: for the Spirit was not yet given; because Jesus was not yet glorified.

On the last day, the most joyous and exultant of the whole celebration, when, at the fetching of the water and the usual libation, Psalms 113–118 and, possibly, Isaiah 12:3 were sung, Jesus spoke these words, standing and crying with a loud voice. They are in a different spirit from those threatening words of warning which, in the preceding section, had been addressed to the rulers. They offer once more a kind and urging invitation to all who truly hunger and thirst after His righteousness. The commonly received interpretation finds here the statement, that the believers, having tasted the goodness of the Lord and being filled with His Spirit, will themselves become springs of life and wells of salvation to the world. (See Matt. 5:13, 14. The disciples, the salt and the light of the world.) But the words of comment which the Evangelist adds to this utterance of the Lord seem to demand a different interpretation. According to John's understanding the "rivers of living water" meant "the Spirit which they that believed on Him were to receive." That Spirit comes from Christ, the "fountain of the Spirit," as Irenæus calls Him, and therefore the words "out of his belly" must not be referred to the individual believer, nor even, in the first place, to the Church, the body of Christ, but to Christ Himself, the Rock (see 1 Corinth. 10:4) of whom it was said (Exodus 17:6): "Thou shalt smite the Rock and there shall come *from within it* waters, and the people shall drink." This meaning of the passage becomes very clear if we adopt a different punctuation, reading as follows, without the slightest change of the original: "If any man thirst let him come [unto Me] and let him that believeth on me, drink; as it is written," etc.[1]

(b.) The Division in the Multitude (7:40–44)

40–44. *Some of the multitude therefore, when they heard these words, said, This is of a truth the prophet. Others said, This is the Christ. But some said, What, doth the Christ come out of Galilee? Hath not the scripture said that the Christ cometh of the seed of David, and from Bethlehem, the village where David was? So there arose a division in the multitude because of him. And some of them would have taken him; but no man laid hands on him.*

The effect of the words of the Lord upon the multitude is here described. The different opinions concerning Christ which are here represented, remind us of the account given by the disciples concerning the thoughts of the people (Matt. 16:14 f.). Some deny His Messianic character because He comes from Galilee. They are sure that Christ must be born in Bethlehem, the city of David, as the Sanhedrim itself, years ago, correctly answered the question of the Magi (Matt. 2:5 compared with Micah 5:2). And yet the very men who are so sure and orthodox concerning Christ's coming from Bethlehem, are ready to "take Him," when the officers were sent for that purpose.

---

[1] This is found in a Strassburg edition of the New Testament of 1524. Bengel calls it a plausible punctuation; and men like Rambach, Francke, Roos and Stier have adopted it.

1. Jesus the Fountain of Life (7:37–52)

(c.) The Chief Priests and Pharisees (7:45–52)

45–52. *The officers therefore came to the chief priests and Pharisees; and they said unto them, Why did ye not bring him? The officers answered, Never man so spake. The Pharisees therefore answered them, Are ye also led astray? Hath any of the rulers believed on him, or of the Pharisees? But this multitude which knoweth not the law are accursed. Nicodemus saith unto them (he that came to him before, being one of them), Doth our law judge a man, except it first hear from himself and know what he doeth? They answered and said unto him, Art thou also of Galilee? Search, and see that out of Galilee ariseth no prophet.*

The officers return without their prisoner but with a remarkable testimony in His favor, showing the deep impression which His words had made upon them. But this testimony arouses the highest indignation and wrath on the part of the Sanhedrim. Never before did they show themselves so arrogant, defiant and overbearing. The example and authority of the "rulers and Pharisees" is laid down as the absolute standard, to be followed blindly by the people. And yet even in this sweeping and passionate statement there is an element of truth, as we find in 1. Cor. 1:26 f. But what a cruel contempt and condemnation of "this accursed multitude which knoweth not the law!" If this charge was correct, who was responsible for this ignorance of the multitude, except they themselves, the teachers and doctors of the law? And how about their own knowledge and observance of the law? Nicodemus has the presence of mind, with a ready sarcasm, to apply the standard of the law to the conduct of the rulers. They certainly know what is written in Exodus 23:1 and Deuteronomy 1:16 ff. How can they judge a man, contrary to the letter and the spirit of the law, without hearing him? But, of course, it is one thing to know the law, another thing to remember it at the right time, and to do it. Nicodemus, though here for the first time taking his stand against the rulers, is still extremely cautious and diplomatic in his dealings with them. He has not a word to say directly of Christ, or for Christ. He takes his position simply on the law, the acknowledged stronghold of the Pharisees themselves. While in his heart he means to defend Christ, by his mouth he only appears as an advocate of the law. But he will not be able to deceive them for any length of time. His true sympathies will betray him sooner or later. With the instinct of partisanship they scent the Galilean in him. With unparalleled effrontery they trample upon the truth: "Out of Galilee ariseth no prophet." And having thus flippantly disposed of plain historical facts, of Jonah, and Elijah, and Nahum, and Hosea, the Galilean prophets of Jewish history, they boldly claim this flagrant perversion of facts as the result of scientific research, and undeniable historical evidence: "Search and see!"

1. Jesus the Fountain of Life (7:37–52)

JOHN 8

1–2. *[And they went every man unto his own house: but Jesus went unto the mount of Olives. And early in the morning he came again into the temple, and all the people came unto him; and he sat down, and taught them. And the Scribes and the Pharisees bring a woman taken in adultery; and having set her in the midst, they say unto him, Master, this woman hath been taken in adultery, in the very act. Now in the law Moses commanded us to stone such: what then sayest thou of her? And this they said, tempting him, that they might have whereof to accuse him. But Jesus stooped down, and with his finger wrote on the ground. But when they continued asking him, he lifted up himself, and said unto them, He that is without sin among you, let him first cast a stone at her. And again he stooped down, and with his finger wrote on the ground. And they, when they heard it, went out one by one, beginning from the eldest, even unto the last: and Jesus was left alone, and the woman where she was, in the midst. And Jesus lifted up himself, and said unto her, Woman, where are they? did no man condemn thee? And she said, No man, Lord. And Jesus said, Neither do I condemn thee: go thy way; from henceforth sin no more.]*

This passage, we are convinced, does not originally belong to the fourth Gospel. It is not found in the best and most ancient manuscripts, such as the Sinaitic (ℵ) the Vatican (B), probably also the Alexandrine (A) Codex. The ancient Syriac version (Peshitto) omits it. The most prominent and learned of the Fathers have no knowledge of it. The language is not that of John. Its whole spirit and character is that of the Synoptists. Even those manuscripts that contain it, show great uncertainty as to the correct text. The twelve verses have more than sixty various readings. Nor is there a full agreement in the place assigned to this section; some have it after John 7:52, others after John 7:36, others at the end of the fourth Gospel, others after Luke 21. The passage clearly interrupts the context of John's Gospel at this point. Without it, there is a steady progress and clear connection between the end of the seventh chapter and the continuation of the Lord's discourses in 8:12, ff. But the event narrated in these verses undoubtedly belongs to the life of Christ. It is a fact and no fiction. Most likely it belongs to the last days after the Lord's entrance into Jerusalem, when He was constantly beset with trying questions, mostly concerning the law, by the Scribes and Pharisees. The Lord's going out in the evening to the Mount of Olives and returning to the temple early in the morning fits exactly into the history of those last days before His passion and death. See Luke 21:37, 38.

We continue our exposition with the following section:

2. Jesus the Light of the World (8:12–20)

12–20. *Again therefore Jesus spake unto them, saying, I am the light of the world: he that followeth me shall not walk in the darkness, but shall have the light of life. The Pharisees therefore said unto him, Thou bearest witness of thyself; thy witness is not true. Jesus answered and said unto them, Even if I bear witness of myself, my witness is true; for I know whence I came, and whither I go; but ye know not whence I come, or whither I go. Ye judge after the flesh; I judge no man. Yea, and if I judge, my judgement is true; for I am not alone, but I and the Father that sent me. Yea and in your law it is written, that the witness of two men is true. I am he that beareth witness of myself, and the Father that sent me beareth witness of me. They said therefore unto him, Where is thy Father? Jesus answered, Ye know neither me, nor my Father: if ye knew me, ye would know my Father also. These words spake he in the treasury, as he taught in the temple: and no man took him; because his hour was not yet come.*

The Lord, in speaking these words, is found essentially in the same surroundings as in the previous section. Possibly the lighting of the large candelabra in the inner court may have suggested this new theme. But it was certainly a scriptural idea, set forth in numerous prophetical passages, such as Isaiah 42:6, 49:6, 9:2, 60:3. (The Messiah "a light of the Gentiles," and "My salvation unto the end of the earth"; "They that dwell in the land of the shadow of death, upon them hath the light shined.") As indicated even in these Old Testament passages, the divine idea of light implies salvation and life for those that are rescued from the dominion of darkness. It is not the light of a purely theoretical knowledge, but has an

3. THE LIFTING UP OF THE SON OF MAN (8:21–30)

eminently practical meaning. To be filled with this light is the end of our walking in darkness and the beginning of having the light of life, following the Lord Jesus as the Saviour and the Leader.

The opposition of the Pharisees is growing more bitter with every new step in the Lord's argument. Their interruptions are becoming more frequent, impatient and venomous. The "Light of the World" is promptly attacked and denounced as a false witness. Light and truth belong together. How can He be the "Light of the World," if His testimony is not true? They deny His authority and right to testify of Himself. But what would the light be, if it did not testify of itself? Who will deny this innate right and power to the "Light of the World"? As the sun shines, so the Light of the World must testify of its own presence and blessed influence; otherwise it would cease to be light; it would become one of the powers of darkness. True, the Lord had once Himself admitted: "If I bear witness of Myself, My witness is not true" (John 5:31). But there He spoke of Himself κατά σάρκα, according to the flesh, simply as man, like other men and teachers. But here He takes a higher stand, asserting His divine authority. Of this He is fully conscious, and it must be part of His testimony to the world and a very important part of it. So He appeals to that same principle of the law, on which His enemies claim to stand: "that the witness of two *men* is true." If that be so, how much more the witness which is borne by Himself and the Father! This appeal is met with the sneering question: "Where is thy Father?" The Lord answers it with a solemn warning: Not to know the Son is not to know the Father. To listen to the Son, to come to Him, to know Him and to have Him is to know and to have the Father. But there men will reject the Father's testimony as well as that of the Son. The two witnesses are lost on them.

3. THE LIFTING UP OF THE SON OF MAN (8:21–30)

21–30. He said therefore again unto them, I go away, and ye shall seek me, and shall die in your sin: whither I go, ye cannot come. The Jews therefore said, Will he kill himself, that he saith, Whither I go, ye cannot come? And he said unto them, Ye are from beneath; I am from above: ye are of this world; I am not of this world. I said therefore unto you, that ye shall die in your sins: for except ye believe that I am he, ye shall die in your sins. They said therefore unto him, Who art thou? Jesus said unto them, Even that which I have also spoken unto you from the beginning. I have many things to speak and to judge concerning you: howbeit he that sent me is true; and the things which I heard from him, these speak I unto the world. They perceived not that he spake to them of the Father. Jesus therefore said, When ye have lifted up the Son of man, then shall ye know that I am he, and that I do nothing of myself, but as the Father taught me, I speak these things. And he that sent me is with me; he hath not left me alone; for I do always the things that are pleasing to him. As he spake these things, many believed on him.

Another and more emphatic reference to Christ's impending departure, which means for many of the Jews the terrible judgment of "dying in their sin"; not the ruin of the nation as such, but the damnation of the individuals, who will persist in their unbelief and thus be lost in their sinful state. The men who are bent on becoming instrumental in His "removal," as they are already planning to murder Him, interrupt Him with a venomous suggestion of suicide, the most horrible and damnable way of "departing" in the eyes of the Jews. The Lord's answer to this infernal charge of His enemies proves, indeed, that He is "from above," while they are "from beneath,"—not simply from the earth, from this world. Deeper, more infernal depths seem to be indicated, from which their thoughts take their origin. See ver. 44, where the full meaning of this "κάτω" ("from Beneath") is revealed in the statement: "Ye are of your father, the devil." In striking contrast to this character of the Jews, the Lord now fully reveals Himself as the Saviour, the Messiah of His people. He is the one who saves men from dying in their sin. And the only way to be delivered from this state of perdition is to believe in Him, to believe that He is the promised Messiah, the way, the truth and the life, as Isaiah says (43:10, 11), "that ye may know and believe Me and understand that I am He; I, even I, am the Lord and besides Me there is no Saviour."

The question of the Jews: "Who art thou?" is not to be taken as the honest question of an inquirer. It is too late for that. Wherever that question had been found in the heart of a true Israelite, without guile, it had been abundantly answered by the Lord in His preceding declarations. But in the mouth of these men it is a contemptuous and

4. Last Words on and after the Feast of Tabernacles (8:31–59)

indignant rejection of Christ's Messianic declaration. The Lord, however, undisturbed by their interruption, affirms even more directly and emphatically, that the word He speaks, and by which He is revealed as the incarnate Word, that "hath declared the Father," is the true answer to their question. I am, He says, principally and absolutely, the very one I claim to be in what I speak, in My words and testimony. But, as He testifies of Himself, He also testifies concerning His antagonists, their sin and their judgment; and this testimony is as true as that which reveals His own person. The time will come when they shall find out who He is, when they have lifted Him up on the cross. The Father who is with Him, even through those darkest hours, will vindicate Him fully by His glorification, declaring Him to be the Son of God with power by the resurrection from the dead (Rom. 1:4). For the "lifting up" of the Lord certainly includes the crown as well as the cross, and it is the glory following the passion that will open the eyes of some of the Jews; though, of course, in lifting Him up on the cross, they never dreamed of becoming the means to His glorification.

4. Last Words on and after the Feast of Tabernacles (8:31–59)

(A.) Whose Servants are the Jews? (8:31–36)

31–36. *Jesus therefore said to those Jews which had believed him, If ye abide in my word, then are ye truly my disciples; and ye shall know the truth, and the truth shall make you free. They answered unto him, We be Abraham's seed, and have never yet been in bondage to any man: how sayest thou, Ye shall be made free? Jesus answered them, Verily, verily, I say unto you, Every one that committeth sin is the bondservant of sin. And the bondservant abideth not in the house for ever: the Son abideth for ever. If therefore the Son shall make you free, ye shall be free indeed.*

The preceding testimony of the Lord had wrought a beginning of faith in a number of Jews. They "believed Him." There was a certain willingness to receive His word, yea, to accept Him as their Messiah, provided that He should satisfy their Messianic notions and expectations. "Believing Jews" is certainly a startling combination in the gospel of St. John, a kind of *contradictio in adjecto*, a paradox. There is a conflict between those two words and it must be settled. Will "the Jew" obtain the victory over that incipient faith, or vice versa? The Lord knows their hearts with the Jewish leaven they still contain. And He at once proceeds to test their faith. Will they *abide* in His word? that is the question. Will they recognize and appreciate the true spiritual liberty, offered and conveyed by His everlasting truth, or will they still cling to their own phantoms of liberty, to be realized by a Messiah after their own heart, in breaking the yoke of Roman bondage? There is a fascination even for the natural man, that has not cast off every ideal, in those two words: truth and freedom. But nowhere are they to be realized except in Christ. Truth first and then freedom. To be bound to God by His everlasting truth, is to be free from the deception of error, from the bondage of sin, and of the laws and traditions of men.[1] But the self-righteous, proud and pharisaic spirit of those "believing Jews" is at once aroused by the Lord's reference to their delivery from a state of bondage. "We have never yet been in bondage to any man." Is it possible that they should have forgotten the bondage of "Abraham's seed" in Egypt, under the Philistines and surrounding nations, in Babylonia and now under Roman rule? It can hardly be that they mean to refer to their national, political independence. But they claim true spiritual liberty and independence in the sphere of religion. They are the Lord's temple, "the guide of the blind, a light of them which are in darkness, having the form of knowledge and of the truth in the law" (Rom. 2:19, 20). The Lord therefore must speak more plainly and directly of the freedom He offers them in His word of truth. He appeals to their conscience by introducing sin and its servitude, for which they, that are under it, are fully responsible, because by their own act they "commit" sin. And the consequence of this bondage to sin is the forfeiture of sonship in the Father's house. The true Son of the house alone, who abideth forever, can free those bondservants and restore them to their position as children.

---

[1] See Luther's two great Reformation-Manifestos of 1520: On the Babylonian Captivity of the Church; and The Freedom of the Christian Man.

4. Last Words on and after the Feast of Tabernacles (8:31–59)

(b.) Whose Children are the Jews? (8:37–47)
(Not Abraham's; not God's; but the Devil's.)

37–47. *I know that ye are Abraham's seed; yet ye seek to kill me, because my word hath not free course in you. I speak the things which I have seen with my Father: and ye also do the things which ye heard from your father. They answered and said unto him, Our father is Abraham. Jesus saith unto them, If ye were Abraham's children, ye would do the works of Abraham. But now ye seek to kill me, a man that hath told you the truth, which I heard from God: this did not Abraham. Ye do the works of your father. They said unto him, We were not born of fornication; we have one Father, even God. Jesus said unto them, If God were your Father, ye would love me: for I came forth and am come from God; for neither have I come of myself, but he sent me. Why do ye not understand my speech? Even because ye cannot hear my word. Ye are of your father the devil, and the lusts of your father it is your will to do. He was a murderer from the beginning, and stood not in the truth, because there is no truth in him. When he speaketh a lie, he speaketh of his own: for he is a liar, and the father thereof. But because I say the truth, ye believe me not. Which of you convicteth me of sin? If I say truth, why do ye not believe me? He that is of God heareth the words of God: for this cause ye hear them not, because ye are not of God.*

The Lord readily admits the historical fact that the Jews are Abraham's seed according to their natural descent. But He denies that they are Abraham's true children in a spiritual sense, because they show a very different spirit from that of Abraham. The difference of spirit points to a difference of origin. On the one side Christ speaking the things which He has by direct intuition from His Father; on the other side the Jews doing the things which they have from their father by hearing his deceitful and malignant suggestions. The manner in which they receive what He tells them from the Father, their opposition to His word, which takes no root and makes no headway with them, proves that they are neither Abraham's nor God's children. Their inspiration is from a different source, as clearly shown by their murderous intentions. Instead of loving Him, the Father's Son and messenger, they seek to kill Him, a man who tells them the truth which He has from God, yea who is Himself of God. What a climax: first homicide, next murdering truth; finally deicide! Such a state of things has only one explanation: they are the children of the devil, in full accord with him, moved by his spirit, filled with his desire to destroy both truth and life, that is, to lie and to kill. By this statement the Lord teaches no Manicheism or Gnostic dualism, dividing the world and the race absolutely and helplessly between God and the devil. He holds them morally responsible for this relation of sonship to the devil. It is their *will* to do his lusts. In the realm of their innermost thoughts and inclinations they place themselves in accord with the devil by their own volition and decision. The nature and spirit of their father, the devil, is fully characterized in the 44th verse. He is the murderer and liar from the beginning, that is, the first to introduce such perversion, the destruction of life and truth, into God's creation, by seducing the first man to sin and thus bringing death upon him. And back of this murderous act of his there is his own attitude and decision with reference to God's truth. "He stood not in the truth," or, as the authorized version and also Luther's have it: "he abode not in the truth." We are aware that a strictly philological interpretation emphasizes the present state and condition of Satan as denoted by the Greek verb here used. Even Bengel insists that the Lord refers, not to the fall, but to the present state ("non lapsus sed status") of the devil. And yet this present "status" clearly implies the idea of his not continuing in the truth, and points to the historical fact of a fall (lapsus) by which it must have been preceded. Thus we are brought back to the authorized version, with which the Latin, German, French, Italian, Dutch and Spanish translations agree. It is now the very nature of the devil to lie, with no idea of a possibility of his ever speaking the truth. For when the devil speaks the truth he is lying most outrageously. And yet there is a difference between this father of liars and his children. When the Jews hate and pervert the truth they speak after their father. When the devil lies "he speaketh of his own." With him it is original and primary, with his children it is secondary and derived. But under the influence of their father these Jews are so far estranged from truth, that they oppose and bate Christ *because* He saith the truth; the very essence of devilry! The whole argument is summed up by the Lord in a purely negative form: "Ye

4. Last Words on and after the Feast of Tabernacles (8:31–59)

are not of God." This is, of course, essentially the same as "ye are of your father, the devil," but it is a much gentler expression, in harmony with the renewed and urgent entreaty: "Why do ye not believe Me?"

(c.) *The Eternal Majesty of Christ (8:48–59)*

48–59. *The Jews answered and said unto him, Say we not well that thou art a Samaritan, and hast a devil? Jesus answered, I have not a devil; but I honour my Father, and ye dishonour me. But I seek not mine own glory: there is one that seeketh and judgeth. Verily, verily, I say unto you, If a man keep my word, he shall never see death. The Jews said unto him, Now we know that thou hast a devil. Abraham is dead, and the prophets; and thou sayest, If a man keep my word, he shall never taste of death. Art thou greater than our father Abraham, which is dead? and the prophets are dead: whom makest thou thyself? Jesus answered, If I glorify myself, my glory is nothing: it is my father that glorifieth me; of whom ye say, that he is your God; and ye have not known him: but I know him; and if I should say, I know him not, I shall be like unto you, a liar: but I know him, and keep his word. Your father Abraham rejoiced to see my day; and he saw it, and was glad. The Jews therefore said unto him, Thou art not yet fifty years old, and hast thou seen Abraham? Jesus said unto them, Verily, verily, I say unto you, Before Abraham was, I am. They took up stones therefore to cast at him: but Jesus hid himself, and went out of the temple.*

In these verses the dispute between the Lord and the Jews reaches its climax, the Jews charging Him with having a demon, and finally throwing stones at Him as a blasphemer. First they call Him a Samaritan, an apostate from the orthodox Israelitic faith, who has separated himself from the covenant of Abraham's seed. To this they add the even more serious charge, that He "has a devil." This is to be distinguished from the Scripture-term which designates those unfortunate ones who were possessed by the devil. It is a clumsy return of His charge that they are the children of the devil. It reminds us of what is said of Judas Iscariot, "Satan entered into him" (John 13:27). But terrible as it may sound, if Christ's words are mere presumption and not absolute truth, then no words of condemnation are too strong for Him. In His answer the Lord makes no reference to the title "Samaritan," not only because He meant to spare the Samaritans, among whom His word had gained many believers, but also because in the fullest sense of the word He is Himself "the good Samaritan" whose picture He drew in Luke 10:30–37. But the other charge He cannot pass unnoticed. He positively rejects and disproves it by the fact that "He honors His Father." And surely, the God who has said: "Them that honour Me, I will honour" (1 Sam. 2:30), must vindicate the honor of Christ. He will seek it and judge. And this vindication consists in the fact, that those who keep Christ's word, believing His doctrine, trusting His promise and obeying His mandate, shall not see death, but have everlasting life and salvation.[1] This assurance of the Lord certainly includes the triumph also over the terrors of physical death on the part of the believer. The Jews, however, misrepresent and twist His words by confining their meaning exclusively to physical death; though they are correct in recognizing in them a claim of superiority over Abraham and the prophets. This is what they are determined to deny under all circumstances, but this is the very center of all the teaching of the Lord. In answer to their charge of unbearable presumption ("What makest Thou Thyself?") the Lord again asserts His humility. It is the Father that glorifieth Him. And to the Father He leaves it. His personal relation to the Father is very strongly emphasized by Him in this connection, over against the pretension of the Jews that "He is their God." "My Father," this is the sum and substance of His testimony from the first word in the temple to the last word on the cross. Having thus established His filial relation to the Father, He explains more particularly His relation to Abraham, showing to the full extent His superiority over him. Two distinct statements are made: "Abraham rejoiced to see His day," when he received the promise concerning his seed and was looking forward in faithful expectancy to its fulfilment. "And he saw it and was glad," referring to Christ's historical advent in the flesh, which was made known to Abraham, as probably to other departed

---

[1] On February 17th, 1546, the day before his death, Luther wrote the following words in the album of a friend: "We must all meet death and depart; but the Christian does not taste nor see death; he is not afraid of it, as other men."

4. Last Words on and after the Feast of Tabernacles (8:31–59)

saints, in the other world. This whole testimony culminates in that wonderful word, which truly reflects the heavenly glory of the everlasting Son: "Before Abraham was, I am." Here is the antithesis of the finite and the Infinite, the creature and the Creator.[1] He who is before Abraham has had His day, came into human existence in space and time (John 1:14). The Jews fully and correctly understood the Lord as claiming in these words divine character and majesty. They therefore promptly proceed to inflict the punishment which the Mosaic law prescribed for the blasphemer (Leviticus 24:16). At this critical moment the Lord disappears from among His people and from their temple, an indication of the impending withdrawal of His presence from Israel, when His word is to be fulfilled: "Behold your house is left unto you desolate" (Matt. 23:38).

---

[1] *Agnoscite Creatorem; discernite creaturam.* Augustine.

JOHN 9

THE CONFLICT WITH THE UNBELIEVING JEWS REACHING ITS CLIMAX (CH. 9 TO 12)

I. THE HEALING OF THE MAN BORN BLIND (CH. 9)

(a.) The Fact itself (9:1–12)

1–12. *And as he passed by, he saw a man blind from his birth. And his disciples asked him, saying. Rabbi, who did sin, this man, or his parents, that he should be born blind? Jesus answered, Neither did this man sin, nor his parents: but that the works of God should be made manifest in him. We must work the works of him that sent me, while it is day: the night cometh, when no man can work. When I am in the world, I am the light of the world. When he had thus spoken, he spat on the ground, and made clay of the spittle, and anointed his eyes with the clay, and said unto him, Go, wash in the pool of Siloam (which is by interpretation, Sent). He went away therefore, and washed, and came seeing. The neighbors therefore, and they which saw him aforetime, that he was a beggar, said, Is not this he that sat and begged? Others said, It is he: others said, No, but he is like him. He said, I am he. They said therefore unto him, How then were thine eyes opened? He answered, The man that is called Jesus made clay, and anointed mine eyes, and said unto me, Go to Siloam, and wash: so I went away and washed, and I received sight. And they said unto him, Where is he? He saith, I know not.*

There is no interval of any consideration between the close of the 8th and the opening of the 9th chapter. The healing of the man born blind took place immediately after the Lord left the temple, when the Jews took up stones to cast at Him; or at least on the same day. There is really no cause why the Lord should not have met that unfortunate man, sitting and begging, somewhere on the street leading from the temple. In this case also, as with the sick man in Bethesda, the initiative to the healing came from the Lord without a petition on the part of the blind man. "He *saw* a man blind from his birth." The Lord's looking at him betrayed that peculiar interest in his case which led to his healing.

I. The Healing of the Man Born Blind (Ch. 9)

As the Lord fixed His eyes upon that man, the attention of the disciples was also attracted. But they look upon this case from a different point of view. The question which occupies their minds is: how did he ever get into this miserable condition? whose fault was it? his own personal fault? or, as he was born blind, rather the fault of his parents? The question of rescue from this condition does not for a moment occur to them. They consider it an utterly hopeless case, simply an object of theological inquiry or speculation, but not of helping and restoring charity. The Lord on the other hand promptly rejects the idea of a special sin of the man himself or his parents, more than the sins of others who are blessed with seeing children. To Christ not the "whence?" but the "whither?" is the principal question in this affliction. And to this He presents a striking and hopeful answer: "That the works of God should be made manifest in him;" in this case clearly not God's work of judgment, but that of life giving, of restoring to light. For this He hath been sent and in such work His disciples must join with Him: "We must work the works of Him that sent Me." How can we bring light to this poor afflicted one? Surely this trial has come upon him not that he should sit in darkness forever, but that he should enjoy the light and the glory of God in a peculiar manner. What a blessed word, full of hope for the blind man: "I am the Light of the world and I am here to work while it is day!" And so the Light of the world dispels the lifelong darkness of this unfortunate one. A new creation-morning dawns upon him. "Let there be light!" and it was light. The process and method of healing however was in this case rather extended and circumstantial; for the double purpose of trying and of training the faith of that man and for hiding His own majesty and miraculous power, as if the softly going waters of Siloam had done it all (Isai. 8:6).

(b.) Investigation by the Pharisees (9:13–34)

The detailed account of the thorough examination of this miracle by the Pharisees, with all the questioning and testifying connected with it, is of special interest, because it presents a rare case of actual, critical inquiry into one of the scriptural miracles, with all the witnesses on hand. It has been repeatedly declared by the opponents of miracles that if they could be convinced by credible witnesses of the reality of such supernatural proceedings, they would at once renounce their infidelity and skepticism and embrace Christianity. But the attitude of the Pharisees clearly proves what an illusion this is, and how true the popular saying, that "a man convinced against his will is of the same opinion still." They remind us of that bold statement of one of the most radical representatives of unbelief (Voltaire), that if a miracle should be performed in one of the public squares of Paris in the presence of a thousand witnesses and himself, he would rather distrust those two thousand and two eyes than believe it!

1. First Appearance of the Man before the Pharisees (9:13–17)

13–17. They bring to the Pharisees him that aforetime was blind. Now it was the sabbath on the day when Jesus made the clay, and opened his eyes. Again therefore the Pharisees also asked him how he received his sight. And he said unto them, He put clay upon mine eyes, and I washed, and do see. Some therefore of the Pharisees said, This man is not from God, because he keepeth not the sabbath. But others said, How can a man that is a sinner do such signs? And there was a division among them. They say therefore unto the blind man again, What sayest thou of him, in that he opened thine eyes? And he said, He is a prophet.

Some busybodies, not necessarily with a design to denounce the Lord, bring the man that had been healed before the Pharisees. But at this first appearance of the man before them, the opposite impressions, which divided the multitude in their opinion concerning Christ, are reflected also in this meeting of the Pharisees. "There was a division among them" (ver. 16). From one and the same historical fact directly opposite conclusions were drawn by the two parties. The plain fact in the case was: the man born blind had been healed on the Sabbath. The one party, starting with the last point of this historical fact ("on the Sabbath-day"), argue from this after this manner: On the *Sabbath-day* some work had been done, which ought not to have been done. Therefore the man who did it or caused it to be done is not of God, but a sinner, to be rejected and condemned, together with his work. The other party argues in this way: There has been a case of *healing*, a most extraordinary case of giving

I. The Healing of the Man Born Blind (Ch. 9)

sight to a man born blind ("a thing never heard of since the world began," ver. 32). This is clearly a manifestation of divine power, and therefore the one who did it is to be received and trusted as a great prophet.

2. Questioning his Parents (9:18-23)

18-23. The Jews therefore did not believe concerning him, that he had been blind, and had received his sight, until they called the parents of him that had received his sight, and asked them, saying, Is this your son, who ye say was born blind? how then doth he now see? His parents answered and said, We know that this is our son, and that he was born blind: but how he now seeth, we know not; or who opened his eyes, we know not: ask him; he is of age; he shall speak for himself. These things said his parents, because they feared the Jews: for the Jews had agreed already, that if any man should confess him to be Christ, he should be put out of the synagogue. Therefore said his parents, He is of age; ask him.

However, the men representing the former view are determined to have their own way, to upset the historical fact of the miraculous healing itself. They "did not believe concerning him, that he had been blind and had received his sight." There has not been a miraculous healing. Surely this man was not really blind; one of the many cases of beggars on public highways, feigning certain physical ailments in order to secure the alms of those that pass by. We will promptly settle the case. Call his parents. They must know all about it. "Is this your son who ye say was born blind? how then does he now see?" His parents answered and said: "We know that this is our son, and that he was born blind," so far their positive evidence. Mark how clearly and directly to the point are all the questions and answers throughout this investigation. We are in the atmosphere of the court-room. The whole proceeding is one of legal exactness. Point after point the evidence is secured and the facts, thus presented, are indeed stubborn things. The foundation of the miracle is clearly established by the testimony of the parents. They are competent to speak of the case. This man is their son and he was born blind. As to the manner and method of his receiving sight, they cautiously withhold their testimony. "How he now seeth, we know not; or who opened his eyes we know not." They were not eye-witnesses to that. But their very refusal to give testimony on what they had not seen with their own eyes makes their evidence on the fundamental fact, that their son was born blind, all the more irresistible. It was a desperate attempt at the very outset to demonstrate the absence of a miracle in this case. And it becomes more desperate than ever as the Pharisees are now compelled to recall the first and principal witness, who alone could answer the question: "how doth he now see?"

3. Second Appearance and Expulsion of the Man Born Blind (9:24–34)

24–34. *So they called a second time the man that was blind, and said unto him, Give glory to God: we know that this man is a sinner. He therefore answered, Whether he be a sinner, I know not: one thing I know, that, whereas I was blind, now I see. They said therefore unto him, What did he to thee? how opened he thine eyes? He answered them, I told you even now, and ye did not hear; wherefore would ye hear it again? would ye also become his disciples? And they reviled him, and said, Thou art his disciple; but we are disciples of Moses. We know that God hath spoken unto Moses: but as for this man, we know not whence he is. The man answered and said unto them, Why, herein is the marvel, that ye know not whence he is, and yet he opened mine eyes. We know that God heareth not sinners: but if any man be a worshipper of God, and do his will, him he heareth. Since the world began it was never heard that any one opened the eyes of a man born blind. If this man were not from God he could do nothing. They answered and said unto him, Thou wast altogether born in sins, and dost thou teach us? And they cast him out.*

"So they called a second time the man that was blind and said unto him: Give glory to God: we know that this man is a sinner,"—a bold unscrupulous attempt to intimidate him. But the simplicity, straightforwardness and courage of the man completely baffle them. "He is of age—said his parents,—he shall speak for himself." And did he not speak for himself and for Him, who made him whole? The Pharisees are aware what a dangerous witness this man is going to be; they therefore move heaven and earth to make him deny his Physician and Saviour. "We know that this man is a sinner," and what "we know," you are expected to accept, and to abide by it without criticism or contradiction. But he will not accept it. "Whether He be a sinner I know not: one thing I know, that,

I. THE HEALING OF THE MAN BORN BLIND (CH. 9)

whereas I was blind, I now see." This is the theology of living facts over against prejudiced dogmatism. The "one thing he knows" is better than all that their wisdom claims to know. The Light of the world has opened his eyes. He has been taught by God. And he proceeds undauntedly to give them a taste of his theology too, after having given his legal evidence in their court of inquiry. "*We know* that God heareth not sinners, but if any man be a worshipper of God and do His will, him He heareth. Since the world began it was never heard that any man opened the eyes of a man born blind. If this man were not from God, He could do nothing." Good sound Mosaic theology and common-sense and logic besides! A regular syllogism, with Major, Minor and Conclusion. Here is the sign, you cannot deny, established beyond the possibility of a doubt by the testimony of eye-witnesses. Will you not draw the correct conclusion, as Nicodemus, your ruler, did: "No man can do these signs, except he come from God, and God be with him"?

There is a wonderful life-realism pictured in the scenes of this chapter. We *see* everything as plainly before our eyes as if we stood in person between those contending parties. We see the reflection of the "Light of the World" beaming on the face of this man whose eyes have been opened. We see the flash of heavenly joy in his bright sparkling eyes, as he exclaims again and again: I received *sight!* (ver. 11); I do *see!* (ver. 15). One thing I know—now I *see!* (ver. 25). He *opened* mine *eyes!* (ver. 30).

But all the light and joy of this testimony is lost on the Pharisees. If they only could, they would gladly force him back to the darkness in which he was born (as they afterwards resolved to kill Lazarus in order to stop the mouth of the testimony of his resurrection). But being unable to do that they cast him out in furious passion.

(c.) Jesus the Saviour of the Blind and the Judge of the Seeing (9:35–41)

35–41. *Jesus heard that they had cast him out; and finding him, he said, Dost thou believe on the Son of God? He answered and said, And who is he, Lord, that I may believe on him? Jesus said unto him, Thou hast both seen him, and he it is that speaketh with thee. And he said, Lord, I believe. And he worshipped him. And Jesus said, For judgement came I into this world, that they which see not may see; and that they which see may become blind. Those of the Pharisees which were with him heard these things, and said unto him, Are we also blind? Jesus said unto them, If ye were blind, ye would have no sin: but now ye say, We see: your sin remaineth.*

Jesus heard that they had cast him out. So He went after him, and finding him, He said: "Dost thou believe on the Son of God?" At the time of the healing the man born blind had not seen the Lord. He had been sent away to the pool of Siloam with his eyes still closed, and immediately after the healing he was dragged before the Pharisees. But now for the first time his eyes rest on the Lord, whom he at once recognizes by the well-known voice. He whom he had learned to know as his great physician, whom he had already confessed before men as a prophet come from God, reveals Himself to him as the very Son of God. "Thou hast *seen Him*, and He it is that speaketh with thee." Thus the man born blind is led from light to light; from the light of the body to the light of the soul; from the knowledge of the great prophet to saving faith in the Son of God.

But He who came as a Saviour for the blind that they might see, is at the same time the judge of those which see "that they may become blind." Those which see not are the same whom the proud Pharisees characterized as "the multitude which knoweth not the law," and whom the Lord Himself speaks of as the "babes." Those which see are the men who are full of their "we know," and whom the Lord characterizes as the "wise and understanding." The amount of knowledge which they actually had, even concerning the Christ, the Son of God, laid a fearful responsibility on them. They were the men of the parable, who, when the Lord of the vineyard sent His beloved Son, reasoned one with another, saying: "This is the heir; let us kill him, that the inheritance may be ours" (Luke 20:9–18). To them applied those words of warning in the sermon on the mount: "The lamp of the body is the eye: if therefore thine eye be single, thy whole body shall be full of light. But if thine eye be evil, thy whole body shall be full of darkness. If therefore the light that is in thee be darkness, how great is the darkness!" (Matt. 6:22).

II. The Discourses Following the Healing of the Man Born Blind (Ch. 10)

JOHN 10

II. The Discourses Following the Healing of the Man Born Blind (Ch. 10)

(A.) First Discourse (10:1–21)
1. Christ the Shepherd (10:1–6)

1–6. *Verily, verily, I say unto you, He that entereth not by the door into the fold of the sheep, but climbeth up some other way, the same is a thief and a robber. But he that entereth in by the door is the shepherd of the sheep. To him the porter openeth; and the sheep hear his voice: and he calleth his own sheep by name, and leadeth them out. When he hath put forth all his own, he goeth before them, and the sheep follow him: for they know his voice. And a stranger will they not follow, but will flee from him: for they know not the voice of strangers. This parable spake Jesus unto them: but they understood not what things they were which he spake unto them.*

As the connection between the 8th and 9th chapters, so also that between the 9th and 10th is close and direct. What the Lord says in the first discourse on the Shepherd, the Door and the Flock will be felt to have a peculiar force, if we remember that by His side was the man who had been so tyrannically treated by the rulers in Israel, who had learned to know the voice of the Good Shepherd and clung to Him undisturbed by those blind leaders of the blind, the thieves and robbers that enter not by the door into the fold, but climb up some other way.

Some think that the Lord was standing by the sheep gate (John 5:2), and as the sun was setting the sheep came flocking in from the valley of the Kidron and the slopes of the Mount of Olives. But we need no such substratum for His parable of the Shepherd. The Old Testament abounds in passages based on this figure, from the Shepherd of Joseph (Gen. 49:24, in the prophecy of Jacob) down to the "idol shepherd that leaveth the flock" (in Zechariah 11). The details of the allegory of the Lord set forth in these verses present no difficulties to the reader. The fold is the theocracy, the people of God chosen and separated from others through God's covenant. Those that lord it over the sheep by cunning or violence (as thieves and robbers) are the ruling Pharisees who approach the sheep by their own arrogant self-appointment, not in God's own proper way, through the door, the office instituted by Him, and Christ the true mediator of all pastoral vocation in Israel. The porter who opens the door and lets the shepherd in to his flock may be the Holy Spirit, or, if we prefer a more concrete historical figure, the forerunner of the Lord, John the Baptist. The Shepherd, even in these first verses, though still spoken of with a certain reserve, is Christ Himself, not the pastors or shepherds in general. His voice the sheep hear. There is something in the very sound of His words that awakens an echo in the hearts of all true Israelites. "Thine are we (2 Chron. 12:18). Thou art our Shepherd." And He calleth His own sheep by name; there is an intimate personal relation between Him and His own; as even in our natural relations it is the exclusive privilege of those nearest and dearest to us to call us (and to be called by us) by the proper name. And He leadeth them *out*"—not simply forth to green pastures, beside the still waters, in the paths of righteousness (Ps. 23), but *out* of the narrow enclosure of the Old Testament theocracy. He brings them forth into a large place. This deliverance from the former state of bondage is not accomplished without considerable labor and effort on the part of the Shepherd. But after He has succeeded in "putting forth all His own" He goeth before them, and they follow Him freely and joyfully whithersoever He may lead them; and no stranger shall disturb them; they would flee from Him rather than follow His voice.

2. *Christ the Door (10:7–10)*

7–10. *Jesus therefore said unto them again, Verily, verily, I say unto you, I am the door of the heep. All that came before me are thieves and robbers: but the sheep did not hear them. I am the door: by me if any man enter in, he shall be saved, and shall go in and go out, and shall find pasture. The thief cometh not, but that he may steal, and kill, and destroy: I came that they may have life, and may have it abundantly.*

II. The Discourses Following the Healing of the Man Born Blind (Ch. 10)

The parabolic saying contained in these verses is by no means identical with the preceding one. "Christ is the door;" this presents an entirely new aspect, different from the figure of the Shepherd. He is "the door of the sheep." Does this mean the door *to* the sheep for those who approach them as their shepherds and pastors? They must enter to the sheep through Christ as the door, in His name, in His Spirit, not in their own name, as thieves and robbers? Or does the term, "the door of the sheep," simply mean the door by which the sheep enter into the kingdom of heaven, finding life and abundance in it? The 8th verse seems to point to the former view. The 9th verse seems as decidedly to point to the latter view. Perhaps they might both be combined: Christ the door for shepherd and flock. No open door for the shepherd to the flock, except through Christ. No open door for the sheep to the life and abundance of the heavenly kingdom except through Christ. Through Him they go in by faith, through Him they go out, confessing their faith and proving it by the love of the brethren.

3. One Flock and One Shepherd (10:11–18)

11–18. *I am the good shepherd: the good shepherd layeth down his life for the sheep. He that is a hireling, and not a shepherd, whose own the sheep are not, beholdeth the wolf coming, and leaveth the sheep, and fleeth, and the wolf snatcheth them, and scattereth them: he fleeth because he is a hireling, and careth not for the sheep. I am the good shepherd; and I know mine own, and mine own know me, even as the Father knoweth me, and I know the Father; and I lay down my life for the sheep. And other sheep I have, which are not of this fold: them also I must bring, and they shall hear my voice; And they shall become one flock, one shepherd. Therefore doth the Father love me, because I lay down my life that I may take it again. No one taketh it away from me, but I lay it down of myself. I have power to lay it down, and I have power to take it again. This commandment received I from my Father.*

This passage, containing the well-known parable of the good Shepherd who layeth down his life for the sheep, illustrates most clearly how the so-called parables in the Gospel of St. John go far beyond the sphere of a real simple parable. A statement like this: "I am the good Shepherd. The good Shepherd layeth down His life for the sheep," ceases to be a parable. It is a literal heavenly reality. Christ is not *like* unto a good Shepherd as He is likened unto a sower, etc. He is emphatically and truly *the* good Shepherd. And in the natural sphere there is no such thing as a shepherd who would willingly, by his own free choice and determination, resolve to lay down his life for the sheep. In looking over the whole passage we at once recognize how difficult, yea impossible, it is, to draw the line between the parabolic or allegorical speech and the direct doctrinal statement. True, there are the shepherd, the sheep, the wolf, the hireling, the fold, the flock,—all figurative terms according to the common understanding. But then: Christ layeth down His life, Christ knows His own; His own know Him; the Father knoweth Him; He knoweth the Father. The Father doth love Him because He lays down His life. He has power to lay it down and has power to take it again. Where is there a parable in all this? These are all plain direct statements of great historical realities. *The* good Shepherd who layeth down His life for the sheep is nowhere to be found in reality, except in the person and in the passion of the Lord Jesus Christ. And this passion and death of Christ is emphatically described as His own free choice and act, done with full power and freedom. His death is the culminating and consummating *act* of His love. It is a remarkable feature of the Gospel of St. John, that the solemn word of the passion of the Lord accompanies us through its whole narrative. It appears earlier in it than in any other Gospel. In the very first chapter we were pointed to the Lamb of God which taketh away the sin of the world. In the 2d it was "the temple of His body" that was to be destroyed. In the 3d the serpent in the wilderness, the type of the lifting up of the Son of Man; in the 5th the Jews seek to kill Him because He called God His own Father; in the 6th, it is His flesh (and blood) which He will give for the life of the world; in the 7th He asks His enemies: Why seek ye to kill Me? in the 8th they take up stones to cast at Him; and here it is the good Shepherd laying down His life.

And these passion-thoughts naturally suggest mission-thoughts. As the Lord afterwards said: "If I be lifted up from the earth I will draw all

II. The Discourses Following the Healing of the Man Born Blind (Ch. 10)

men unto Myself," so He speaks of "other sheep not of this fold: them also I must bring and they shall hear My voice; and there shall be one flock and one shepherd." Mark well: the only means to bring others to His flock, to unite them all, Jews and Gentiles, under the one good Shepherd, is the hearing of His voice. No true Mission work except through His voice. No true Union work except through His voice. Where men refuse to listen to His voice, there men may be gathered to men, but they are not brought to Him, and the flock is in reality one flock only as far as it is one in the faith in the good Shepherd.

4. Impression of these Words on the Jews (10:19–21)

19–21. *There arose a division again among the Jews because of these words. And many of them said, He hath a devil, and is mad; why hear ye him? Others said, These are not the sayings of one possessed with a devil. Can a devil open the eyes of the blind?*

The words of the Lord made essentially the same impression which we found on different occasions before this. "There was a division among them." On the one side He is charged with having a devil (demon) and people are warned: Do not hear Him! On the other side some are ready to draw a similar conclusion to that of the blind man whom He had healed: "Can a devil open the eyes of the blind?"

(B.) Second Discourse (on the Feast of Dedication)
1. Historical Introduction (10:22–24)

22–24. *And it was the feast of the dedication at Jerusalem: it was winter; and Jesus was walking in the temple in Solomon's porch. The Jews therefore came round about him, and said unto him, How long dost thou hold us in suspense? If thou art the Christ, tell us plainly.*

Two months intervene between the festival of tabernacles and the feast of the dedication, the former being kept in the month of October, the latter in December. In the interval the Lord was absent from Jerusalem, but it is hard to decide where He spent the time between those two dates. He may have gone back to Galilee, or He may have stayed in the neighborhood of Jerusalem, but certainly He did not show Himself in the city. The feast of the dedication was not one of the ancient Mosaic institutions. It was introduced at the time of the Maccabees in memory of the re-consecration of the temple after its profanation by Antiochus Epiphanes (1 Maccab. 4:50 f.; 2 Maccab. 10:6 ff.). It was called the feast of the lights, from the magnificent illuminations with which it was celebrated. Jesus was walking in the temple in Solomon's porch, on account of the inclemency of the weather. This porch was on the east side of the temple plateau, on a steep precipice overhanging the valley of Jehoshaphat; it was said to be one of the few remnants of the ancient Solomonic temple and, at the time of Christ, belonged to the court of the Gentiles. There He was walking, as if to indicate that He was ready to take leave of His people and offer His salvation to the Gentiles. There the Jews surrounded Him, demanding, as they said, a plain and direct answer to the question: "Art Thou the Christ?"

2. First Section of the Discourse: I. and the Father are One (10:25–31)

25–31. Jesus answered them, I told you, and ye believe not: the works that I do in my Father's name, these bear witness of me. But ye believe not, because ye are not of my sheep. My sheep hear my voice, and I know them, and they follow me: and I give unto them eternal life; and they shall never perish, and no one shall snatch them out of my hand. My Father, which hath given them unto me, is greater than all; and no one is able to snatch them out of the Father's hand. I and the Father are one. The Jews took up stones again to stone him.

What answer should He return to their question? By a plain affirmative He would have surrendered Himself to their carnal ideas of the Messianic kingdom. By answering in the negative He would have denied His own divine mission. He knows that their question is not one of honest inquiry, coming from a sincere desire to have light on a dark and hitherto unintelligible subject. It is not His fault that they are not in the clear on this point; but it is their own unwillingness to accept and believe Him. He therefore simply refers to His former testimony and that of His works. "I told you—My works witness of Me—but ye believe not." There is no lack of testimony; but there is no faith on their part. They are

II. The Discourses Following the Healing of the Man Born Blind (Ch. 10)

not of His sheep. They do not know His voice, though they hear His words; and consequently they do not follow Him, nor enjoy the life and safe protection of His faithful and strong pastoral hand. My sheep, He says, are in My hand. The Father has given them unto Me. I have not assumed power and authority over them, without commission from on high. They are in the Father's hand; in one hand, for I and the Father are one. The word "one" in the original of the New Testament is neuter, which is lost in the English (and French) translations; while it is preserved in the Latin ("unum"), in the German (eins), in the Italian (una stessa cosa) and in the Spanish (una cosa). The Father and the Son are one in power and authority and this only because they are one in divine nature and essence. "We are," He says, against any attempt to wipe out the distinction of persons "one"; (one essence, one nature), He says against a mere moral oneness in spirit; and against any attempt to rob the Son of His full, co-equal divinity. The answer of the Jews to this statement of Christ, is clear beyond the possibility of a misunderstanding. "They took up stones again to stone Him." They heard and understood correctly. They did not put anything into His words which was not there by His own meaning and intention. He claims oneness with the Father, equality with the great Jehovah. They hold that He has no right to this claim; that He is guilty of blasphemy and deserves the penalty of death. And if Jesus of Nazareth is what ancient and modern humanitarians say of Him, however profusely they may compliment Him for the purity and loftiness of His moral and religious principles and doctrines, then the Jews were right and were bound by the law of Moses to stone Him to death. There is no third possibility. Either Christ *is* what He claims in these words, and then adoration and worship are due Him as the Eternal Son of the living God, our King and our Saviour. Or Christ is not what He says, and then: Down with Him! Stone Him to death, for all the talk of His moral loftiness is scattered to the wind by that one horrible accusation: "He being a man made Himself God." To our conceited and arrogant generation it may seem a small matter to claim co-equality with God. But it is *the* diabolical sin, the very essence of devilry, that the creature makes himself God.

JOHN 10

3. Second Part of the Discourse: Christ's Defense against the Charge of Blasphemy (10:32–39)

32–39. *Jesus answered them, Many good works have I shewed you from the Father; for which of those works do ye stone me? The Jews answered him, For a good work we stone thee not, but for blasphemy; and because that thou, being a man, makest thyself God. Jesus answered them, Is it not written in your law, I said, Ye are gods? If he called them gods, unto whom the word of God came (and the scripture cannot be broken), say ye of him, whom the Father sanctified and sent into the world, Thou blasphemest; because I said, I am the Son of God? If I do not the works of my Father, believe me not. But if I do them, though ye believe not me, believe the works: that ye may know and understand that the Father is in me, and I in the Father. They sought again to take him: and he went forth out of their hand.*

The Lord disarms His enemies yet for a little while, in the first place by pointing to His good (beautiful) works, which He has shown them from the Father. The works are referred to as manifestations of His union with the Father, of His Messianic commission and His true Sonship. And yet those very works, instead of proving to them Christ's true character, excited their hatred, stirred up the conflict, and finally caused the council to put Him to death.

Again He points them to their "law," to that scripture which "cannot be broken," to show that on the indisputable authority of good theocratical language, the principle cannot be established, that it would be blasphemy under all circumstances to speak of a man as God? It is the very A B C concerning the idea of the Godman to which He introduces them. Psalm 82:6, it was said to the rulers and judges in Israel: "Ye are gods," though they "judge unjustly" and "shall die like men." Thus these sinful men, the incumbents of a theocratic office, are called "gods" because their office was instituted by God and their authority is from on high. But the Messiah is the theocratical office-bearer in the absolute sense. All offices are united in Him, He is prophet, priest and king. From Him emanate and in Him culminate all the offices of the Old Covenant. He is sent, sealed, sanctified and consecrated for His Messianic work by

II. The Discourses Following the Healing of the Man Born Blind (Ch. 10)

the Father Himself. Can He be charged with blasphemy, because He says: "I am the Son of God?" The term "Messiah" and the name "Son of God" are by no means identical. The title "Messiah" reveals His divine commission, it specifies His work, which He was sent to accomplish. And the works He is doing must demonstrate Him as the great divine office-bearer, the Anointed of God. But if He is proved to be the Messiah by His works, He is also entitled to the name "Son of God," not as an ornamental title, without reality; but in the full sense of His essential union with the Father: "the Father in Me and I in the Father."

4. Christ's Retreat to Peræa (10:40–42)

40–42. *And he went away again beyond Jordan into the place where John was at the first baptizing; and there he abode. And many came unto him; and they said, John indeed did no sign: but all things whatsoever John spake of this man were true. And many believed on him there.*

The response to this testimony of the Lord is another attempt "to take Him" on the part of His enemies. But He "went forth out of their hand, away beyond Jordan," that is, into Peræa. The Synoptists also speak of this sojourn of Christ in that region shortly before His coming to Jerusalem at the last Passover. Both Matthew (19:1-2) and Mark (10:1) tell us of great multitudes that followed Him and of His healing them there and teaching them as He was wont. This is in full accord with John's record in verses 41 and 42: "Many came unto Him, and many believed on Him there." After all the sad and disheartening experiences with "His own" in Jerusalem, there was yet some harvest joy in store for the heavenly Sower. Believers in Samaria, believers in Galilee, and now believers also in Peræa. As we approach the end of the Lord's public ministry, there is once more a precious testimony for John the Baptist, his memory is kept fresh and green by the Evangelist, his former pupil, from the beginning to the close of his Gospel. The people of that region where John was at the first baptizing have not forgotten the revered prophet. "John indeed did no sign." For good reasons God had not granted them to Christ's forerunner. There would have been even greater danger of confounding him with

Christ, and thus the difficulty in coming from John to Christ would have been considerably increased. "But all things whatsoever John spake of Christ were true." They were true, at the time they were spoken, though the people did not at that time recognize and appreciate them in their full meaning. Truth is truth, even should there be not a single soul to accept it and believe it. Could anything greater and more creditable be said of John the Baptist or of any other messenger and witness of the Lord than this simple testimony: "All things whatsoever he spake of this man were true"?

JOHN 11

III. THE RAISING OF LAZARUS.—THE CRISIS IN JUDÆA (CH. 11)

(A.) Sickness and Death of Lazarus and Message to Jesus (11:1–16)

1–16. *Now a certain man was sick, Lazarus of Bethany, of the village of Mary and her sister Martha. And it was that Mary which anointed the Lord with ointment, and wiped his feet with her hair, whose brother Lazarus was sick. The sisters therefore sent unto him, saying, Lord, behold, he whom thou lovest is sick. But when Jesus heard it, he said, This sickness is not unto death, but for the glory of God, that the Son of God may be glorified thereby. Now Jesus loved Martha, and her sister, and Lazarus. When therefore he heard that he was sick, he abode at that time two days in the place where he was. Then after this he saith to the disciples, Let us go into Judæa again. The disciples say unto him, Rabbi, the Jews were but now seeking to stone thee; and goest thou thither again? Jesus answered, Are there not twelve hours in the day? If a man walk in the day, he stumbleth not, because he seeth the light of this world. But if a man walk in the night, he stumbleth, because the light is not in him. These things spake he: and after this he saith unto them, Our friend Lazarus is fallen asleep; but I go, that I may awake him out of sleep. The disciples therefore said unto him, Lord, if he is fallen asleep, he will recover. Now Jesus had spoken of his death: but they thought that he spake of taking rest in sleep. Then Jesus therefore said unto them plainly, Lazarus is dead. And I am glad for your sakes that I was not there, to the intent ye may believe; nevertheless let us go unto him. Thomas therefore, who is called Didymus, said unto his fellow-disciples, Let us also go, that we may die with him.*

With the eleventh chapter we now come to the greatest of all the signs of Jesus, the raising of Lazarus, which matured the crisis in Judæa, just as the feeding of the 5,000 had a similar effect in Galilee. It is acknowledged on all sides that this miracle of the Lord eclipses everything else. It is the last, most brilliant flash of the Light of the World before sunset.[1]

But why are the other three Gospels silent on this greatest and most impressive of all the miracles of the Lord? There must have been weighty reasons for passing it by. We must remember that the Synoptists represent the earliest tradition of the life and work of the Lord as it was told and retold in the gathering of the first Christian congregations, and in their regular services from Lord's day to Lord's day. This tradition, as it began to take a fixed form since the day of Pentecost, only a few weeks after the events here recorded, avoided for good and weighty reasons any special reference to the quiet little family in Bethany, and particularly to Lazarus, who had been raised from the dead. The avowed design of the rulers and Pharisees, to kill Lazarus also (12:10) is in itself sufficient to explain this silence. And then, great as the miracle in Bethany was, it was in its turn eclipsed by the greater one in Joseph's garden on Easter morning. The resurrection of the Lord formed the one prominent theme on which all the rays of the synoptical record unite. If the raising of Lazarus helped to cause and to accelerate the death of the Lord, the resurrection of Christ was the great victory of the Messiah-King, which is supreme in the Synoptical account.

The little village of Bethany (house of the poor, the suffering), situated on the eastern slope of the southern part of Mount Olivet, is designated as the home of Mary and Martha, though the names of these sisters had never before been mentioned in the fourth Gospel,—an evidence that they were supposed to be known to all the readers. Though Martha was evidently at the head of the little family in Bethany, Mary's name is mentioned first in this connection, on account of her significant anointing of the Lord, which is told in the next chapter. The message by which the sisters inform the Lord of their brother's sickness is framed in the most tender and delicate manner. "Lord, behold, he whom Thou

---

[1] Spinoza said of this miracle, if he could be convinced of the historical reality of the raising of Lazarus, he would willingly demolish his whole philosophical system and accept the common Christian faith.

III. THE RAISING OF LAZARUS.—THE CRISIS IN JUDÆA (CH. 11)

lovest is sick." They do not despair of His love, or find fault with Him, because he whom He loves is sick. They know that those whom the Lord loves may, yes must, have their share in the sufferings and trials of this life. They do not ask the Lord to come, though, of course, it is their firm belief, if only the Lord were here, the brother would not die.

The Lord's attitude in the face of this touching appeal seems rather strange at first sight. "This sickness is not unto death, but for the glory of God, that the Son of God may be glorified thereby,"—and then "He abode at that time two days in the place where He was." And, as if to solve the riddle, contained in these two sentences, the Evangelist inserts between them the assuring statement: "Now—however strange this may seem to you—Jesus loved Martha and her sister and Lazarus." But "the Son can do nothing of Himself." He is bound to the hour which the Father will show Him. At the hour when the message from Bethany reached the Lord, Lazarus was dying or, most likely, dead already, and then, according to Oriental custom,[1] he was buried on the very same day when Christ heard of his sickness. Two days after this the Lord startled His disciples with the sudden announcement: "Let us go into Judaea again." They dread it as the place where His life is in manifest danger. But Christ knows His time and His safety in the way of His calling. True, the last hour of the day of His life is approaching; but He still walks in the light of His day; under the Father's guidance and protection. Thus it is impossible for Him to stumble (ver. 9, 10). At last He tells His disciples, who did not understand the heavenly terminology, "Our friend Lazarus is fallen asleep;" in plain earthly language, "Lazarus is dead." And immediately the heavenly victory of faith and life over the temporary conquests of death bursts out again triumphantly in the following words: "I am glad for your sakes that I was not there, to the intent ye may believe; nevertheless, let us go unto him." But the disciples are not yet able to catch the spirit of their triumphant Master. Peter, the always ready spokesman, is speechless at this point. In his heart there is another "Be it far from Thee,

---

[1] Not, however, the ancient custom of the Patriarchs or the Egyptians, but of later origin; possibly arising from an anxiety to avoid the contact with the dead, and thereby to become unclean according to the Levitical law.

Lord," but he suppresses it, remembering the rebuke received before. Another must speak for the twelve this time. It is Thomas, the one who of all the disciples is inclined to see the darkest side and to cling with morbid tenacity to his gloomy, desperate forebodings. Lazarus dead! The Lord going to Judaea and sure to be killed there! Every light extinct! Nothing left to us, but to go also and to die with Him! If there is not much faith in these words, there is certainly a heroic devotion in them, ready to go into death for the beloved Lord.

(B.) *The Miracle of the Raising of Lazarus (11:17–44)*

1. *Arrival of Jesus and Conversation with Martha (11:17–27)*

17–27. *So when Jesus came, he found that he had been in the tomb four days already. Now Bethany was nigh unto Jerusalem, about fifteen furlongs off; and many of the Jews had come to Martha and Mary, to console them concerning their brother. Martha therefore, when she heard that Jesus was coming, went and met him: but Mary still sat in the house. Martha therefore said unto Jesus, Lord, if thou hadst been here, my brother had not died. And even now I know that, whatsoever thou shalt ask of God, God will give thee. Jesus saith unto her, Thy brother shall rise again. Martha saith unto him, I know that he shall rise again in the resurrection at the last day. Jesus said unto her, I am the resurrection, and the life: he that believeth on me, though he die, yet shall he live: and whosoever liveth and believeth on me shall never die. Believest thou this? She saith unto him, Yea, Lord: I have believed that thou art the Christ, the Son of God, even he that cometh into the world.*

By the time that Jesus arrived in Bethany Lazarus had been in the tomb four days. (The first, the day when Jesus received the message; the second and third were the days of His delay in Peræa; the fourth the day of His journey). The distance from Peræa to Bethany was about twenty miles, so that, starting early in the morning, He could reach the village on the afternoon of the same day. During these days before the Lord's arrival "many of the Jews had come to Martha and Mary to console them concerning their brother." These friends of the family evidently belonged to the ruling party in Jerusalem, and it is not impossible that they used

III. The Raising of Lazarus.—The Crisis in Judæa (Ch. 11)

the affliction which had come upon the sisters, to try their influence with the bereaved household against Jesus, who, to all human appearances, was tarrying unnecessarily in Peræa and leaving the sisters to their sorrow.

Martha, whose character all through this chapter is in striking harmony with her portraiture in Luke 10:38–42, is the first to meet the Lord on His arrival: "Lord, if Thou hadst been here my brother had not died. And even now I know that whatsoever Thou shalt ask of God, God will give Thee." And to the prompt, positive assurance of the Lord: "Thy brother shall live again," she answers: "I know that he shall rise again in the resurrection, at the last day." There is in these expressions of Martha a mixture of light and darkness, strength and weakness. She makes no complaint against the Lord on account of His absence. She expresses an implicit and heroic confidence in Him. His presence would have kept the destroyer from their threshold. And even now there is no limit to what He may still obtain from God, on His asking. In all this we recognize the elements of strong faith in the words of Martha. But the way she speaks of His asking God (αἰτεῖν θεόν) is rather indefinite, and not up to the standard of His divine majesty. And her answer to the Lord's direct promise—"Thy brother shall live again"—is a considerable falling off from the exalted position her faith seemed to have taken before. What the Lord sets before her, so to speak, within present reach, she pushes off to a distant future. And what He offered as a special gift and privilege from Himself she treats as a sort of commonplace, which it needed no prophet to tell her. She knew that herself. All the Jews could tell her that, who had come to console them concerning their brother. But here is another comforter. He has infinitely more to give than this abstract reference to a future day of resurrection. "*I am* the resurrection and the life; He that believeth on Me, though he die, yet shall he live, and whosoever liveth and believeth on Me shall never die." Here again is that great, ever recurring "*I am*," the living water for the Samaritan woman, the living bread from heaven for the Jews in Capernaum; and here "the resurrection and the life" for Martha and Mary and Lazarus and whosoever will believe on Him. It is the very soul and centre of this whole chapter. What an advance from that indistinct, far-off "he shall rise again on the resurrection at the last day" to this positive, direct, personal "I am the resurrection and the life—believest thou this?" Here is the great point for Martha, the "one thing needful" on this occasion. To look to the present Saviour; to grasp and to have life in Him by faith even now in the face of death and the tomb; not simply looking forward with resignation to a distant future, and hoping for something better to come, but having and possessing now, in the midst of the darkest, dreariest present, Him who is the resurrection and the life. This is the true faith of the Christian, this is what Martha ought to believe.

Christ is the resurrection because He is the life. In Him is life and in Him the constant victory of life in its conflict with death, that is resurrection. He is the Life of the living and the resurrection of the dying. Through Him we reverse the old song, "In the midst of life we are in death," and say: "In the midst of death we have life through Jesus Christ our Lord." Believing in Him we draw His life, with all its victorious power over death, into the very centre of our personality, so that death cannot touch it. Whosoever has been awakened to new life by faith in Christ, has nothing to fear from death; he lives a life which death itself, so far from harming it, can only bring to its fullest, most glorious development. He says with Paul: "To me to live is Christ and to die is gain."

Martha's response to these mighty words of the Lord is another plain but comprehensive confession added to those of the Samaritan woman (4:29), Simon Peter (6:68–69), and the man that was born blind (9:36–38): "Thou art the Christ, the Son of God, even He that cometh into the world." Comparing it with the question of the Lord (v. 26), we observe that this is not an exact answer to that question. She is not yet ready and able to take in all the rich treasures contained in the statement of the Lord: "Resurrection—life—believing on Him—never dying." But she can grasp Him in whom all this is treasured up; who has it all and gives it all, Jesus, her Lord. Of Him she takes hold and clings to Him, the Christ, the Son of God, the Saviour of the world. In Him she has the one and all she needs.

III. The Raising of Lazarus.—The Crisis in Judæa (Ch. 11)

2. Meeting with Mary (11:28–37)

28–37. And when she had said this, she went away, and called Mary her sister secretly, saying, The Master is here, and calleth thee. And she, when she heard it, arose quickly, and went unto him. (Now Jesus was not yet come into the village, but was still in the place where Martha met him.) The Jews then which were with her in the house, and were comforting her, when they saw Mary, that she rose up quickly and went out, followed her, supposing that she was going unto the tomb to weep there. Mary therefore, when she came where Jesus was, and saw him, fell down at his feet, saying unto him, Lord, if thou hadst been here, my brother had not died. When Jesus therefore saw her weeping, and the Jews *also* weeping which came with her, he groaned in the spirit, and was troubled, and said, Where have ye laid him? They say unto him, Lord, come and see. Jesus wept. The Jews therefore said, Behold how he loved him! But some of them said, Could not this man, which opened the eyes of him that was blind, have caused that this man also should not die?

The Master must have asked for Mary, for Martha called her out to meet Him. He was unwilling to come into the house for fear of creating an excitement. But He could not be hidden. The Jews in the house followed Mary first to the Lord, then to the tomb. At the meeting with the Lord we hear from Mary the same words which had been on the sisters' lips all through those weary and anxious hours at the sickbed and deathbed of Lazarus: "Lord, if Thou hadst been here, my brother had not died." More she cannot say; she sinks down under the weight of her sorrow at the feet of Jesus. Nor has the Lord anything to say to her. Seeing her weeping and the Jews also weeping, He "was moved with indignation in the spirit and troubled Himself." This emotion must not be confounded with the weeping of the Lord (V. 36). The marginal note of the Revised Version gives us the full meaning of the original. Christ was filled with indignation. The woe and misery of this world, particularly the destruction and sorrows of death, the source from which all this weeping sprang, the sin of the world, and behind all this the prince of this world, with the power of death, to whose bondage even His beloved ones were subject, so that their eyes were holden, that they could not see the glory of God,—all these thoughts provoked in His spirit a holy wrath and indignation. He masters His emotion with the question: "Where have ye laid him?" And they lead Him to the tomb with that suggestive invitation: "Come and see." He came, He saw, He conquered. But before the glory of the God-man is thus manifested, His true human heart, His tender feeling and compassion is revealed. Jesus wept. And even here in this sanctuary of the holy narrative, once more a division among the Jews;—some, deeply moved by the tears of the Lord, the testimony of His love for Lazarus; others, finding fault with "this man" even at this point, for not preventing the death of Lazarus.

3. Jesus at the Tomb (11:38–44)

38–44. *Jesus therefore again groaning in himself cometh to the tomb. Now it was a cave, and a stone lay against it. Jesus saith, Take ye away the stone. Martha, the sister of him that was dead, saith unto him, Lord, by this time he stinketh: for he hath been dead four days. Jesus saith unto her, Said I not unto thee, that, if thou believedst, thou shouldest see the glory of God? So they took away the stone. And Jesus lifted up his eyes, and said, Father, I thank thee that thou heardest me. And I knew that thou hearest me always: but because of the multitude which standeth around I said it, that they may believe that thou didst send me. And when he had thus spoken, he cried with a loud voice, Lazarus, come forth. He that was dead came forth, bound hand and foot with graveclothes; and his face was bound about with a napkin. Jesus saith unto them, Loose him, and let him go.*

Gradually, step by step, the Lord leads them up to the greatest of all His signs. Whatever human hands can do in assisting and preparing the way for Him they are allowed to do: "Take ye away the stone." But Martha half interferes with this order of the Master, quite overcome with the natural horror at the thought that the body should be brought out at this stage, for a last parting look of the Friend and Master. Her faith is at its lowest ebb in the face of the fearful realities of death which obtrude themselves on the senses. There is not a trace left in her words of that trust, "that whatsoever He shall ask of God, God will give Him." Every hope is finally relegated to "the last day." The answer of the Lord is a direct, though gentle rebuke of her lack of faith: "Said I not unto thee that

III. The Raising of Lazarus.—The Crisis in Judæa (Ch. 11)

if thou believedst, thou shouldest see the glory of God?" Where our natural senses perceive nothing but death and destruction, with all its horror and humiliation, there the Lord calls in that "sixth sense," as faith has sometimes been named, "to *see* the glory of God." Faith and nothing but faith is the organ to perceive the glory of God. The natural man desires first to see and then to believe, Christ reverses the order: first believe and thou shalt see! Believing is seeing the glory of God in His present word. Therefore the Lord reminds Martha pointedly of His word: "Said I not unto thee—" He had said so in the message returned to Bethany: "This sickness is not unto death but for the glory of God that the Son of God may be glorified thereby." He had said so, when He assured Martha, "he that believeth on Me, though he die, yet shall he live." (See also 2:11 and 1:14)

And now, the stone being taken away, Jesus lifted up His eyes and said: Father, etc. (ver. 41 and 42). This praying of Jesus with eyes lifted up to the hills whence cometh our help, together with the weeping of Jesus (ver. 36), marks the true human nature of the incarnate Word, which in this narrative of the glorification of the Son of God is again and again most graphically brought out. What a reminder this prayer was to Martha of that highest flight of her faith, when she had said, "I know that whatsoever Thou shalt ask of God, God will give Thee." And yet, what a correction and advance beyond Martha's ideas. Instead of "God," it is the "Father." Instead of asking, it is "I thank Thee." How far above the petitions to which Martha referred, is this triumphant "Father, I thank Thee that Thou heardest me and I know (knew) that Thou hearest Me always."

And "the multitude" also, "which standeth around," is in the Lord's mind, as He utters this prayer. In spite of their opposition and unbelief, with which they grieved Him so often, it is the yearning of His heart, that, if it were possible, even now they might be enabled to catch the inspiration of this hour and join in "seeing the glory of God." Never was there such an opportunity for the Lord, in the face of death and corruption, surrounded by a multitude which filled the very air with the miasma of unbelief,—to make the boldest and most solemn appeal to the

Father, to testify of the Son, to glorify Him before the world, to give Him that most impressive of all His works, which would enable them to believe that the Father did send Him. There is only one parallel to the crisis of this scene in the whole compass of sacred history; it is Elijah on Mount Carmel, standing before the altar, surrounded by the multitude and crying to the Lord, God of Abraham, Isaac and Jacob: "Hear me, O Lord, hear me, that this people may know that Thou art the Lord God." But the scene at Lazarus' tomb is a New Testament scene, and its glory is not that of fiery Elijah, like a great and strong wind, rending the mountains, breaking the rocks in pieces, and bringing inexorable judgment upon the enemies of Jehovah. It is the glory of the only begotten Son of the Father full of grace and truth. And therefore, before He manifests this glory that their eyes may see it, the Son of God is willing to grant to their hearts an insight into His relation to the Father and the wonderful communion between the Father and the Son. The multitude, as far as it was possible to admit them to it, received in that prayer at Lazarus' tomb a taste of those treasures and mysteries unfolded to the disciples in the parting discourses and in the mediatorial prayer (John 13–17). "And when He had thus spoken, He cried with a loud voice: "Lazarus come forth." Nothing could be more majestic than the simplicity of the two little words which in the original embody the command of the Lord to Lazarus. There is not even a verb in them. "Hither! Out of there!" that is all. *Out* of the tomb, the darkness, dishonor and corruption; *hither* to Christ, to resurrection and life, to light and glory imperishable and undefiled! "He that was dead came forth, bound hand and foot with graveclothes; and his face bound about with a napkin." Every little touch of that memorable scene noticed by the eye-witness, photographed on the spot in the memory of the beloved disciple. And "Jesus saith unto them: Loose him and let him go!" The last word of the Lord, sealing His triumph over death and the tomb, "Let him go." He knew what the breaking of this tomb, the loosing of Lazarus' bonds meant for Himself! It was His own death warrant. A few days, and Christ Himself will be "bound hand and foot with graveclothes," and the stone and seal will lock the tomb in Joseph's garden. But it is "the resurrection and the life" which they enclose in that tomb. It is

III. The Raising of Lazarus.—The Crisis in Judæa (ch. 11)

impossible that it should hold Him. Again a few days and Peter and John and those devout women find the stone rolled away—this time by angels' hands—from the sepulchre. They enter in, no odor of corruption there; they behold the linen cloths lying, and the napkin, that was upon His head, rolled up in a place by itself. Other hands had attended to the "loosing" there. And angels greet them with the Easter-message: "Why seek ye the Living among the dead? He is not here. He is risen!"

(C.) The Effect of the Miracle (11:45–57)

1. On those Present at the Tomb (11:45–46)

45–46. *Many therefore of the Jews, which came to Mary and beheld that which he did, believed on him. But some of them went away to the Pharisees, and told them the things which Jesus had done.*

The Evangelist has not a word to say of the effect which the miracle in Bethany had on the members of that little family itself, on Martha and Mary and Lazarus. It belongs to those things which can be better felt than described. But he speaks of the multitude which had witnessed that sign. Some hold that those verses mean to say: "The impression made by the raising of Lazarus was the same on all those that were present; even those that went away to the Pharisees and told them the things which Jesus had done," believing on Jesus and trying to convince the Pharisees of His true Messianic authority and character. But the manifest contrast between the "many" that believed and the "some" that went away to the Pharisees, seems to forbid this interpretation. We find here again the well-known "division" among the Jews. Those that went to the Pharisees, being probably the same who found fault even when the Lord was weeping at the tomb, did not make their report to the rulers in a kindly spirit, nor in a neutral attitude, simply asking for their opinion, but with hostile intention.

2. Effect on the Chief Priests (11:47–53)

47–53. *The chief priests therefore and the Pharisees gathered a council, and said, What do we? for this man doeth many signs. If we let him thus alone, all men will believe on him: and the Romans will come and take away both our place and our nation. But a certain one of them, Caiaphas, being high priest that year, said unto them, Ye know nothing at all, nor do ye take account that it is expedient for you that one man should die for the people, and that the whole nation perish not. Now this he said not of himself; but being high priest that year, he prophesied that Jesus should die for the nation; and not for the nation only, but that he might also gather together into one the children of God that are scattered abroad. So from that day forth they took counsel that they might put him to death.*

The Chief Priests and the Pharisees on hearing the news of the raising of Lazarus, "gathered a council and said: What do we? for this man doeth many signs." Note the testimony which, however, unwillingly, they give here, as on other occasions, concerning the Lord and His powerful manifestations. "This man doeth many signs." It reminds us of the concession and confession with which Nicodemus introduced himself to the Lord. But of these "many signs" even the last and greatest only proves that icy death and the tomb itself will yield to the power of Jesus, rather than the unbelieving hearts of the Pharisees. "If we let Him thus alone," they continue, "all men will believe on Him, and the Romans will come and take away both our place and our nation." The logic of this high-sounding patriotism sounds rather forced and obscure. Why should the believing on Christ bring the Romans upon them and involve the nation in a catastrophe? It could only be understood on another premise which remains hidden in their hearts: Believing on Christ means falling away from the authority of the rulers and chief priests. And to this threatened loss of their influence they will not quietly submit. There will be a disturbance, and thus an opportunity will be offered to the Romans to wipe out finally the national independence of Israel. This last part of their statement is correct enough in itself. It is a true prophecy, unconsciously uttered, like that of Caiaphas which follows. "The Romans will come and take away their place and their nation," but not because they believe on Jesus of Nazareth and accept Him as the Messiah, but because they knew not the time of their visitation and rejected the stone, of which it is written: "Every one that falleth on that stone shall be broken to pieces; but on whomsoever it shall fall, it will scatter him as dust" (Luke 20:18).

III. THE RAISING OF LAZARUS.—THE CRISIS IN JUDÆA (CH. 11)

"But a certain one of them, Caiaphas, being high priest that year, said unto them: Ye know nothing at all, nor do ye take account that it is expedient for you that one man should die for the people and that the whole nation perish not." These are the words of the heartless, unscrupulous politician, an overbearing, domineering character of one-sided cold intellectualism, to whom men are only means to reach his own selfish ends. By destroying the man who claimed to be the Messiah, he advises them to secure the favor and good-will of the Romans. And the people, being involved in the killing of the Messiah, would then be freed from His powerful influence, and bound more firmly than ever to Pharisaic leadership. This was the logic of the astute politician in the see of the highpriest, and history showed that it was correct enough as far as it went.

But his words had a significance, far beyond what Caiaphas meant and was conscious of, for Christ Himself and His everlasting kingdom. "This he said not of himself: but being highpriest that year, he prophesied that Jesus should die for the nation; and not for the nation only, but that he might also gather together into one the children of God that are scattered abroad." There are some passages in the Old Testament indicating that, under certain circumstances, the highpriest in his official capacity asked counsel before the Lord for leading men "after the judgment of Urim" (Exod. 28:30; Numb. 27:21, in Joshua's case. 1 Sam. 22:10, the priest inquired of the Lord for David. 1 Sam. 30:7, David himself inquiring of the Lord, in the highpriest's ephod), and thus became a mediator of divine revelation for certain specified cases. But in later times there is no trace of such revelation through the highpriest. The office of prophesying belonged to the prophet, whenever there were prophets in Israel. But Caiaphas "being highpriest that year prophesied." Every time, when Caiaphas is mentioned, that year is emphasized (ver. 49, 51, and ch. 18:13). The Evangelist does not mean to tell his readers (as some have interpreted him) that the office of the highpriest changed its incumbent from year to year. He is too much of a Jew to make such a misstatement. He knows that the office of the highpriest according to the Mosaic law was to be for life. But he also knows that in those days, owing to constant political disturbances and outside influences, there were frequent changes of incumbents of that office. Still Caiaphas held it for at least eleven years (25–36 A. D.). And holding the highest theocratic office in that year of the death of Christ, he designated Jesus as the sacrifice for the people. There is a deep divine irony in the fact, that "the perishing priesthood, against the knowledge and the will of the office bearer," had thus to announce the one true atoning offering of the New Testament Highpriest, by which all the sacrifices and the priesthood itself of the Old Testament were to be fulfilled and abolished for ever; as Daniel said "to finish the transgression and to make an end of sins and to make reconciliation for iniquity and to bring in everlasting righteousness; He shall cause the sacrifice and the oblation to cease" (Ch. 9:24, 27).

But this great New Testament principle "one died for all" (see 2 Cor. 5:14), reaches far beyond the limits of the Jewish nation, "not for the nation only, but that He might also gather together into one the children of God that were scattered abroad." So far from bringing ruin upon His people, as the Pharisees said, He will spread salvation and blessing among the Gentiles and add to the true spiritual Israel those that were far off and strangers from the covenants of the promise, making them fellow-citizens with the saints and of the household of God (Eph. 2:11–19).

Thus the unwilling and unconscious prophecy of the highpriest of the Jews forms the most appropriate and striking introduction to the history of Christ's passion. Through the open door of that council-room of the Sanhedrim in Jerusalem we are permitted to cast a glance into the heavenly council chamber, where "the determinate counsel and foreknowledge of God" (Acts 2:23) ordained, that it "behooved the Christ to suffer these things and to enter into His glory;" and we are assured that, whatsoever human and satanic craft and wickedness may plan in those days, God's counsel of salvation will overrule it all, bringing light out of darkness, and glory and victory out of what seemed to be shame and defeat.

III. The Raising of Lazarus.—The Crisis in Judæa (ch. 11)

3. The Lord's Retreat into Ephraim (11:54–57)

54–57. *Jesus therefore walked no more openly among the Jews, but departed thence into the country near to the wilderness, into a city called Ephraim; and there he tarried with the disciples. Now the passover of the Jews was at hand; and many went up to Jerusalem out of the country before the passover, to purify themselves. They sought therefore for Jesus, and spake one with another, as they stood in the temple, What think ye? That he will not come to the feast? Now the chief priests and the Pharisees had given commandment, that, if any man knew where he was, he should shew it, that they might take him.*

The exact situation of Ephraim, to which place the Lord retired, cannot be determined. It was evidently to the north-east of Jerusalem, on the borders of the wilderness of Judah, giving the Lord a choice between the Easter-caravans from Galilee or from Peræa, whenever He was ready to join the pilgrims to that last Passover. The excitement, caused by the raising of Lazarus, continued unabated even after the Lord's departure. There are the pilgrims from the country, on their arrival in Jerusalem, standing around in groups on the temple area, the questions as to Jesus of Nazareth and His coming to the feast being the principal theme of their conversation. "What think ye? Will He come? Or will He not come to the feast?" Thus they continually asked, until these questions found their final answer by the multitude itself in their jubilant: "Hosanna! Blessed is He that cometh in the name of the Lord, even the King of Israel." Such an open, public entrance, the enemies of Christ would fain have prevented. They planned to take Him quietly before the feast, and to deliver Him up in Jerusalem as a criminal. A Jewish tradition (Babyl. Gemara, about 550 A. D.) says, that for forty days before the passover a court-crier publicly proclaimed: "He must be stoned to death, that man who leads the people astray by His deceptions. Whosoever has anything to say in His defence, let him come forward and speak. But nothing being found to defend Him, He was crucified on Passover evening."—(Lightfoot, quoted by Godet.)

JOHN 12

IV. THE END OF THE PUBLIC MINISTRY OF CHRIST (CH. 12)

(A.) *The Supper at Bethany (12:1–8)*

1–8. *Jesus therefore six days before the passover came to Bethany, where Lazarus was, whom Jesus raised from the dead. So they made him a supper there: and Martha served; but Lazarus was one of them that sat at meat with him. Mary therefore took a pound of ointment of spikenard, very precious, and anointed the feet of Jesus, and wiped his feet with her hair: and the house was filled with the odour of the ointment. But Judas Iscariot, one of his disciples, which should betray him, saith, Why was not this ointment sold for three hundred pence, and given to the poor? Now this he said, not because he cared for the poor; but because he was a thief, and having the bag took away what was put therein. Jesus therefore said, Suffer her to keep it against the day of my burying. For the poor ye have always with you; but me ye have not always.*

From Ephraim the Lord went down to Jericho and there joined one of the caravans of pilgrims coming up from Peræa for the Easter festival in Jerusalem. Having arrived with them in the neighborhood of the city, probably on Friday evening, in the week previous to His death, He stayed in Bethany while the other travellers at once proceeded to Jerusalem. The Supper which was there prepared for Him took place on the Sabbath preceding the Passover. It was not in the house of Martha, nor arranged by her family exclusively, but by the larger circle of friends in Bethany, believers on Christ, who thereby boldly expressed their devotion to Him in the face of the hostility and persecution, instigated by the Rulers in Jerusalem. Of course Martha was there and Lazarus and Mary, each of them in that peculiar place and attitude ascribed to them respectively in the Gospel: Martha serving, Lazarus sitting at meat with Him, and Mary coming in with the precious ointment.

Matthew and Mark record this anointing of the Lord after His entrance into Jerusalem; using it as a most beautiful opening of the Passion-history, in striking contrast to the betrayal of Judas. But their

IV. The End of the Public Ministry of Christ (Ch. 12)

arrangement here, as on other points, is more with reference to matter than to time; whilst the fourth Gospel is most exact in its chronological statements. Especially here, where we come to the last week of the Lord's life before His death and resurrection, we find the Gospel of St. John as careful and detailed in its dates as in the first week of the Lord's public ministry, described in the first two chapters. The incident at the Supper in Bethany is most fully recorded by John, and its connection both with the raising of Lazarus and the death and resurrection of the Lord, is clearly indicated in this Gospel.

The anointing of the Lord with that precious spikenard the value of which, so well known to Judas, was about fifty dollars of our money, was prompted in part by Mary's feeling of gratitude to the Lord for all that He had done for her family, for the restoration of her brother, for the spiritual blessings which He had showered upon them. Nothing is too precious and expensive, let it all go in the service and for the glory of her Lord and Master. As the odor of that ointment filled the whole house, so her very soul is poured out in fervent devotion to Jesus. She is indifferent even to the possible charge of a lack of modesty, for unloosing her hair and wiping the feet of the Lord with the ornament of her womanhood. Mary's action was however severely criticised on the part of the disciples. Matthew and Mark only tell us of an indignation among them and the objections made by "some." But John marks the one who was the author of this attack, and who, of all the apostles and guests at the table in Bethany, was certainly least fitted and disposed to appreciate the act of Mary,—Judas Iscariot, the betrayer and the thief. His unkind criticism arose not simply from that spirit of covetousness which was his besetting sin, but he was provoked by all these manifestations of love and devotion for the Lord, and ever since the Lord had designated him as the "devil" (John 6:70), he was ready for an outburst at any time. His opportunity in this case was well chosen. The plain practicable principle of utility, dressed up in the garb of charity for the poor, carried away even a number of disciples. Certainly not John. He came nearest to understanding Mary, and he saw deepest into the lie and hypocrisy of Judas, who did not in reality care for the poor, but for the bag which he carried, and in which he took away what was put therein.

The Lord Himself takes up the defence of Mary. Hers was a beautiful work, done to Him, not without deep meaning and for a good purpose. The very thing which Judas denies, the Lord asserts in a manner particularly severe for the man whose heart was filled with thoughts of betrayal. If Judas was planning the preparatory steps for the death of the Lord, Mary was getting ready for the burial of Him whom Judas killed. "It was right that she kept this against the day of My burying." Not that Mary was conscious of the full prophetical and typical meaning of her act. Her love to Christ makes her a prophet, as Caiaphas had turned prophet through his hatred to Him. But apart from that beautiful significance in Mary's act, anticipating His death and burial, the Lord in His defence points out some principles of abiding value for His church of all times. One is, when He tells His disciples: "The poor ye have always with you," with ample opportunity and constant obligation to do them good. But the idea, that Mary should turn her precious ointment into money, and that the 300 pence realized thereby should be given to the poor, thus contributing towards the wiping out of the difference between the rich and poor, is a Judas-idea, not approved of by the Lord, however practical, useful and taking it may appear even to the disciples. Whatever human sin and selfishness may do to widen the distance between rich and poor, and to drive them into two hostile camps threatening destruction to the whole fabric of society, the difference (not the alienation, the enmity, the cruel indifference and bitter hatred) between rich and poor is of divine appointment, and no utopian plans of to-day or of "two hundred years from to-day" will ever wipe out this plain statement of the Lord: "The poor ye have always with you."

The other point is this: that over against the principle of barren utilitarianism, the Lord pleads in favor of Mary's wastefulness: "She has done a beautiful work to Me" (on Me). Whatever beautiful and precious earthly treasures the tender devotion of His own may lay at Jesus' feet, in the service of God's house, this He will accept and call it a beautiful work, provided that it be a work done in the spirit of Mary, proceeding from a

IV. The End of the Public Ministry of Christ (Ch. 12)

devout and truly believing heart, seeking Christ and His glory alone and not the honor of self and family.

(B.) Excitement among the Common People and Counsel of the Chief Priests to put Lazarus to Death (12:9–11)

9–11. *The common people therefore of the Jews learned that he was there: and they came, not for Jesus' sake only, but that they might see Lazarus also, whom he had raised from the dead. But the chief priests took counsel that they might put Lazarus also to death; because that by reason of him many of the Jews went away, and believed on Jesus.*

At the news of the presence of Christ in Bethany many of the common people went out to see not only Him but also Lazarus, whom He had raised from the dead. And this seeing of the risen Lazarus resulted in leading many to faith in Christ. For this reason the unscrupulous rulers determined that Lazarus also should die. Nothing could prove more strongly the significance of that last and greatest miracle of the Lord, than this desperate scheme of putting Lazarus back into the tomb to stop the mouth of this testimony of Him, who is the resurrection and the life.

(C.) Entrance into Jerusalem (12:12–19)

12–19. *On the morrow a great multitude that had come to the feast, when they heard that Jesus was coming to Jerusalem, took the branches of the palm trees, and went forth to meet him, and cried out, Hosanna: Blessed is he that cometh in the name of the Lord, even the King of Israel. And Jesus, having found a young ass, sat thereon; as it is written, Fear not, daughter of Zion: behold, thy King cometh, sitting on an ass's colt. These things understood not his disciples at the first: but when Jesus was glorified, then remembered they that these things were written of him, and that they had done these things unto him. The multitude therefore that was with him when he called Lazarus out of the tomb, and raised him from the dead, bare witness. For this cause also the multitude went and met him, for that they heard that he had done this sign. The Pharisees therefore said among themselves, Behold how ye prevail nothing: lo, the world is gone after him.*

If the supper in Bethany was held on the Sabbath, the following day, on which the entrance into Jerusalem took place, was the first day of the week, our Sunday, the traditional day for keeping the memory of this glorious manifestation of Christ as the Messiah. Thus far every attempt on the part of the followers of Christ, to make a public demonstration in His favor, had always been promptly frustrated by the Lord. But now, the hour of His passion and death having arrived, He is willing to be publicly known and proclaimed as the promised Messiah, that cometh in the name of the Lord, the King of Israel. He even takes Himself an active part in the arrangement of this procession which is to make Him known as the one in whom all the prophecies are fulfilled. No one in the excitement and enthusiasm of that hour would ever have thought of the young ass on which the Messiah-King was to ride into His own city. But He thought of it and "found it," as John briefly but comprehensively says: He found it, because He sent for it; He needed it for the exact fulfilment of the passage in Zechariah (9:9). Not on the stately, warlike horse, nor on the mule, as some of the illustrious kings of the Old Testament dispensation, but on the despised ass did He enter Jerusalem,—the emblem of the lowliness and humility of this King, and of the peaceful character of His kingdom, since the earliest times an object of ridicule and sneering on the part of His adversaries. The disciples themselves do not seem to have caught the exact significance of this feature, at that time. They were still dreaming of glorious thrones in the Messianic kingdom. But the multitude, if they were not ready to read Zechariah (9:9) into this event, still had sufficient light shed upon it by their jubilant antiphones taken from the 118th psalm, which was commonly acknowledged and accepted as Messianic. They greet Him with palm branches and with their devout and joyous "Hosannah," which has been fittingly called the theocratic "God save the king" (for in its original meaning it is a prayer: Help now, help then, O Lord)—one of the words of that heavenly language, which have found their way to all nations, tongues and books, equally used and understood by all the lovers of God's kingdom the world over, expressing the same joy, devotion, adoration, praise and trust for all (like Allelujah, Kyrie, Immanuel, Jehovah, Amen).

In this connection also the fourth Gospel points out the influence of the miracle of Bethany on the multitude in the procession. This jubilee

IV. The End of the Public Ministry of Christ (Ch. 12)

was a testimony on the part of those that were "with Him when He called Lazarus out of the tomb and raised him from the dead" (17). And the same cause moved the multitude which "went" out from Jerusalem and "met Him" (ver. 18). The two streams meeting on the slope of Mount Olivet originally sprang from the same source—the deep impression of the raising of Lazarus was the common source. Of course there were other "mighty works which they had seen," and over which they might rejoice and praise God with a loud voice at the descent of the Mount of Olives (Luke 19:37). But foremost of all was that last miracle; it was in every body's mouth. They "met Him, for that they heard that He had done this sign."

To the Pharisees it was an occasion of utter disgust and discouragement. They stand aside, but in sulking isolation, like the elder brother, angry at the sound of music and dancing on the return of the prodigal. Oh, how those Hosannas grate on their ears! It is all in vain! "Ye prevail nothing. Lo the world is going after Him." Another prophecy, dictated by bitter hatred and yet true to the end of the world. Yea, the world is gone after Him. It counts its very years as "Annos Domini." This is the victory that hath overcome the world, even our faith (1 John 5:4). And "in the name of Jesus every knee shall bow, of things in heaven and things on earth and things under the earth, and every tongue shall confess that Jesus Christ is Lord, to the glory of God the Father" (Phil. 2:10, 11).

D. The Greeks Knocking at the Door of the Kingdom (12:20–36)

1. The Historical Fact (12:20–22)

20–22. *Now there were certain Greeks among those that went up to worship at the feast: these therefore came to Philip, which was of Bethsaida of Galilee, and asked him, saying, Sir, we would see Jesus. Philip cometh and telleth Andrew: Andrew cometh, and Philip, and they tell Jesus.*

On the feast of Tabernacles the Jews had sneeringly asked of the Lord: "Will He go among the Greeks and teach the Greeks?" (John 7:35). Here is the answer in a request coming from the Greeks. It is at the same time a striking illustration how that unwilling and unconscious prophecy of the Pharisees:—"All the world gone after Him"—is already beginning to be fulfilled. There is something wonderfully striking and significant at this point in this plain, modest petition: "We would see Jesus." The men who uttered it were Greeks, not Jews among the Gentiles ("Hellenists"), but real Gentiles themselves, who had been drawn, in the deeper yearning of their heart, to the covenant people of the Old Testament, to its revelation, its sanctuary and services, and who came from year to year, or at longer intervals from time to time, to worship in Jerusalem in the court of the Gentiles. "We would see Jesus." The one great theme which was on the lips of every one in those days had also taken possession of their hearts; but will they like Him as He was to be seen before the end of that week, lifted up on the cross, with the words written in *Greek* over His head: "Jesus of Nazareth the king of the Jews"? Or will it be with them as the prophet of old wrote: "When we shall see Him there is no beauty that we should desire Him"? (Isaiah 53:2).

Their wish, which certainly implied a personal interview with the Lord, was first modestly communicated to Philip. With his characteristic deliberateness, bordering on indecision, he does not reach a conclusion for himself. He hesitates to bring the Lord into contact with these Gentiles at the very point, when, for the first time, His own people had publicly received Him as the Messianic King of Israel. So Philip lays the question before Andrew, who is much more resolute and prompt in coming to a decision. Thus the two Apostles with Greek names, Philip and Andrew, lay this question of the Greeks before the Lord. It is difficult to say at what exact date between the Lord's entrance and the last supper this took place. It is the only incident recorded in the Fourth Gospel out of the many important dialogues and discourses belonging to this period, and narrated by the Synoptists. From Monday till Wednesday of that week we have the second purifying of the temple, the cursing of the figtree, the disputes with Pharisees, Sadducees and scribes, probably the case of the adulterous woman (John 8:1), the great discourse against the Pharisees (Matt. 23) and the prophecies of the Lord concerning the last things, the judgment over Jerusalem and the world. The interview with

IV. The End of the Public Ministry of Christ (Ch. 12)

the Greeks is differently placed, from the day of the Lord's entrance down to Thursday in Passion week, which was most likely spent in the quiet retreat of Bethany. John does not tell us directly whether the request of the Greeks was granted by the Lord. It would be strange, indeed, if it was not. But of much greater interest to the Evangelist is the deep and manifold significance of this request of the Greeks, and this is set forth most fully in the following verses (23–36).

2. Significance of this Fact (12:23–36)

(a.) For the Lord Himself (12:23–30)

23–30. And Jesus answereth them, saying, The hour is come, that the Son of man should be glorified. Verily, verily, I say unto you, Except a grain of wheat fall into the earth and die, it abideth by itself alone; but if it die, it beareth much fruit. He that loveth his life loseth it; and he that hateth his life in this world shall keep it unto life eternal. If any man serve me, let him follow me; and where I am, there shall also my servant be: if any man serve me, him will the Father honour. Now is my soul troubled; and what shall I say? Father, save me from this hour. But for this cause came I unto this hour. Father, glorify thy name. There came therefore a voice out of heaven, saying, I have both glorified it, and will glorify it again. The multitude therefore, that stood by, and heard it, said that it had thundered: others said, An angel hath spoken to him. Jesus answered and said, This voice hath not come for my sake, but for your sakes.

Jesus answered "them," the disciples and the Greeks with them. The Lord sees in this appeal of the Greeks an indication that the hour for His glorification, which His mother and His brothers have long been so anxious to see (John 2, John 7) has at last arrived. The scripture is being fulfilled which said: "I shall give Thee the heathen for Thine inheritance, and the uttermost parts of the earth for Thy possession" (Ps. 2:8). The Son of Man, rejected by the Jews, is accepted by the Gentiles,—this is the first stage of His glorification. But the very fact of His rejection by the Jews, which precedes and introduces His acceptance on the part of the Gentiles, involves His passion and death. "Except the grain of wheat fall into the earth and die, it abideth by itself alone; but if it die it beareth much fruit." The great law of heaven, which His whole life has upheld and realized, is the mystery of love, giving up Himself for the welfare of others. But this mystery of *love* is at the same time the mystery of *life*; it is the law of nature also that the sacrificing of the grain, its burial and death in the ground is the indispensable condition of a new abundant harvest. Here then we have, in the sphere of nature, implanted in it by the Creator's hand and by the Logos through whom all things were made, the very earliest prophecy and type of the mystery of redemption and the atoning sacrifice of Christ. The Lord metes out the mysteries of God's redeeming love to different classes of men in different forms and figures. The serpent in the wilderness for Nicodemus, the Old Testament scholar and teacher; but the grain of wheat for the Greeks, those children of nature, who had no knowledge of Moses and the Prophets, but who, in their mysterious services, especially the worship of Ceres (Demeter) in Eleusis, acknowledged "the principle of a new life after death, founded on the process of nature by which seed sown in the ground must first die and rot before it can yield new life, a process which the annual going and coming of Persephone, the daughter of Demeter was designed to illustrate" (Encycl. Brit. "Ceres," Vol. V. 345). But this principle of self-sacrificing love, as identical with the principle of new life out of death, is announced by the Lord as one that must be applied to all His followers. They must all be ready to sacrifice self, for he that loveth his life loseth it, and he that hateth his life in this world shall keep it unto life eternal. "If any man serve Me, let him follow Me. And where I am—in the humiliation of the cross and the glory of resurrection—there shall also My servant be." These words were of peculiar emphasis and solemnity in this connection, spoken in the presence of the Greeks, whose fundamental conception of this world and human life in it, was based, not on the principle of self-denial and sacrifice, but on that of self-indulgence and enjoyment.

But this reference to His sufferings and the glory hereafter, fills the Lord with deepest anguish and horror at the thought of what is before Him, the "hour" which now has come, the "cup" which He must take and drink. The fourth Gospel passes by the agony in the garden, but in this

IV. The End of the Public Ministry of Christ (Ch. 12)

scene it gives an anticipation of its woe and sorrows, its struggles and prayers. "Now is My soul troubled; and what shall I say: Father, save Me from this hour? (Thus the marginal reading of the Rev. Version correctly suggests.) But for this cause came I unto this hour.' Therefore, My only prayer shall be: *'Father, glorify Thy name.'* What are My trouble and sorrows, if only Thy name be glorified and Thy council be accomplished." There is a remarkable and close parallelism between the conflict and its solution, here and in Gethsemane. "Not Mine, but Thy will be done."

For the third time in the life of the Lord there is a heavenly "Amen" of recognition, in the voice of the Father. As in the hour of His baptism, and again on the mount of transfiguration, so here the Father distinctly testifies in words which say of the Son's prayer: "Yea, yea, so shall it be." The prayer was: "Father, glorify Thy name." The answer is: "I have both glorified it and will glorify it again." The reality of this sign, the voice from heaven, is not in the least affected by the different attitude of the hearers with regard to it. To some it was nothing but a sound of distant thunder; to others it seemed like angels' voices; to the Son, and no doubt to the Evangelist also, who was there as a witness, the words themselves were as distinct as those of any speaker uttered before human ears. There were different grades of ability to perceive and understand it; but the sign was acknowledged by all,—a voice, a sound from heaven.

(b.) For the World (12:31–33)

31–33. *Now is the judgement of this world: now shall the prince of this world be cast out. And I if I be lifted up from the earth, will draw all men unto myself. But this he said, signifying by what manner of death he should die.*

The hour of the glorification of the Son of Man means an hour of "crisis," of judgment for the world: "Now is the judgment of this world: now shall the prince of this world be cast out." It is the most momentous time in the history of the human race. The cross on Calvary marks the point from which the ways of individuals and of nations separate. There, as old Simeon had said, the thoughts of many hearts shall be revealed (Luke 2:35). The final judgment is only the confirmation and publication of this separation and judgment which divided men all along, on the principle of believing or rejecting the word of the Cross.

But, apart from this subjective judgment in the hearts of men there is also, in this hour of the glorification of the Son of Man, an objective judgment executed against the prince of this world. At the moment of Christ's elevation on the cross, he is dethroned, cast out. His power is broken. The crucifixion of the Son of God was the most daring piece of satanic craft and power; it was, in its purport and intention, deicide itself. And yet in its final effect it was not more than bruising the heel of the woman's seed, whilst in that very act the serpent's *head* was crushed. Satan being thus dethroned, the Son of Man will be exalted on His throne, to rule and draw the hearts of men. But the throne with which His reign begins, on which it is firmly established, is the *cross*. "If I be lifted up from the earth I will draw all men unto Myself." There is a wonderful power of attraction and of separation in the cross of Christ. It draws all men to Him, it is the concentration of God's world-redeeming love. But it draws men to a crucified Saviour. It separates forever the world, with all that it holds great and noble and wise and good, from the kingdom of Christ. The cross is the wall between the world and the Church, as Paul glories in "the cross of Christ through which the world hath been crucified unto me and I unto the world" (Gal. 6:14). And again that same cross of Christ breaks down forever the partition walls of ancient creeds and nationalities. As Jews and Gentiles had joined hands in executing the satanic design of killing Christ, so they are to join hands in the common inheritance of all the blessings purchased by the Prince of Life with His own precious blood. There is henceforth "no distinction between Jew and Greek: for the same Lord is Lord of all, and is rich unto all that call upon Him" (Rom. 10:12). Here, then, in this blessed assurance: "I will draw all men to Myself," is the distinct and direct answer of Christ to the application of the Greeks: "We would see Jesus."

(c.) *For Israel (12:34–36)*

34–36. *The multitude therefore answered him, We have heard out of the law that the Christ abideth forever; and how sayest thou, The Son of man must be lifted up?*

IV. The End of the Public Ministry of Christ (Ch. 12)

who is this Son of man? Jesus therefore said unto them, Yet a little while is the light among you. Walk while ye have the light, that darkness overtake you not: and he that walketh in the darkness knoweth not whither he goeth. While ye have the light, believe on the light, that ye may become sons of light. These things spake Jesus, and he departed and hid himself from them.

The multitude, representing, of course, the Jewish hearers of the Lord, refer to a certain difficulty in their way concerning the kingdom of the Messiah. They have learned to consider it, as they think, on the authority of Scripture, as an everlasting, visible kingdom on earth. How does this accord with Christ being lifted up from the earth, literally "out of the earth?" (Margin. reading R. V.). Is this Son of Man really identical with the Messiah? Who is this Son of Man?

Jesus therefore "said" unto them: "Yet a little while is the light among you," etc. His words were not an answer to their question. That answer had been given time and again. But the Lord does give them a last and solemn warning. The sun of salvation is about setting in Israel. The night will soon overtake them. Then Israel will grope in the darkness, knowing not whither it goeth,—the wandering Jew forever without light, peace and home. This is Christ's parting word to the multitude of Israel.

(E.) Final Review of the Unbelief of the Jews (12:37–43)

1. Their Unbelief Prophesied by Isaiah (12:37–41.)

37–41. *But though he had done so many signs before them, yet they believed not on him: that the word of Isaiah the prophet might be fulfilled, which he spake,*
Lord, who hath believed our report?
And to whom hath the arm of the Lord been revealed?
For this cause they could not believe, for that Isaiah said again,
He hath blinded their eyes, and he hardened their heart;
Lest they should see with their eyes, and perceive with their heart,
And should turn,
And I should heal them.
These things said Isaiah, because he saw his glory; and he spake of him.

What the Gospel of John had indicated in the Prologue already, that though "He came unto His own, His own received Him not," is now once more at the end of the whole narrative stated as a historical fact, and both the guilt and the responsibility of the people and the judgment of God in this fact are shown forth. The point has been reached, when the Lord has finished His whole testimony to His people. He now departs and hides Himself from them. The time of the manifestation of His glory in His words and His many signs (only six of which John had narrated) is passed; and passed without bringing the people as a people to belief on Christ. The Gospel of John here deals with the same difficult and momentous theme to which Paul devoted those three chapters (9–11) in his Epistle to the Romans, the unbelief of Israel. And here, as in other passages of the New Testament, where this attitude of God's chosen people is referred to, the fundamental prophecy of Isaiah is introduced, which presents the unbelief of Israel in the light of divine judgment (Matt. 13:14, Acts 28:26, 27). The respective import of these two distinct quotations from Isaiah must be well marked. The first, from Isa. 53:1, states the unbelief of Israel as the responsible act and guilt of the people themselves. To the wise and great in this world there was "no form nor comeliness" in the appearance of the Messiah, "no beauty that they should desire Him." For this reason they were not willing to believe on Him and to receive Him. But there is another aspect yet to this unbelief, as set forth in the second passage from Isaiah 6. They could not and should not believe on Him. There was a divine judgment in this. Having hardened their hearts and closed their eyes against God's gracious revelation in Christ, their eyes are blinded and their hearts are hardened by God's own righteous act of punishment.

2. *Cowardly Fear of the Pharisees* (12:42, 43)

42–43. *Nevertheless even of the rulers many believed on him; but because of the Pharisees they did not confess it, lest they should be put out of the synagogue: for they loved the glory of men more than the glory of God.*

That this judgment of God upon Israel as a whole did not exclude individuals from coming to Jesus, appears from the following verses.

IV. The End of the Public Ministry of Christ (Ch. 12)

"Nevertheless even of the rulers many believed on Him." The way was open, if they only had been strong and courageous enough to come out boldly for the Lord, as Joseph and Nicodemus did when their time came. But the conflict with the Pharisees was too much for them. After all they loved the glory of men more than the glory of God. And this was the very sin of the Pharisees and the principal obstacle of faith, as the Lord had said of them long before this, "How can ye believe which receive glory one of another, and the glory that cometh from the only God ye seek not?" (John 5:44).

(F.) Summing up of the Lord's Testimony (12:44–50)

44–50. *And Jesus cried and said, He that believeth on me, believeth not on me, but on him that sent me. And he that beholdeth me beholdeth him that sent me. I am come a light into the world, that whosoever believeth on me may not abide in the darkness. And if any man hear my sayings, and keep them not, I judge him not: for I came not to judge the world, but to save the world. He that rejecteth me, and receiveth not my sayings, hath one that judgeth him: the word that I spake, the same shall judge him in the last day. For I spake not from myself; but the Father which sent me, he hath given me a commandment, what I should say, and what I should speak. And I know that his commandment is life eternal: the things therefore which I speak, even as the Father hath said unto me, so I speak.*

If we have followed attentively the narrative of the fourth Gospel to this point, if we remember the positive statement verse 36 that after that last discourse, occasioned by the appearance of the Greeks, Jesus departed and hid Himself from them, the question naturally suggests itself at the opening of the 44th verse: When and where, under what circumstances did Jesus deliver this last discourse, if such it be, contained in verses 44–50? We fail to find any special occasion for it, such as the fourth Gospel clearly states in the introduction of every other discourse of the Lord. After the climax of the Lord's testimony to the Jews, verses 35 and 36, there is no room in the historical order of events, recorded in the fourth Gospel, for this section, verses 44–50, as a historical discourse of Christ, delivered then and there during those last days before His passion and death. We therefore believe that in these verses the Evangelist presents a brief summary of the principal points of the testimony of Christ; every word of it spoken by the Lord before or after this, but at this point arranged by John himself as a final offset to the unbelief of the Jews. The Evangelist cannot part from that picture of Israel's hopeless unbelief without pointing out once more, in a sort of epilogue, how clearly, solemnly and fully Christ had testified before their ears, and offered them all the light and help they needed to come out of their unbelief and to embrace Jesus as the Saviour of the world. The absolute dignity and authority of Christ's person and work is briefly and pointedly summed up in this section: Christ the Son of God, sent by the Father, to save the world. His word the absolute divine message to the world. Whosoever rejects it, will be judged by that same word on the last day.

IV. The End of the Public Ministry of Christ (Ch. 12)

THIRD PART. CHAPTERS 13–21

THE TRIUMPH OF FAITH.—THE INCARNATE WORD GLORIFIED AMONG HIS OWN

JOHN 13

I. Historical Introduction to the Parting Discourses of the Lord (13:1–30)

1. Jesus Washing the Disciples Feet (13:1–17)

1–17. *Now before the feast of the passover, Jesus knowing that his hour was come that he should depart out of this world unto the Father, having loved his own which were in the world, he loved them unto the end. And during supper, the devil having already put into the heart of Judas Iscariot, Simon's son, to betray him, Jesus, knowing that the Father had given all things into his hands, and that he came forth from God, and goeth unto God, riseth from supper, and layeth aside his garments; and he took a towel, and girded himself. Then he poureth water into the bason and began to wash the disciples' feet, and to wipe them with the towel wherewith he was girded. So he cometh to Simon Peter. He saith unto him, Lord, dost thou wash my feet? Jesus answered and said unto him, What I do thou knowest not now; but thou shalt understand hereafter. Peter saith unto him, Thou shalt never wash my feet. Jesus answered him, If I wash thee not, thou hast no part with me. Simon Peter saith unto him, Lord, not my feet only, but also my hands and my head. Jesus saith unto him, He that is bathed needeth not save to wash his feet, but is clean every whit: and ye are clean, but not all. For he knew him that should betray him; therefore said he, Ye are not all clean.*

So when he had washed their feet, and taken his garments, and sat down again, he said unto them, Know ye what I have done to you? Ye call me Master, and Lord: and ye say well; for so I am. If I then, the Lord and the Master, have washed your feet, ye also ought to wash one another's feet. For I have given you an example, that ye also should do as I have done to you. Verily, verily, I say unto you, A servant is not greater than his lord; neither one that is sent greater than he that sent him. If ye know these things, blessed are ye if ye do them.

With the thirteenth chapter we reach the third and last section of the Gospel of St. John, setting forth the triumph of faith; the incarnate

I. Historical Introduction to the Parting Discourses of the Lord (13:1–30)

Word glorified among His own. The first half of this section (chapters 13 to 17) stands in striking contrast to the preceding middle section of this Gospel. There we saw the fierce conflict between the Lord and His adversaries growing hotter and hotter until it reached its climax in the determination to kill both Him and Lazarus. Here we leave this battlefield and enter into that quiet, peaceful sanctuary in which the Lord is closeted with His disciples for the last parting hours. Being delivered from that one antagonistic element, which had still been defiling that sanctuary, Judas Iscariot, they are at last alone among themselves in full harmony. And now the deepest lessons are taught to the disciples. They are introduced into the profoundest mysteries of the Holy Trinity. Their knowledge, faith and love expand and are strengthened as never before. Now they "believe that He came forth from God" (16:30).

The fourth Gospel, whilst it refrains from recording for a fourth time the history of the institution of the Lord's Supper, supplements the Synoptical account at this point with that most significant and valuable narrative of the washing of the disciples' feet.

John in introducing this history by a sort of prologue presents the heavenly aspect of the case. It was now that Easter on which Christ was to be given as the true Paschal Lamb. The hour was come that He should depart out of this world unto the Father. Fully conscious of this, and knowing that the Father had given all things into His hands and that He came forth from God and goeth unto God—He riseth from supper and layeth aside His garments; and He took a towel and girded Himself; then He poureth water into the bason and began to wash the disciples' feet and to wipe them with the towel wherewith He was girded. In full sight of His divine majesty and glory this deepest humiliation of ministering to His disciples as a servant! This is the divine, the heavenly aspect of this act. But there is still another side to it, a lower earthly aspect, which must be considered in order to realize fully the character of that scene. The Gospel of St. Luke (ch. 22) furnishes us the most important features in this respect. The Lord had taken special care, as the house-father of His family of twelve, to have that supper properly prepared. Peter and John had been directed by Him to make all the arrangements in detail. And when the hour was come, He sat down and the apostles with Him. And He said unto them: "With desire I have desired to eat this passover with you before I suffer." But over against this heavenly frame of mind, in which the Lord sat down, what a different spirit in the hearts of those men who met with Him at that table! Here was one of the twelve who had made up his mind by this time, to reward the Lord for all the love received from Him during the past three years, by betraying Him. Here were eleven of the twelve who after their three years' intimate communion with their Master, the most meek and lowly in heart, at this very time entered upon those solemn evening hours with "a contention among them, which of them is accounted to be greatest." If we follow Luke in his 22d chapter down to the end of the 27th verse, we at once recognize the connection between that contention and the Lord's acting "in the midst of them as he that serveth," that is, by washing their feet. Upon Peter and John, to whom all the arrangements for the supper had been committed, the duty devolved, to see also to the washing of the feet of the company; and, if there was no servant present, to attend to it themselves, or secure the service of one of the apostles for this work. But here the contention arose. No one was ready to stoop down to this menial service. And thus the only-begotten Son of the Father, the Lord and King of heaven and earth, Himself rises from His couch, and being "the chief becomes as he that doth serve." This He does in the first place, as He distinctly states, as an example: "If I, the Lord and Master, have washed your feet, ye also ought to wash one another's feet. For I have given you an example, that ye also should do as I have done to you." It was Christ's love to His own, a love without limit, loving "to the uttermost" (εἰς τὸ τέλος, ver. 1) which He had demonstrated in this act and the example of this love He means to impress upon their hearts. It is, in the most graphic and telling form, that new commandment: "That ye love one another, even as I have loved you, that ye also love one another" (ver. 34, 35). This love must be ready and willing to minister to the need of the brother in outward acts of service, not shrinking even from the meanest, most uncommon and repulsive, wherever the necessity arises. But, as the Lord Himself, as we will

I. Historical Introduction to the Parting Discourses of the Lord (13:1–30)

presently see, gave to the outward, bodily washing a deeper spiritual significance, so the application of this example must also be in the sphere of that spiritual washing and cleansing, which Paul describes in Gal. 6:1, 2. "Brethren if a man be overtaken in any trespass, ye which are spiritual, restore such a one in a spirit of meekness;—bear ye one another's burdens and so fulfil the law of Christ." Such service can be effectively done only in that spirit of true humility, which acts on the principle "if any man would be first, he shall be last of all and minister of all" (Mark 9:35).

But this washing of the feet is also a type of Christ's work of redemption. This deeper spiritual meaning of the foot-washing comes out fully in the dialogue between the Lord and Peter, resulting from his refusal to have his feet washed by his Master. The one principal aim of the whole work of Christ in all His words and deeds was, not to establish a glorious kingdom before the eyes of men, or to proclaim profound philosophical truths before the ears of men, but to absolve and cleanse the hearts of men from sin and guilt, and this work of absolution and cleansing He can only accomplish by His own deepest self-humiliation; even as the Son of Man came not to be ministered unto, but to minister and to give His life a ransom for many. The blood of Jesus cleanseth us from all sin. This is the meaning of that most comprehensive and solemn word to Peter: "If I wash thee not thou hast no part with Me." Not what men may do in their admiration and enthusiasm for Christ, gives them a position in the kingdom of God; but that one great experience: "I am washed and cleansed by Jesus." Without it I cannot have part with Him, and having once obtained pardon through Him, I must still be washed by Him from day to day, not forgetting the cleansing from daily sins.

2. Judas Iscariot Forced to Withdraw (13:18–30)

18–30. I speak not of you all: I know whom I have chosen: but that the scripture may be fulfilled, He that eateth my bread lifted up his heel against me. From henceforth I tell you before it come to pass, that, when it is come to pass, ye may believe that I am he. Verily, verily, I say unto you, He that receiveth whomsoever I send receiveth me; and he that receiveth me receiveth him that sent me.

When Jesus had thus said, he was troubled in the spirit, and testified, and said, Verily, verily, I say unto you, that one of you shall betray me. The disciples looked one on another, doubting of whom he spake. There was at the table reclining on Jesus' bosom one of his disciples, whom Jesus loved. Simon Peter therefore beckoneth to him, and saith unto him, Tell *us* who it is of whom he speaketh. He leaning back, as he was, on Jesus' breast saith unto him, Lord, who is it? Jesus therefore answereth, He it is, for whom I shall dip the sop, and give it him. So when he had dipped the sop, he taketh and giveth it to Judas, *the son of* Simon Iscariot. And after the sop, then entered Satan into him. Jesus therefore saith unto him, That thou doest, do quickly. Now no man at the table knew for what intent he spake this unto him. For some thought, because Judas had the bag, that Jesus said unto him, Buy what things we have need of for the feast; or, that he should give something to the poor. He then having received the sop went out straightway: and it was night.

From the beginning of this chapter the Evangelist has repeatedly directed our attention to the fact, that the betrayer is still present with the twelve; that there is no peace and comfort among them so long as this thorn is felt in the flesh; and that the crisis has now come; it is time to have it extracted and the body freed from its disturbing influence. In the introduction already (ver. 2) the Evangelist refers to the fact that "the devil put it into the heart of Judas Iscariot to betray Him." In the tenth verse there is the second reference to him in the words of the Lord: "Ye are clean but not all, for He knew him that should betray Him." Again in the 18th: "I speak not of you all: I know whom I have chosen: but that the Scripture may be fulfilled: He that eateth My bread, lifted up his heel against Me." Then in the 21st the direct announcement by the Lord: "One of you shall betray Me." And at last the final marking of the traitor: "He it is for whom I shall dip the sop and give it him. So when He had dipped the sop He taketh and giveth it to Judas, the son of Simon Iscariot. And after the sop then entered Satan into him,"—an evident climax as

I. Historical Introduction to the Parting Discourses of the Lord (13:1–30)

compared to the statement in the second verse. "He then having received the sop went out straightway: and it was night."

It is the satanic character of the sin of Judas, which is most strongly emphasized in the fourth Gospel. But this does not forbid an attempt on our part to comprehend in some measure the psychological development of that son of perdition. We think it most probable that Judas, besides his mean love of money, was burning with a desire to see the establishment of a glorious Messianic kingdom which would force itself upon the people by the display of signs and wonders. Even now, in betraying the Lord, Judas may have indulged in the hope that he would thereby compel Christ to overwhelm His adversaries by a miraculous manifestation of His power and glory. We remember the scene on the pinnacle of the temple, at the temptation of Christ, when Satan said to Him: "If Thou art the Son of God, cast Thyself down." But Judas, by his betrayal, pushes the Lord off from the pinnacle, expecting to see Him spread the pinions of His miraculous power, and save Himself from the catastrophe of an ignominious fall. He did not believe that the Lord was seriously ready and willing to die. Had He not thus far carefully avoided, and successfully escaped from all the attempts on His life made by His persecutors? Judas felt sure that He would be fully able to cope with all the power and cunning of His adversaries, and therefore he did not see much danger in delivering Him into their hands. They would be double losers in the end. Their money safe in Judas' bag; their prisoner safe out of their hands. Thus nothing would be lost ultimately to Christ or to himself. But if these were his calculations, he soon enough found himself undeceived. As he pushed off the Lord by his betrayal, to his utmost horror and dismay he saw Him sink and sink; submit to the power of His enemies in absolute self-surrender. Despair seized him. Everything lost in this bold, unscrupulous game. So he brought back the thirty pieces of silver, the price of blood, to the chief priests and elders and went away and hanged himself.

John 13

II. First Parting Words Addressed to the Eleven (13:31–14:4)

1. *The Son of Man Glorified (13:31–32)*

31–32. *When therefore he was gone out, Jesus saith, Now is the Son of man glorified, and God is glorified in him; and God shall glorify him in himself, and straightway shall he glorify him.*

Being freed from the presence of the traitor, though the departure of Judas Iscariot means the hour of passion and death for Himself, the Lord enjoys a foretaste of the glory in store for Him. He actually enters upon the road to His immediate glorification. "Now is the Son of Man glorified,"—this is the grand and glorious beginning of the parting discourses of that evening; a shout of victory at the very opening of the battle, in the night in which He was betrayed. Not less than five[1] times in these two short verses the word "glorify" is used. The Son of Man is glorified,—in looking back over His past life He can boldly claim that His whole life-work was nothing but glorifying the Father, and thereby He Himself is glorified. The Son of Man is glorified in that present hour as He now willingly takes up the cross to seal and to crown His life-work by His obedience unto death. The Son will be glorified, and that without delay, by His exaltation to the right hand of the Father.

2. *The Imminent Departure (13:33)*

33. *Little children, yet a little while I am with you. Ye shall seek me: and as I said unto the Jews, Whither I go, ye cannot come; so now I say unto you.*

The Lord addresses His disciples in the most affectionate manner as dear little children. The great human heart of the true man Jesus feels most tenderly the impending separation. He cannot spare them the same hard truth, which He had before announced to the Jews. He goes and they cannot come, whither He is going. They will miss Him. And they will seek Him, but, different from the Jews, they will find Him again. They will not, as it was said to the Jews, die in their sins. They will live through Him and in Him and with Him in glory, though for the present they cannot possibly go with Him. The passion and the death of atonement are

---

[1] Four times in the reading accepted in the Revised Version.

II. First Parting Words Addressed to the Eleven (13:31–14:4)

exclusively His own. No one can share with Him the agony of these hours; but they shall share with Him the glory in His Father's mansions (14:3).

3. The New Commandment (13:34–35)

34–35. *A new commandment I give unto you, that ye love one another; even as I have loved you, that ye also love one another. By this shall all men know that ye are my disciples, if ye have love one to another.*

In their sorrow over the Lord's departure, the disciples are to find comfort in fulfilling this new commandment of loving one another even as He had loved them. The question naturally presents itself: What is the new feature in this love, with which the disciples are charged? For, certainly, the love of God and of our fellow-men was as old as the Old Testament law itself. Nor can the newness of this commandment of love be found in a concentration upon the narrow circle of believers, the "philadelphia," or brotherly love, of which we read a good deal in the Epistles. The characteristic feature of this new commandment of love must be found in the words: "even as I have loved you." The Christlike love is the original and new feature in this "new commandment" of the New Testament. It is love learned from the example of Christ; love inspired by His redeeming love; love begotten of the wondrous love of the Saviour, for this end has He "loved His own to the uttermost end" (13:3) that they might love one another. Christ's love, apprehended by faith, is the quickening power of the love of His disciples. Men cannot honestly exalt love, and Christianity as "the religion of love," and yet at the same time cast out faith, the only hand that grasps the love of the God-man.

4. Peter's Interruption Answered by the Lord (13:36–38)

36–38. *Simon Peter saith unto him, Lord, whither goest thou? Jesus answered, Whither I go, thou canst not follow me now; but thou shalt follow afterwards. Peter saith unto him, Lord, why cannot I follow thee even now? I will lay down my life for thee. Jesus answereth, Wilt thou lay down thy life for me? Verily, verily, I say unto thee, The cock shall not crow, till thou hast denied me thrice.*

This conversation with Peter, or one very similar to it, is recorded by Matthew and Mark at a later period of the passion history, on the way to the Garden. But the account of Luke (22:33, 34) seems to support John. And why should it be impossible that similar words were spoken more than once on that memorable evening, when Peter's heart was full to overflowing with devotion to his Lord and anxiety about His departure? It seems to us, the question of Peter at this point is so directly connected with the immediately preceding statement of the Lord: "Whither I go ye cannot come," that it cannot be detached from it without doing violence to the whole context.

Peter is the same as we found him at the washing of the feet, rash, forward, full of self-reliance, enthusiastically devoted to his Lord, but lamentably misjudging his own strength. The Lord in the first place does not directly answer Peter's question. He simply reaffirms His former statement: "Whither I go thou canst not follow." But He qualifies it by the addition of the "now" and the further explanation: "thou shalt follow afterwards." His time will come; it has not yet arrived;[1] but it is sure to come, when Peter once begins to deny himself, to give his old Adam into death; as a mature Christian he will even be honored with a martyr's death (as prophesied also John 21:18, 19).

---

[1] *Quid festinas, Petre? nondum te Suo Spiritu soliaavit Petra.* (Why in such a hurry, Peter? the Rock (*Petra*) has not yet established or confirmed thee with His Spirit. (AUGUSTINE.)

II. First Parting Words Addressed to the Eleven (13:31–14:4)

JOHN 14

5. The Disciples Comforted Concerning the Lord's Departure (14:1–4)

1–4. *Let not your heart be troubled: ye believe in God, believe also in me. In my Father's house are many mansions; if it were not so, I would have told you; for I go to prepare a place for you. And if I go and prepare a place for you, I come again, and will receive you unto myself; that where I am, there ye may be also. And whither I go, ye know the way.*

At the opening of this chapter Luther says of this and the following discourses: "Here the Lord has abundantly poured out those precious consolations, which all Christians enjoy, and which men ought to seek in all their trials and tribulations. Moreover we have here a summary of all the principal articles of Christian doctrine, most powerfully established, as nowhere else in the Scriptures, such as: the doctrine of three distinct Persons in the Trinity; of the divine and human nature of Christ and His eternal, indivisible Person; also of the righteousness of faith and the true consolation for an anxious conscience."

As in the question of Peter, so here in these assuring words of Christ we recognize the close connection with the announcement of His imminent departure which had considerably disturbed and discouraged the disciples. The one great panacea against such tribulations is faith, faith in God and faith in Christ. We prefer the translation in the marginal note of the R. V., taking the two verbs as two emphatic imperatives: "Believe in God, believe also in Me." Faith in God is the foundation of faith in Christ. But faith in Christ is the only way to a truly saving and crowning faith in God, that really gives Him all His due honor. In demanding the same faith for Himself, as is due to God, Christ unmistakeably claims co-equality with God.

The Lord has now reached that point in the history of His life when the world will refuse Him a place. In a few hours Jerusalem will resound with the cry: Away with Him! Cast Him out! Crucify Him! And in the face of this He speaks with perfect peace and assurance of heavenly mansions for Himself and His own, abiding-places, where no one will be disturbed or expelled. "If it were not so I would have told you." These words are generally understood as a simple affirmation of His positive statement, on which His disciples can absolutely rely. A better meaning of this sentence, however, is obtained, by reading it as a question: "If it were not so, would I have said to you that I am going to prepare a place for you?"

His going, then, is for the benefit of His disciples, to prepare a place for them in the Father's house. But He will come again and receive them unto Himself, that they may be where He is. When and where is this coming of the Lord and this receiving of His disciples realized? Is it on Easter, when the risen Saviour appears to His disciples? or on Pentecost when He sends down His Spirit from on high? or at the hour of their death, when He delivers them from all evil and takes them to Himself, to be forever with the Lord? is it on His second advent when the new heaven and the new earth shall greet the glorified saints? Combine all these in one grand perspective: He comes to His people whenever and wherever they need Him, so that they on their part may be fully prepared to enter His heavenly mansions.

III. Further Interruptions of the Disciples Answered by the Lord (14:5–11)

1. *Thomas (14:5–7)*

5–7. *Thomas saith unto him, Lord, we know not whither thou goest; how know we the way? Jesus saith unto him, I am the way, and the truth, and the life: no one cometh unto the Father, but by me. If ye had known me, ye would have known my Father also: from henceforth ye know him, and have seen him.*

Thomas is the "pessimist" among the disciples. Being by nature of a gloomy, melancholy disposition, he finds it difficult to come to a simple, childlike faith. But at the same time he is a most earnest and sincere inquirer, who will surely find the right way in the end according to the Lord's own promise: "Seek and ye shall find." At this point he is the

III. FURTHER INTERRUPTIONS OF THE DISCIPLES ANSWERED BY THE LORD (14:5–11)

mouthpiece of all the Apostles, expressing their consternation and perplexity at the Lord's impending departure. Therefore the answer to his question is in reality addressed to all the disciples, who still fail to comprehend Christ's peculiar relation to the Father, and are consequently anxious concerning His future. In the Lord's answer the principal idea, to which everything else is subordinate, is evidently that of *the way*. He is the way to the Father and to the Father's house, not the guide to point out the way, but the Way itself; and the only way, to the exclusion of all other ways and means of coming to the Father. He is the Way, because He is the Truth, the absolute fullness and reality of God's revelation to man and man's reconciliation with God. Being the Truth, He is also the Life. Divine Truth, as represented by Him, personified in Him. is a quickening power, begetting and preserving life.[1] Even in His death, yea, through His very death, He is the Life of the world. As He was now ready to depart for His passion and death, the disciples needed to be strongly impressed with the fact that He is the Life, all the developments of the next twenty-four hours to the contrary. No justice is done to this brief and comprehensive statement of the Lord, if we divest it of all reference to His mediatorial office, His passion and death. Mark also the divine character and truly heavenly majesty shining forth in these words. No mere man could ever speak thus of himself without insane presumption and conceit. At the close of the Lord's answer (ver. 7), there is both a rebuke and an encouragement for the disciples; a rebuke, because they do not yet know Him as they ought to know Him by this time; an encouragement, that even now they are further advanced in their Christian knowledge than they themselves realize.

2. *Philip (14:8–11)*

8–11. *Philip saith unto him, Lord, shew us the Father, and it sufficeth us. Jesus saith unto him, Have I been so long time with you, and dost thou not know me,*

---

[1] See John 6:63. Also the twofold meaning of the German word: zeugen—testify and beget.

Philip? he that hath seen me hath seen the Father; how sayest thou, Shew us the Father? Believest thou not that I am in the Father, and the Father in me? the words that I say unto you I speak not from myself: but the Father abiding in me doeth his works. Believe me that I am in the Father, and the Father in me: or else believe me for the very works' sake.

The naïve request of Philip undoubtedly contains precious elements of truth. He is ready to accept Christ as the way to the Father, as the only one who can show the Father; and with Christ's revelation of the Father he declares himself perfectly satisfied. To see the Father, as shown by Christ, would be to Philip the climax of earthly happiness; all the yearning and thirsting of the human soul after God would be completely quenched, if Christ would only "show the Father." And yet there is a decided tone of rebuke in the gentle answer of the Lord. Philip was yet far from realizing the experience, described in the prologue of the Gospel (John 1:14): "We beheld His glory,—as of the only-begotten Son of the Father, full of grace and truth." In this petition that the Father should be shown, Philip may have meant something after the manner of the Old Testament Theophanies. But his very demand for something or some one *to see,* in addition to Christ, betrays a lack of faith and of a correct appreciation of the true relation between Christ and the Father. He that hath seen Him hath seen the Father. While the line of distinction between the person of the Father and the person of the Son is clearly maintained, yet it is stated with equal distinctness that the Father is in the Son and the Son in the Father. The Son is the absolute revelation of the Father. Whatever can be *shown* of the Father, so as to bring men to a personal knowledge of and communion with the Father, is shown in the Son and in Him alone. Behold the Father's power and majesty in the works of the Son; the Father's love in the words of the Son; the Father's holiness in the life of the Son. Outside of Christ there is no saving knowledge of the Father.[1]

---

[1] Cf. Luther's repeated and vigorous protest: I know and will know of no other God, except the One that lieth in the manger and is nailed to the cross, etc.

IV. THE PARTING WORDS CONTINUED (14:12–31)

And there is only one way to realize this: it is by *believing* that Christ is in the Father and the Father in Him, on the testimony of His works, and particularly His words. The correct petition therefore must now be addressed to the Spirit: "Show us *the Son*, for if we know and see the Son, we know and have the Father."

IV. THE PARTING WORDS CONTINUED (14:12–31)

1. *The Disciples Doing the Works of Jesus (14:12–14)*

12–14. *Verily, verily, I say unto you, he that believeth on me, the works that I do shall he do also; and greater works than these shall he do; because I go unto the Father. And whatsoever ye shall ask in my name, that will I do, that the Father may be glorified in the Son. If ye shall ask me anything in my name, that will I do.*

The questions, by which Thomas and Philip interrupted the Lord's discourse, having been answered, Jesus proceeds with the principal theme—the encouragement and consolation of His disciples in view of His impending departure. As in the preceding verses (10 and 11), so here also everything is based upon faith: "He that believeth on Me." In the power of that faith, works, great works, are to be done. The reference to work is in itself wholesome medicine for hearts aching with sorrow over the loss of one so near and dear. But the Lord uses the very strongest language to magnify the life-work of the disciples. Not only shall His work be continued by them, but they shall even do greater works. It is His going to the Father, His passion, death and glorifycation, that paves the way for these greater works to be done by the disciples. Strange as this may seem, it is literally true. The work of the Lord's public ministry on earth, with its miracles and preaching, had its clearly defined limitations. "He was not sent but to the lost sheep of the house of Israel." And in addition to these theocratical, national and geographical barriers there was the all-important fact, that the Holy Spirit had not yet been shed abroad, for Jesus was not yet glorified. But now, after His going to the Father, what a manifestation of power from on high through the Apostles! The result of Peter's one Pentecostal sermon, far surpasses everything that was ever given to Christ during the three years of His public ministry. The same is true of St. Paul's mission-work from Damascus and Arabia to Spain. "The Apostles' work reached further than Christ's," says Luther. "They filled the whole world; Christ only a little corner."

These works of the disciples, however, are in reality Christ's own works. He continues to be at work: "The works that *I do*" are works carried on in the present, not merely works done in the past. Now these greater works are given to the disciples by the glorified Christ in answer to their prayers which they offer in His name. Thus the "Ora" (pray) and "Labora" (work) are beautifully and permanently blending in the life-work of the disciples. Such prayer is to be in the name of Jesus, that is, in living faith in God's revelation in Christ, praying at His command, by His authority, pleading His intercession as the only mediator through whom we may come to the Father; praying after His own mind, in His spirit, for the cause of His kingdom; and finally, even calling upon Christ Himself, our Saviour, as the true God. This last feature we maintain even though the pronoun "me" in the 14th verse ("If ye shall ask *Me* anything in My name") should be eliminated from the text, as we believe it ought to be.[1]

2. *Praying for Another Comforter (14:15–17)*

15–17. If ye love me ye will keep my commandments. And I will pray the Father, and he shall give you another Comforter, that he may be with you for ever, even the Spirit of truth: whom the world cannot receive; for it beholdeth him not, neither knoweth him: ye know him; for he abideth with you, and shall be in you.

There is a close connection between the 15th and the following verses. In making the precious promise (vers. 16 and 17) the Lord insists on a condition: the disciples must love Him and, in proof of this love, keep His commandments. Then He will ask the Father to give them another "Paraclete," the Spirit of truth. This is the first full and direct announcement by the Lord of that great Pentecostal fact, the coming of

---

[1] Though Teschendorf and Westcott retain it on the testimony of the Sinaitic and Vatican MSS.

IV. The Parting Words Continued (14:12–31)

the Holy Ghost, that had been referred to on former occasions as the best gift which God's children could possibly ask from their heavenly Father.

Here, as in all the subsequent utterances of the Lord on this subject, the personality of the Spirit is strongly emphasized. He speaks of Him as "another Paraclete or Advocate," implying that in the first place Christ Himself was the Comforter, that is, the Advocate of the disciples, as He is represented in 1 John 2:1. As the "Logos" in the gospel of St. John is clearly a divine person, so also is the "Paraclete," who carries on the work of the Logos. All the verbs in this context, which describe the different acts of Jesus, of the Father and of the Comforter, bear a decidedly personal character. They represent throughout acts that can be predicated only of persons: the *praying* or asking on the part of the Son; the *giving* on the part of the Father; the *abiding* on the part of the Spirit.

The "Paraclete," the one who is called in, or called upon for assistance, is the "Advocate," the counsel and assistant, to plead one's cause, to represent one and to make intercession. Thus Luther explains the term: "One, who is the advocate or support (Beistand) of the accused, who takes charge of his case, to defend him, to plead his cause, to assist him with his counsel, admonition, instruction and encouragement, as it may be needed."[1]

This Paraclete is the Spirit of truth. In addition to the word which Christ left to the disciples they shall also have the Spirit Himself, the Spirit of grace, of faith, of adoption, of prayer, of love, of holiness, power and glory. In the midst of the discomfort which the Lord's departure causes to the disciples, there comes this blessed assurance to them that this other Comforter shall abide with them, yea, in them forever; of course not in the sense of a gift that could under no circumstances be lost. However great and precious a privilege it was to have the Lord as personal

---

[1] The German word "Tröster" which is used in Luther's version for "Comforter," in its ancient meaning corresponds very closely to the Greek "paracletos." It is related to "trauen" (trust) and means a protector on whom we may rely. The same meaning is attached to the English term "Comforter," as first used by Wicliff in his version of the Bible. The "Comforter" in the language of ancient English law is one who gives support or assistance.

friend and counsellor during His life on earth, it is a greater gift that henceforth the disciples were to have the Paraclete in their own hearts. Thus they will truly become Christian characters, ripened into full Christian manhood.

This possession of the "Paraclete" is the characteristic mark of the disciples over against the world, which cannot receive Him and does not behold nor know Him. As it would not receive the Logos (John 1:10, 11), it will have nothing to do with this "other Paraclete." It will not look to Him for light, advice or assistance. It looks away from Him, having its eyes fixed upon the visible, tangible things of God's creation, and ignoring the heavenly, invisible gifts and graces of God's redemption.

3. The Lord Coming with the Father (14:18–21)

18–21. *I will not leave you desolate: I come unto you. Yet a little while, and the world beholdeth me no more; but ye behold me: because I live, ye shall live also. In that day ye shall know that I am in my Father, and ye in me, and I in you. He that hath my commandments, and keepeth them, he it is that loveth me: and he that loveth me shall be loved of my Father, and I will love him, and will manifest myself unto him.*

As the Lord had before addressed His beloved disciples as "little children" (13:33), He now describes their condition after His departure as that of desolate orphans. And such indeed was their state between the passion and the resurrection of Christ. Though lasting only "a little while," it was a perfect abyss of despondency through which they had to pass in those hours. But here are His promises: "I come unto you. Ye behold Me. I live." Their fulfilment began with the re-appearance of the risen Lord on Easter-day, and culminated, for the Apostles in their lifetime, on the day of Pentecost. But the coming of the Lord and the coming of the promised Paraclete are not absolutely identical. It must never be forgotten that in distinction from the presence of the Spirit the glorified Christ is still true man, with a full human nature, including even a human body, which shares in His divine glory. It is the one, undivided Christ, in His state of glory, that promises to come to, and to be with His disciples.

IV. THE PARTING WORDS CONTINUED (14:12–31)

When He shows Himself as the living One to His desolate disciples, when He brings His peace from the tomb, their hearts are filled with joy, their doubt and unbelief is ended, they begin to live in a new and heavenly sense of that word. And when on the day of Pentecost they are all filled with the Holy Ghost, they realize what it is to live through Christ, in Christ, for Christ. The reality and fullness of this new life is unfolded before our eyes in the Book of Acts. Compare those men, as we know them from the narrative of the Acts since the day of Pentecost, with their attitude in the history of the Gospels. Truly, those men, their words and discourses, their acts and lives, have become immortal through the living Christ, whom they witnessed. Their names are written on the walls of the heavenly Jerusalem (Revelation 21:14). They are live men through their living Saviour.

In that day the disciples shall gain that true insight into the relation between the Father and the Son and between the Son and themselves: "I in My Father. Ye in Me. I in you." For this is life eternal that they should know the only true God and Him whom He did send, even Jesus Christ (John 17:3).

4. To whom will He manifest Himself? (14:22–24)

22–24. Judas (not Iscariot) saith unto him, Lord, what is come to pass that thou wilt manifest thyself unto us, and not unto the world? Jesus answered and said unto him, If a man love me, he will keep my word: and my Father will love him, and we will come unto him, and make our abode with him. He that loveth me not keepeth not my words: and the word which ye hear is not mine, but the Father's who sent me.

Another interruption or interpellation on the part of the disciples, this time by Judas Lebbæus or Thaddæus. With undisguised naïve astonishment he asks: "What in the world has happened, that Thou wilt manifest Thyself unto us and not unto the world?" He is evidently not conscious of the sharp contrast between the spirit of the world and the spirit of Christ's disciples. So far from judging the world for its alienation from God, he shows a certain humility in his amazement that the disciples should be so much nearer to the Lord than the world. But there is yet another side to this question of Judas. It reminds us somewhat of the demand of Christ's unbelieving brothers that He should manifest Himself to the world (John 7:4). The difficult problem before the eyes of Judas is this: Shall the manifestation of Christ be confined to the small circle of disciples, and shall the world be shut out from it? What, then, becomes of the Messianic kingdom in this world? "What sort of a king is He to be, who will show Himself to no one and will manage His kingdom in such a mysterious, secret way, that no one shall see Him or know Him, except the few who love Him?" (Luther).

Over against this question and the spirit which underlies it, the Lord, without entering fully into it, simply emphasizes the internal, spiritual character of His revelation and of His kingdom. The mark of His disciples as over against the world, is their loving the Lord and keeping His word. And these are the souls in which the Father and the Son will take up their abode through the Pentecostal coming of the Spirit,—the full New Testament realization of the Old Testament Shekinah. "A true and glorious day of Pentecost and a powerful demonstration of the Spirit, a heavenly gathering or concilium in two directions: the hearts being enlightened and filled by the Holy Spirit with the love of Christ; and again the love of Christ and of the Father shining forth manifesting itself toward the believers" (Luther). This passage indeed sets forth the true idea and definition of the Church of Christ: the assembly of Saints and Believers, gathered around the word of Christ, who love the Lord, who are the beloved of the Father, and with whom the Triune God is dwelling, they themselves being temples of the Holy Ghost. It is therefore a most appropriate selection by which this passage (John 14:23–30) was taken for the Gospel of the day of Pentecost.

5. *The Teaching of the Holy Spirit* (14:25, 26)

25–26. *These things have I spoken unto you, while yet abiding with you. But the Comforter, even the Holy Spirit, whom the Father will send in my name, he shall teach you all things, and bring to your remembrance all that I said unto you.*

The Lord refers here again to His imminent departure. The time of those direct personal communications between Christ and His

IV. The Parting Words Continued (14:12–31)

disciples is now at an end. But their learning, studying and growing in knowledge is not ended. As the parting Lord gives them over to the instruction of the Paraclete, the Spirit of truth, now definitely called "the Holy Spirit," their knowledge of Christ's truth will be better developed and increased than during the days of their Master's visible presence. The Holy Spirit is to be sent by the Father in Christ's name, that is, not simply by His request, through His mediation, but in His place, to manifest and to glorify the Son. His work is to teach the disciples and to remind them of all that Christ said unto them. These two statements, describing the work of the Spirit, must not be separated from each other, much less be considered as in any way antithetical to each other. The Holy Spirit in teaching the disciples all things does not introduce absolutely new doctrines of which they never heard before. All His teachings are based upon Christ's. They are the development of the seed sown by Christ. The real character of the Spirit's teaching is to repeat, to freshen, to expand, to deepen the knowledge of truth received before in the words of the Master. "Nothing is to be taught" says Luther, "in the Christian Church by the Holy Spirit, but what the Apostles had heard from Christ." Most vigorously does he protest against the Romanist's claim, that their "traditions" contain a great deal of what the Holy Spirit had to teach after the Apostles' times, which they themselves had never known or taught.

6. The Peace of Jesus (14:27)

27. Peace I leave with you; my peace I give unto you: not as the world giveth, give I unto you. Let not your heart be troubled, neither let it be fearful.

Possibly after a short pause the Lord begins with this "Farewell," the salutation commonly used in the Orient to the present day on coming or going. The term is taken from the Old Testament "Shalom," which signifies not a subjective feeling of pleasure or happiness, but an objective state of health, a condition of absolute well-being (Isaiah 53:5). This peace is more fully characterized as Christ's peace: "My peace I give unto you." This is not simply a repetition, but an explanation. It is the peace which no one has to give but the Lord Jesus Christ, who has obtained it for us by His going to the Father. His whole salvation is included in this word (Acts 4:12). This gift is essentially different from the world's way of giving. Of course, *what* the Lord gives is not what the world gives. But here it is more the *how* the Lord gives, that differs from the world's giving. The world says: Peace! Peace! and yet there is no peace, for the wicked have no peace. But while the world in hollow phrases boasts of peace, Christ gives a heavenly reality, a peace that passeth all understanding. Holding first to this peace, the disciples' hearts must not be discouraged, though they may be disturbed for a time. The greatest disturbance awaited them within the next day in the passion and death of their Lord. And yet, out of the wreck of all their earthly, carnal aspirations, the "peace" of Christ was saved to them by the triumph of Easter-day.

7. *The Believers' Joy in Christ's Departure (14:28, 29)*

28–29. *Ye heard how I said unto you, I go away, and I come unto you. If ye loved me, ye would have rejoiced, because I go unto the Father: for the Father is greater than I. And now I have told you before it come to pass, that, when it is come to pass, ye may believe.*

Divine thoughts and human thoughts are the very reverse of each other. The disciples think that because they love Him they cannot but sorrow over His departure. The Lord thinks, if they love Him they must rejoice over it. For it means His going to the Father, from a state of humiliation and suffering to a state of exaltation, of glory. This is what He intends to say by the statement: "The Father is greater than I." There is no comparison in these words between the divinity of the Father and the human nature of the Son, but the Lord compares, as Calvin also explains, "His present state with the heavenly glory" to which He is going. Before going to the Father He was, as Luther says, "a poor, miserable, suffering Christ, but now with the Father He is a great, glorious, living and almighty Lord over all creatures."

IV. THE PARTING WORDS CONTINUED (14:12–31)

8. Jesus and the Prince of the World (14:30, 31)

30–31. *I will no more speak much with you, for the prince of the world cometh: and he hath nothing in me; but that the world may know that I love the Father, and as the Father gave me commandment, even so I do. Arise, let us go hence.*

Satan is the Prince of the World (sometimes even called the God of this world), not *de jure* (of right), but *de facto* (as a matter of fact). In the unlimited self-reliance of this position he comes to try his power even against the Holy One of Israel. He attacks Him in the dark hours of His passion, not only through those men who acted as his tools, but in that mysterious personal conflict (Luke 22:53), which took place in Christ's agony in the garden before any of His captors laid their hands on Him (Heb. 2:14, 18). But though the enemy may attack and molest Him he will gain nothing. He has no hold on Him; there is no sin, no weakness that would give him any claim on Christ. Of this the Lord is fully conscious, and by this thought He encourages and strengthens Himself against the Prince of darkness. Though it might look as if He was, for a time, helplessly overpowered by the Evil One, still in this very conflict the world shall find the greatest demonstration of Christ's love to the Father and His faithfulness in carrying out the Father's commission. It is not through the overwhelming attack of the enemy that He is forced into His passion, but it is His loving obedience to the Father that leads Him to the cross and to the tomb.

JOHN 15

V. NEW PARTING DISCOURSE (CH. 15 AND 16)

1. The Vine and the Branches (15:1–8)

1–8. *I am the true vine, and my Father is the husbandman. Every branch in me that beareth not fruit, he taketh it away: and every branch that beareth fruit, he cleanseth it, that it may bear more fruit. Already ye are clean because of the word which I have spoken unto you. Abide in me, and I in you. As the branch cannot bear fruit of itself, except it abide in the vine: so neither can ye, except ye abide in me. I am the vine, ye are the branches: He that abideth in me, and I in him, the same beareth much fruit: for apart from me ye can do nothing. If a man abide not in me, he is cast forth as a branch, and is withered; and they gather them, and cast them into the fire, and they are burned. If ye abide in me, and my words abide in you, ask whatsoever ye will, and it shall be done unto you. Herein is my Father glorified, that ye bear much fruit; and so shall ye be my disciples.*

After the concluding words of the preceding chapter the question naturally presents itself as to the circumstances and surroundings under which the words contained in chapters 15 to 17 were spoken. After the positive order, given by Christ: "Arise, let us go hence," we cannot doubt that the disciples did arise, ready to start with their Lord for any place of destination to which He might lead them. The most common explanation ever since the time of Chrysostom is, that at that point the Lord left the upper room, where He had spent the evening, to go to Gethsemane, and that the following discourses were spoken on the road to the garden, or at a quiet, secluded spot on the slope from the eastern wall of the city to the valley of the Kidron. Some interpreters even go so far as to suggest, that, "stopping on the way before a vine covered with branches," the Lord took up the theme of the parable of the vine. But we find it extremely difficult to think of a place quiet enough for the following discourses, and particularly for the sacerdotal prayer, on the road through the city to Gethsemane; especially if we remember that during this pass-over-week all Jerusalem, including its immediate neighborhood, was crowded with

V. New Parting Discourse (Ch. 15 and 16)

pilgrims from all parts of the country. We are therefore more inclined to picture the scene, following the fourteenth chapter, in this manner: that the disciples, after rising from the table, remained standing, grouped around their Master in that upper room, and that then and there the words in ch. 15 to 17 were spoken.

The contrast between the opening of the fifteenth chapter and the conclusion of the fourteenth is quite striking. After the reference to "the old bitter foe" lurking in the darkness ready to assault the Lord, this peaceful picture of the vineyard and the quiet work of the husbandman on the branches of the vine! We need not look around for any outward objects suggesting the fruitful theme of this parable. The Lord's Supper, with its cup of blessing, which had just been instituted, would indeed have been suggestion enough. But even apart from this, the figure of the vine was perfectly familiar to the Israelites, not only because the vine was one of the chief products of their country, but because the Old Testament scriptures repeatedly use the vineyard with its work and its fruit as an illustration of the Israelitic theocracy (Psalm 80:9 ff.; Isaiah 5:1ff.; Jeremiah 2:21; Ezekiel 19:10).[1] And now, at the very time when His judgment was ready to fall upon His Old Testament vineyard, God makes a new beginning, in choosing and preparing this vine of the New Testament by whose fruitful branches He is to be better praised and glorified than by the sour grapes of the former dispensation.

The Father the husbandman, the Lord Jesus the true vine, the disciples the branches,—these are the leading points of the parable. The Father plants this vine in His own vineyard, giving His only-begotten Son into this world, making Him the life and salvation of a lost race through His passion, death and resurrection; giving to the Son those that are to believe in Him, and watching over their growth and development as living, fruitful branches. The Son, as the true vine, stands between the husbandman and the branches. He belongs to both, as the vine planted

---

[1] At the benediction of the first cup of the Passover the Israelites offered the following prayers: "Blessed art Thou, Lord God, the King of the World, who hast created the fruit of the vine." And "Blessed art Thou, Lord God, the King of the World, who has chosen us above every nation."

by the husbandman and as the vine on which the branches grow. It is impossible for the husbandman to have branches that will bear fruit for His honor and glory, without having that particular vine planted for that purpose; that is, speaking without figure, it is only through the incarnation and the redemption wrought by the Son, that the Father will have a kingdom, accomplishing the salvation of immortal souls. The relation of the branches to the vine is not the outcome of a natural process, such as our natural birth. It is the result of our being engrafted into Christ through baptism for a real, personal life-union.

Thus this parable of the true vine contains the whole secret of true Christianity. It is far more than having Christ for a teacher or example, more even than having Him for our Mediator and Highpriest; it is life from Him, through Him, with Him and in Him, as Paul says (Gal. 2:20): "I live, and yet no longer I, but Christ liveth in me."

The detailed accounts concerning the relation of the branches to the vine and their development, are full of solemn warning, admonition and encouragement to the disciples. The fate of the unfruitful branches is pictured with terrible clearness: "taken away (ver. 2), cast forth, withered, gathered, cast into the fire, burned" (ver. 6). A judgment, beginning already in this life and extending into eternity, reminding us strongly of the preaching of John the Baptist: "Every tree that bringeth not forth good fruit is hewn down and cast into the fire" (Matt. 3:10). To avoid this the branches must be subject to the pruning discipline of the husbandman. It is either αἴρειν or καθαίρειν; either the things that are evil must be taken away, and thus the branches cleaned, or we ourselves will be cut off. On the other hand, those branches that begin to bear fruit have the promise of being watched over and constantly improved by the pruning, purifying discipline of the Father. In this the Son also has His share, for it is through Christ's word that the disciples are being cleaned. With His words abiding in them and the open access to the throne of grace through Him, the disciples will be kept as such in the spirit of true discipleship, bringing forth much fruit to the honor and praise of the Father.

V. New Parting Discourse (Ch. 15 and 16)

2. Abiding in His Love by Keeping His Commandments (15:9–17)

9–17. *Even as the Father hath loved me, I also have loved you: abide ye in my love. If ye keep my commandments, ye shall abide in my love; even as I have kept my Father's commandments, and abide in his love. These things have I spoken unto you, that my joy may be in you, and that your joy may be fulfilled. This is my commandment, that ye love one another, even as I have loved you. Greater love hath no man than this, that a man lay down his life for his friends. Ye are my friends, if ye do the things which I command you. No longer do I call you servants; for the servant knoweth not what his lord doeth: but I have called you friends; for all things that I heard from my Father I have made known unto you. Ye did not choose me, but I chose you, and appointed you, that ye should go and bear fruit, and that your fruit should abide: that whatsoever ye shall ask of the Father in my name, he may give it you. These things I command you, that ye may love one another.*

The life-union between the vine and the branches is substantially a union of love. It is true, this love makes its demands upon the disciples and must be evidenced by keeping His commandments, but it is not, in the first place, the result of an outward, legal commandment. It springs from that unspeakable gift of love which the disciples have received in Christ: "I have loved you." Here is the beginning of this loving union between Christ and His own, as between the vine and the branches. And with what manner of love has He loved them! "Even as the Father hath loved Me." Here is the true head-spring of all love, the love existing from eternity between the Father and the Son. All the love between Christ and His own is simply the outcome of the Father's love to Him and in Him; the flowing over of that divine love upon men, who thus receive a taste of the loving communion between the Father and the Son, and become aware that they owe their life and salvation to this love which brought the everlasting Son into this world of sin and death.

To abide in this loving union with Christ, the disciples must needs keep His commandments. A great deal is included in this comprehensive term *"my love:"* His love to us; our love to Him; our love to the brethren which binds us together in spiritual union with our fellow-believers. The keeping of His commandments in this connection certainly has nothing of a legalistic bondage in it. There is an inspiring parallelism and example to it, when the Lord says: "Even as I have kept My Father's commandments and abide in His love." The love of the Father has moved the Son to undertake the work of redemption. "Lo, I come: I delight to do Thy will" (Psalm 40:7, 8). Down to the very end of His earthly life, through all the details of His life, passion and death, Christ has this unbroken testimony with Him of an absolute, loving, faithful submission to the will of the Father. (See the opening of John's account of the passion, of Christ at the beginning of chapter 13, and especially the agony in the garden of Gethsemane with the prayer: "Thy will be done.") Thus also the love of the disciples to Christ is to be demonstrated and preserved in a similar manner by keeping His commandments.

With the love of Christ also the joy of Christ will be the blessed inheritance of the disciples. "These things have I spoken unto you, that *My joy* may be in you and that your joy may be fulfilled." This means neither His joy in them or over them, nor their rejoicing in Him, but it refers to that quiet, holy, inward cheerfulness, which characterized Christ during the years of His life on earth. Though we have no record of special manifestations of great outward joy, but rather the distinct testimony, that the Lord wept, at least, on three different occasions, still the picture of Christ's life on earth, as drawn by the Evangelist, gives us the impression, that through all the conflicts of His life He was full of a heavenly peace and joy, of which the world had no conception. This joy of His sprung from His consciousness of the love of God, His unity with the Father, and it does not leave Him even now on the way to the cross. Such heavenly joy is to pass over to the disciples, so that they may, in this respect, be like their Master, and enjoy a perfect, heavenly peace, surpassing all the happiness they may have had before.

Christ Himself is the headspring and the example of every good and perfect thing which His disciples are to have. Their joy is to be like His joy; their love is to be like His love. In order to give His disciples an approximate idea of that love from which their own brotherly love is to draw its inspiration, the Lord condescends to a truly human comparison: "Greater love hath no man than this, that a man lay down his life for his

V. New Parting Discourse (Ch. 15 and 16)

friends." These words are, in this connection, not meant to bring out the full purpose and meaning of His death, as an atonement for the sins of the world. We know that Christ died not only for these, His friends. "He is the propitiation not for our sins only, but for the sins of the whole world" (1 John 2:2). And "God commendeth His love toward us, in that, while we were yet sinners, Christ died for us" (Rom. 5:6–8). But in speaking of the sacrifice of His life the Lord here simply describes His unbounded devotion to those beloved ones, whom He honored with His love and friendship then and there. Of course, the general character and bearing of Christ's love, as manifested in His atoning death, must at once be recognized, when the question is raised: "How is it that these weak, erring, sinful men ever became the 'friends' of the Holy One of Israel?" We answer, with Luther: "Formerly they were His enemies, but now they are friends, simply because He counts them as such. Not that they had done Him any good, but He is doing them all the good He can. For such 'friends' He layeth down His life, who never did Him any good; but He loved them and made them friends."

While the Lord insists that, in order to abide in His friendship, the disciples must "do the things which I command you," He nevertheless strongly emphasizes the honor of the title "friend" over against the title and position of "servant." "Ye are My friends,—no longer do I call you servants." Abraham, the father of believers, enjoyed this high honor of being called the friend of God (Jas. 2:23). Once before the Lord had, indeed, called the disciples "friends" (Luke 12:4), but not with that clearly defined distinction from "servants," as in this passage. And certainly in the narrative of the Synoptical Gospels the disciples appear throughout in the attitude of servants. But now, in these last discourses, when they are drawn so closely to the heart of their departing Master, they are honored with the position of "friends." The fact that the fullest and most confidential communications are passed from person to person, is everywhere among men recognized as an evidence of close friendship. The same is here mentioned by the Lord to prove the intimate relation into which He has admitted the disciples. "I have called you friends; for all things that I heard from My Father, I have made known unto you."

They are to have a full insight into God's plan of redemption. It is, of course, one thing, and the first thing, that the Lord should communicate to the disciples those things which He has heard from the Father. But it is another thing, and also essential to the continuation of that honored and privileged position of friends, that the disciples must show an interest in these revelations, and strive to penetrate into an ever fuller and deeper understanding of God's mysteries. The statement that the Lord made known to the disciples all things that He heard from His Father is not in conflict with what we read in chapter 16:12: "I have yet many things to say unto you, but ye cannot bear them now." His communications to them were necessarily all along conditioned by their capacity to grasp them; and a most important part of these communications is the doctrine, that the Paraclete will come to take the Lord's place and to guide them into all truth.

Having thus magnified the privileged position of His disciples, the Lord adds another statement which will have the effect to keep them humble, by reminding them of the origin of their relation as friends. There is no equality here, and reciprocity as in the usual relations of human friendship. The distance is too great between the disciples and their "friend" whom they more and more learn to recognize as their Lord and their God. The initiative in forming this friendship-relation is altogether with Christ. They did not choose Him but He chose them. How vividly did John remember all the details of that first call! (See the personal reminiscences contained in John 1:37–41) The choosing of the Twelve which the Lord here so strongly emphasizes as His own act and decision, was a very solemn and important event in His life. "He went out into the mountain to pray; and He continued all night in prayer to God; and when it was day, He called His disciples" (Luke 6:12, 13). And how much patience, condescension, compassion and intercession was needed through those three years of His public ministry, to keep them from falling away, to hold them steadfast in their relation as friends!

Having chosen them, the Lord "appointed them that they should go and bear fruit and that their fruit should abide." They must "*go.*" Thus far they stayed with Him and clung to Him, as their friend, instructor and

V. New Parting Discourse (Ch. 15 and 16)

rector, whose eyes were constantly upon them, and to whom they could look for advice and oversight. But now the time is coming when they themselves must go. They must face a hostile world. They must stand up in mature manhood and fight their own battles. They go forth, no longer servants, who receive their order from day to day, from hour to hour, but friends, who understand their friend at the right hand of the Father. Of course this new position of manly responsibility is not one of loose and unbounded independence and subjectivism. They go, but they keep close to His word and Spirit, thus abiding in His truth.

Thus going they shall *bear fruit*. Their lifework is not to be the doing of certain outward things, mechanically, here a little, there a little after an atomistic fashion; it is *bearing fruit*: there is to be a coherent, organic growth on the tree of their Christian character, a unit of unbroken development.

And the fruit which they bear shall *abide*. There is eternity in this word. Whatever influence may have been gained by prominent men in the history of the world, lasting possibly through many centuries, as in the case of the ancient greek poets and philosophers, all this dwindles into nothing before this word of Christ: "fruit that shall abide." It abideth not only after they are gone, or after their generation is gone, but after this present world is gone. It is fruit following them into eternity and abiding there for ever and ever! However lowly his outward position in this world may be, every Christian that is faithfully working out his salvation with fear and trembling, and conscientiously doing his duty towards God's kingdom, is bearing fruit for eternity.

3. The World's Hatred against the Disciples (15:18–25)

18–25. *If the world hateth you, ye know that it hath hated me before it hated you. If ye were of the world, the world would love its own: but because ye are not of the world, but I chose you out of the world, therefore the world hateth you. Remember the word that I said unto you, A servant is not greater than his lord. If they persecuted me, they will also persecute you; if they kept my word, they will keep yours also. But all these things will they do unto you for my name's sake, because they know not him that sent me. If I had not come and spoken unto them, they had not had sin: but now they have no excuse for their sin. He that hateth me hateth my Father also. If I had not done among them the works which none other did, they had not had sin: but now have they both seen and hated both me and my Father. But this cometh to pass, that the word may be fulfilled that is written in their law, They hated me without a cause*

In the preceding verses the Lord has drawn a picture of the wondrous love which has its heavenly and everlasting source in the union between the Father and the Son, which is revealed on earth through the Son, which is reflected in the disciples: the Father loves the Son; the Son loves the disciples, whom the Father has given Him; the disciples recognize the Father's love through the Son. But there is a strange and unexpected antithesis to this manifestation of love. These beloved disciples are hated by the world. In them Christ is hated by the world, and in Christ the Father; a continuous revelation of hatred from below, over against the revelation of love from above. The Lord must speak to the disciples most fully and directly of this hatred of the world, in order to guard them against taking offence in this unexpected experience that awaits them. They are to be forewarned and forearmed. They must not look upon it "as though a strange thing happened unto them" (1 Peter 4:12). The fact that Christ's own people are hated by the world, must not be a discouragement for the disciples, but rather the reverse: it proves that they are not of the world, but of Christ.

It would indeed be a bad sign for the disciples if the world should not hate them. For in this case the world would recognize "its own" in them, and this worldly spirit would be agreeable and lovable to the world. We find in this term an indication of that deep-seated egotism of the world, which, even where it seems to love, does not really and truly love the person, but only its own principles, its anti-godly, anti-christian spirit. Herod and Pilate may recognize and love in each other the common aversion and opposition to God's kingdom, they may thus for a while be united against Christ, but at the bottom of their heart they are bitterly opposed to each other, they hate each other personally.

The Lord is very careful in defining the reason why the disciples will be hated by the world. It is because they are not of the world, because

V. New Parting Discourse (Ch. 15 and 16)

He has chosen them out of the world. This principle must be most conscientiously applied to individual cases. Wherever Christians meet with the enmity and hatred of the world, they must carefully examine themselves, whether it is not through their own faults, sins and shortcomings that the animosity and hostility of the world is drawn out against them. Certainly "the name of the Lord" and Christianity as such, should not be charged with what is due to their own personal perversity. Peter, by his own sad experience, had learned to draw this line of distinction very carefully. "Let none of you suffer as an evildoer—but if a man suffer as a Christian, let him not be ashamed; but let him glorify God in this name. Blessed are ye if ye are reproached for the name of Christ" (1 Peter 4:14–15). This blessed name, the open confession of Christ as the Son of the everlasting God and the Messiah, sent by His Father, must be the true and real cause of the world's enmity which they have to encounter.

The Lord reminds the disciples of His words, spoken before, that the servant is not greater than his Lord, nor the disciple above his Master. They will fare no better than He. And this very experience of the hatred of the world is part of the "perfecting" of the disciples in the likeness of their Master (Luke 6:40). It is certainly to the encouragement of the disciples that these words are spoken. As surely as the world recognizes in them the Master's likeness, so surely will they receive the very same treatment as Christ. If it persecuted Him, it will also persecute the disciples; if it kept His word, it will keep theirs also. But did the world ever keep His word? What is the evidence on this point as the disciples had it before their eyes? Did not the Lord Himself declare to His enemies: "Ye do not understand My speech even because ye cannot hear My word" (John 8:43). Must we then take this reference of Christ to the keeping of His word as a bitter irony, which meant to state the very opposite, namely a sharp complaint that the world, as world, never received and kept His word, and that the disciples must not expect anything better? Some commentators, however, still hold that these words of the Lord are to be taken in their direct, literal meaning, that after all there were some men in the midst of an unbelieving world, who did receive and keep His word, and that the disciples also might expect the same result from their preaching and teaching. While this is certainly true and fully borne out by the testimony of the Book of the Acts, we might still question whether this idea would, in this connection, be in its proper place.

With peculiar emphasis the Lord brings out the responsibility of the world for its refusal to receive His word. If He had not spoken,—if He had not done among them the things which none other did, they had not had sin; but now they are without excuse. The world cannot possibly plead ignorance. They know all about Jesus, who has testified before their ears again and again concerning His divine character and mission. But they hardened themselves against His testimony in the fixed determination not to yield to Him, not to accept His word; thus showing their opposition and hatred against Him and the Father who sent Him. And in addition to the testimony of His words there is that of His works, done among them, before their eyes, undeniable facts, which proved too strong even for their searching criticism, as in the case of the man that was born blind (John 9). But even this testimony is lost on them. What a monstrous conclusion, in conflict with logic and philosophy, as well as religion. They have seen His works and seen Him in those works, the exponent of the Father's love for our fallen and dying race, and—they hate both Him and the Father! This is that great "new sin," as Luther calls it, "the sin against His word" and testimony, for which there is absolutely no excuse.

But this very opposition is to be understood as a direct sign and evidence of Christ's Messianic character and position. It was all foreseen and foretold by the spirit of prophecy. The sixty-ninth Psalm, to which the Lord here refers, was commonly accepted as a Messianic psalm by the Jewish scholars in the days of our Lord. It is one of the psalms most frequently quoted in the New Testament, particularly in connection with the passion of the Lord. Being thus assured from the word of God, in the Old Testament, concerning the enmity of the world against the Messiah, the disciples are sufficiently fortified against the danger of taking offence in this experience. The hatred of the world appears in the light of God's word, as a testimony both for the Messiah and for His disciples: No true

V. NEW PARTING DISCOURSE (CH. 15 AND 16)

Christ without the hatred of the world; no true Christians without the hatred of the world.

JOHN 16

4. Jesus Sending the Spirit (15:26–16:15)

15:26–27. *But when the Comforter is come, whom I will send unto you from the Father, even the Spirit of truth, which proceedeth from the Father, he shall bear witness of me: and ye also bear witness, because ye have been with me from the beginning.*

16:1–15. *These things have I spoken unto you, that ye should not be made to stumble. They shall put you out of the synagogues: yea, the hour cometh, that whosoever killeth you shall think that he offereth service unto God. And these things will they do, because they have not known the Father, nor me. But these things have I spoken unto you, that when their hour is come, ye may remember them, how that I told you. And these things I said not unto you from the beginning, because I was with you. But now I go unto him that sent me; and none of you asketh me, Whither goest thou? But because I have spoken these things unto you, sorrow hath filled your heart. Nevertheless I tell you the truth; It is expedient for you that I go away: for if I go not away, the Comforter will not ome unto you; but if I go, I will send him unto you. And he, when he is come, will convict the world in respect of sin, and of righteousness, and of judgement: of sin, because they believe not on me; of righteousness, because I go to the Father, and ye behold me no more; of judgement, because the prince of this world hath been judged. I have yet many things to say unto you, but ye cannot bear them now. Howbeit when he, the Spirit of truth, is come, he shall guide you into all the truth: for he shall not speak from himself; but what things soever he shall hear, these shall he speak: and he shall declare unto you the things that are to come. He shall glorify me: for he shall take of mine, and shall declare it unto you. All things whatsoever the Father hath are mine: therefore said I, that he taketh of mine, and shall declare it unto you.*

The Lord Himself departing, and the hatred of the world impending, what could be more welcome to the disciples at this point than the renewed promise of the coming of the Paraclete (advocate,

V. New Parting Discourse (Ch. 15 and 16)

comforter) of whom the Son had spoken before? Two distinct statements are made concerning this "Spirit of Truth." First: The Lord "will send Him unto the disciples from the Father." Second: "He proceedeth from the Father." These two statements are not identical. The one is in the future tense, referring to the outpouring of the Spirit on the approaching day of Pentecost. The other is in the present tense, referring to the never-changing present of Eternity; the Spirit's relation to the Father being described as an everlasting proceeding from the Father. As the Father is included in the act of sending the Spirit on the day of Pentecost, the Son is not excluded in the everlasting "proceeding" of the Spirit. The Nicene creed rightly says of the Holy Spirit, "Who proceedeth from the Father and the Son," though there is no direct literal reference to the latter in the passage here before us.

The Holy Spirit shall "bear witness" of Christ,—another distinctly *personal* activity ascribed to Him. He is to be a witness of Christ in the first place to the apostles themselves. In the face of the hatred of the world, the disciples are to be strengthened and comforted by the Holy Spirit assuring them, that in spite of the hostility of the world, Jesus is the Christ, the Way and the Truth and the Life. It is through this influence of the Holy Spirit that the disciples themselves come to that full and clear understanding of Christ, and that bold and correct utterance, which makes them true witnesses of the crucified and risen Lord. By His inspiration their testimony is made sure and infallible. But there is a clear distinction between two kinds of testimony in these words of the Lord. The Spirit testifies, and the apostles testify. And they hold this position as witnesses even now, before the day of Pentecost. Before their preaching went forth into the world, before their epistles and gospels were written, the disciples were called and in some measure enabled to be the witnesses of the Lord. "That which we have heard, that which we have seen with our eyes, that which we beheld and our hands handled—declare we unto you" (1 John 1:1). "We were eye-witnesses of His majesty. We ourselves heard the voice come out of heaven, when we were with Him on the holy mount" (2 Peter 1:16–18). Two features then are beautifully and inseparably blending in the testimony of the apostles: the human factor and the

John 16

divine; their knowledge of Christ as eye-witnesses of His life, and their knowledge of Christ through the inspiration of the Holy Ghost. As mere men the apostles are credible witnesses, being plain, honest, conscientious men, who simply report what they have seen and heard. And as the inspired organs of the Holy Spirit they have a right to insist that their message be accepted "not as the word of men, but as it is in truth, the word of God" (1 Thess. 2:13).

16:1. The aim of the Lord in all these statements is, that the disciples should not be made to "stumble," when these violent persecutions which are here predicted, should fall upon them. It was indeed a terrible thought for the sincere and faithful Israelite, to be put out of the synagogue, as "the Jews had agreed already that if any man did confess that He was Christ, he should be put out of the synagogue" (John 9:22). This was the very thing that kept many of the chief rulers from confessing Him "lest they should be put out of the synagogue by the Pharisees" (John 12:42). But not only excommunication but proscription and death itself awaited them. And, worst of all, the fanaticism of their persecutors glories in these acts of violence against the Christians as a veritable "service unto God," though the Lord protests that they arise from not knowing the Father nor the Son.[1]

On former occasions the Lord had indeed already referred to such experiences of His disciples. See Matt. 5:10–12; 10:17–21 ff, 36; Luke 6:22; 12:11 ff. But the real principle of all these persecutions had never before been so fully declared, namely, the hatred of the world against God Himself.

In view of all these revelations it is no wonder that the hearts of the disciples should be filled with sorrow on account of the departure of

---

[1] Luther, the faithful and devoted child of the Mediaeval Church, tasted this bitter cup to the very dregs. His remark on this passage "they will sing a Te Deum laudamus over these things" proved to be an exact prophecy with regard to the massacre of St. Bartholomew, Aug. 24, 1572. When the news of this horror reached Rome, the Pope, attended by the Cardinals and other ecclesiastical dignitaries, went in long procession to the Church of St. Louis, where the Cardinal of Lorraine chanted a Te Deum. (See Henry White: The Massacre of St. Bartholomew, p. 466.)

V. New Parting Discourse (Ch. 15 and 16)

their Lord. But the full meaning, the aim and end of this departure (the "whither?") was not yet understood by them. And thus it could happen, that the very same words which for centuries have been an inexhaustible fountain of consolation and joy for thousands of believers, filled the hearers with sorrow when they were first spoken. The disciples were overwhelmed with the Lord's going *away from them;* but His *going to the Father* was nothing to them. For this season the Lord emphasizes the "Whither?" They ought to enquire into the aim and end of His way, and they would find that His going to the Father means going to a state of exaltation, to heavenly glory.

The Lord then proceeds to unfold before the disciples the blessings resulting from His departure. "If I go not away the Comforter will not come unto you; but if I go I will send Him unto you." Only after the Lord has been glorified by His death and resurrection can the Spirit come (John 7:39). And only when they are deprived of the visible, bodily presence of the Lord will the apostles themselves be in a proper condition to receive the Holy Ghost and to be benefited by His great deepening work in their souls. Thus far outward, visible things and material conceptions of God's kingdom had engrossed their minds, but now they will become truly spiritual.

The work of the Paraclete will have two objects: the world and the hearts of the disciples. The world will be convicted by Him in respect of sin and of righteousness and of judgment. In whatever form and in whatever circles "the world" may be found, it will be thus, attacked, reproved, convicted by the testimony of the Spirit, whether it will submit to it by repentance and faith, or harden itself against it. Of *Sin* the world will be convicted, *"because they believe not on Christ."* This is indeed a new definition of sin, not recognized in the world. At the very best "the world" will count as sinful the things forbidden in the second table of the decalogue. The sphere of "believing" or not believing is generally regarded by the world as a matter of freedom and indifference, for which men ought not to be held morally responsible. But now, under this new testimony of the Holy Spirit, the refusal to accept Christ and to believe in Him is to be considered the one great culminating sin above all others.

All the sin of the world, however heinous the transgression of the divine law may be, can be overcome and wiped out, men can be delivered from its guilt, its power and condemnation through God's grace in Christ. But where Christ is refused, men will remain in their sin, in spite of the Gospel, and thus bring upon themselves everlasting ruin. Of *righteousness* the world is to be convicted *"because I go to the Father, and ye behold Me no more."* This also is a new and startling definition. We know what an important place the idea of "righteousness" held in the teaching of the Jewish doctors, and in the practice of the chief rulers, scribes and Pharisees, at the time of Christ's public life on earth. We also know how severely Christ condemned "the righteousness of the Pharisees and scribes" (Matt. 5:20; Matt. 6; Matt. 23; Luke 18:9). But now, to find out what righteousness is, the eyes of the world are directed to that same Christ, in whom they would not believe, whom they cast out and rejected, but who went to the Father, through the shame of the cross to the glory of resurrection and ascension. "The Holy and Righteous One whom the Jews denied, the Prince of Life whom they killed, was raised from the dead" (Acts 3:14, 15). Thus He was "justified in the Spirit" (1 Tim. 3:16), "declared to be the Son of God with power, according to the spirit of holiness, by the resurrection of the dead" (Rom. 1:4). Christ's going to the Father implies then, in the first place, His own personal vindication and justification, as the One who knew no sin, who did not suffer and die for His own sin. But He was made sin on our behalf, that we might become the righteousness of God in Him (2 Cor. 5:21). Our righteousness then is, to "believe on Him that raised Jesus our Lord from the dead, who was delivered up for our trespasses, and was raised for our justification" (Rom. 4:24, 25). Thus Christ's going to the Father establishes not only His own personal vindication, but at the same time our justification before God through faith in the crucified and risen Saviour. It is a righteousness not of works, but of faith, not of seeing, but of believing on Him who went to the Father through His passion, death and glorification. Of *judgment* the world is to be convicted by the Spirit of truth, *"because the prince of this world hath been judged."* In the passion and death of Jesus Christ there was indeed an act of judgment passed before the eyes of the world. Jesus of

V. New Parting Discourse (Ch. 15 and 16)

Nazareth seemed to be judged and cast out as a criminal, even as the great Plato divined in his famous description of the treatment of the "righteous" one, if he should ever appear in this world.[1] But in reality it is not Christ, the Prince of Life, who is judged, but the Prince of this world. His power is broken. The serpent's head is bruised. His cause is lost. With him the world is doomed. The final and eternal judgment awaits it, and every one will fall under it who does not find delivery from his sin in the righteousness of Christ.

Besides this work of convicting the world of sin, righteousness and judgment, the Paraclete finds a great deal to do in the hearts of the believing disciples: He shall guide them into all truth, He shall glorify Christ in their hearts. There are yet many things the Lord has to say to the disciples, but they cannot bear them now. From different sides the enemies of truth have tried to shield themselves behind these words. Here the Romanists seek to establish the authority of their innumerable traditions, decrees and decisions set up by their councils and the "infallible" bishop of Rome. But if those things are the truth that were taught in the councils of the mediaeval church, "Then," says Luther, "the apostles have never come into possession of the full truth." On the other hand, modern Rationalism has claimed this passage in favor of what it calls "a progressive Christianity." The gospel of Christ, with the plain facts of the Apostles' Creed, it is said, must be developed into the "gospel of the Spirit," meaning thereby the spirit of the time, to which, one after another, the old truths are to be sacrificed, leaving nothing but a sort of molluscous Christianity, without the strong backbone of the great Gospel-facts.

---

[1] Plato, De republ. II., 361 ff. in a passage which has often been quoted by ancient and modern writers on evidences of Christianity, says: "First of all he must be deprived of his good name,—next, of all his possessions, except righteousness; he must be brought into conflict with his rulers, so that he is actually treated as the most unrighteous, though he has done nothing unrighteous whatsoever. Such a righteous one would be bound, scourged and his eyes put out, and having endured all these tortures, he would be nailed to the pole, so that it would be manifest that he was anxious not to appear as righteous, but to be so in reality."

Over against such views we hold that the Spirit did *"guide the disciples into all truth"* and that this word of our Lord assures to us both the credibility and the sufficiency of the apostolic testimony in the canon of the New Testament. Moreover the Lord lays down the standard, by which whatever claims to be the Spirit's witnessing must be tested: *"He shall not speak of Himself; He shall take of Mine; He shall glorify Me."* Even as the Son Himself did not speak of His own, but revealed what He had from the Father, so the Spirit continues that same revelation of the Father and the Son. And as the Spirit is a spirit of prophecy, it is naturally His province to *"declare the things that are to come."* Though the Lord Himself, especially in His eschatological discourses (Matt. 24 and 25) had dwelt on the last things, still there were many points concerning the consummation of Christ's kingdom, which were to be fully brought out by the Apostles, as taught by the Holy Spirit. (See 1 Thess. 4:13; 2 Thess. 2:1–12; Rom. 11:25, 26; 1 Cor. 15:50; 2 Peter 3:10 and the Book of Revelation.) The passage closes with one of the most direct and comprehensive testimonies as to the divinity of Christ and His co-equality with the Father, whose throne and whose glory belong likewise to the Son, in whom dwelleth all the fulness of the Godhead bodily (Col. 2:9). Nothingness than this is contained in this statement: *"All things, whatsoever the Father hath, are mine."*

5. Last Words to the Disciples (16:16–33)

16–33. *A little while, and ye behold me no more; and again a little while, and ye shall see me. Some of his disciples therefore said one to another, What is this that he saith unto us, A little while, and ye behold me not; and again a little while, and ye shall see me: and, Because I go to the Father? They said therefore, What is this that he saith, A little while? We know not what he saith. Jesus perceived that they were desirous to ask him, and he said unto them, Do ye inquire among yourselves concerning this, that I said, A little while, and ye behold me not, and again a little while, and ye shall see me? Verily, verily, I say unto you, that ye shall weep and lament, but the world shall rejoice: ye shall be sorrowful, but your sorrow shall be turned into joy. A woman when she is in travail hath sorrow, because her hour is come: but when she is delivered of the child, she remembereth no more the anguish, for the joy that a man is born into the world. And ye therefore now have sorrow:*

V. New Parting Discourse (Ch. 15 and 16)

but I will see you again, and your heart shall rejoice, and your joy no one taketh away from you. And in that day ye shall ask me nothing. Verily, verily, I say unto you, If ye shall ask anything of the Father, he will give it you in my name. Hitherto have ye asked nothing in my name: ask, and ye shall receive, that your joy may be fulfilled.

These things have I spoken unto you in proverbs: the hour cometh, when I shall no more speak unto you in proverbs, but shall tell you plainly of the Father. In that day ye shall ask in my name: and I say not unto you, that I will pray the Father for you; for the Father himself loveth you, because ye have loved me, and have believed that I came forth from the Father, I came out from the Father, and am come into the world: again, I leave the world, and go unto the Father. His disciples say, Lo, now speakest thou plainly, and speakest no proverb. Now know we that thou knowest all things, and needest not that any man should ask thee: by this we believe that thou earnest forth from God. Jesus answered them, Do ye now believe? Behold, the hour cometh, yea, is come, that ye shall be scattered, every man to his own, and shall leave me alone: and *yet* I am not alone, because the Father is with me. These things have I spoken unto you, that in me ye may have peace. In the world ye have tribulation: but be of good cheer; I have overcome the world.

The first question in the consideration of this passage is, what is implied in the promise of Christ to the disciples: "Ye shall see Me?" Is it His return after His resurrection? or His coming through the Paraclete on Pentecost? or His second Advent to judge the quick and the dead? or are we to combine all these three dates, in order to do full justice to this promise of the Lord? There can hardly be any doubt that with the words: "A little while and ye behold Me no more" the Lord refers to His imminent death. And consequently it seems most natural and in keeping with the context to think of the re-appearance of the risen Lord when He says: "And again a little while and ye shall see Me." The "little while" before His departure and "the little while" between His departure and His re-appearance would thus be most evenly balanced.

These words of the Lord, however, were evidently a great mystery to the disciples. Their perplexity is graphically described in verses 17, 18, culminating in the confession: "We know not what He saith." Most tenderly does the Lord meet them in their difficulty by repeating the very question that agitates their hearts. And yet in the following argument He does not really and fully enter upon an explanation of the "little while," but He gives them a graphic description of the wonderful change which those two experiences represent: first not beholding Him, and then seeing Him again. It is a change from weeping and lamenting, in sorrow over the beloved dead, into joy. The antagonism between the disciples and the world which has before been described in the hatred and persecution of the disciples, is once more manifested in this connection: The world rejoicing and the disciples sorrowful, and *vice versa*. These two different impressions and experiences on the part of the world and the disciples are not simply simultaneous in time, but they are based on one and the same fact. The very same thing that makes the world rejoice, makes the disciples lament: The departure of the Lord, His death and disappearance. Not to see Christ, is the joy of the world and the sorrow of the disciples. The world is glad that He is dead and buried out of sight. But on Easter morning the scales are turned. The empty tomb becomes the joy of the disciples, and the terror of the world.

Again: the great change from sorrow into joy is not simply a new and opposite experience following the first one. There is the closest connection between the sorrow that precedes and the joy that follows. It is not only one *after* another, but one *out of* the other. Their sorrow itself shall be turned into joy—"as the water was turned into wine," says Bengel, so that the very thing that was first the cause of sorrow and lamentation, shall be recognized by them as a wonderful source of joy and happiness. When the disciples shall have learned to understand the full meaning of the cross of Christ, the very passion and death of the Lord will be to them the object of boundless joy and glorying (Gal. 6:14). "Worthy is the Lamb that hath been slain to receive the power, and riches, and wisdom, and might, and honour, and glory, and blessing" (Rev. 5:12).

The most realistic illustration not only of this sudden transition from sorrow to joy, but of the fact that the woe itself is turned into joy, is given in the figure of the woman in travail. Out of the hour of anguish,

V. New Parting Discourse (Ch. 15 and 16)

peril and pain comes the great joy, "that a man is born into the world." Though with these words the Lord meant to illustrate the experience of the disciples only, there is a striking parallelism between His own experience and theirs from Good Friday to Easter morning. The very agony through which He passed in the garden of Gethsemane and on the cross of Calvary when His hour had come, brought into life that glorious victory of Easter morning, by which He triumphed over sin, death and the devil. Thus the Lord's own anguish was turned into joy. But the real and direct application of this figure is to the disciples. To them those dark hours of the passion of their Lord, brought the most terrible experience of their life. Never before were the apostles so overwhelmed with the consciousness of their unworthiness, never before did they suffer such bitter pangs of despair and of judgment over their sin, as in the night when the Lord was betrayed, when they all forsook Him, when Peter denied Him. And never was the healing, quickening grace of their Lord and Saviour greater before their eyes, than when He met them with the Easter-greeting of forgiveness and reconciliation: Peace be with you! Out of that deep sorrow of repentance came that grateful, joyful faith, which grasped the risen Saviour, and found in Him, who had been delivered up for their sins, a full and abiding justification, the very righteousness of God (Rom. 4:25; 2 Cor. 5:21).

    This great change from sorrow to joy is altogether due to the Lord. He takes the initiative: *"I will see you again."* His promise had been that in Galilee He would appear again to His disciples and gather anew His scattered flock. But after the great victory is won, the good Shepherd cannot wait so long. He looks after His distressed disciples[1] on the very day of His resurrection, in the City of Jerusalem. And the joy He brings them is of a twofold character. It is a joy for their *hearts* and it is an *imperishable* joy which no one taketh away from them. This cannot be said of any of the so-called joys of the world. They leave the very centre of the human personality, the heart, unhappy and dissatisfied. But the disciples have the promise, that their heart shall rejoice and that it shall be a lasting

---

[1] Remember also the saving look Christ gave to Peter after his denial (Luke 22:61).

joy in an "inheritance incorruptible and undefined and that fadeth not away," "a joy unspeakable and full of glory" (1 Pet. 1:4, 6, 8). There is a special comfort and encouragement in this assurance of the Lord. With the antagonism existing between the disciples and the world, they must be prepared to have their joy meet with the interference and opposition of the world. It is an offence to the world and if it only could, the world would fain rob them of their joy. But no one shall take it away from them.

Two important features are mentioned by the Lord as characteristics of that perfect joy which He promises to His disciples. In the first place: a clear insight into the whole plan of salvation, as it will be understood by them in the light of Christ's resurrection, making it unnecessary for them to ask any more of such questions as they had hitherto been addressing to the Lord. And then: an open access to the throne of the Father, in the name of the Son, that is, such privileges in their prayers as the beloved children, as they have never enjoyed before. This latter point is introduced by the Lord in that solemn "Verily, Verily" (ver. 23) which always indicates a matter of particularly grave importance or of special difficulty for the understanding of the disciples. There had, indeed, been no lack of references to prayer in the teachings of the Lord up to this point. From the very beginning of His public utterances the Lord had dwelt on the necessity and the blessings of prayer and the assurance of an answer from the heavenly Father. The Sermon on the Mount already contains the model prayer for the disciples, "the Lord's Prayer" (Matt. 6:9–13), as well as those positive and direct promises: Every one that asketh, receiveth; and he that seeketh findeth; and to him that knocketh it shall be opened (Matt. 7:7–9). New features are added to these in Luke 11:1–13; Luke 18:1–8; Matt. 18:19; 21:22, and in a number of passages in these last discourses, John 14:13, 14; 15:7, 16. But at this point we have the culmination of all the former statements of the Lord concerning the prayers of His disciples. He tells them plainly that hitherto they have "asked nothing in His name." Their prayers up to this point, at their very best, were like the prayers of the Old Testament Saints. But a higher stage is to be reached: Praying in the name of Jesus. Through the passion, death and resurrection of the Lord the full and free access has been opened to

V. New Parting Discourse (Ch. 15 and 16)

the Father's throne. Now begins the true New Testament kind of prayer. The work of reconciliation must be completed, the spirit must be given, before there can be truly a prayer in the name of Jesus, the prayer of a reconciled child of God, assured of the Father's love, a prayer addressed to God as the Father, in the name of His only begotten Son, our only Mediator. The New Testament Church has most beautifully and appropriately established the rule to close all her prayers, particularly those precious and comprehensive collects, with the expressed and distinct appeal to the Lord: "through Jesus Christ, Thy Son, our Lord." But beautiful and correct as this usage is, we know that the mere addition of these words will not make our prayer in reality a prayer in the name of Jesus. To be such in spirit and in truth it must be offered by a heart believing in the redemption of Christ, and filled with the spirit of Christ, having the same mind which was also in Jesus (Phil. 2:5) and which was manifested in His prayer in the garden. To such a prayer there is, in reality, no limitation or condition set by the Lord. "If ye shall ask *anything* of the Father He will give it you in My name." No wonder that to such a privilege of a praying child the promise is attached of a perfect and boundless gratification: "Ye shall receive, that your joy may be fulfilled." Any gift that had been earnestly desired, hoped for and asked for, brings joy to the heart of the recipient. And here is promised to the believing child of God the consummation of his deepest yearnings, his loftiest hopes and aspirations,—that is, a perfect joy and satisfaction.

As the Lord had, in the preceding words, spoken to the disciples of a new and higher stage in their prayerful communion with God, so He now (ver. 25) also holds out to them a higher stage with reference to His communication to them. Hitherto He spoke unto them "in *proverbs*," but the hour is coming, when He shall "tell them *plainly* of the Father." There is evidently here a distinction between a more indirect, obscure, primitive form of teaching, and one direct, full and plain, leading them into the very centre of God's revelation. In the former class we must include even these discourses to which the disciples had now been listening, and which contained so much that was yet dark and unintelligible to them. The second stage of communications will be reached after the resurrection of the Lord, and particularly with the day of Pentecost, when the Paraclete, the Spirit of truth, shall teach them all things and bring to their remembrance all that He said unto them (John 14:26). This higher stage of knowledge and the higher stage of prayer shall be simultaneous. The time when they shall know "plainly" of the Father will be the time when they shall speak directly to the Father: "I say not unto you, that I will pray the Father for you" (ver. 26). This seems somewhat strange and unexpected in the light of such passages as 1 John 2:1, Rom. 8:34, and Heb. 7:25, which represent Christ as the advocate of His people before the Father, who is at the right hand of God, who also maketh intercession for us, who is able to save to the uttermost them that draw near unto God through Him, seeing He ever liveth to make intercession for them. And certainly there are times and conditions when the disciples in the future also will need the intercession of Christ's mediatorial prayers. But when they approach the Father in the name of the Son, as reconciled and beloved children, they have Christ already on their side and in their very prayers, being assured of the Father's love through Him. Surely these are "great and wonderful things, that we are to be like Christ and His brothers and the Father's own dear children, beloved by Him for Christ's sake" (Luther).

Such a state, however, can only be thought of where the relation between the disciples and their Master implies the following features (ver. 27): (1) the Father Himself loveth them; (2) they have loved Christ; (3) they have believed that He came forth from the Father. If we reverse the order of these statements, we find the following facts and experiences, which, in successive order, lead up the disciples to that blessed state: (1) Christ cometh forth from the Father; (2) the disciples believe this, and thus they believe in Him, not only in His divine mission, but also in His divine nature, as the everlasting Son of the everlasting Father; (3) the disciples love Christ; (4) the Father loveth the disciples.

Thus the Lord has reached the point where He can sum up in one short, comprehensive statement, all that He had to say in these parting discourses, in fact, all that He had ever taught the disciples. He does this in the words: "I came out from the Father, and am come into the world:

V. New Parting Discourse (Ch. 15 and 16)

again I leave the world and go unto the Father" (ver. 28). Here is, in the briefest form, the whole testimony of Christ concerning His person and work, everything that the Church confesses of His eternal pre-existence and co-existence with the Father, His incarnation, His mediatorial office, His humiliation and exaltation, His passion, death and glorification. We are inclined to think that this was really intended as the conclusion of these discourses. But the subsequent naive remarks of the disciples called for some additional closing words of a more personal, pastoral character. The disciples show (vers. 29 and 30) that the words of the Lord have made a deep impression upon them. At this moment everything seems perfectly clear to them. They think they understand Him now, as speaking "plainly" and not in "proverbs." They come out with a cheerful, hearty confession of faith: "We believe that Thou earnest forth from God." Beautiful and touching as all this may be, there is no doubt that the disciples were mistaken in their judgment of their state of mind, their progress in the faith. The very reason they give for their present understanding and believing, shows that there is no real progress in this respect, no real grasping of the great and comprehensive truths which the Lord had communicated to them. The fact that the Lord had anticipated their questions, thus proving that He "knoweth all things," was the real cause of their present readiness to believe. But even now the contents of their faith, by their own statement, are quite fragmentary, if compared with the testimony of the Lord. Their confession of faith contains only one half of what the Lord had just set forth. They stop with this sentence: "that Thou camest forth from God." They are silent on the other half of His testimony, those very words around which everything had clustered that the Lord had communicated to them that evening: "I leave the world and go unto the Father." The mystery of this departure still hangs over them, waiting for its fuller explanation and understanding in the great events of His death and resurrection. They do not like to touch this point. Or did they possibly imagine this leaving the world and going to the Father as a sort of triumphant exodus and entrance, in utter ignorance of the impending terrors of that very night in which He was betrayed? (Grau).

The Lord's answer to the last remarks of the disciples unmistakably shows, that He had not much confidence in their faith at that stage. The revised version, with many prominent commentators, takes the words ἄρτι πιστεύετε (ver. 32) as a question. In this case it would be the expression of a doubt concerning the sincerity or at least the stability of their faith; possibly even with a touch of irony in it. We prefer to take the words as a positive statement: "Now ye believe." But even in this case we find here a criticism of the faith they had so boldly professed. *Now* there is something like faith, with all its inspiration and enthusiasm. But it will not prove very strong and enduring. That very night they shall be scattered, every man to his own, leaving Him alone!

But, while He found Himself constrained to shake their confidence at that point and to prepare them for a most painful experience of want of faith, He ends with sweet and tender words of consolation and of peace. Though left by the disciples, He is not alone. The Father is with Him. This He says not only for His own strengthening and encouragement under the trials of that night; but also and chiefly for the sake of His disciples. However difficult it may be for them to realize it, that the outcast and condemned Jesus of Nazareth has the Father with Him, on His side,—it is the one light in the darkness of that night, for Christ and His disciples.

And now, once more, as a parting word, the Lord sums up everything that His disciples need, in that precious "Peace," which He is going to secure for them, and of which He meant to assure them through every word He spoke that evening. He knows and admits that *in the world they have tribulation*. By this He does not mean the common sorrows and afflictions to which all mortals are subject in this life. He refers to those special tribulations which are inflicted by the world on the disciples, because they are Christ's and not of the world. Thus the tribulation itself proves their heterogeneity as over against the world, and is in reality a comforting and assuring feature in the experience of the disciples. And more than that! They have every reason to take courage and "be of good cheer." For their Lord has *overcome the world*. Thus He anticipates the great

V. New Parting Discourse (Ch. 15 and 16)

Τετέλεσται (it is finished) of Calvary, and with the word of victory on His lips He goes forth into battle!

Christ's victory appropriated by faith becomes our own victory, as John himself interprets and applies this passage: "This is the victory that hath overcome the world, even our faith" (1 John 5:4). Whatever we may yet have to suffer and to struggle, is not a real battle any more, but simply our share in the spoils and in the glory of His victory (Luther).

JOHN 17

VI. THE HIGH PRIEST'S PRAYER

1. *Introductory Remarks*

In taking up the exposition of this chapter, containing the "High Priest's Prayer," we hear the words, spoken by the Lord from the burning bush to Moses, resounding in our hearts: "The place whereon thou standest is holy ground." It is the "Holiest of Holies" even in this Gospel of St. John, on which we here enter. Our greatest theologians have always looked up to this chapter with special reverence, and almost with a kind of awe, that made them despair of their ability to do justice to this passage, in their attempts to interpret it. Even Luther shrank from it with the confession: "I am afraid I shall not be able to bring out the true character and power of this prayer; it is so deep, so rich and comprehensive, that no man can possibly fathom and exhaust it.—It is the prayer, in which the Son poured out the very depths of His heart before His God and Father." Melanchthon delivered his last lecture to his students in Wittenberg, on this chapter (April 2, 1560), saying: "There have never been heard, in heaven or on earth, more exalted, holy, wholesome and pathetic words than these." Spener, who had never in his life had the courage to preach on this chapter, had it read three times in his dying hours. John Gerhard said, that "this wonderful and peculiar prayer exceeded all human understanding." And yet Bengel is right when he characterizes it in these brief and pithy words: "Verbis facillimum, sensibus profundissimum—(quite easy in its words, most profound in its meaning)."

One thing must never be forgotten in reading this chapter or in trying to interpret it: It is, from beginning to end, *a prayer* and not an address, like the preceding discourses to the disciples. The opening words of the chapter clearly characterize its contents as a prayer: "Jesus, lifting up His eyes, said: Father, etc." It is the Lord's Prayer in an emphatic

VI. THE HIGH PRIEST'S PRAYER

sense, while what we are accustomed to call by that name is in reality the disciples' prayer, the prayer of those who are, through Christ, the children of their heavenly Father and brethren in their relation to each other. Christ's prayerful communion with the Father, which we know to have been a regular occurrence every day and many a night, was, as a rule, without witnesses, and has not therefore been recorded in words which men could hear and preserve. But in this particular case the disciples were privileged to hear the very words He prayed, and to treasure them in their memory for all time to come, for their own and the Church's comfort and edification. But, we insist, it is not a discourse for the instruction, admonition and encouragement of the hearers, but a true and genuine prayer, an appeal addressed by the Son to the Father, with certain clearly defined petitions, with a strong purpose to obtain from the Father everything He asked for.

While John Gerhard calls it "the prayer before the agony" (εὐχὴ προαγώνιος) its commonly accepted title is "the sacerdotal prayer" or "the High Priest's prayer," which is used by Luther already (not first by Chytræus, as is sometimes stated). In what sense then is it called "the High Priest's prayer"? Jesus, "the Apostle and High Priest of our confession" (Hebrews 3:1), is ready to enter, "not into a holy place, made with hands,—but into heaven itself, now to appear before the face of God for us" (Hebrews 9:24). He gives an account of His apostleship to the Father (rationem reddit Christus coram patre. John Gerhard). And on the ground of His well discharged *apostolic* function He brings His claims and appeals before the Father, and declares Himself ready to enter upon the highest function of His *sacerdotal* office, the offering of the atoning sacrifice for the sin of the world. He is now coming to the Father as the High Priest (accessu sacerdotali. Bengel on verse 11). And this is the prayer of initiation. It is therefore not exactly on the same level with the prayers with which Christ in His present state of glory, at the right hand of the Father, makes intercession for His people. It has a unique place in the history of our Lord, just as the sacrifice itself has, which He was then ready to offer. "By *one* offering He hath perfected forever them that are sanctified" (Hebrews 10:14. Also verse 12).

However reluctant we may feel to submit the wonderful organism of this prayer to the attempt of human logic and dialectics to map out a full and detailed disposition of this chapter, we see no reason to reject the commonly accepted division into three parts: first:[1] Christ's prayer for Himself (vers. 1–5); secondly: Christ's prayer for His disciples, as there assembled before Him (vers. 6–19); thirdly: Christ's prayer for those, who, through their word, will be brought to believe in Him (vers. 20–24). The two remaining verses of the chapter form the conclusion of the prayer.

In taking up its exposition in detail, we are mindful of Luther's advice, always to consider "who the Man is that offers this prayer; who He is to whom the prayer is offered; how great the things are which are asked for."

2. The High Priest Praying for Himself (17:1–5)

1–5. *These things spake Jesus; and lifting up his eyes to heaven, he said, Father, the hour is come; glorify thy Son, that the Son may glorify thee: even as thou gavest him authority over all flesh, that whatsoever thou hast given him, to them he should give eternal life. And this is life eternal, that they should know thee the only true God, and him whom thou didst send, even Jesus Christ. I glorified thee on the earth, having accomplished the work which thou hast given me to do. And now, O Father, glorify thou me with thine own self with the glory which I had with thee before the world was.*

Thus far the Lord had kept His eyes fixed upon His disciples whom He had been addressing. Now He lifts them up to heaven, addressing the Father, whose name runs like a golden thread through the whole prayer. (It is mentioned six times, verses 1, 5, 11, 21, 24, 25, twice with the adjectives: holy and righteous.) The hour, to which He refers in the opening sentence of His prayer, is the hour of glorification. It is the hour in which Christ's whole earthly life culminates, including both His

---

[1] This first part is extended by some commentators so as to include verses 6–8; beginning the second part with the ninth verse; the intercession in behalf of the disciples being marked by the words: "I pray for them." See Weizsæcker, Das Neue Testament, 1888.

VI. The High Priest's Prayer

deepest humiliation and His glorious exaltation.[1] He knows what this hour will bring to Him, and He thus formally and solemnly offers Himself for all this; He goes even so far as to ask for it directly with this petition: Father, glorify Thy Son. But this glorification of the Son is only an instrumentality. The great final aim and end is the glory of the Father Himself, the recognition of His glory, the honoring of His name (John 12:28) among men, the full realization of that "Gloria in Excelsis Deo" with which the incarnation of the Son was heralded on Bethlehem's field. If it is a divine work of the Father to glorify the Son, it is likewise a divine work of the Son to glorify the Father.

The claim of this comprehensive petition, "Glorify Thy Son," is based upon the fulfilment of the task allotted to Him. He renders His account before the Father, and in doing so, He, first of all, remembers the charge He had received: Authority over all flesh—to give them eternal life. Both a power and a commission are implied in the term authority (ἐξουδία) as in John 10:18, the power and the commandment to lay down His life and to take it again are combined (ἐξουδία and ἐντολή). It is the Incarnate Son of God to whom such power and authority over all flesh are given. The Logos must become flesh, to have a saving power over all flesh. For this term "all flesh" represents an ocean of human misery and wretchedness. "All flesh is grass and all the goodliness thereof is as the flower of the field. The grass withereth, the flower fadeth, because the Spirit of the Lord bloweth upon it: surely the people is grass" (Isaiah 40:6 f.); a "corruptible seed" as Peter calls it (1 Pet. 1:23). To give eternal life to this perishing flesh, is the task committed to the Son, with the corresponding power; a power not to bring death and destruction, but life and salvation to all that come unto Him, being given unto Him by the Father.

This life eternal the Son declares to be "that they should know Thee the only true God and Him whom Thou didst send, even Jesus Christ." It is natural that a statement like this has frequently been treated

---

[1] See John 13:1. Jesus knew that His hour was come that he should depart out of this world unto the Father.

as if it were a piece of information, intended for the disciples, instructing them as to the way by which to reach eternal life. But we insist on preserving the character of a prayer, addressed to the Father, also in this sentence. It is a solemn declaration of the Son to the Father, concerning the manner in which He discharged His duty of giving eternal life to all flesh. Here is His conception of eternal life. Men can receive it only with the full light of revelation concerning the one true God and Him whom He did send, even Jesus Christ. "In Him was life and the life was the light of men. That was the true light, which lighteth every man that cometh into the world" (John 1:4, 9).[1] We find then in the statement of this third verse an account of His stewardship, rendered by the Son to the Father. So much concerning the true conception of the form of this statement. And now a few remarks on its contents. Here we observe first of all, that this definition of "eternal life" brings this precious gift clearly and distinctly into this present time. Eternal life is here not represented as a distant good, to be hoped for as a future inheritance in another life, it is described as a present possession and enjoyment, within the reach of man in this world.

But how can "eternal life" be identical with a certain *knowledge*, however great and precious the truths may be, that are made known to men? The scriptural term "to know," especially as used in this connection by the Saviour, is by no means a purely intellectual grasping of certain abstract, impersonal truths, it is not a knowledge of books, of arithmetical tables, of facts and dates, of creeds and doctrines. It is to know a person or persons, as a friend knows the friend, a child the mother, a husband his wife. It is a personal relation; an affectionate knowledge, which is most fruitful and effective (*nosse cum affectu et effectu*). And in this case this knowledge is absolutely dependent on the fact, that the one true God makes Himself known to man through Him, whom He did send, even Jesus Christ. It is thus that men come to know the Father. "The only-begotten Son which is in the bosom of the Father, He hath

---

[1] "The prayer of the High Priest is the real source of the Prologue of St. John's Gospel" (F. L. STEINMEYER).

VI. The High Priest's Prayer

declared Him" (John 1:18). To receive His testimony, to accept God's love as revealed in Christ (John 3:16), to be thus re-united with the Father through the Son, to be restored to a personal relation of union and communion with Him, this is to know the only true God and Him whom He sent, even Jesus Christ, and this, indeed, is eternal life. To have lost this union, this personal and intimate acquaintance, knowledge and communion with God, was and is death, everlasting death, because it implies separation from God, the source of all life.

Everlasting life then is bound up with the absolute revelation of the one true God through Jesus Christ His Son, over against all false religions, religionisms and philosophies, whether Jewish, Pagan or modern "Christian." The charge made by Socinians and others that this text claims divinity only for God the Father as "the only true God" and that it denies it to Him, whom the Father sent, has well been met by Luther already, when He says: "Christ binds Himself up with that same one divine being, power and majesty, because He wants to be known, together with the Father, as the one that gives everlasting life." Certainly, in speaking of Himself as the one who was sent by the Father, the Lord does not place Himself on the same level with other Apostles and prophets, like Moses, Elijah, St. Paul. It would be impossible in this sentence to substitute one of these names, or any other name of man for that of Jesus Christ. For He is not simply an "agent," a messenger and Apostle of that saving knowledge, which is life eternal; He is Himself the "object" of that knowledge, the same as the Father Himself (Godet). In this connection the full name "Jesus Christ" is used with special emphasis by the Lord. He often spoke of Himself in the third person, as the "Son of Man" or "the Son." "Christ" He uses twice (Mark 9:41 and Matt. 23:10). "Jesus" He never uses alone. And here for once "Jesus Christ," the full name in which His humility and His majesty are both combined; that precious name, which, being preached by His servants and confessed by His church, is henceforth the name in which God's saving revelation to this world is comprehended, namely, that Jesus is the Christ the Son of God, and that believing, men might have life in this name. (See also 1 John

5:20, that we may know Him that is true; and we are in Him that is true, even in His Son Jesus Christ. This is the true God and eternal life.)

The Son will glorify the Father, when, in His state of exaltation, He will send down the Spirit to gather men into the everlasting Kingdom of God. But the Son has already glorified the Father in His prophetic and apostolic work on earth. He has accomplished His work. In spite of the frequent pain and sorrow caused by the indifference and hostility of men (see John 5:40), His heart is cheered in looking over the little band of believers who did take everlasting life from Him, and who will soon carry His life-message all over the world. And now, having finished this task, the God-man asks that He may sit at the right hand of the Father, with the same divine majesty, glory and power, which He had from everlasting with the everlasting Father, above the world, before the world, its time and space.

This "glorify Me" is the sum and substance of the High Priest's prayer for Himself. Now we turn to His prayer for the disciples gathered around Him.

3. The High Priest Praying for the Disciples (17:6–19)

6–19. I manifested thy name unto the men whom thou gavest me out of the world: thine they were, and thou gavest them to me; and they have kept thy word. Now they know that all things whatsoever thou hast given me are from thee: for the words which thou gavest me I have given unto them; and they received them, and knew of a truth that I came forth from thee, and they believed that thou didst send me. I pray for them: I pray not for the world, but for those whom thou hast given me; for they are thine: and all things that are mine are thine, and thine are mine: and I am glorified in them. And I am no more in the world, and these are in the world, and I come to thee. Holy Father, keep them in thy name which thou hast given me, that they may be one, even as we are. While I was with them, I kept them in thy name which thou hast given me: and I guarded them, and not one of them perished, but the son of perdition; that the scripture might be fulfilled. But now I come to thee; and these things I speak in the world, that they may have my joy fulfilled in themselves. I have given them thy word; and the world hated them, because they are not of the world, even as I am not of the world. I pray not that

VI. The High Priest's Prayer

thou shouldest take them from the world, but that thou shouldest keep them from the evil one. They are not of the world, even as I am not of the world. Sanctify them in the truth: thy word is truth. As thou didst send me into the world, even so sent I them into the world. And for their sakes I sanctify myself, that they themselves also may be sanctified in truth.

The direct prayer of the High Priest for His disciples begins only at ver. 9, "I pray for them." The preceding vers. 6–8 introduce the subject, presenting the disciples themselves to the Father, telling what had been done for them thus far, what stage of their spiritual development they had now reached through the work of the Son during those past three years. On this basis, then, the petition is offered in behalf of the disciples, that they should be kept in the Father's name, kept from evil, sanctified in the truth.

Whatsoever Christ did on earth was done to *manifest the Father's name*. Eternal life is to know the Father. But to know the Father we must have His name manifested to us. It is a significant fact that in the language of the New Testament the word "to know" (γινώσκω) and the word "name" (ὄνομα) have one common root. The name of the Father naturally suggests the revelation of the Father, it is His nature and being as known and revealed in this world. This manifestation of the Father-Name through Jesus Christ must, however, be correctly understood. It is quite true that this name reveals God as love. (See John 3:16 and 1 John 3:1.) It is "that true name by which we are to know God, that is, see His very heart, will and work" (Luther). But it is not, in the first place, "God as our Father" that is referred to by this manifestation of His name. It is God as the *Father of the Lord Jesus Christ*, who gave His only-be-gotten Son for the life of the world.

The disciples to whom this Father-Name was first manifested by Christ are described as "the men whom Thou gavest Me out of the world," not by an absolute, eternal decree of predestination, but by the means described in the following statements. *"Thine they were"* not simply in that universal sense in which all creatures are His who made them. It includes all those preliminary educational steps, by which these men were, under the Father's special care, brought out of the world and led to the Son. In the case of the disciples this implies their Old Testament covenant relation as honest Israelites, looking, like Simeon, for the consolation of Israel (Luke 2:25). With a number of them this culminated in their connection with John the Baptist, whom they joined as disciples and as candidates for the Kingdom of heaven which he announced. Christ's testimony *"they have kept Thy word"* therefore points to the Old Testament word of the Father as distinct from the New Testament words which Jesus Himself gave unto them in His personal teaching. This reference to the Father's word is particularly significant in this connection, as it "promptly puts an end to any anxiety and dispute concerning the secret council and decree of God by which some men are troubled and tormented" (Luther). How these men, after all that the Old Testament dispensation and the preventing grace of God had done for them, were individually drawn to Christ, is beautifully illustrated in the narrative John 1:35–51.

From their preparatory department, so to speak, in the knowledge of the Father, they have then been advanced to the full New Testament knowledge through the testimony of the Son: *"Now they know,"* etc. They recognized in Christ the One whom the Father sent and endowed for His great Mission. His words they *received*, and *knew* and *believed* that the Father did send the Son. These three stages, then, receiving, knowing, believing, are inseparably connected in this whole development of saving knowledge. See Peter's testimony: "We have believed and know that Thou art the Holy One of God" (John 6:69).

With the ninth verse the prayer itself begins which the High Priest offers for His disciples. It opens with an emphatic Ἐγώ, *I* pray for them, I the God-man, who have given them the Father's words and have brought them to their present state of faith. He prays for them; but what He asks from the Father for them is not introduced until the eleventh verse. At present the Lord prepares the way for His particular petition. It is based upon the fact that the disciples stand in sharp antithesis to the world and in close intimate union with Himself. He prays *"not for the world,"* which persists in its hostile attitude towards Him. Of course there is no decree of reprobation to be found in these words. Though some

VI. The High Priest's Prayer

predestinarians strain them even so as to contain the declaration, that, as He will not even pray for the world, much less will He die for the world! We know that on other occasions the Lord did indeed pray for the world. (See Luke 23:34 on the cross.) And charged His disciples also to pray for the hostile world (Matt. 5:44). But here He confines Himself to those whom the Father has given Him and who are the Father's own at the same time, in whom He is glorified. He is the Saviour of all men, but especially of them that believe (1 Tim. 4:10). And of those He now says with special emphasis to the Father: *"they are Thine."* This is more than the previous statement: "Thine they were" (ver. 6). Now they are really, fully and eternally His, as those given by the Father to the Son and brought through the Son to the Father. From the persons, the disciples, that are the Father's and the Son's, the Lord rises to a wider and more comprehensive outlook: "All things that are Mine are Thine, and Thine are Mine." If He only said the first part of this sentence, "all things that are Mine are Thine," it would not, says Luther, be such a remarkable and wonderful thing. For every one must say in a certain sense that whatever we have is God's. But this is truly great and marvellous that He reverses it, saying: "Thine are Mine." This no creature can say before God.

In the eleventh verse the Lord at last utters the petition in behalf of the disciples: "Holy Father, keep them in Thy name." This prayer is offered by Him who is going to leave the disciples in a world of sin, conflict and temptation. Out of this world they had been given to Him. And now He is anxious to see them preserved from falling back into this world and kept intact through the mercy and care of the Father. The Lord, in these words, clearly anticipates His departure. He knew what it was to be in this world. And the next hours were to give Him a full taste of the sorrow and shame which the world was determined to heap upon Him. But He is coming to the Father. This is the one thought that is now uppermost in His mind. It lifts Him up above the world. "I am no more in the world; but these are in the world." They need the Father's sheltering care and protection. For them He prays: *"Holy Father, keep them."* It is only in this one passage of the New Testament that God is addressed by this name. The term "Holy" which is so frequent in the Old Testament, is comparatively rarely found as an attribute of God in the New Testament, which, however, has a great deal to say of God's people, as the "Saints" (ἅγιοι) It designates not only the sinless purity and majesty of God, but also the idea that the pure and holy God is determined to purify the sinner, to bridge over the gulf that separates Him from the sinful world, and to save the sinner. It combines His self-assertion and His condescension. (See Luke 1:49, 50 and the frequent connection in the Old Testament, of this attribute of God with His grace and mercy; Isaiah 57:15, 16; 41:14, and other passages.)

The Holy Father, who preserves and sanctifies His people, is asked to keep them *"in His name, that they may be one."* Being kept in the Father's name, the disciples are in the unity of one knowledge, faith and confession, in one word and sacrament, in one Lord Christ, and therefore they are kept together, so as to be one in Him. Hitherto the Lord Himself, in His personal bodily presence with the disciples, was their keeper and guardian, watching over them, admonishing and warning them, praying for them, that their faith fail not (Luke 22:32). This work He now commits to the Father. His petition simply amounts to this: "Do Thou henceforth, what I myself have been doing hitherto," another striking proof of the union between the Father and the Son. The Son's work of keeping and guarding His own has been perfectly successful, with only one apparent exception, "the son of perdition" whose memory follows the Lord even into this prayer. But it is part of the account He gives to the Father of His stewardship, that He must refer to that lost one. He owes it to Himself to testify, in that solemn hour, that as far as He was concerned, nothing was left undone. Judas Iscariot received the same pastoral care as the other disciples. No reproach rests on his Master. But he refused to accept and keep His words, as the others accepted and kept them. There is one consolation for the Lord in this sad case, and that is *the fulfilment of Scripture* even in the fate of the traitor. But it is not Christ's fault, nor the Scripture's, nor the Father's, that Judas is lost. Looking upon it in this light, even this terrible reminiscence cannot now interfere with the serene, heavenly joy of the Lord and of His disciples.

VI. The High Priest's Prayer

The first petition which the Lord offered for the disciples is intensified (in ver. 15) in this form: I pray that Thou shouldst keep them from the evil. The reference to the traitor suggests the great danger to which the disciples are exposed as long as they are in this world, which hates them and persecutes them. Their relation to the world has become totally changed since they accepted the word which the Lord has given them. Through this acceptance of His word they are placed in a position of antagonism to the world, even as Christ Himself is "not of the world." For their personal feeling it might seem to be the most desirable thing that, together with their Lord, they might be taken out of this world and be at rest forever. But this cannot be. And the Lord cannot pray for this. He has a great work for them to do in this world, and even for their own personal development and sanctification it is good and necessary for them to remain and fight the good fight of faith. But they do need the power and protection of the Father to keep them from evil in this wicked world.[1]

Thus far the Lord asked for His disciples that the Father should keep them in His name and should keep them from evil. Now He offers the positive petition: "Sanctify them in the truth," basing it upon the great fact of His atoning passion and death: "for their sakes I sanctify Myself, that they themselves also may be sanctified in truth." These verses (17–19) represent the very centre and heart of the whole prayer. Both the personal and the official consecration of the disciples, as God's children, ambassadors of Christ, is included in this sanctification. The powerful means by which this is to be effected is the word. Over against the world with its darkness and satanic lies, the disciples have the word of light and truth, which Christ has given them. It is the whole saving truth of God, the only power that will prevail against the prince of this world. But here

---

[1] The question is, whether ἐκ τοῦ πονηροῦ (as in the seventh petition of the Lord's Prayer, Matthew 6:13) is to be taken as masculine, the evil one, or as neuter, the evil. The former view is held by Bengel, Wesley, Luthardt, Weiss, Keil, Westcott, Dwight, Weizsæcker, and the Revised Version; the latter by Stier, Lange, Alford, Godet and Luther's Version. Apart from deeper reasons against the masculine πονηρός in this context, the prepositio ἐκ seems to us clearly to decide the case in favor of the neuter.

again let us not forget to take even such a sentence ("Thy word is truth") as a true prayer, both in its form and spirit. The Son, at the close of His personal prophetical work on earth, says to the Father, in this solemn hour and in the hearing of His disciples: "Thy word is truth!" He confesses and declares with praise and thanksgiving to the Father, what His word has been even to Him in His experience as a teacher and prophet among the people. And His Apostles, whom He sends out into the world, will make the same experience of the truth of the word, and of its sanctifying, conquering power over against all the opposing forces of the world around them and in them. But the one, true foundation of the sanctification of Christ's people is the fact that He has sanctified Himself for them. He sacrificed Himself for us in the consecration of His whole life, culminating in His passion and death (Philippians 2:8, becoming obedient even unto death, yea, the death of the cross). Thus through the sacrifice of Christ the guilt of sin is wiped out, its power broken, the gift of the Holy Spirit, the sanctifier, secured. "By one offering He hath perfected forever them that are sanctified" (Hebrews 10:14).

4. The High Priest Praying for all Believers (17:20–24)

20–24. Neither for these only do I pray, but for them also that believe on me through their word; that they may all be one; even as thou, Father, art in me and I in thee, that they also may be in us: that the world may believe that thou didst send me. And the glory which thou hast given me I have given unto them; that they may be one, even as we are one; I in them, and thou in me, that they may be perfected into one; that the world may know that thou didst send me, and lovedst them, even as thou lovedst me. Father, that which thou hast given me, I will that, where I am, they also may be with me; that they may behold my glory, which thou hast given me: for thou lovedst me before the foundation of the world.

The view of the praying High Priest expands. From the little band around Him He looks out over the whole world, and forward over all the centuries of its history. He prays for all believers of all times and nations, who through the Apostolic word, as written and preached by the

VI. The High Priest's Prayer

disciples, believe[1] on Christ. It is, in so far, again a prayer for the disciples, as it asks and insures the Father's blessing upon their testimony and the success of their Apostolic ministry. As the history of the Church progresses, those that believe on Christ through the word of the Apostles will differ in nationality, language, culture, sex and age. But the Lord prays that, in spite of these natural and outward differences, they shall all be one. Believing through the word of the Apostles, they are by such faith united with Christ, and in Christ with the Father. But that same faith binds them together in the unity of the Church, an organic unity with Christ as its head, though possibly connected with different outward organizations. Such unity is a real oneness of life, resulting from the fact that all true believers have their share in God's life. It is more than unity in doctrine and confession, though it can only be a unity in the truth, in one faith, one Lord, one Baptism.[2] "What Christ prayed for in this place, He obtained," says John Gerhard. "Since then the Apostles are one in unity of faith; that is, since there is the most perfect harmony of Apostolic doctrine, as set forth in their writings, let us hold fast by the Apostolic doctrine as the foundation of true and sound unity in the Church, for by this will true unity flourish among us too." And Luther says: "We are made one thing with Christ and through Him with the Father also; so that just as little as Christ can be separated from the Father, just so little is it possible that the Christian Church and each individual member thereof can be divided from Him, and therefore that all is attached and bound together, the one to the other."[1]

---

[1] Present, not Future, as the received reading has it.

[2] To blame those who are zealous for the truth as the basis of Christian union is directly in conflict with this whole prayer of the Lord, which recognizes no other instrumentality for the sanctification, unification, and glorification of God's people than the truth of God's word.

[1] "To refer this sublime intercessory prayer, as do Romanists and others, to mere external unification, is not only to externalize everything, but to represent the all-prevailing intercession of the God-man in a light not much higher than the petitions of ordinary men. When He prayed that they all might be one He obtained what He asked." George Smeaton, D.D., a prominent theologian of the Free Church of Scotland, in a pamphlet on Scriptural Union, Edinburgh, 1871.

This union of believing Christians under one Lord, in one Spirit, is to be a testimony before the *world*, that it may *believe* and (ver. 23) that it may *know* that the Father did send the Son. This, after all, will always be the desire of the Lord concerning the world, that it should believe and be saved. (See John 3:17; 1:7.) And with this ideal aim and desire the Church is to carry her testimony into the world. Though the historical reality in the attitude of the world towards Christ and His Gospel will never go beyond the fact: "believed on in the world" (1 Tim. 3:16).

The unification of the believers appears, in verses 22 and 23, as a feature of the glory which they receive from Christ. *The glory*—I have given unto them, *that they may be one*. Christ means not only the salvation of individual believers here and there, but the bringing together into an organic union of a whole assembly of believers. All the many different members in which His grace has been manifested, represent the full glory of Christ's Body only in their union, for which the Lord here prays.

Through all the humility and lowliness with which our Apostle and High Priest Jesus Christ, in the first part of this prayer, gave an account of His stewardship, His divine majesty has been shining forth more and more clearly. But the revelation of His heavenly majesty reaches its climax in the 24th verse, when the Son comes before the Father with that firm and positive claim: *"Father, I will that, where I am, they also may be with Me."* How different this "I will" from the language used shortly afterwards in the agony of Gethsemane: "Not what I will, but what Thou wilt." The turning point in the High Priest's prayer from His lowliness to this bold and majestic self-assertion is to be found in the 19th verse; "For their sakes I sanctify Myself." On this complete self-sacrifice, culminating in His obedience unto death, rests His claim: "Father, I will." (See also Philippians 2:6–9, the connection between the humiliation of Christ vers. 6–8, and His exaltation ver. 9.) What He demands as being due Him from the Father on account of His sacrifice is, that His own "may *behold His glory*," which the Father hath given Him. This alone is the true conception of the perfect glory and bliss of His people in the future world, to behold Christ's glory. Nothing else would satisfy them fully even there.

5. *Conclusion of the High Priest's Prayer* (17:25, 26)

VI. The High Priest's Prayer

25–26. O righteous Father, the world knew thee not, but I knew thee; and these knew that thou didst send me; and I made known unto them thy name, and will make it known; that the love wherewith thou lovedst me may be in them, and I in them.

The prayer concludes with another sharp antithesis between the world on one side, and the Lord with His loved ones on the other, and with an appeal to the righteousness of the Father who will, no doubt, do what is right and just, by the world and the disciples. The title *"righteous Father"* which is only used at this place combines the two prominent attributes of God, on which the whole work of redemption is based: His love and His justice. But it is the latter on which the emphasis rests in this connection. The righteousness of the Father is not known by the world. It will be the principal work of the Paraclete to convict the world in respect of sin and of righteousness and of judgment (John 16:8). Least of all does the world realize the righteousness of God as revealed in the Gospel of the Lord Jesus Christ, showing God as being "just and the justifier of him that hath faith in Jesus" (Romans 3:26). But the Son knoweth the Righteous Father. He knows how the Father's righteousness will have to deal with Him, who was made sin for us, how He will be "smitten of God and afflicted;" how "the Lord" will "lay on Him the iniquity of us all" (Isaiah 53:4, 6). The bitter cup of Gethsemane and the bloody cross of Calvary tell the tale of that righteousness, which the Son had to taste. And "if they do these things in the green tree, what shall be done in the dry?" (Luke 23:31).

But there is a great deal of consolation for the disciples in this appeal to the righteous Father. The claim put forth in ver. 24, "Father, I will," etc., is sure to find recognition. The Father cannot, in justice, withhold any of those great and glorious things which the Son here asked for His believers. They know Him as the Son of God and the Saviour of the world. They know the Father's name and will steadily grow in such blessed knowledge. They will be perfectly safe in the Father's love and in the love of their Saviour. They may rest "assured that such petitions are acceptable to the heavenly Father and are heard by Him. Amen, Amen, Yea, Yea, it shall be so" (Small Catechism).

JOHN 18

THE TRIUMPH OF FAITH CONTINUED IN THE HISTORY OF THE PASSION AND RESURRECTION OF THE LORD

It is evident that the fourth Gospel does not intend to give anything like a complete account of the Lord's Passion. Even a hasty comparison merely of the outward extent of the narrative of John, with the accounts of Matthew, Mark and Luke, must at once convince us of this. The two passion-chapters in John have only 82 verses over against 141 in Matthew; 119 in Mark; 127 in Luke, making in all 387 verses in the synoptical account of Christ's Passion. There is undoubtedly the design in the record of the fourth Gospel, to supplement in some important points the narrative of the Synoptists which are supposed to be known to the readers. But there is yet another idea pervading the passion-account of the Gospel of St. John. It is the fundamental idea, the real theme of the whole Gospel: The glory of the incarnate Word, and on the one side the faith that receives Him, on the other the unbelief that rejects Him. This glory, lighting up with its heavenly rays the darkness and humiliation of the passion and the cross; and manifesting itself particularly in that perfect freedom, with which the Lord gives Himself up to suffering and death; that faith of His own, recovering itself from the severe shock of those trying hours and coming out triumphantly, with the full assurance that this Jesus of Nazareth is indeed the Christ, the Son of God, and that believing in His name they have everlasting life; and lastly, the unbelief of Israel, reaching its climax in the open surrender of every Messianic hope: We have no king but Cæsar!

I. THE CAPTURE OF JESUS (18:1–11)

1. Arrival of the Band (18:1–3)

1–3. *When Jesus had spoken these words, he went forth with his disciples over the brook Kidron, where was a garden, into the which he entered, himself and his*

I. The Capture of Jesus (18:1–11)

disciples. Now Judas also, which betrayed him, knew the place: for Jesus oft-times resorted thither with his disciples. Judas then, having received the band of soldiers and officers from the chief priests and the Pharisees, cometh thither with lanterns and torches and weapons.

From the lofty heights of the last discourses of the Lord (14–16), from the heavenly peace pervading His prayer as the High Priest (17), the fourth Gospel takes us with one step into the actual beginning of the sufferings of Christ. Omitting the agony in the Garden, its passion-history opens with the account of the capture of the Lord in that same garden of Gethsemane, so clearly described in the first verse, one of the three gardens, so prominent in the Scripture, Eden, where sin entered into the world, Gethsemane, where it was fought and overcome, Joseph's garden, where it was buried in the tomb. To Gethsemane the Lord led forth His disciples over the brook Kidron, not the brook of Cedars (as the marginal note in the R. V. suggests), but the dark, the black brooklet, which served as a sort of drainage for the City of Jerusalem, carrying off its impurities down to the Dead Sea. It was the same Kidron which David crossed when he fled from rebellious Jerusalem, and his ungrateful son Absalom, and the treachery of Ahithophel's counsel; the same brook Kidron into which, at the time of Hezekiah's reformation, "all uncleanness that they found in the temple of the Lord" had been carried. To the garden on the left (or eastern) bank of the brook Kidron, at the foot of the Mount Olivet, Judas, the betrayer, led the band of soldiers, that is, the Roman cohort, dispatched for this purpose by the Governor, and the officers of the chief priests and the Pharisees. There is an unmistakable touch of irony in the description of this powerful force arriving with lanterns and torches and weapons, to catch the "Light of the World," to make Him a prisoner, who said: "No one taketh My life from Me, but I lay it down of Myself. I have power to lay it down and I have power to take it again."

2. Jesus Meeting the Band (18:4–9)

4–9. Jesus therefore, knowing all the things that were coming upon him, went forth, and saith unto them, Whom seek ye? They answered him, Jesus of Nazareth.

Jesus saith unto them, I am he. And Judas also, which betrayed him, was standing with them. When therefore he said unto them, I am he, they went backward, and fell to the ground. Again therefore he asked them, Whom seek ye? And they said, Jesus of Nazareth. Jesus answered, I told you that I am he: if therefore ye seek me, let these go their way: that the word might be fulfilled which he spake, Of those whom thou hast given me I lost not one.

The manner in which the Lord meets His captors demonstrates most forcibly that freedom of His action which is so strongly emphasized in the Gospel of John. Jesus, *knowing* all the things that were coming upon Him, went forth—"and saith unto them, Whom seek ye?" It was the first word of Jesus, recorded in the fourth Gospel, addressed to those inquiring disciples: What seek ye? Here it is one of His last words, addressed to His enemies: Whom seek ye? He is the one central figure of the world's history, sought by friend and foe. All the misery, distress and helplessness of this forlorn and benighted world seek Him as the only helper and physician: "Of whom may we seek for succor but of Thee, O Lord?" And all the enmity against God and His word and salvation seeks Him as its central object of attack, with the fixed determination: "We will not that this man reign over us" (Luke 19:14). But at the same time God's righteous judgment, in dealing finally with the sin of the world, seeks Him. As the voice of the Lord God once after the fall called unto Adam, hidden under the trees of the garden, "Where art thou?" so it calls now in this great hour of reckoning for the second Adam, seeking Him, who was made sin for us.

"*I am He;* "this is the Lord's own answer to that great central question: "Whom seek ye?" More than once before the Lord had made this declaration. But never was it spoken with more emphasis and majesty than here at the moment when the Lord gave Himself up unto passion and death. "*I am He,*" He says to divine justice; the sin, the guilt, all on Me; take Me, strike Me and let these go their way! *I am He,* He says to the life-and-light-seeking world, your wisdom, and righteousness, and sanctification and redemption, the way, and the truth, and the life! *I am He,* He says also to the enmity and hatred of the world: I am Jesus whom ye persecute; it will be hard for you to kick against the goads; ye shall yet

I. The Capture of Jesus (18:1–11)

see Him whom ye have pierced, "the Son of Man sitting at the right hand of power and coming on the clouds of heaven." And was not the effect of this "I am He" at this point a clear foreshadowing of the hour of the Lord's final revelation, when before the throne of His majesty all his enemies shall be made His footstool?

3. Peter Striking with the Sword (18:10, 11)

10–11. *Simon Peter therefore having a sword drew it, and struck the high priest's servant, and cut off his right ear. Now the servant's name was Malchus. Jesus therefore said unto Peter, Put up the sword into the sheath: the cup which the Father hath given me, shall I not drink it?*

Whatever there was to be, at that point, of a demonstration of the Lord's power, whatever of battle and of victory, had all been revealed and been brought to bear upon the enemies of Christ as they were lying prostrate at His feet. Truly there was no need of displaying any physical force and carnal zeal on the part of the disciples. So far from aiding the cause of their Master they could only hurt it by resorting to violence. We do not believe that Peter rushed upon the prostrate enemy to enjoy a cheap and easy victory, by striking with the sword those whom the word of His majesty had felled to the ground. It was, when the Master Himself had invited them to come forward and take Him and let His disciples go, when those in the front rank of the enemies having risen to their feet, first laid their hands upon Jesus, then Peter's blood was up, he threw himself upon them, striking down the first he met. Thus he intended to make good his word, and to demonstrate his devotion to the Master beyond the possibility of a doubt. But with this carnal zeal he did all in his power to rob his Master's kingdom of its true glory, and to make it impossible for the Lord to maintain that position before the Governor: "My kingdom is not of this world. If My kingdom were of this world, then would my servants fight that I should not be delivered to the Jews" (18:36). Moreover, Peter by this rash act of his burdened himself with an evil conscience, which, in the hour of his severe trial, will throw him helpless into the clutches of the enemy. He stands henceforth under the fear of that sentence of the Master Himself: "All they that take the sword shall perish with the sword." Striking Peter is denying Peter. There is a deep inward connection between the two events. The very fact of his striking with the sword at that hour was a denial of the true, spiritual nature of the Kingdom of Christ.

There are a few touches in this account of the scene in the Garden, peculiar to the fourth Gospel and strongly marking its character as one of historical exactness and minuteness. The Synoptical account, representing the earliest tradition of these events in the church, does not mention Peter's name, but only speaks of one of "them that were with Him." But the Gospel of John for the first time names the disciple, Simon Peter; inserting the old name of the carnal man, who once more asserted himself in this act. Again the name of the High Priest's servant, Malchus, is here mentioned for the first time.

II. JESUS BEFORE THE HIGH PRIEST (18:12–27)

1. *Jesus Taken to Annas (18:12–14)*

12–14. *So the band and the chief captain, and the officers of the Jews, seized Jesus and bound him, and led him to Annas first; for he was father in law to Caiaphas, which was high priest that year. Now Caiaphas was he which gave counsel to the Jews, that it was expedient that one man should die for the people.*

2. *First Denial of Peter (18:15–18)*

15–18. *And Simon Peter followed Jesus, and so did another disciple. Now that disciple was known unto the high priest, and entered in with Jesus into the court of the high priest; but Peter was standing at the door without. So the other disciple, which was known unto the high priest, went out and spake unto her that kept the door, and brought in Peter. The maid therefore that kept the door saith unto Peter, Art thou also one of this man's disciples? He saith, I am not. Now the servants and the officers were standing there, having made a fire of coals; for it was cold; and they were warming themselves: and Peter also was with them, standing and warming himself.*

II. Jesus before the High Priest (18:12–27)

3. Hearing of Jesus before Annas (18:19–24)

19–24. *The high priest therefore asked Jesus of his disciples, and of his teaching. Jesus answered him, I have spoken openly to the world; I ever taught in synagogues, and in the temple, where all the Jews come together; and in secret spake I nothing. Why askest thou me? ask them that have heard me, what I spake unto them: behold these know the things which I said. And when he had said this, one of the officers standing by struck Jesus with his hand, saying: Answerest thou the high priest so? Jesus answered him, If I have spoken evil, bear witness of the evil: but if well, why smitest thou me? Annas therefore sent him bound unto Caiaphas the high priest.*

4. Second and Third Denial of Peter (18:25–27)

25–27. *Now Simon Peter was standing and warming himself. They said therefore unto him, Art thou also one of his disciples? He denied, and said, I am not. One of the servants of the high priest, being a kinsman of him whose ear Peter cut off, saith, Did not I see thee in the garden with him? Peter therefore denied again: and straightway the cock crew.*

There is again an unmistakable touch of irony in this account of the actual capture of Christ, the fulness and circumstantiality with which all the parties are enumerated who, having recovered their courage after their ignominious prostration, now rush upon the Lord, to make sure of this dangerous man: "the band, and the chief captain, and the officers of the Jews,"—Jews and Gentiles united in the very first act of physical violence to Christ—seized Jesus and bound Him and led Him to Annas first, who was not only the father-in-law of Caiaphas, but also, as it is generally supposed, his predecessor in the office. This hearing before Annas, who lived in a separate wing of the High Priest's palace, is again one of the distinctive features of the fourth Gospel, the Synoptists giving only the official inquest before Caiaphas. But the "disciple that was known to the High Priest," that is undoubtedly John, had the best opportunity to know about this. And that he was not ignorant of the hearing before Caiaphas appears clearly from the statement (ver. 13), "they led Him to Annas first," and again from the 24th verse, "Annas sent Him bound unto Caiaphas the High Priest."

This preliminary hearing before Annas and a few members of the Sanhedrim was not of an official character. No sentence was passed there, because there was no authority to pass it. The purport of this meeting seems to have been to elicit some statement from the Lord by which He would commit Himself, and which might be used against Him in the official inquiry that followed. Thus they meant to make good use of the time which was needed to call a regular meeting of the Sanhedrim.

The insidious questions of Annas as to His *disciples*, that is, the formation of a party of adherents, and as to His *doctrine*, that is, the heresy with which He is charged, indicate clearly the two lines on which the prosecution hoped to make out a case against Christ. Before the Roman magistrate He was to be denounced as the head of a dangerous party, which at any time might create a political disturbance. Before the Sanhedrim the charge was to be His heretical teaching, His blasphemy. The counter-question of the Lord: "Why askest thou Me?" and the whole tenor of His response prove that He did not recognize any rightful authority of this court of investigation. His dignified answer simply appeals to the publicity of His ministry, and calls in all the Jews as witnesses of what He did and taught. At the same time it strongly reminds those who were at home in Old Testament Scripture of that word put in the mouth of the Messiah by Isaiah the prophet: "I have not spoken in secret from the beginning, from the time that it was, there am I, and now the Lord God and His Spirit hath sent Me" (Is. 48:16).

The rebuke administered to Annas in these words of the Lord is felt keenly by the whole company, and one of the officers, anxious to help his master out of the embarrassing situation, rudely strikes the Lord in the face (either with the hand or with a rod) a significant indication of the course which this whole process of inquiry is bound to take; instead of argument and testimony, bodily violence, to silence the mouth of this witness. But the hour for His final silence had not yet come. He still speaks to show this offender his wrong: "If I have spoken evil, bear witness of the evil; but if well, why smitest thou Me?" The question has sometimes been asked by those who are always ready to criticise the Lord, whether His action in this case was in accord with His own teaching in

II. Jesus before the High Priest (18:12–27)

the Sermon on the Mount: "Resist not him that is evil; but whosoever smiteth thee on thy right cheek, turn to him the other also." But did Christ really refuse to be smitten on the other cheek also? Did He not willingly, humbly and patiently offer His whole body to every stroke and torture which His cruel enemies chose to inflict upon Him? But whilst His hand did not strike back, His mouth could not and did not keep silent at the outrage which was committed. In all meekness, and yet most pointedly and directly, He testifies against it, to convince the sinner of the error of his ways and thus, if it were possible, to enlighten his mind and change his heart.

In the order of the three different denials of Peter the fourth Gospel again exhibits the exactness of its chronological arrangement, as compared to the Synoptists. Even Renan admits that everything is told more fully and explained more satisfactorily in the account given by St. John.

We learn here, what none of the Synoptists told us, that through the good services of another disciple, undoubtedly John himself, "who was known unto the High Priest," Peter found admission into the court of the palace. Both had followed the Lord at the same time to the same place; and yet no harm came of it to John, while to Peter is threatened the very loss of his soul. It is the old adage: Two men may do the same thing and yet it is not the same. John had not the same prohibitory command from the Lord, and therefore had a clear conscience in following Him. He went along as a matter of course, as the beloved disciple, never thinking of himself and his personal safety. Peter, as we are told in the Gospel of St. Luke, followed "afar off." He was at a distance from the Lord internally, as well as outwardly. He was disregarding His express commandment by his very act of following Him. He did it with a divided, uncertain, and consequently with an uneasy heart. He still loved his Lord, but at the same time he was looking out for himself. After the repeated promises he had made, he thought he owed it to himself, to his own reputation for manliness and truthfulness, that he must go with Him. He had undertaken too much, as he did on another occasion, when, leaving the boat in which the others were safe, he ventured to the Lord on the water.

Unconsciously he was already under the curse of that fundamental law of God's kingdom: "Whatever is not of faith, is sin."

Again, Peter stood with the servants and officers at the fire and warmed himself. Nowhere do we read of John as being in this company; but Peter was there accepting their hospitality in the cold night and trying to preserve his incognito by appearing as cool and indifferent as possible. Think of the sneering and slandering, the calumnies and blasphemies against his Lord to which Peter listened in the company around that fire! And he never opened his mouth. The confessor, otherwise so quick and ready with his speech, keeps silent in the midst of his Master's reviling enemies. Had not Peter denied the Lord already before he uttered one of those terrible words?

And now the denial itself. Never did a greater fall come from a more trifling occasion. It was the simple question addressed to Peter, first by the maid that kept the door, and afterwards by other servants and officers: "Art thou also like John, who was there in the palace, in perfect safety and unconcern—one of this man's disciples?" It was a splendid occasion for brave, heroic Peter to do what he had done so nobly before this, to confess his Lord and Master as the Son of the living God, and himself as His devoted and believing disciple. True, it is one thing to answer such a question in the presence of the Lord, surrounded by believing and loving disciples, and another to answer it in the face of a Christ-hating, sneering world. And so Peter denied it and said: I am not! He thus first denied himself, before he even denied his Lord, and having thrown away himself, the former bold confessor, it was only a little way to deny the Lord directly, "I know not this man of whom ye speak." This form of direct denial of Christ Himself is not given in John's account, which presents Peter's fall in the mildest form, whilst the Gospel of St. Mark, written most likely under Peter's personal influence, narrates the fall in the most aggravated manner.

Was there ever a greater triumph of Satan against the Lord and His Kingdom than this fall of Peter? There in the hall before Annas, stood Jesus appealing, in answer to the questions about His disciples and His doctrine, to those "that heard Him": "Ask them, behold they know what I have said." And here is the answer of the foremost of them "that heard Him" and who ought to know the Master and what He said unto them. His answer is: "I am not one of His disciples. I know not this man." In striking Peter, Satan most severely struck the Lord Himself. Had He not said once in answer to Peter's confession of faith: "Thou art Peter, and upon this rock I will build My Church and the gates of hell shall not prevail against it?" Not prevail? echoes the derisive laughter of triumphant hell. Where is your Peter now, where his confession, the rock upon which the Church is to be built? Where is that Church itself? Peter the head and chief confessor overthrown by the casual remark of a damsel! What kind of a church, what sort of a kingdom, to be built of such material as this? The Lord's divinity denied by the very man who had first confessed it, and thus the very foundation of the Church destroyed,—this is what Satan meant with his victorious assault upon Peter.

III. JESUS BEFORE THE GOVERNOR PILATE (18:28–19:16)

1. First Charge of the Jews (18:28–32)

28–32. They lead Jesus therefore from Caiaphas into the palace: and it was early; and they themselves entered not into the palace, that they might not be defiled, but might eat the passover. Pilate therefore went out unto them, and saith, What accusation bring ye against this man? they answered and said unto him, If this man were not an evil-doer, we should not have delivered him up unto thee. Pilate therefore said unto them, Take him yourselves, and judge him according to your law. The Jews said unto him, it is not lawful for us to put any man to death: that the word of Jesus might be fulfilled, which he spake, signifying by what manner of death he should die.

The struggle between the Jews and the Roman Governor, by which the former seek to obtain from the latter the sentence of death against Jesus, is most fully and graphically described in the fourth Gospel, which is, particularly in this scene, an indispensable supplement to the Synoptists. We distinguish four different attempts on the part of the Jews to make the Governor a tool for the execution of their designs: there is first the general, tumultuary demand that the evil-doer, delivered up to the Governor, should be put to death (28–32). The next attempt is the political charge, that He made Himself King of the Jews (ver. 33–19:6); the third is the accusation of blasphemy, that "He made Himself the Son of God" (19:7–12). The fourth and last attempt to which the Governor succumbs is the threat: "Thou art not Cæsar's friend" (19:13–16).

Pilate held the office of Governor of Judæa about the same length of time as Caiaphas that of the High Priest (26–36 A. D.). He usually resided in Cæsarea. At festival seasons he came up to Jerusalem, and there made a dazzling display of Roman splendor. His character has been judged quite differently by different writers. Some call him haughty, stubborn, self-willed. Others speak of him as a good and efficient officer. Serious charges being brought against him before Vitellius, the governor of Syria, he is said to have taken his own life in exile under Cæsar Caligula.

The Jews approach him first with the peremptory demand that he should consent to become their executioner. Their Sanhedrim having decreed that "He is worthy of death," Pilate is expected to carry out the sentence, even as the church-tribunals of inquisition in the middle ages, having passed their sentence upon the heretic, delivered him up to the sword of the secular power, washing their hands in innocence with the hypocritical assurance: "Ecclesia non sitit sanguinem." But in this case the Governor sees through their scheme, and politely returns their prisoner with the sarcastic remark: "Take Him yourselves and judge Him according to your law." It was a painful humiliation for them to be forced to admit: "It is not lawful for us to put any man to death." With this loss of the right to inflict the penalty of death, the Jews had actually lost their sovereignty as a nation; and it was as bitter for them to concede this before the Roman Governor, as it had been bitter to be told by the Lord only a few days before this: "Render unto Cæsar the things that are Cæsar's."

2. Jesus the King (18:33–38^a)

33–38. Pilate therefore entered again into the palace, and called Jesus, and said unto him, Art thou the King of the Jews? Jesus answered, Sayest thou this of thyself,

III. Jesus Before the Governor Pilate (18:28–19:16)

or did others tell it thee concerning me? Pilate answered, Am I a Jew? Thine own nation and the chief priests delivered thee unto me: what hast thou done? Jesus answered, My kingdom is not of this world: if my kingdom were of this world, then would my servants fight, that I should not be delivered to the Jews: but now is my kingdom not from hence. Pilate therefore said unto him, Art thou a king then? Jesus answered, Thou sayest that I am a king. To this end have I been born, and to this end am I come into the world, that I should bear witness unto the truth. Every one that is of the truth heareth my voice. Pilate saith unto him, What is truth?

The next point of attack on the part of the Jews is indicated in this Gospel in the question of Pilate (ver. 33), "Art Thou the King of the Jews?" But in order to make this fully clear and intelligible, John must here be supplemented by Luke, who shows how Pilate was led to ask this question (Luke 23:2). The Jews had brought the definite charge: "We found this man perverting our nation and forbidding to give tribute to Cæsar, and saying that He Himself is Christ, a King." And this is followed in the Gospel of St. Luke by the same question, which we have here in John: "Art Thou the king of the Jews?" This title could have a double meaning in the history of those days. As understood by the Roman it naturally implied the idea of rebellion against Cæsar, it was a "king" in the political sense of the word. As understood by the believing Israelite the title had a spiritual meaning, designating the Messiah, the Lord of God's kingdom, of righteousness, peace and joy in the Holy Spirit, "the righteous Branch of David who shall execute judgment and justice in the earth" (Jerem. 23:5), the "Prince of Peace, of whose government there shall be no end upon the throne of David" (Isaiah 9:6, 7), from whom the Roman Emperor had as little to fear as Herod from the babe in Bethlehem. The Lord, therefore, was not ready without further explanation to answer the question as to His kingship either in the affirmative or in the negative. (See the question of the Jews, 10:24.) He therefore answered: "Sayest thou this of thyself, or did others tell it thee concerning Me?"—is the term "king of the Jews" used in the Roman, that is, the political sense, or in the Israelitic, that is, the theocratic sense?

But there is another more important feature in this counter-question of the Lord. It reveals the kindly personal and pastoral interest which Christ takes in Pilate. On this memorable occasion when the Saviour of the world is for the first time brought into direct contact with the representative of Rome, He offers Himself even to this proud Roman Governor as the one great physician of the soul. He means to deal with him pastorally, as He dealt with Nicodemus and with the Samaritan woman. For this reason the tables are promptly turned, and when Pilate had called Jesus into the palace and was alone with Him, the accused at once questions the judge and inquires into his moral standing and character. The Lord, who "knew what was in man," lays His finger upon the weak point in Pilate's character. "Sayest thou this of thyself, or did others tell it thee concerning Me?" Here was the dangerous rock on which he was shipwrecked, and here was the danger-signal and warning of the Lord in His very first word addressed to Pilate. With all his haughtiness and conceit, with all his consciousness of the power and authority of his office, the Governor was in danger of being influenced by what "others tell him concerning Christ." He lacked in moral courage and determination to maintain what he said in this case "of himself." Wherever, throughout this mock-trial, Pilate really spoke his own mind, it was invariably the declaration of Christ's innocence; and when, in spite of this his better conviction, he ultimately delivered up Christ to be crucified, he yielded to what "others told" him to do. For this reason the Lord means to detach him from those outside influences. If He could only have him alone, to speak to him eye to eye, undisturbed by the insidious tales of the chief priests and Pharisees, Pilate would not be altogether inaccessible.

But it is a characteristic feature of those moral weaklings who are least able to form and maintain a judgment of their own, and most dependent on outside influence, that they are always over-anxious to preserve the appearance of absolute freedom and independence in their decisions. While in reality they are the helpless reed shaken by the wind, the wave of the sea, driven and tossed by the storm, they pretend to be the rock, standing immovable amidst the foaming surf. Thus the proud Roman will not submit to this pastoral dealing on the part of his prisoner. He resents it with the cold and haughty: "Am I a Jew?" and with the formal

III. Jesus Before the Governor Pilate (18:28–19:16)

and official question of the judge to the criminal: "What hast Thou done?" And now the Lord "before Pontius Pilate witnessed the good confession" (1 Tim. 6:13), affirming that He is king indeed, and describing the true character of His kingdom: "My kingdom is not of this world: if My kingdom were of this world, then would My servants fight, that I should not be delivered to the Jews,"—thus clearly maintaining the unpolitical and even anti-Jewish character of His kingdom. Pilate therefore said unto Him: Art Thou a king then? Jesus answered: Thou sayest it: I am a king. To this end I have been born—as the Son of Mary—and to this end am I come into the world—as the Son of God—that I should bear witness unto the truth. Every one that is of the truth heareth My voice.

There He stands, the King of truth, in a perishing world of lies and vanities, declaring, out of the bosom of the Father, the everlasting and saving truth of God. Before Him, they have been seeking it, "if haply they might feel after Him;" and now that He has come, "the way, the truth and the life," they criticise and reject Him! And yet: "Every one that is of the truth heareth His voice." Wherever there is an honest yearning in a human heart for God's truth it is bound to come to Christ, to hear His voice.

What an appeal to Pilate, to his conscience, to the human soul in him! Was there no spark of truth left in Him to be kindled by these words of Jesus? Was it not truth that Pilate spoke, once and twice, and six times: I find no guilt in Him? And being conscious of this and witnessing it publicly, should it have been so difficult for him to "hear His voice"? But men must first listen to the truth from above and submit to it, before they can speak it and possess it. Thus their persons, their life, their walk and talk, their words and deeds, become purified, renewed through the sanctifying power of that truth. They become "truth" themselves.

Pilate, however, turns away from the King of truth, before him, with the question: "What is truth?" The representative of ancient paganism, with all its culture and philosophy, acknowledges the complete loss and utter despair of truth; he thus declares the total bankruptcy of the ancient world. It is a remarkable fact that the three Roman governors, whom we know somewhat more fully from the New

Testament, Pilate, Felix and Festus, all meet the testimony of the truth with the same carelessness and indifference of the worldly skeptic, shrugging their shoulders in pity and contempt for such enthusiasts and martyrs of truth as Jesus of Nazareth and Paul of Tarsus.[1]

3. Jesus and Barabbas (18:38–40)

38–40. *And when he had said this, he went out again unto the Jews, and saith unto them, I find no crime in him. But ye have a custom, that I should release unto you one at the passover: will ye therefore that I release unto you the King of the Jews? They cried out therefore again, saying, Not this man, but Barabbas. Now Barabbas was a robber.*

Being convinced of the innocence of Jesus and yet lacking the courage to act up to this conviction and to give a decision in favor of the prisoner, Pilate tries a number of methods to shift the responsibility upon others, in order to get rid of Jesus and of the Jews without deciding between them. His first attempt in this line is the sending of Christ to Herod, as recorded in St. Luke (23:6–12). The second is briefly referred to by John but more fully told by the Synoptists. It is the proposition that the people, according to their custom, probably in memory of their delivery from bondage in Egypt, should have the release of the prisoner for whom they asked. He had no doubt that after the enthusiastic reception of Jesus on His recent entrance into Jerusalem He would be the choice of the multitude, all the more so, as he knew, that the chief priests and rulers had delivered Him for envy. But in vain. The same men who had delivered

---

[1] There is a great deal of this Pilate-spirit in modern men, who, while they are constitutionally afraid of the full blaze of the truth, make so much of their everlasting inquiry and search after truth. Cf. Lessing's word, so frequently quoted and praised: "If the Almighty, holding in His right hand truth itself, and in His left search after truth, gave me the choice between the two, I would humbly take the left saying: 'Give me the search; full truth is for Thee alone!'" "The late Dr. Duncan of Edinburgh said once of this statement: "It contains the essence of all devilry. It may amount to the willingness to be eternally without God. It is delight in the mere *activity* of the *faculties* that is chosen, the *search* that is fearless and free, unimpeded and irrestricted, forever to pursue an endless chase, to prove all things, but hold fast nothing. It is the maxim of eternal revolt and independence." See Colloquia peripatetica, 5th ed., pp. 35, 36.

III. Jesus Before the Governor Pilate (18:28–19:16)

Him up, persuaded the multitude that they should ask for Barabbas. They cried out therefore saying: Not this man, but Barabbas!

JOHN 19

4. Scourging and Mocking of the King of the Jews (19:1–3)

1–3. Then Pilate therefore took Jesus, and scourged him. And the soldiers plaited a crown of thorns, and put it on his head, and arrayed him in a purple garment; and they came unto him, and said, Hail, King of the Jews! and they struck him with their hands.

5. Behold the Man (19:4–6)

4–6. And Pilate went out again, and saith unto them, Behold, I bring him out to you, that ye may know that I find no crime in him. Jesus therefore came out, wearing the crown of thorns and the purple garment. And Pilate saith unto them, Behold, the man! When therefore the chief priests and the officers saw him, they cried out, saying, Crucify him, crucify him. Pilate saith unto them, Take him yourselves, and crucify him: for I find no crime in him.

Another attempt of Pilate to rescue Christ from the hands of His cruel enemies! "He took Jesus and scourged Him" and afterwards presented to them the bleeding Jesus, wearing the crown of thorns and the purple garment, with the words: "Behold the man." The scourging as a rule preceded crucifixion. It was in itself a punishment so severe, that in some cases it ended in death and made crucifixion superfluous. Here Pilate inflicts it as a measure of compromise. He expects them to be satisfied with this cruel punishment, which in his own opinion inflicted far more upon the prisoner than He deserved. There is in fact a twofold attempt on the part of the Governor in this scene. Their merciless desire for the punishment and blood of Jesus, is to be met by the cruel scourging. The remaining feeling of humanity and compassion, if there be such a thing left in their hearts, is to be touched by the presentation of the bleeding victim of their persecution, for whom even the heartless Roman pleads mercy: "Behold the man!" What a contradiction and inconsistency in this double act, first scourging the innocent as if He were guilty; and

III. Jesus Before the Governor Pilate (18:28–19:16)

then pleading for the scourged one as if He were innocent! First gratifying the bloodthirsty beast with a taste of the blood that was craved, and then appealing to a human soul in the beast that had tasted blood! A Roman governor who had gone so far had really given himself away completely. Henceforth he will be an easy prey to the cruel determination of the enemies of Christ whom nothing short of death can satisfy.

For a moment, however, Pilate seems as determined not to submit to their dictation as they were to obtain the penalty for Jesus. Highly provoked and indignant over the failure of his last attempt, the Governor meets their inexorable "Crucify Him" with the stern irony: "Take Him yourselves and crucify Him; for I find no crime in Him;"—if there is any meaning in this last clause it must be: "I cannot and will not do it."

6. Jesus the Son of God (19:7–11)

7–11. *The Jews answered him, We have a law, and by that law he ought to die, because he made himself the Son of God. When Pilate therefore heard this saying, he was the more afraid; and he entered into the palace again, and saith unto Jesus, Whence art thou? But Jesus gave him no answer. Pilate therefore saith unto him, Speakest thou not unto me? knowest thou not that I have power to release thee, and have power to crucify thee? Jesus answered him, Thou wouldest have no power against me, except it were given thee from above: therefore he that delivered me unto thee hath greater sin.*

The Jewish rulers, being aware that they are checked and repulsed at this point, try an approach from another side. Much against their own wish,—because it implied the sacrifice of a great principle on their part,—they find themselves compelled at last to bring the religious charge of blasphemy also before the Governor, to whose domain it certainly did not belong. "We have a law and by that law He ought to die, because He made Himself the Son of God." This law, they claim, has never been interfered with by the Romans. They have it still and they insist on its being respected. It demands the death of the blasphemer who makes Himself equal with God! The light-hearted skeptic, on hearing this, is seized with superstitious dread of having before him one of the gods (as

Paul and Barnabas were taken for Jupiter and Mercurius in Lystra, Acts 14:11 ff.). He withdraws from the multitude, enters the palace again and saith unto Jesus: "Whence art Thou?" But Jesus gave him no answer. Was it because by telling the Governor the truth on this point He would have made it impossible for him to pass the sentence of death? or was it simply because Pilate by this time had heard enough of Him? But the silence of the Lord again irritates the Governor. He feels deeply offended and bursts out in savage indignation: "Speakest Thou not unto me? Knowest Thou not that I have power to release Thee and have power to crucify Thee?" This is no doubt the worst thing Pilate ever said, the saddest exhibition of the low standard to which the much and deservedly praised Roman jurisdiction could be degraded, in the hands of an unscrupulous, despotic governor. But I am inclined to say, Pilate was not quite as bad as this word of his. If he had been satisfied from the beginning of having such power, in that absolutely arbitrary sense of the word, he would never have troubled himself so much about taking a stand against the Jews, as he had done up to this point.

The answer of the Lord is full of majesty and gentleness at the same time. Over against the "power" claimed by Pilate, He points to the higher One who gave it to him from above. And then the wonderful kindness and gentleness, the touch of hearty sympathy with poor Pilate in the words: "He that delivered Me unto thee hath greater sin." The Lord gives him to understand that He appreciates the difficulty and embarrassment of his position, and that He knows where to locate the moral responsibility in this case with perfect impartiality. He tells him, what Pilate has been telling himself, that there is sin, great sin in this whole process. He cannot and does not exonerate Pilate. But He knows also that Pilate is not the original instigator of this thing. It has been thrust upon him against his own will and desire, and all his efforts to get rid of the case have been in vain. The greater sin is with those that delivered Jesus to him, Caiaphas, the High Priest of that year, and the rulers of Israel in general, including the "one of the twelve who betrayed Him."

III. Jesus Before the Governor Pilate (18:28–19:16)

7. Cæsar's Friendship. The Governor Yields (19:12–16)

12–16. *Upon this Pilate sought to release him: but the Jews cried out, saying, If thou release this man, thou art not Cæsar's friend: every one that maketh himself a king speaketh against Caesar. When Pilate therefore heard these words, he brought Jesus out, and sat down on the judgment seat at a place called The Pavement, but in Hebrew, Gabbatha. Now it was the Preparation of the passover: it was about the sixth hour. And he saith unto the Jews, Behold, your King! They therefore cried out, Away with him, away with him, crucify him. Pilate saith unto them, Shall I crucify your King? The chief priests answered, We have no king but Caesar. Then therefore he delivered him unto them to be crucified.*

This third charge then of the Jews, introducing their law against blasphemy is another failure. It only had the effect that "Pilate sought to release Him" (ver. 12). Consequently their last mine is sprung which shatters to pieces the Governor's defense bringing him to unconditional surrender. "If thou release this man, thou art not Cæsar's friend: every one that maketh himself a king, speaketh against Cæsar." They intimate that they will denounce him to the Emperor as one who spared a dangerous rebel, a king of the Jews. And Pilate knew well enough, that such a threat was indeed a serious matter with a ruler like Tiberius, of whom the historians (particularly Suetonius) say that the laws concerning offences against the majesty of Caesar were executed by him in the most cruel and unsparing manner. Even the good conscience of a spotless character would have offered poor chances of escaping the consequence of such denunciations. And such a character was not that of Pilate. He therefore yielded, and delivered Him unto them to be crucified. But in doing this against his own conscience he will at least have the satisfaction of revenging himself on these contemptible Jews, after his own mind. Sitting on the judgment seat, ready to pass the final sentence, the Roman Governor taunts the raging Jews with the cruel sneer: "Behold your king! Shall I crucify your king?" The fearful effect of these words upon the Jews reveals the crisis which had now been reached in the history of that nation, the divine nemesis upon God's chosen people, who in surrendering their Messiah to the Gentiles actually dishonored and destroyed their own glory and life as a nation. All through this process, in spite of their conceit and arrogance, they had most ignominiously lowered themselves before the Roman. The only Jew for whom he showed a particle of respect was the prisoner in bonds, Jesus of Nazareth. For the rest of them he had nothing but contempt, which grew all the more bitter as he allowed himself to be dragged down to the level of this murderous crowd. But now he has his revenge. "Here is what you want. The cross for your King! Ye shall have it! Let the King of the Jews be crucified!"

"We have no king but Caesar!"—this is the desperate, furious answer of the Jews. It is the public and formal renunciation, made on the feast of the Passover, made before the judgment seat of the Roman governor, of all their Messianic hopes and expectations. What a judgment upon those people who were haunted night and day by the one thought and desire, how to put an end to Roman rule and Cæsar's reign, with the help of a Messiah after their own heart, that they must now be brought to this formal, public declaration: "We have no king but Caesar." Of a truth they had no king but Cæsar. The king of Israel, "who had visited and brought redemption for His people, and had raised up a horn of salvation for them in the house of His servant David" (Luke 1:68, 69), Him they rejected, saying: "We will not have this man reign over us" (Luke 19:14). They have chosen Cæsar. And Caesar shall be all that is left to them, Cæsar's sword, Cæsar's legions, Cæsar's eagles, which are hovering over them ready to devour the carcass of what had once been God's chosen and beloved people.

IV. THE EXECUTION (19:17–42)

1. *The Crucifixion (19:17–18)*

17–18. *They took Jesus therefore: and he went out, bearing the cross for himself, unto the place called The place of a skull, which is called in Hebrew Golgotha: where they crucified him, and with him two others, on either side one, and Jesus in the midst.*

Thus we have reached the scene on Calvary and here particularly the principle is to be observed, which we found in John's presentation of the Passion-history in general, viz. that only a few, but most significant

IV. The Execution (19:17–42)

and characteristic features are given. "He went out,"—"that He might sanctify the people through His own blood, He suffered without the gate. (Let us therefore go forth unto Him without the camp, bearing His reproach." Heb. 13:12.) The bearing of the cross by Jesus Himself is also one of the features peculiar to John, while the Synoptists tell us that when they reached the outskirts of the city the cross was laid on Simon of Cyrene, to carry it after Jesus. It was customary to lead those condemned to crucifixion through the most populous streets and places; the criminal in chains preceded by a herald who called out the charge of which he had been found guilty; frequently a tablet was tied round the neck of the condemned man, containing the statement of his guilt. Crucifixion itself was the most ignominious, and at the same time the most painful and cruel death penalty that could be inflicted. It was an exceedingly slow process of torture, resulting in death at the earliest in about twelve hours and sometimes not before the third day.

2. The Inscription on the Cross (19:19–22)

19–22. *And Pilate wrote a title also, and put it on the cross. And there was written, Jesus of Nazareth, the King of the Jews. This title therefore read many of the Jews: for the place where Jesus was crucified was nigh to the city: and it was written in Hebrew, and in Latin, and in Greek. The chief priests of the Jews therefore said to Pilate, Write not, The King of the Jews; but, that he said, I am King of the Jews. Pilate answered, What I have written I have written.*

All the Synoptists have a brief statement concerning the title which Pilate wrote and put on the cross: "Jesus of Nazareth, the King of the Jews," but the fourth Gospel gives the fullest account of the circumstances connected with this inscription, setting forth its full significance both for the Lord and His enemies. It is evident that this was an afterthought, occurring to Pilate in his burning desire to have his revenge on those men, to whom he had yielded against his conscience. And truly a greater insult could not be offered to them and the people represented by them, than to fix over the head of that man of sorrows, the helpless, naked, bleeding outcast, this title: "The King of the Jews." On the day of their highest festival, in the midst of the vast assembly gathered in

Jerusalem on that occasion, the defamation of the Jews was thus publicly proclaimed in the three principal languages of the ancient civilized world! No wonder the chief priests of the Jews keenly felt the sting of that inscription. But it was the title which they themselves had fastened upon Jesus; and to give it over to the shame of the cross together with its bearer was simply to publish, ratify and seal their own declaration: "We have no king but Cæsar." What was most offensive to them was the objective historical form of that inscription, which fixed and proclaimed it for all time as a historical fact, that Jesus of Nazareth, the King of the Jews, was nailed to the cross! If it could only be presented as a statement and imagination of His own, that "He said I am king of the Jews," a claim and pretension which did not deserve to be credited. They proposed this change to the Governor, confidently expecting that he would make no difficulty in yielding this little point, having yielded everything they wanted. But this time the shaking reed is found to be an immovable rock. "What I have written I have written." If it had not been his spite against the Jews, it was the Roman law itself, which forbade him to alter one jot or tittle of the formal and official sentence thus published. Rome has spoken. Rome has written. And God has spoken and God has written through this Governor. This writing shall abide. All the scribes and doctors of Israel shall not alter this scripture, which enrols Pilate with Moses and all the rest, as one of the writers of God's revelation, even as Caiaphas has been enrolled with Isaiah and the others as one of the prophets. Roman hands, by order of Cæsar Augustus, for the first time entered that blessed name of Jesus into the lists of the empire. Roman hands wrote and affixed over the head of the dying Jesus the name which is above every name, the one name under heaven given among men wherein we must be saved. This title, John significantly says, was read by many Jews, and it was written in Hebrew and in Latin and in Greek. Being written it was read. The writing being finished the reading begins. But the question is: "How readest thou?" (Luke 10:26). "Understandest thou what thou readest?" (Acts 8:30). Being written in Hebrew and in Greek and in Latin, its reading was not confined to the Jews, but it could

IV. The Execution (19:17–42)

be read and understood by the Gentiles as well, who happened to be in Jerusalem.

It was written in Hebrew, thus far the language of revealed religion; of the patriarchs, priests and kings, who had, centuries ago, been looking for this king; in the language of the Psalms and services which sang of Him, and prophesied and typified Him in the Old Testament.

It was written in Greek, the language of wisdom and learning, of highest culture and art in the ancient world, the language of the first translation of the Old Testament, the Septuagint.

It was written in Latin, the language of the ruling nation, of the great organizers and administrators, of order and discipline, whose spirit was inherited by the Mediaeval Church, which, in raising the stupendous structure of the Roman Hierarchy, was the most powerful instrumentality in bringing the Gentiles to the obedience of faith.

Here then is the first polyglot on the name of the crucified Jesus, a commentary to His word, which we read in the 12th chapter, "And I when I am lifted up from the earth will draw all men unto Myself;" an anticipation of Pentecost, when Jews and proselytes and strangers heard the disciples "speaking in their own tongues the mighty works of God" (Acts 2:11). The three tongues there are a prophecy of the three hundred, in which the name of Jesus is read and proclaimed at the present time.

3. Dividing His Garments (19:23, 24)

23–24. *The soldiers therefore, when they had crucified Jesus, took his garments, and made four parts, to every soldier a part; and also the coat: now the coat was without seam, woven from the top throughout. They said therefore one to another, Let us not rend it, but cast lots for it, whose it shall be: that the scripture might be fulfilled, which saith,*

>*They parted my garments among them,*
>*And upon my vesture did they cast lots.*
>*These things therefore the soldiers did.*

This feature of the Passion-history is only very briefly referred to by the Synoptists, who place it before their account of the inscription. But in John the narrative is much fuller, showing the hand of the Apostle who was present at the scene as an eyewitness. At the same time he points out the significance of this fact as a direct and literal fulfilment of the 22d Psalm. The Synoptists have no reference to this; not even Matthew, who is richest in references to Old Testament prophecies fulfilled in Christ. (See the Revised Version, Matt. 27:35, which simply omits the reference to the Psalm as a later insertion from John.)

4. Last Will of Mary's Son (19:25–27)

25–27. But there were standing by the cross of Jesus his mother, and his mother's sister, Mary the wife of Clopas, and Mary Magdalene. When Jesus therefore saw his mother, and the disciple standing by, whom he loved, he saith unto his mother, Woman, behold, thy son! Then saith he to the disciple, Behold thy mother! And from that hour the disciple took her unto his own home.

Of the seven words on the cross the Gospel of John records three: The third, to Mary and John: "Woman, behold thy Son! and behold Thy mother!" the fifth: "I thirst," and the sixth: "It is finished." Matthew and Mark have the fourth only: "My God, My God! why hast Thou forsaken Me?" St. Luke gives the first two and the seventh: "Father, forgive them for they know not what they do." "Verily I say unto thee today shalt thou be with Me in Paradise," and "Father, into Thy hands I commend My spirit."

Standing by the cross, faithful to the last, fearless even in the midst of that sneering and reviling crowd, we find the women. When Peter and James and Philip and Andrew, and Thomas and Nathanael and all the rest had fled, the women stood, and stood by the cross! And with them one solitary apostle of all the twelve, the beloved disciple. It is not necessary to refute the vagaries of Romish commentators who try very hard to prove from Mary's presence under the cross, and from the words addressed to her by the dying Saviour, that she was a kind of assistant of the Lord in the work of redemption, laboring with Him for the salvation of mankind. The very first word, the title or address given to her in this testament of her Son, overthrows all such theories. It is the same word "woman," with which He addressed her at the marriage table in Cana,

IV. The Execution (19:17–42)

assigning to her her proper position in her relation to Himself. Here under the cross she is in an emphatic sense nothing but the "woman," the frail, helpless woman that needs the strong supporting arm of a faithful and devoted son. And this the Lord provides for her in committing her to the care of His beloved John. Having made intercession even for His enemies in the first word on the cross as the High Priest and having opened the gate of Paradise to the dying thief in the second, as the King and Lord forever, He now makes His last will and testament for Mary His mother. But what can He possibly leave to her? There He hangs on the cross, stripped of everything, even His garments divided among His executioners, nothing left to Him that He could leave to Mary. And yet there is a rich capital, honestly earned by Him in His life of love, and wonderfully increasing in those very hours of His severest trial and passion, it is the love of those whom He calls His own. It was both His gift and His command that they should love one another even as He had loved them unto death. Blessed John to whom the dying Lord gave such an evidence of His undying affection for His beloved disciple, that He committed to his charge His nearest and dearest on earth. Blessed Mary, who inherited such a rich legacy in the tender love and care of the disciple thus honored by the Lord!

5. Death of Jesus (19:28–30)

28–30. *After this Jesus, knowing that all things are now finished, that the scripture might be accomplished, saith, I thirst. There was set there a vessel full of vinegar: so they put a sponge full of the vinegar upon hyssop, and brought it to his mouth. When Jesus therefore had received the vinegar, he said, It is finished: and he bowed his head, and gave up his spirit.*

The bodily sufferings of the incarnate Word culminate in the burning thirst which compels Him for the last time to humble Himself before His enemies and murderers, and to ask from them a moistening of His parched lips. But even this feature of the Lord's passion appears in the light of an exact fulfilment of scripture prophecy. The twenty-second Psalm, which the Lord has used to give expression to the deepest agony of His soul, also described the bodily suffering of the crucified Saviour:

"My strength is dried up like a potsherd; and my tongue cleaveth to my jaws" (Ps. 22:15; cf. also Ps. 69:21, in my thirst they gave Me vinegar to drink). There is no doubt that no other part of the O. T. Scripture was so much in the mind of Christ during those terrible hours when He was suspended on the cross, as the twenty-second Psalm. In remembrance of this Scripture and in full assurance that every particle of it was to be fulfilled and that this fulfillment was now reaching its climax, He said: "I thirst." And this burning thirst of His body at the same time typified the craving of His soul to see His work finished, to bring salvation to a perishing world. As it had been His meat all through this life to do the will of Him that sent Him and to accomplish His work (John 4:34), so He was now longing to be refreshed according to the word of Isaiah: "He shall see the travail of His soul and shall be satisfied" (53:11).

His burning lips being moistened by the vinegar on the sponge, He received strength to utter with "a loud voice" (as Mark distinctly says, 15:37) the great word of victory: "It is finished." All the preceding words had their special address to which they were directed. This one is without such an address and yet its meaning and direction are easy to understand. It is the word of consummation and victory in the fullest and absolute sense. It is His achievement, His victory, and yet He does not say: "I have finished it," as He had a right to say, but, as the humblest performer of the greatest work for time and eternity, He simply and modestly says: "It is finished"—the passion, the action, the whole obedience of His life even unto death, the scripture, with its prophecies, its types, its law, its covenants, the will of the Father, the redemption of mankind, all is finished. No one can add to this, no one can detract from this. Christ has finished it and Christ alone! And Christ announces and proclaims it to the world. Having poured out His soul unto death He is entitled to be the first herald and preacher of the victory of the cross, declaring "His righteousness unto a people that shall be born, that He hath done it" (Ps. 22:31). Again, He says it to the Father: "It is finished, what Thou hast given Me to do. I glorified Thee on the earth, having accomplished the work which Thou hast given Me to do" (John 17:4). Again: He proclaims His victory to hell and all the powers of Satan: It is

IV. The Execution (19:17–42)

finished: Death where is thy sting? Hell, where is thy victory? Here is the stronger one that overcame the strong man fully armed and guarding his court. He taketh from him his whole armor wherein he trusted and divideth his spoils. The battle is over, the victory secured. It is finished! And lastly, this loud voice of the dying Saviour goes up into the heavens and makes them resound with the Alleluias of those that rejoice over one sinner that repented. It fills them with that song of praise which shall not cease to all eternity: "Worthy is the Lamb that hath been slain, to receive the power, and riches, and wisdom, and might, and honor, and glory, and blessing."

6. Piercing His Side (19:31–37)

31–37. *The Jews therefore, because it was the Preparation, that the bodies should not remain on the cross upon the sabbath (for the day of that sabbath was a high day), asked of Pilate that their legs might be broken, and that they might be taken away. The soldiers therefore came, and brake the legs of the first, and of the other which was crucified with him: but when they came to Jesus, and saw that he was dead already, they brake not his legs: howbeit one of the soldiers with a spear pierced his side, and straightway there came out blood and water. And he that hath seen hath borne witness, and his witness is true: and he knoweth that he saith true, that ye also may believe. For these things came to pass, that the scripture might be fulfilled, A bone of him shall not be broken. And again another scripture saith, They shall look on him whom they pierced.*

In the midst of the deepest humiliation of the Lord the Gospel of St. John continues to point out certain features indicating His Messianic dignity. The day of the Lord's death was "The Preparation," that is, the day before Sabbath, and in this case the day before the great Passover Sabbath. The Jews therefore were anxious that the bodies of the crucified men should not be left hanging on the cross. This was the custom of the Romans, who left the bodies of crucified criminals as a prey for wild beasts. But the Jewish law (Deut. 21:22, f.) ordered that the bodies of men, executed by hanging, should not remain all night upon the tree, but should be buried that day, that the land might not be defiled. This provision of the Mosaic law may properly be applied to those also who died on the cross, "the accursed tree," though crucifixion was not the usual form of capital punishment among the Jews. This then was one demand, with which the Jews appeared before Pilate, "that those bodies might be taken away" before the beginning of the great Sabbath Day. But they could not be taken away, unless there was official evidence of actual death. To obtain this, they also demanded "that their legs might be broken." This was also a Roman form of punishment, not always connected with crucifixion, and even not always resulting in immediate death. The piercing with the spear would have secured that end more promptly, and with much less torture to the dying criminal. But it seems the Jews were not yet satisfied with the sufferings which their victim had endured on the cross. They asked for this crurifragium (breaking of the legs) as the last bitter cup for Jesus, in addition to all the torments heaped upon Him on that day. But here they were met with a divine "Thus far and no further." Their demand was not fulfilled as far as Christ's person was concerned. "When the soldiers came to Jesus and saw that He was dead already, they brake not His legs;" but one of them pierced His side with a spear. By this unexpected turn, for which there was no order given by any human commander, in a most remarkable manner two prophecies concerning the Messiah, the Lamb of God, find their fulfilment at the same time; the one, referring to the Passover-Lamb (Exodus 12:46), "A bone of him shall not be broken;" the other, spoken by the prophet Zechariah (12:10), "They shall look on Him whom they pierced." Though the spear was thrust by the hand of a Gentile, it was in reality Israel that rejected, murdered and pierced the divine Messiah. But, says the prophet, the day shall come, when they will "look on Him whom they pierced," meaning, not the day of judgment, to which Revelation 1:7 refers, but the day of grace when Jerusalem shall turn to Him with true repentance and anxious supplications, as on Pentecost when three thousand Israelites recognized their Saviour and Redeemer in the pierced Christ.

  The result of the spear thrust in the Saviour's side is fully described by John: "Straightway there came out *blood and water.*" Some commentators find in this flow from the side of Jesus the natural result of the breaking of the pericardium. But the majority of theologians ever

IV. The Execution (19:17–42)

since the patristic period hold that there was, in this flow of blood and water, something not in the line of the common laws of nature, but of a miraculous, supernatural character. "Christ's body," says Luther, "is flesh and blood even as our own body, and dies; but His flesh and blood being without sin, He dies in such a manner, that even in His death there is an indication of life. For while our blood in death becomes cold and ceases to flow, in Christ's body it remains in a fluid condition." This view is essentially adopted by such modern commentators as Godet, Grau and others. Certain it is that the eyewitness John marks this detail as one of special importance and significance for the Church. Even if we hesitate to find a direct connection between this passage and 1 John 5:6 (This is He that came by water and blood, even Jesus Christ; not with water only, but with the water and the blood),[1] there can be no doubt that the blood and water from the side of Jesus have a rich symbolic meaning for His Church. "Christ's blood is the treasure of our redemption, the ransom and satisfaction for our sins" (1 John 1:7) (Luther). Here we find the daily washing and cleansing from all our iniquities, in the forgiveness of our sins. And these blessings are conveyed and sealed to us through the means of grace, Baptism, the Word of the Gospel, and the Sacrament of the body and blood of Christ.

The manner in which this whole scene is described and the assurance of the writer that "his witness is true: and he knoweth that he saith true, that ye also may believe," has always and justly been considered as one of the strongest evidences of the Johannean origin of this Gospel, in spite of the attempts of modern critics to prove, at this very point, a distinction between the writer of the Gospel, and the eyewitness under the cross, the Apostle John.

7. The Burial of Christ (19:38–42)

38–42. *And after these things Joseph of Arimathæa, being a disciple of Jesus, but secretly for fear of the Jews, asked of Pilate that he might take away the body of Jesus: and Pilate gave him leave. He came therefore, and took away his body. And*

---

[1] Bugge finds here a reference to the beginning and the end of Christ's mediatorial office: His baptism in the river Jordan, and His death on the cross.

there came also Nicodemus, he who at the first came to him by night, bringing a mixture of myrrh and aloes, about a hundred pound weight. So they took the body of Jesus, and bound it in linen cloths with the spices, as the custom of the Jews is to bury. Now in the place where he was crucified there was a garden; and in the garden a new tomb wherein was never man yet laid. There then because of the Jews' Preparation (for the tomb was nigh at hand) they laid Jesus.

The burial of the Lord as described in this section is, as Calvin calls it, a fitting prelude to His glorious resurrection on Easter morning. The Jewish custom of throwing the bodies of executed criminals into a common ditch had to give way to the more humane Roman practice, which had been particularly favored by Caesar Augustus, of returning such bodies to their friends and families, whenever application was made for them.[1] All the four Evangelists introduce Joseph of Arimathaea in connection with the burial of the Lord. While John only speaks of him as a secret disciple of Christ, the others give additional details as to his character, social standing, wealth, etc. He was a rich man (Matthew), a councillor of honorable estate (Mark), a good man and a righteous who was looking for the kingdom of God, and who, as a member of the Sanhedrim, had not consented to their counsel and deed (Luke). His home had been in Arimathaea, the Ramah, or Ramathaim-Zophim, on Mount Ephraim, in the tribe of Benjamin, known in the Old Testament as the city of Samuel. He had moved to Jerusalem not many years before these events, and had there secured the garden with the burial-place for his family, which had not yet been used. Joseph had not been present on Calvary during the agony and death of the Lord. He appeared on the scene when all was over. And now, he had the boldness, as Mark says, to go to Pilate and ask for the body, thus professing himself openly as a friend and disciple of Jesus. There was hardly any risk in this step as far as his relation to the Roman Governor was concerned. But it required great courage to do this, at that time, in the face of the Pharisees and the Sanhedrim, of which he was a member. His fear of the Jews, which had

---

[1] Tiberius, it is true, had been acting contrary to this; but in the provinces the milder practice prevailed even during the reign of that cruel emperor.

IV. The Execution (19:17–42)

thus far kept him from a public confession of Christ, was well grounded. For "they had agreed that if any man should confess Him to be Christ, he should be put out of the synagogue" (John 9:22). And so he had been one of the "many rulers" who "believed on Him, but, because of the Pharisees they did not confess it, lest they should be put out of the synagogue" (John 12:42). But now, the Saviour's dying love has wrought this miracle in him, and made him the first to cast away all human considerations and to come forward as a bold, devout confessor, when Peter and Thomas and the rest had fled and forsaken their Lord. Nor is his case the only one. He is at once joined by Nicodemus, also a councillor, also, heretofore, a secret disciple of Jesus, who at the first came to Him by night. Where the first have become last, the last now become first. In the most scrupulous way these two men make provision for the burial of the Lord, buying linen and myrrh and aloes, and wrapping the body up in those spices according to the Jewish custom of burying. This is emphatically said in distinction from the Egyptian custom, which, with its radical treatment, reduced the body to a mummy. At the manger of the new-born king of the Jews the Magi from the East appeared with their treasures of gold, frankincense and myrrh, to provide for the journey to Egypt. Here the two Sanhedrists appear with their homage before the dead king of the Jews, to contribute from their wealth to His last journey to that silent tomb in Joseph's garden.

Thus ends the passion of the Lord with the dawn of glory upon it. The Easter-Sun is ready to rise over the tomb which could not hold its captive.

JOHN 20

V. The Resurrection of Jesus (Ch. 20)

1. Peter and John at the Tomb (20:1–10)

1–10. *Now on the first day of the week cometh Mary Magdalene early, while it was yet dark, unto the tomb, and seeth the stone taken away from the tomb. She runneth therefore, and cometh to Simon Peter, and to the other disciple, whom Jesus loved, and saith unto them, They have taken away the Lord out of the tomb, and we know not where they have laid him. Peter therefore went forth, and the other disciple, and they went toward the tomb. And they ran both together: and the other disciple outran Peter, and came first to the tomb. And stooping and looking in, he seeth the linen cloths lying; yet entered he not in. Simon Peter therefore also cometh, following him, and entered into the tomb; and he beholdeth the linen cloths lying, and the napkin, that was upon his head, not lying with the linen cloths, but rolled up in a place by itself. Then entered in therefore the other disciple also, which came first to the tomb, and he saw, and believed. For as yet they knew not the scripture, that he must rise again from the dead. So the disciples went away again unto their own home.*

Concerning the history of the resurrection itself and its first announcement through the angel and the tomb, the Gospel of St. John has nothing to say. It is evident that the Evangelist is familiar with the record of this fundamental fact of Christianity as found in the Synoptists. The points with which John supplements their narrative show how utterly unconcerned he is about seeming difficulties or disagreements in consequence of his statements. The principal object with him is in perfect keeping with his whole Gospel. The *faith* of the disciples in their glorified and risen Lord is to be shown. And the prominent figures represented in this argument are Mary Magdalene, Peter, John and Thomas. Mary Magdalene was Mary of Magdala[1] on the west coast of the Lake of Galilee,

---

[1] In the Western Church, chiefly through the influence of Gregory the Great, she was, without any historical evidence, identified with the great sinner (Luke 7:37–50), and this

V. The Resurrection of Jesus (Ch. 20)

near Tiberias (Matt. 15:39). She is spoken of as the woman from whom seven devils had gone out (Luke 8:2; Mark. 16:9). Mary Magdalene had gone to the sepulchre early in the morning in company with the other women; each Evangelist mentioning those by name that were to him the most prominent. But the testimony of all the four Gospels agrees in making her the main figure. There is no real conflict in the different statements as to the time of their going to the sepulchre. John says "while it was yet dark," Luke, "at early dawn," Mark, "They came to the tomb when the sun was risen." Considering the distance they had to go, the time needed for their meeting each other, and the fact that the transition from night to daylight is very quick in that latitude, we can readily understand how Mary Magdalene could have left her house "while it was yet dark" and reached the sepulchre just at sunrise. At the sight of "the stone taken away from the tomb" Mary Magdalene is completely bewildered. She turns and runs, without waiting for consultation with the other women, to tell the chief disciples of this awful discovery. Her words to Peter and John leave no doubt as to the thought that was, at the moment, uppermost in her mind. "*They* have taken away the Lord out of the tomb." She mentions no name. But we know whom she means. The Jews, the Rulers and Pharisees, in their unrelenting enmity against the Lord, have desecrated even the quiet resting-place of the beloved Master. They have broken into it, of course to take away His body and cast it off, in dishonor and shame, somewhere without burial! "And *we* know not where they have laid Him." With these words she clearly shows that she was not alone when that discovery was made. Others were with her,—the very women whose names are given by, the Synoptists; and speaking of herself and those companions she says: "*We* know not."

Though "the disciple whom Jesus loved" is mentioned in the second place, we are inclined to think that it was to his house she went,

---

idea has ever since been inseparably connected with her name, the "Magdalene." Sometimes even Mary of Bethany was found in that same person, and thus three distinct women of New Testament history were thrown together into one; quite contrary to the usual practice of Roman legends, to multiply, rather than to diminish, the number of their Saints and their precious relics.

and there she found Peter with John. A good place for fallen Peter, to be with John, the beloved disciple, and with Mary, the mother of the Lord, whom John had taken into his house. And a good testimony for John, that he did not shut out Peter in the sorrow of his broken and contrite heart, but received him kindly and offered him the sympathy and good counsel of a true friend and brother.

The effect of the astounding message which Mary Magdalene carried to these apostles was instantaneous. Without the slightest delay they start for the sepulchre. They run both together, though John, the younger, with the easier conscience, outruns Peter, who, in addition to his years, is burdened with a heavy load of sin and guilt. But while John is the first to reach the tomb, he hesitates to enter in. He is filled with awe and perplexity at the thought of strange and conflicting possibilities. Should His enemies really have carried their hatred so far as to violate the sacredness of His tomb as Mary thought? Or is there another possibility?—a heavenly interference? Meanwhile Peter also arrives. He is the practical man, of resolute action. Without losing time in reflection or discussion with John, he at once enters into the tomb. He surveys the condition of things in detail: There, the linen cloths lying, and the napkin, that was upon His head, not lying with the linen cloths, but rolled up in a place by itself. He calls out this report to John. There is, then, no evidence of violence, or spoliation; everything as orderly and undisturbed as if one had quietly risen from his slumber and had laid off these cloths which were no longer needed.[1] Thereupon John also enters in "and he saw and believed." What did he believe? That "they had taken away Christ's body" as Mary Magdalene had reported? This is the view held by some of our greatest commentators, like Luther, Gerhard, Bengel and others. But we cannot in this case agree with them. "*He believed*" is entirely too strong and too comprehensive a term to confine its meaning to the acceptance of that statement of Mary. John was the first to believe the great fact of

---

[1] Bengel thinks that this proper adjustment of the linen and napkin in the tomb was owing to the ministrations of the angels who, even then were present in the tomb, though unseen by Peter and John.

V. The Resurrection of Jesus (Ch. 20)

Christ's resurrection, on the evidence of what *"he saw."* First he saw and then he believed. And in writing this short, comprehensive statement, John well remembered, what Jesus said to Thomas in His criticism of the faith of that disciple: "Because thou hast seen Me, thou hast believed: blessed are they that have not seen and yet have believed" (John 20:29). He has therefore no reason whatever to be particularly elated over this first faith of his. He is, indeed, honest and humble enough to add another word of criticism concerning his own and Peter's position at that time. "As yet they knew not the scripture; that He must rise again from the dead." There was still, even in John's case, a lack of understanding the scripture. And whatever there was of faith, it was not that plain, direct scripture-faith, taking the word and holding on to it. It was a faith that still needed the assistance of sight, instead of planting itself fairly and squarely upon the revealed word of God.

But what of Peter's condition of mind at that point? The statement, "He saw and he believed," is so clearly confined to John, that we cannot possibly include Peter in it. In Luke (24:12) we read: "He departed to his home *wondering* at what had come to pass." And possibly before he reached home the Lord Himself appeared to him and assured him of the great fact which crowned the work of redemption and sealed to Peter the forgiveness of his great sin. John also went to his "own home." Even for him the news of that morning was overwhelming. He needed some time of quiet meditation and self-collection, to realize in its full extent what had happened. And he might rest assured that the living Lord would not be long in demonstrating to His own disciples that He was risen indeed.

2. Mary Magdalene (20:11–18)

11–18. But Mary was standing without at the tomb weeping: so, as she wept, she stooped and looked into the tomb; and she beholdeth two angels in white sitting, one at the head, and one at the feet, where the body of Jesus had lain. And they say unto her, Woman, why weepest thou? She saith unto them, Because they have taken away my Lord, and I know not where they have laid him. When she had thus said, she turned herself back, and beholdeth Jesus standing, and knew not that it was Jesus. Jesus saith unto her, Woman, why weepest thou? whom seekest thou? She, supposing him to be the gardener, saith unto him, Sir, if thou hast borne him hence, tell me where thou hast laid him, and I will take him away. Jesus saith unto her, Mary. She turneth herself, and saith unto him in Hebrew, Rabboni; which is to say, Master. Jesus saith to her, Touch me not; for I am not yet ascended unto the Father: but go unto my brethren, and say to them, I ascend unto my Father and your Father, and my God and your God. Mary Magdalene cometh and telleth the disciples, I have seen the Lord; and how that he had said these things unto her.

Having informed the two disciples, Peter and John, of the condition of the tomb as found by the women, Mary Magdalene herself returned to the sepulchre in Joseph's garden, alone, not in company with the two Apostles, who were too quick for her. She probably arrived at the tomb after John and Peter had left it. Certainly she was there alone, after the disciples had gone home, staying there, as Bengel says, "majori perseverantia" (with greater perseverance). Her state of mind is that of one completely overwhelmed with grief, and quite inaccessible to any other thought than that of her bereavement. Having first lost the living Christ in the tomb which shut Him in, she is now made doubly wretched by the empty sepulchre, having lost even the dead Christ out of the sepulchre. Even the heavenly apparition of the two angels, like the cherubim at the ark of the covenant, one at the head and one at the feet, where the body of Jesus had lain, makes no impression whatever on her. There is no sign of astonishment, or of terror, as in the case of the other women (Mark 16:5). She is so wrapt up in her sorrow that she becomes indifferent to everything. The question addressed to her by those heavenly guardians is not so much an expression of sympathy, but rather a gentle rebuke to her, like the words, spoken by the angels to the women: "Why seek ye the living among the dead?" (Luke 24:5). There is in reality no cause for weeping at this empty tomb. Indeed, if she had found the dead body in the sepulchre, then she might have had good reason for her tears. In answer to the question of the angels she repeats, in a sort of mechanical way the same dreary statement, which she had, before, carried to the disciples: "They have taken away my Lord, and I know not

V. The Resurrection of Jesus (Ch. 20)

where they have laid Him,"—with the characteristic little change, however, that it is now: "I know not" (instead of "we know not"), because she is now alone with the angels. In her despondency she expects no consolation from any comforter and, without waiting for an answer, turns her back to the angels, when she sees another figure facing her outside the tomb. This time it is Christ Himself whom she does not, at first, recognize; her eyes veiled with tears, her heart with despair and unbelief, she is looking, not for a living Christ, but for a corpse. Moreover there must have been something strange, uncommon, not heretofore known to the disciples, in the manner and appearance of the risen Lord. He is the same and yet not the same, like a king, who has, for a number of years, done menial service in a foreign land, and is now ready to take full possession of his kingdom (Tholuck).

The question of the angels is repeated by the Lord: "Woman, why weepest thou?" with the addition of that tender and sympathetic "Whom seekest thou?" indicating a knowledge of her personal longing for a dear lost one. There is a rich and striking significance in these very first words from the lips of the risen Saviour: "Woman, why weepest thou?" Not only that the weeping one, the one most weary and heavy laden, is first and specially remembered by the risen Lord,[1] who is anxious to bring His peace to those that need it most. But it is *woman*, to whom the joy and triumph of resurrection is first appropriated. It is her sex that is thus considered and honored by the Lord. As woman, being first beguiled, had fallen into transgression, and had her fullest share in the misery and degradation resulting from sin and death, she is first to be cheered and comforted by the victory of the Saviour over sin and death. Mary Magdalene, supposing Him to be the gardener, saith unto Him, "Sir, if thou hast borne Him hence, tell me where thou hast laid Him, and I will take Him away." No name—there is only one of whom she thinks and whom she seeks, and she speaks of Him as if every one must know without a question whom she means. There is confusion in every word of hers, and deepest love and devotion in every word. The sympathy of the

---

[1] Cf. the message of the angel to the women: "Tell his disciples *and Peter.*"

stranger, "the gardener," has touched her heart and she confides her trouble to him. We discover a certain progress in a positive and hopeful direction, in the new theory which she now advances concerning the disappearance of her Lord's body. Possibly this removal is not an act of enemies, but done by friendly hands, for some good purpose.[1] But after all what Lord is that whom Mary serves, if any one can "take Him away" by guile or might? Or, whither will she, frail woman, carry Him to keep Him in a place of safety, if this rock-sealed tomb in the garden of His friend was no sufficient protection?

But now her Lord ends all this perplexity with one word: "Mary." How truly human this word of recognition with its gentle rebuke and its infinite tenderness! The "gardener" reveals himself as the good shepherd who had said of His sheep (John 10:4, 27, 28). "They hear and know His voice, they follow Him and no one shall snatch them out of His hand." With the old familiar "Rabboni" she throws herself down at Jesus' feet, to clasp them and hold Him, as if she were afraid that any one might snatch Him out of her hand! When the other women met the Lord for the first time after His resurrection, "They came and took hold of His feet and worshipped Him" (Matt. 28:9). When the terrified and affrighted disciples supposed that they beheld a spirit, at the first appearance of the Lord, He said to them: "See My hands and My feet, that it is I Myself: handle Me and see; for a spirit hath not flesh and bones, as ye behold Me having" (Luke 24:37–40). When doubting Thomas first met the risen Lord, Jesus said unto him: "Reach hither thy finger and see My hands; and reach hither thy hand and put it into My side: and be not faithless but believing." But when Mary Magdalene threw herself down before her Lord in the joy of her impulsive and affectionate heart, the Lord promptly checked that overflow of sentiment with His command: "Touch Me not." All the others needed encouragement to come nearer and to realize that their Lord was risen indeed. And with all the encouragement they received, they still were conscious of the majesty of their glorified

---

[1] Christ Himself has borne His body out of the grave and takes it up to the throne in heaven. (AUGUSTINE.)

V. The Resurrection of Jesus (Ch. 20)

Saviour. The women "worshipped" Him. Thomas said unto Him: "My Lord and my God!" But Mary's "Rabboni" was of a different character. However respectful this title may have been in bygone days, it fails to do justice to the risen Lord who must be recognized in His divine majesty. The former familiar intercourse based upon His visible presence, must yield to another relation. But to Mary Magdalene the concrete reality of that visible, bodily presence of Christ is so much even at that moment, that she is bent on retaining this and holding on to it, in utter ignorance of the great change that has taken place through the resurrection of the Lord.

"Touch Me not," saith the Lord, "for I am not yet ascended unto the Father." The reference to the ascension as the closing and culminating scene of this glorification on earth is clear enough in this connection. But there is a difficulty in the combination of that command with the statement "not yet ascended," and this statement given as the reason for that command (οὔπω γὰρ ἀναβέβηκα). Is it that the Lord means to comfort and to quiet Mary Magdalene with the assurance that she need not fear to lose His visible, bodily presence as yet, inasmuch as He is to stay yet for a little while before He will ascend to the Father? But the emphasis in this utterance of the Lord seems to us to be not on His staying yet for a while, but on the announcement of His approaching ascension. Mary Magdalene needs no assurance concerning the reality of Christ's resurrection. But she does need a reminder of His ascension in the near future. And this is the message she is to carry to the disciples: The risen Lord is not going to stay with us in this visible and tangible bodily presence, but He will soon ascend to the Father, thus consummating His glorification. This short period of the forty days between resurrection and ascension must therefore serve the purpose of weaning the disciples from that kind of intercourse with their Master (Rabbi) which they had hitherto enjoyed, and preparing them for the truly spiritual, and yet at the same time most realistic, manner of grasping, holding and enjoying their Lord and God through His Spirit, His Word and Sacraments, by which even the real presence of His body and blood is secured to them.

The careful distinction made in the words of the Lord between "*My Father* and your *Father*, *My God* and your *God*," is quite significant. Though it is His life-work to reveal the Father to us and to bring the wayward children back to the Father, to enjoy the Father's love, in the Father's house, though He goes so far as to call the disciples His "brethren," He never includes Himself with us, in speaking of God or to God as "*Our* Father." Whenever He refers to "the Father" in a personal way it is always with the claim of standing in a peculiar and unique relation to the Father. As the first word of Jesus in the temple (Luke 2:49) expressed His determination of clinging to "the Father" in a peculiar sense, over against the claims of a purely human affection (of Mary and Joseph), so does this emphatic reference to "the Father" in one of the very last utterances of the God-man on earth. Ever since Cyrillus, Ambrose and Augustine, the significance of these words of Christ has been marked and commented on by the fathers.[1] "*My* father," they say, "by nature, *yours* by grace; *My* God under whom I also am as a man; *your* God, whom I reconciled to you as the mediator between you and Him." There is special tenderness in the name "brethren" given to the disciples by their risen Lord. All through the shame and torture of His passion, the Lord stands before His captors and judges as a true king, whom they shall see sitting at the right hand of power, and coming on the clouds of heaven (Matt. 26:64; John 18:6). But now, in the glory of His resurrection, He calls His disciples "brethren." He is not ashamed to call them brethren (Hebrews 2:11), though by their desertion and denial they had cut themselves loose from Him. He brings them back and binds them to Himself again by that precious name, thus being in reality "the firstborn among many brethren" (Romans 8:29).

3. First Appearance before the Disciples (20:19–23)

19–23. When therefore it was evening, on that day, the first day of the week, and when the doors were shut where the disciples were, for fear of the Jews, Jesus came

---

[1] Non ait Patrem nostrum; aliter ergo meum, aliter vestrum: natura meum, gratia vestrum; Deum Meum, sub quo et Ego sum homo; Deum vestrum, inter quos et ipsum mediator sum. (AUGUSTINE.)

V. The Resurrection of Jesus (Ch. 20)

and stood in the midst, and saith unto them, Peace be unto you. And when he had said this, he shewed unto them his hands and his side. The disciples therefore were glad, when they saw the Lord. Jesus therefore said to them again, Peace be unto you: as the Father hath sent me, even so send I you. And when he had said this, he breathed on them, and saith unto them, Receive ye the Holy Ghost: whose soever sins ye forgive, they are forgiven unto them; whose soever sins ye retain, they are retained.

The sun of that first Easter-Day had gone down already. It was evening, and, no doubt, late in the evening, not far from midnight; for the two, returning from Emmaus (Luke 24:33–35), could not have reached Jerusalem before a very late hour. The little band of disciples were assembled, probably in the same upper room, where the Lord had addressed to them His parting discourses. The Easter-light is still struggling against the darkness of doubt and unbelief in their hearts. From early morning, as the day went on, one message after the other had reached them, announcing the resurrection, but "they believed not, their words appeared in their sight as idle talk" (Luke 24:11). Their lack of faith is shown by their "fear of the Jews." What had the disciples of a risen Christ to fear from the Jews? And, if their Lord was not risen, what protection would the closed doors afford against those enemies who had just succeeded in nailing Christ to the cross and sealing Him up in the tomb? But with the characteristic inconsistency of unbelief "the doors were shut—for fear of the Jews." And yet, with all their lack of faith, the disciples were gathered together that evening, in the name of their Lord, and they were to experience the blessed promise that "there is He in the midst of them" (Matt. 18:20).

"*Jesus came and stood in the midst.*" We can readily dismiss all attempts to explain Christ's entrance in a natural way. The exact process of His entering was not seen or closely observed by the disciples. All at once He stood among them. As His glorified body had left the tomb before the stone was rolled away, so He enters this room while the doors are shut. This proves, as Luther says, "that after His resurrection, in His kingdom on earth, He is not bound to time and space, but must be believed in and known as One who rules in omnipresent might, and is both willing and able to be with us whenever and wherever we need it, notwithstanding the world and all its power."

Having thus suddenly appeared among the disciples, the Lord greets them with the words: *"Peace be unto you."* It had been one of His last words on the evening before His passion: "Peace I leave unto you; My peace I give unto you" (John 14:27), it is the first word at their meeting again. As stated before, it is the customary Old Testament salutation, which these words contain. But even in the mouth of a devout Israelite of old it was more than an every-day salutation, it was a devout prayer, a benediction, when he said: "Peace be unto you." Out of the fullness of the Covenant-God he wished for him whom he thus saluted, all the blessings, the full salvation of His kingdom. But here, in the mouth of the risen Saviour, this word far surpasses any salutation ever used among His people. The whole victory of the crucified and risen Lord is contained in this word. The great work of reconciling the world unto God (2 Cor. 5:18, 19) is accomplished. This reconciliation is applied to and conveyed to the disciples personally. The word, "Peace be unto you," is to them their own personal absolution and justification, the individual appropriation of Christ's whole salvation.

And now "He showed unto them *His hands and His side.*" Luke even adds: His feet. This was done not simply to convince them of the reality of His bodily presence, the identity of His person, the indisputable fact of the resurrection itself; but to prove the direct connection between His wounds and the peace which He brought from the sepulchre. He has been in battle, and the peace He brings has been dearly bought by His own life-blood. "He was wounded for our transgressions, He was bruised for our iniquities; the chastisement of our peace was upon Him, and with His stripes we are healed" (Isaiah 53:5). These very wounds were the means to accomplish our atonement. And the living, glorified Christ will always bear the marks of that battle, He will always be known, and even *seen* in eternity, as the Crucified One. We can fully understand how the heart of the Evangelist warms at the remembrance of that scene, how the disciples were glad when they saw the Lord, when His promise was so literally fulfilled: I will see you again and your heart shall rejoice."

V. The Resurrection of Jesus (Ch. 20)

Having thus assured them of their personal forgiveness and salvation, the Lord repeats the words: *"Peace be unto you,"* with reference to the ministry of reconciliation which is committed to them. Being themselves children of peace, they are to be henceforth messengers of peace. As the Lord gave this peace into the hearts of His disciples, so they are to carry it into the hearts of men, by preaching forgiveness in the name of the crucified and risen Jesus of Nazareth. (See Isaiah 52:7; Romans 10:15. How beautiful are the feet of them that bring glad tidings of good things.) In a wider sense it is the work of every Christian to spread throughout the world the news and the power of the resurrection of Christ. Christians as such are to be "the light of the world" (Matt. 5:14). But in a special sense this charge is committed to the Apostles and the ministers of the word. The institution of the ministry of the Gospel is the direct fruit of the resurrection of Christ. *"As the Father hath sent Me, even so send I you."* The authority to send forth special commissioners or apostles is the same with the Son as it is with the Father. And the character of their commission is the same as that of Christ's, namely, to bear witness unto the truth. They must be willing to be sent, even as Christ had been sent by the Father. Their duty as apostles must be discharged in the same spirit, and under the same experiences, as Christ Himself went through in discharging His office as the great apostle of our heavenly calling: through the cross to the crown, through shame to glory. Thus they are to build up a spiritual kingdom, using no carnal weapons to uphold and to spread it, but simply preaching the Gospel of Jesus Christ, and thus helping to deliver men from sin and death.

When the Messiah Himself was "sent to preach good tidings to the meek" (Isaiah 61:1), "the Spirit of the Lord God was upon Him; the Lord had anointed Him." This same Spirit must be upon the disciples, if they are to be sent even as Christ was sent by the Father. He therefore *"breathed on them and saith unto them: Receive ye the Holy Ghost."* Another and most emphatic sign of life from the living Christ. He had before pointed them to His hands and side and feet, to His flesh and bone, and now they feel even the breath of His mouth, the very life of His soul, gently touching their cheeks. This "still small voice" of the breath of the Lord will be swelled, on the day of Pentecost, to the "rushing of the mighty wind which filled all the house where the disciples were sitting" (Acts 2:2).[1] They now receive a sign and pledge, a foretaste of the full gift of the Spirit that awaits them on the day of Pentecost.[2]

In the power of this Spirit of Christ the disciples are to discharge their office in the ministry of the word in a twofold direction: "*Whose soever sins ye forgive they are forgiven unto them; whose soever sins ye retain they are retained.*" Their ministry is to be valid in both directions as to forgiveness of sins and retention of sins. On whom then is this power here conferred? Is it on a special class or order of men, the clergy, as Rome and all Romanizers teach? But when this power was conveyed by the Lord, the apostles were not all present; nor were those present on this occasion all apostles. John clearly distinguishes between the twelve (ver. 24) and the disciples (ver. 19). And Luke tells us distinctly that others were gathered with the disciples (Luke 24:33) on that evening. Luther therefore is right in saying: "This power is given to all Christians. Whosoever hath the Holy Spirit to him this power is given, that is, to him who is a Christian. But who is a Christian? he that believeth. He that believeth hath the Holy Spirit. Every Christian therefore has the power, claimed by Pope and Bishops, of forgiving or retaining sins. Well, then, some might say, we can pronounce absolution, baptize, preach, administer communion? No, indeed. St. Paul says: 'Let all things be done decently and in order' (1 Cor. 14:40). We all have this power, but let no one presume to exercise it publicly, except he be called and chosen for this office by the congregation. But in private we may use this power. If, for instance, my brother comes to me, saying: 'Dear Brother, I am vexed in my conscience, give me a word of absolution,' I am free to do this and tell him the Gospel, how that he should take hold of Christ's work, believing that the

---

[1] One of the many features which prove that the gospel of John is at the same time the most realistic and the most spiritual of all.

[2] John Gerhard distinguishes between three different kinds of receiving the Spirit: First, for their own personal sanctification, the disciples had received the Spirit already; second, for their ministerial office they receive it at this point; third, for the miraculous gifts with which they are to be endowed, they shall receive it on the day of Pentecost.

V. The Resurrection of Jesus (Ch. 20)

righteousness of Christ is truly his own; and that his own sins are truly Christ's. This is, indeed, the greatest service I may do to my fellowman."

This power is, of course not to be limited to the actual word of absolution, in the stricter sense of that term. It includes the whole ministry of the Gospel, in the preaching and teaching of the word and the administration of the sacraments. Ecclesiastical jurisdiction with excommunication comes in under this word only as a last and extreme measure, in the case of those who wantonly and stubbornly resist the word and means of grace.

4. Second Appearance before the Disciples, including Thomas (20:24–29)

24–29. *But Thomas, one of the twelve, called Didymus, was not with them when Jesus came. The other disciples therefore said unto him, We have seen the Lord. But he said unto them, Except I shall see in his hands the print of the nails, and put my finger into the print of the nails, and put my hand into his side, I will not believe.*

And after eight days again his disciples were within, and Thomas with them. Jesus cometh, the doors being shut, and stood in the midst, and said, Peace be unto you. Then saith he to Thomas, Reach hither thy finger, and see my hands; and reach hither thy hand, and put it into my side; and be not faithless, but believing. Thomas answered and said unto him, My Lord and my God. Jesus saith unto him, Because thou hast seen me, thou hast believed: blessed are they that have not seen, and yet have believed.

Thomas or Didymus (that is, "Twin") was not with the disciples when Jesus came on the day of His resurrection. The Evangelist seems to indicate that this absence was not purely accidental, as some think, on account of the greater distance of his home (Bengel), or because he had some very urgent business that detained him (Grotius). From what we know of the character of Thomas we must come to the conclusion that his absence was quite significant. We remember his words (John 11:16) when the Lord announced His purpose after the death of Lazarus of Bethany, "to go unto him." "Let us also go," said Thomas, "that we may die with

Him." Now the very worst had come to pass. Though Lazarus was alive again, Christ Himself had died, died on the cross, His hands and feet pierced by nails, His side riven by the spear. That dreadful picture, with all its details, haunts his mind. With his deep affection for the Lord and his naturally gloomy and melancholy disposition, he had fully tasted the very dregs of that bitter cup, that after the smiting of the Shepherd, they should be scattered every man to his own and should leave Him alone (Matt. 26:31; John 16:32). A terrible feeling of isolation and loneliness has come over him. He cannot believe the rumors of Christ's resurrection. His death is the all-absorbing reality for him. And with the death of Christ everything is lost to him. His withdrawal from the company of the Apostles is an acknowledgment of his utter despair and hopelessness.

But the disciples do not leave him alone. They remember the commission with which the Lord had entrusted them on the day of His resurrection. They are to be the messengers of peace to all weary and downcast hearts. And here is one of their own number who needs this message of peace first and most of all. They therefore hasten to him with the news: *"We have seen the Lord."* In fact, they could say, and undoubtedly did say, much more than that. They had not only seen the Lord, they had touched His hands and His side, had felt His breath on their cheeks, they had heard His message of peace, they had received His great commission, to go forth as messengers of peace into an unbelieving world. All this they told Thomas. But their testimony makes no impression on him. "Whatever may have happened to Christ, now it is all over with Him. My companions are great fools to be thus impressed by the talk of these women and the visions they have seen." In these words Luther forcibly describes his state of mind. He meets the statements of the disciples with the most outspoken and determined incredulity. It is impossible that they have seen anything, or that their observation has been correct. He will accept the testimony of his own ten fingers rather than that of the ten Apostles (Valerius Herberger). While we must give Thomas credit for his unreserved openness and honesty, and look upon this as a hopeful feature in his attitude, showing the hidden wish of his innermost heart, that he might see and believe, we cannot defend him. His case is "as bad

V. The Resurrection of Jesus (Ch. 20)

as Peter's denial" (Luther). He knew the Apostles and their character for veracity. He saw the great change that had come over them since that Easter evening when they had seen the Lord. And yet he positively refuses to accept their testimony, given with the full assurance of their Easter-faith and Easter-joy. Yet he presumes to prescribe to the Lord Himself the exact conditions under which He must meet him, to cure him of his unbelief. Surely this was a bitter and trying experience for the Apostles themselves, and rather discouraging for the great work of their life, to be witnesses of the Crucified and Risen One. What prospect had their testimony before a hostile world if one of the twelve treated them in this manner? And yet, the depression and humiliation for the disciples' hearts caused by this attitude of Thomas was wholesome and well deserved. When they themselves had been called upon to receive the first news of the Lord's resurrection with believing hearts, they had treated those women-messengers somewhat after the same manner. Their words had "appeared in their sight as idle talk of unbelief and they disbelieved them." Having been delivered from this state of unbelief by the personal appearance of the Lord Himself, they were in a position to realize the difficulties of Thomas, and to have compassion for him, who thus far shut himself out from the Easter blessing they had received.

During the week between Easter and the following Sunday there were no new apparitions of the Lord. But one great point is gained by the disciples in their dealings with Thomas, that he at last consents to meet once more with them.[1] Thus he has entered upon the road to that blessing: "Where two or three are gathered together in My name there am I in the midst of them" (Matt. 18:20); instead of "forsaking the assembling of ourselves together" (Heb. 10:25).

The fact that at this second meeting the doors were also shut must not be explained, as the week before, from "fear of the Jews." For

---

[1] We doubt whether this meeting was arranged by the disciples to commemorate the octave of Easter Day, as Luthardt holds. The Church had hardly reached that point already in her appreciation of that day. We rather think that the re-appearance of the Lord on the same day, a week afterwards, had a direct influence toward making that day henceforth "the day of the Lord."

these words are now significantly omitted. It may have been done by the disciples simply to be undisturbed in their meeting. Or had they prayed, and did they hope, for a re-appearance of Christ, for Thomas's sake, under exactly the same conditions as the week before? At any rate, the Lord honors the assembly of His believing disciples by showing Himself to Thomas for the first time in their midst, and not in a private, separate appearance, as He had done in Peter's case. He corroborates their testimony in every single detail by appearing exactly in the same manner, as they had experienced and reported it to Thomas; thus bringing resistless conviction to the doubting disciple from the very first moment. For it was altogether for Thomas's sake that the Lord appeared this time. The salutation "Peace be unto you" was chiefly for his unbelieving, restless heart. The forgiveness and salvation of the Crucified and Risen Christ was thereby directly offered and imparted to him. Moreover there is the overwhelming evidence of Christ's omnipresence and omniscience in the fullness and exactness with which He takes up all the conditions presented by Thomas, in his conversation with the disciples, but never reported to Christ. Surely Christ's treatment of Thomas is most gentle, kind and loving, and at the same time most efficient, turning the skeptic into the most vigorous confessor, and thus establishing and strengthening the faith of future believers. For Gregory the Great truly says: "The unbelief of Thomas has been of more use to us, to help our faith, than even the faith of the believing disciples." And yet, the heavenly physician did not refrain from using the sharp knife also in the treatment of His skeptical disciple. Look at that exquisite irony in His invitation to Thomas, to *see* with his *finger!* "Reach hither thy finger and see My hands." And then that solemn warning: "*Be not faithless but believing*" or in the strict language of the original: "Do not become faithless, but believing." Thomas still, with all the doubt and uncertainty of his mind, had a certain faith in Christ, to whom he was sincerely attached. But now his difficulties concerning the fact of the resurrection threatened to affect his very faith in Christ Himself. Thus far, his unbelief had been only partial, concerning one single fact in the life of Christ; but, of course, this very fact which he doubts is of fundamental importance for the person

V. THE RESURRECTION OF JESUS (CH. 20)

and work of Christ. Therefore the direct command and solemn warning of the Lord, which proves that He holds Thomas responsible for his unbelief.

John does not indicate by a single word that Thomas made use of the permission given him by the Lord and actually touched His hands and His side. We do not believe that he did so, though many of the Fathers from Ambrose to Gregory the Great, and even Calvin and Bengel, have entertained this view. Thomas is completely overwhelmed by the appearance of the Lord, by His majesty as well as His tender kindness. He could not have handled Him in the manner in which he had intended to do. The Lord had commanded him to lay aside his doubts and to become a believer. The Lord immediately afterward testified: "Thou hast believed." The confession "My Lord and my God" was a confession of faith. Thomas had reached a point where he could cheerfully throw aside all his conditions. He does not need to touch or to handle, he simply believes. And what he now holds and believes he expresses in this short and comprehensive confession: *"My Lord and my God."* "This," says Luther, "is the power of the resurrection of Christ, that Thomas, formerly more stubborn in unbelief than all the rest, is suddenly changed into a different man, who now fully confesses, not only that he believes the fact of Christ's resurrection, but that Christ is his Lord, true God and Man. Thus Thomas is turned from an unbelieving, obstinate and ignorant pupil into an excellent theologian and doctor who has the correct and proper knowledge of Christ's person and office." Whatever Christ had spoken before concerning His divine dignity, now rises up before Thomas in heavenly clearness and majesty. He recognizes Him as truly Lord and God from heaven. And this Lord and God has said to him personally: "Peace be unto Thee." He is therefore not against him, but for him. And Thomas boldly grasps Him as his Saviour: "My Lord and *my* God," appropriating unto himself all that is Christ's and thus believing unto salvation.

"Because thou hast seen Me thou hast believed," says the Lord to Thomas. It is of the greatest importance that the Lord thus distinctly recognizes the utterance of Thomas as a confession of faith, and his

present state of mind as that of a believer. But the words also imply a gentle rebuke to Thomas on account of the manner by which he came to his faith. Seeing, of course, was to a certain degree indispensable to establish the faith of the Church. There must have been eyewitnesses to the great facts on which our salvation depends. And their testimony is to the present day the means of producing and preserving faith. But Thomas had discredited the testimony of just such eyewitnesses, and had insisted on his own personal seeing against the fundamental law of God's kingdom that "belief cometh of hearing, and by the word of Christ" (Rom. 10:17). The Lord, therefore, strongly emphasizes this great principle of the New Testament, which is henceforth to rule supremely: *"Blessed are they that have not seen and yet believe."* For faith in its very nature and essence is the assurance of things hoped for, the proving of things not seen (Heb. 11:1). And "we walk by faith and not by sight" (2 Cor. 5:7). The object of such blessed faith in this context, when the word "believe" is used absolutely without modification, cannot be anything but the Christ, in whom Thomas had thus learned to believe, the incarnate Word, the crucified and risen Saviour.

We have thus been led by the hand of the Evangelist to a point where, in the confession of Thomas, the whole Gospel itself seems to have reached its culmination. Throughout the various scenes in which St. John has shown us the incarnate Logos, between the unbelieving world that rejects Him and the believers that receive Him, there is none that represents a more glorious triumph of the God-man, none that contains such a full recognition and such unreserved homage to Him, as this crowning confession from the mouth of skeptical Thomas: My Lord and my God. With this the Gospel-narrative properly ends.

5. Conclusion (20:30, 31)

30–31. *Many other signs therefore did Jesus in the presence of the disciples, which are not written in this book: but these are written, that ye may believe that Jesus is the Christ, the Son of God; and that believing ye may have life in his name.*

The Evangelist has reached the end of his narrative, and as he is ready to lay down his pen he looks back over the whole life of Christ and

V. The Resurrection of Jesus (Ch. 20)

the many signs "He did in the presence of His disciples." This reference is by no means to be confined to the events narrated in the last chapter, as if the "other signs" meant additional apparitions of the risen Lord before His disciples. St. John refers to such other miracles as have been recorded by the Synoptists. Out of their great number only a few have been told by John. And those have been selected and written for a twofold purpose of proving to the readers that Jesus is the Christ the Son of God, and of communicating to them eternal life through faith in His name. This Gospel itself, as written by John, is a monument of the Holy Spirit's work of glorifying Christ. In all the deeds and discourses of the Lord which it contains, it shows that He is indeed the only-begotten Son of the Father, full of grace and truth. The very existence and the whole character of this fourth Gospel verifies the promise of Christ, that the Paraclete should guide the disciples into all truth (16:13). Its comprehensive testimony of the God-man is thus recorded that men may *believe*. The last word of Christ, up to this point, and the last word of the Evangelist speak of *faith*. Why do we believe? not because we have seen the Lord with the eyes of our body, as Thomas and the disciples did, but because we have their written record concerning the person and work of Christ, they themselves and the Holy Spirit with them bearing witness of Him. And what do we believe? Not, in the first place, a certain set of doctrines, theories, rules and principles, but the great central fact of the person of the God-man; viz., that Jesus is the Christ, the divinely sent Messiah, who did His work as God's anointed prophet, high priest and king; and that He is the Son of the Father, very God of very God, but God incarnate, in whose humanity we find the living God, our Saviour. And what is to be the result and outcome of our believing? "that believing we may have life in His name." A real faith brings us into life-union with Him; and such personal contact and union with Him guarantees true and real life, spiritual life in this world, eternal life in a glorified body in the world to come, as Paul also sums up the whole Gospel in the brief statement, that the righteous shall *live* by faith.

This Epilogue, or final summing up of John's Gospel record, leads our thoughts back to the Prologue and the first chapter. There already it was said: "As many as received Him, to them gave He the right to become children of God (a new divine life!), even to them that believe on His name" (1:12). There already we hear Andrew's joyful confession: "We have found the Messiah (which is interpreted *the Christ*)" (1:41). And soon afterwards Nathanael adds to this: "Thou art *the Son of God*" (1:49). It is Jesus, the Christ, the Son of God, whom Thomas in the fulness of his faith confesses as "My Lord and my God."

VI. Appendix. The Appearance of Christ at the Lake of Galilee (21)

JOHN 21

VI. Appendix. The Appearance of Christ at the Lake of Galilee (21)

1. *The Draft of Fishes (21:1–8)*

1–8. *After these things Jesus manifested himself again to the disciples at the sea of Tiberias; and he manifested himself on this wise. There were together Simon Peter, and Thomas called Didymus, and Nathanael of Cana in Galilee, and the sons of Zebedee, and two other of his disciples. Simon Peter saith unto them, I go a fishing. They say unto him, We also come with thee. They went forth, and entered into the boat; and that night they took nothing. But when day was now breaking, Jesus stood on the beach; howbeit the disciples knew not that it was Jesus. Jesus therefore saith unto them, Children, have ye aught to eat? They answered him, No. And he saith unto them, Cast the net on the right side of the boat, and ye shall find. They cast therefore, and now they were not able to draw it for the multitude of fishes. That disciple therefore whom Jesus loved saith unto Peter, It is the Lord. So when Simon Peter heard that it was the Lord, he girt his coat about him (for he was naked), and cast himself into the sea. But the other disciples came in the little boat (for they were not far from the land, but about two hundred cubits off), dragging the net full of fishes.*

Inasmuch as the last two verses of the preceding chapter are evidently the conclusion of the original Gospel of St. John, this chapter, forming a kind of appendix, must have been added at a later period. But, as it is found in all the earliest manuscripts and versions and is known to the ancient fathers, it must have been added very soon after the completion of the original Gospel narrative, and before it was circulated among the churches. It is "nearly contemporaneous" with the preceding twenty chapters, as Renan says. And as the whole spirit and language of this chapter is undoubtedly Johannean, we see no reason to think that another hand had written these lines.[1]

Of the ten apparitions of the Lord after His resurrection this is the seventh; among the appearances before an assembly of disciples it is the third, as John himself distinctly states (21:14). It was probably several weeks after the meeting with Thomas, and most likely on another Lord's Day, that the Lord manifested Himself to the disciples in Galilee. There they had been directed to expect Him by positive orders before and after His resurrection (Matt. 26:32; Mark 14:28; Matt. 28:7–10; Mark 16:7).

At the Lake of Galilee, where, in bygone days, the disciples had enjoyed the most blessed and delightful communion with their Lord, we find seven of them *"together,"* either in one house or in one town or village, such as Capernaum or Bethsaida. The order in which their names are recorded in this connection is quite significant. Peter and Thomas are at the head of the list. The restored denier and the believing skeptic, forever the most striking illustrations of the power of Christ's resurrection. After them follow Nathanael, the sons of Zebedee and two other of His disciples, possibly Andrew and Philip. The place which in this list is assigned to the "sons of Zebedee," one of them the writer of this Gospel, seems to us a very strong evidence that John himself wrote this addition to his Gospel. Any disciple of his, or presbyter of the Church at Ephesus, would have given another place in this list to the last survivor of the Apostles, the revered and beloved John.

---

[1] Grotius was the first to introduce another theory concerning the authorship of this chapter, which in recent times was strongly supported by the late Professor Grau of Koenigsberg. They find the occasion for the addition of this section in the traditional "saying among the brethren that that disciple should not die" (21:23). As the church in Ephesus had received the explanation of the origin of that legend from the Apostle John himself, and as "the saying" continued among the Christians even after his death, the presbyters thought it best to add John's account in his own words to his gospel. But even if this theory should be correct it would in reality only explain the addition of two verses (22 and 23), without covering the rest of this chapter. The majority of commentators therefore, including quite opposite types of theology, are decidedly in favor of the Johannean origin of this chapter. (Richard Simon, Calovius, Wegscheider, Guericke, Credner, Tholuck, Lange, Ebrard, Stier, Luthardt, Hengstenberg, Godet and others.)

VI. Appendix. The Appearance of Christ at the Lake of Galilee (21)

After the last meeting with the Lord in Jerusalem, after the solemn commission they received from Him (20:21–23), we are hardly prepared for such a trivial everyday proposition as that of Peter: "I go a fishing." And, what is perhaps even more astonishing, they all with one accord agree to his motion, and even John and Thomas join the rest: *"We also come with thee."* This resolution, however, presents to us a significant feature of truthfulness in the character and life of the Apostles. Those plain, practical fishermen from the shores of the Galilean Lake, whom the Lord had called to be His coworkers in the building up of His kingdom, are no dreamers, but active men whose very life it was to work. With all the light and happiness which the resurrection of Christ had brought them, they were now at a somewhat trying period of waiting and expectancy. The ascension of their Lord and the coming down of the promised Paraclete were the two great facts to which they were looking forward, and which, after a meeting with Christ in Galilee, might at any time become a reality. And just at this time the sober proposition of Peter was eminently happy and appropriate. Their hearts filled with the great things they have seen and heard, and looking forward to the greater things still in store for them, they quietly settle down to the practical every-day work of their former life. And they do this in common. It would have been a different thing if one alone had taken up his former trade, separated from the others. But there was a protection and a blessing in the very fact of their associating for this fishing expedition. Though the lake, and shore, and net and boat were the same as of old, the men were new men. Their thoughts are with their risen Lord, their conversation is of Him, while their sinewy arms are wielding the oar and hauling the net. Whenever He appears He finds them at work, even though their heavenly call to become "fishers of men" may seem, for a time, to be suspended.

At first, however, this fishing expedition seems to be a failure. *"That night they took nothing:"* a strong reminder of another night's experience, three years ago, on that same lake of Galilee (Luke 5:1–11). This, as well as the order of the Lord about casting the net, together with other details, was particularly intended for Peter, who was to be prepared for a full and formal re-instating in his Apostolic office. At daybreak Jesus appears, standing on the shore, but not recognized by the disciples. He opens a conversation in full accordance with the situation in which He found them: *"Children, have ye aught to eat?"* referring to the fishes they might possibly have caught during the night. Their short, blunt answer "No," betrays their disappointment after an unsuccessful night's work, and perhaps even an unwillingness to be disturbed, as they are busily occupied with their work. It was, no doubt, a frequent occurrence with the Galilean fishermen that some one at the shore, waiting for the boat to come in, greeted them from afar with the question, whether anything could be bought from them "to eat," literally something to eat with the bread, προσφάγιον, a relish, which, in the language of the people around the Lake, meant nothing but fishes.

But the stranger who wants to buy fish where they have none to sell, continues his conversation with the advice: "Cast the net on the right side of the boat and ye shall find." The prompt compliance with this suggestion of the unknown stranger is most remarkable, especially as there is not a word said about it by any of the Apostles. Was there a remembrance of the similar order: "Put out into the deep and let down your nets for a draught" (Luke 5:4), and a divination concerning that person on the shore, in the hearts of the disciples? According to our text there is only one among them who at this point already begins to realize the truth. When the net was cast and they were not able to draw it for the multitude of fishes, John said to Peter: *"It is the Lord."* He is always nearest to the Lord in his thoughts and meditations. He is first in contemplation, intuition, recognition. Peter is foremost in action. And those two stand side by side, closely united here, as in the night of the Lord's passion, on the morning of His resurrection, and afterwards in the first demonstrations of the life and activity of the Pentecost Church (Acts 2–8). Without waiting for the slow movement of the boat, heavily dragging the overburdened net, Peter throws himself into the water to swim to the shore, a distance of a little over one hundred yards. But with all his zeal, there was this time no inconsiderate haste in what Peter did, nor did he

VI. Appendix. The Appearance of Christ at the Lake of Galilee (21)

forget the proper reverence towards his Lord. "He girt his coat about him and thus he cast himself into the sea."

2. The Feast Prepared for the Disciples (21:9–14)

9–14. *So when they got out upon the land, they see a fire of coals there, and fish laid thereon, and bread. Jesus saith unto them, Bring of the fish which ye have now taken. Simon Peter therefore went up, and drew the net to land, full of great fishes, a hundred and fifty and three; and for all there were so many, the net was not rent. Jesus saith unto them, Come and break your fast. And none of the disciples durst inquire of him, Who art thou? knowing that it was the Lord. Jesus cometh and taketh the bread, and giveth them, and the fish likewise. This is now the third time that Jesus was manifested to the disciples, after that he was risen from the dead.*

Nothing is said in the narrative of the Evangelist concerning what transpired between the Lord and Peter, before the other Apostles reached the shore. There was not much of an interval between his arrival and that of the boat with the other disciples. Certainly Peter did not assist the Lord in preparing and arranging that table, to which they were invited. Nor is there any indication of angels ministering unto the Lord in those preparations. John simply tells us of everything being ready for them, "*a fire of coals there and fish laid thereon and bread,*" and the impression, evidently intended by this statement, is that of a miraculous provision made by the omnipotent Lord Himself. And yet, with all that the Lord had provided, the disciples are permitted and requested to bring in also of the fish which they had now taken. Their number, one hundred and fifty-three, has been most marvellously interpreted by the fathers in fanciful allegories, which we will spare our readers.

It is remarkable how few words are uttered during this whole scene. The short invitation of the Lord: "*Come and break your fast,*" is all that is spoken. The disciples were by this time fully convinced that it was the Lord whom they here met so unexpectedly. But they would have liked to receive an affirmation from Himself on this point. They expected it, as the Lord had always given it on former occasions. And yet they had not the courage to solicit such an assurance of His identity. They observed a reverent silence; and only when the Lord in His accustomed manner acted as host they ventured to partake of that mysterious meal. How important this experience was to them and how sweet the remembrance, is shown in Acts 10:41, where Peter in his address before Cornelius of Cæsarea says: "We did eat and drink with Him after He rose from the dead."

There can be no doubt that both the miraculous draught of fishes, and this mysterious meal on the shore of the Lake of Galilee, have a symbolical meaning for the Church of Christ, and in particular for the work and experience of the Apostles and their successors in the ministry of the word. The two events remind us of two well-known miracles told in the Gospel history: The miraculous draught of fishes preceding the call of Peter and John to the Apostolic office as fishers of men (Luke 5:1–2), and the miraculous feeding of the five thousand which is told by all the four Evangelists. Thus here also the draught of fishes foreshadows the work of the Apostles, as fishers of men, with the assurance from their Lord of abundant success for their labor and toil. The mysterious meal, following the draught of fishes, symbolizes the spiritual and temporal support, the strengthening and refreshing which the disciples may surely expect from their glorified Lord, who is on shore, watching over them and providing for them while they toil on the sea of this world.

3. Peter and John (21:15–23)

(a.) Peter (21:15–19)

15–19. *So when they had broken their fast, Jesus saith to Simon Peter, Simon, son of John, lovest thou me more than these? He saith unto him, Yea, Lord; thou knowest that I love thee. He saith unto him, Feed my lambs. He saith to him again a second time, Simon, son of John, lovest thou me? He saith unto him, Yea, Lord; thou knowest that I love thee. He saith unto him, Tend my sheep. He saith unto him the third time, Simon, son of John, lovest thou me? Peter was grieved because he said unto him the third time, Lovest thou me? And he said unto him, Lord, thou knowest all things; thou knowest that I love thee. Jesus saith unto him, Feed my*

VI. Appendix. The Appearance of Christ at the Lake of Galilee (21)

sheep. Verily, verily, I say unto thee, When thou wast young, thou girdedst thyself, and walkedst whither thou wouldest: but when thou shalt be old, thou shalt stretch forth thy hands, and another shall gird thee, and carry thee whither thou wouldest not. Now this he spake, signifying by what manner of death he should glorify God. And when he had spoken this, he saith unto him, Follow me.

After the meal the Lord had a special message yet for Peter on account of his fall. There was not, by this time, any doubt among the disciples, that, in spite of the denial of Peter, his relation to the Lord, as well as to the circle of the disciples, had been fully re-established. They knew how sincerely penitent he was ever since that terrible fall, when he had gone out and wept bitterly. And knowing this penitent state of his mind and remembering their own weakness and instability, they had never ceased to look upon him as one of their own number. A significant evidence on this point is the close association between Peter and John which we can trace all through the history of those days (see John 20:2–10). The disciples, of course, knew of the special reference to Peter in the first Easter-Message of the angel at the tomb (Mark 16:7). Moreover the Lord had appeared to him first of all the Apostles (Luke 24:34; 1 Corinth, 15:5), and we may well take it for granted that at that private meeting Peter received his personal absolution, the full assurance from the Lord Himself of the pardon of his grievous sin. Even the gift of the Spirit, when the Lord breathed upon them, and the commission of the ministry of the Gospel, on the first evening after the resurrection, included Peter as well as the rest. So far then everything seemed to be in order, the transgression blotted out and the fallen Apostle restored to the grace of his Lord, the confidence of his brethren, and even to the honor and responsibility of his ministerial office.

And yet, the offence of Peter had been of such a character, that a public and formal rehabilitation seemed to be called for in his case. It was to take place before witnesses, and in such a manner that it would at once be understood as an offset to Peter's denial. And we have no hesitation in saying that, however painful the scene may have been to him, it was Peter's own desire to have such an opportunity of submitting to a well-deserved humiliation, and of making amends for the offence of his denial, by a threefold confession of his love for his Lord. Only in this way he would be enabled after his restoration to "stablish his brethen," as the Lord had predicted even before his fall.

In opening the conversation with Peter the Lord calls him "*Simon son of John*" (Joanes, Jonah, Matt. 16:17). He goes back to Peter's original name, the name of the natural man, as it appears in John 1:42 and as the Lord used it with great emphasis when he warned Peter against the danger of his denial (Luke 22:31, Simon, Simon, behold Satan has asked to have you, etc.). For the fall was really Simon's and not Peter's, and the illustrious surname "Peter" (Cephas) had been forfeited by his attitude during the passion of Christ, especially by his denial.

If there was an element of discipline in this very address, there is more of it in the comparison which the question of the Lord introduces: "*Lovest thou Me more than these?*" This was unmistakably a sharp reminder of Peter's presumption in the night of Christ's betrayal, when he claimed to be more faithfully attached to the Lord than all the rest, and ready to do and to suffer more for Him than the other disciples: "If all shall be offended in Thee I will never be offended (Matt. 26:33; Mark 14:29). I will lay down my life for Thee" (John 13:37).[1] Or was there even a gentle reference to the fact that at that very moment Peter's affectionate heart had pushed ahead of the others when he threw himself into the sea; when Peter's love first reached the Lord on the shore, while John's love had first recognized Him from afar? But in the fact that Peter's *love* to the Lord is the one great theme of this examination, there was certainly a great deal of encouragement and assurance for the Apostle. And the language and spirit of Peter's answer shows him in the most favorable light. It is full of the gentleness and humility of a broken and contrite heart. No translation is able to do full justice to it, because it cannot reproduce the change of words which Peter makes in speaking of his love to Christ. In

---

[1] An opportunity was thus offered to Peter to make amends not only to the Lord whom he had grieved by his denial, but also to his fellow disciples whom he had slighted and hurt by his overbearing conduct—in both direc tions a highly instructive "example of ecclesiastical discipline." (GROTIUS).

VI. Appendix. The Appearance of Christ at the Lake of Galilee (21)

the question of Christ: *"Lovest thou Me more than these?"* the Greek verb ἀγαπᾷς denotes the highest, most perfect kind of love (diligere), implying a clear determination of will and judgment, and belonging particularly to the sphere of divine revelation. In his answer Peter substitutes the word φιλῶ, which means the natural human affection, with its strong feeling or sentiment, and is never used in scripture language to designate man's love to God.[2] While the answer of Peter then claims only an inferior kind of love, as compared to the one contained in Christ's question, he nevertheless is confident of possessing at least such love for his Lord. There is something very touching in this humble appeal to the Lord: *"Thou knowest that I love Thee."* He hardly trusts himself in this important matter. He has found out by bitter experience that he does not know his own heart sufficiently; that he is apt to deceive himself even where he means to be most sincere in his feelings and utterances. But the Lord knows his heart. And with this appeal to His knowledge he feels himself perfectly safe. "Thou knowest, *that* I love Thee." There is, indeed, no uncertain sound in this. With all his diffidence in himself and his caution not to think of himself more highly than he ought to think, there is a positive assurance on the main point of the question: "Yea, Lord."

After this answer the Lord commits to Peter the care of His flock. *"Feed My lambs."* First the "halieutics" (catching the fish), then the "pastorate" (feeding the flock). It is a testimonial of the confidence which the Lord places in him. Without saying it in direct words, He accepts the confession of Peter's love. For only to a loving one will He commit His beloved lambs which He has purchased with His own blood. They are His own; He Himself being the Chief-Shepherd, who needs no vicars or substitutes to look after His flock, but faithful, humble and loving servants. The little changes made in the threefold commission of the Lord, either in the verb or in the noun are all significant. "Feed My lambs" He says the first time. "Tend My [little] sheep" (προβάτια) the second

---

[2] In John 16:27, the Lord uses it, both of the Father's love for the disciples and their love for Him.

time; "feed My sheep" the third time; (πρόβατα, as the Sinaitic and other manuscripts read). The change of verbs describes the different functions of the pastoral office: *"feeding,"* providing healthy nourishment and thus sustaining life; and *"tending,"* ποιμαίνειν, ruling, watching over the flock, guiding and protecting it. The change of nouns indicates the different classes or conditions of the members of the flock, from the little ones who are beginners in the faith, to the adult members of the organized congregation. It is evident that what the Lord here means in describing Peter's commission are the ordinary functions of the ministry of the word. The very same words are used afterwards by the Apostles themselves in charging the bishops or presbyters of the Churches with the duties of their office. Thus Paul says to the elders of the Church at Ephesus: "Take heed unto yourselves and to all the flock, in the which the Holy Ghost hath made you bishops, to feed the Church of God, which He purchased with His own blood" (Acts 20:28). And Peter himself exhorts the elders of the Churches in Asia Minor as a fellow elder and a witness of the sufferings of Christ: "Tend the flock of God which is among you" (1 Peter 5:2). It is essentially the same work which had been assigned to all the Apostles on the evening of the Lord's resurrection (John 20:19 ff.).

When the Lord asked for a second time: "Simon, son of John, lovest thou Me?" He omitted the comparative reference to the other disciples, which had been in His first question ("more than these?"). This time the question confines itself to Peter's love exclusively. Thereby the Lord seems to indicate His satisfaction with Peter's answer on this point, his silence on the measure of his love as compared with others. Peter has given up those ambitious comparisons. He has enough to do with himself. But the great question itself: "Lovest thou me?" is repeated. It is always the fundamental question in Christ's dealings with His people, and for the pastor in particular it is the great theme of self-examination, showing the one powerful and abiding motive for true faithfulness in the holy office.

But the Lord asks even a third time. *"And Peter was grieved because He said unto him the third time: Lovest Thou Me?"* This third question completed the direct reminder of the three denials. This is a painful

VI. Appendix. The Appearance of Christ at the Lake of Galilee (21)

reminiscence for Peter, full of humiliation and godly sorrow. But there is another feature in this question of Christ, which was, no doubt, strongly felt by Peter, though it is entirely lost to us in the translation of this passage. While in the first two questions the Lord had used the higher word for love (ἀγαπᾷς) He now, in this third question, accepts the word used in the two previous answers of Peter (φιλεῖς), which, as stated above, signifies a lower grade of love. Does then the Lord question even this human affection on Peter's part? Does even this kind of love need careful examination, deepening and maturing? We can understand that this third question, in this particular form, was really the deepest humiliation for Peter. His answer, consequently, is more emphatic than before: *"Lord, Thou knowest all things,"*—my whole life, my sinful heart, my pride and imprudence, my repentance and conversion, my love and devotion, all that Thou hast done for me, all that has enabled me to make this confession, at this time—*"Thou knowest that I love Thee."*

The solemn examination and the formal re-instatement of the fallen disciple having thus been completed, the Lord for a moment lifts the veil from the future course of Peter's life, and shows him that suffering and a martyr's death will be, with him also, the climax of his "glorifying God." In order fully to appreciate the following verses (18 and 19) in their close connection with the preceding passage, we must remember the whole history of Peter's fall, and go back to the very beginning of that sad experience. We find it at the point (John 13:36, 37) when Peter had asked the Lord: "Whither goest Thou?" and Jesus answered: "Whither I go, thou canst not follow Me now, but *thou shalt follow afterwards.*" Peter was quite unwilling to submit to this decision and said unto Him: "Lord, why cannot I follow Thee now? I will lay down my life for Thee." To this the Lord answered with the revelation of his imminent denial.

Now that Peter is restored from his grievous fall the Lord Himself takes up the broken thread again. After all these experiences of the fall, the examination and restoration, Peter is now in a condition to *follow* the Lord to suffering and to a martyr's death. If his denial had betrayed a tendency to escape from such hardships, and even an unfitness, for the time, to undergo such trials, this revelation of the Lord concerning the end of his life may well be considered as an acknowledgment of his fitness to seal his ministry of the Gospel with a martyr's death, and an encouragement to persevere and to be faithful unto death. It is a question of subordinate importance whether, in the details of this prophecy, the Lord intended to indicate crucifixion as the mode of Peter's death. But certain it is that he predicts a time of suffering and a violent death for him. Over against the independence and impulsiveness of his younger days, the time is coming when he will have to surrender to another will, and be led and carried whither he would not. And perhaps we ought not to limit the meaning of this prophecy to the actual martyrdom of Peter, with its bodily sufferings. Henceforth it was the great lesson and test of his life to have the old Simon with his natural Ego crucified in steady self-denial. True pastors, such as Peter was called to be, in order to lead, must themselves be led in humble submission to their Lord. And every Christian, as he advances in years, ought to grow in the likeness of his Lord whom he is called to follow. But this will be possible only under the same condition under which Peter is here placed, viz. the yielding of our own will and the corresponding readiness to say: "Thy will be done."

(b.) John (21:20–23)

20–23. *Peter, turning about, seeth the disciple whom Jesus loved following; which also leaned back on his breast at the supper, and said, Lord, who is he that betrayeth thee? Peter therefore seeing him saith to Jesus, Lord, and what shall this man do? Jesus saith unto him, If I will that he tarry till I come, what is that to thee? follow thou me. This saying therefore went forth among the brethren, that that disciple should not die: yet Jesus said not unto him, that he should not die; but, If I will that he tarry till I come, what is that to thee?*

After the words of re-instatement and of prophecy addressed to Peter the Lord starts to go, and orders Peter to follow Him. This command, then, besides its far-reaching symbolical meaning, to which we referred in the preceding section, must also be taken in a literal and local sense. In obedience to it Peter goes after the Lord. But he at once,

VI. Appendix. The Appearance of Christ at the Lake of Galilee (21)

"turning about," notices John, who also follows them. There was no presumption in this on the part of the beloved disciple. The close relations between Peter and John, and more than that, the intimate relation between the Lord and John, fully explain and justify the action of John. This is meant by the significant reference at this point to the well-known evidences of that intimacy between Jesus and the beloved disciple "which also leaned back on His breast at the supper, and said, Lord, who is he that betrayeth Thee?"

On seeing John also following, Peter asks the Lord: "And what shall this man do?"[1] or, as the marginal note of the Revised Version has it: "And this man, what?" What of him? What is in store for him? This question of Peter seems quite natural, especially if we remember the close friendship between these two apostles. Peter had received from the Lord the revelation concerning the end of his life, his sufferings and martyr's death. And in his sympathy for John, and the anxiety about the future of his friend, the question would readily suggest itself: What is ordained for John? What will be his fate? John himself has no undue desire to penetrate into the unknown future, he is satisfied to rest in the Lord and to follow "the Lamb whithersoever He goeth" (Revelation 14:4). But while John is silent, Peter takes it upon himself to ask the Lord in behalf of his friend, as formerly John had put a question to the Lord in behalf of Peter (John 13:24). From the character of Christ's answer we are forced to think that, with all the kindly interest in the future development of the life of John shown by Peter's question, there must have been in it something which met with the decided disapproval of the Lord. And this was undoubtedly the undue curiosity of Peter, who concerned himself about the affairs of his companion, and desired to penetrate into the mystery of his future, at a time when the Lord had given him such a solemn and important revelation concerning his own life, in which he might have found, just at that time, ample material for earnest, concentrated meditation.

---

[1] This word referring to a "doing" on the part of John is particularly ill chosen, both in the text of the Revised and of the Authorized Version.

The answer of the Lord, however, while in its pointed shortness and in the direct words: "What is that to thee?" it is an unmistakable reproof for Peter, after all gives some information on the very point about which He had been asked: *"If I will that he tarry till I come."* A number of commentators do not find any positive statement in this sentence. They take it in a purely hypothetical sense, emphasizing the "if" so strongly, that they conclude: it was by no means the real intention of the Lord that John should tarry till He comes.[1] But we cannot accept this interpretation. There is, and we believe it to be intentionally so, a certain mysteriousness hanging over these words of Christ. But He does not simply silence Peter. He makes a statement concerning the future of John, and He makes it in close connection with what He has just before revealed to Peter; and, moreover, He frames His words in such a way that we are driven to find in them a contrast to the martyrdom of Peter. The Lord, in whose hand are the lives of His servants, says to Peter: Go, die, seal thy ministry with a martyr's death; and to John: Stay, tarry till I come. If the death of Peter was the central thought of the prophecy concerning his future, the prolonged life of John is the centre of this communication concerning the beloved disciple. There was no mistake in this starting point of the traditional legend of the early church, however much it erred in drawing from it the inference: "That that disciple should not die." But what is meant by the words of Christ: *"till I come?"* The true meaning of the whole statement evidently depends on the interpretation of that one word of the original ἔρχομαι (I come). Does the Lord here mean His coming to John in an easy, natural death, over against the pains and tortures of Peter's martyrdom?[2] Or does His coming signify His second advent at the

---

[1] Thus Erasmus substitutes "velim" instead of "volo"—"if it should be my will" instead of "if I will;" losing entirely that remarkable dignity and majesty with which the Lord here positively asserts His absolute power over the life and death of His own. The latest commentary of Bugge also defends this position of an unreal hypothesis.

[2] This is the interpretation of Augustine, Grotius, Olshausen, Lange, Grau, really amounting to the statement that John should tarry, that is should live until he should die a natural death.

VI. Appendix. The Appearance of Christ at the Lake of Galilee (21)

end of the world, when He shall come to judge the quick and the dead?[1] Neither of these two interpretations is in harmony with the context. But we find in Matt. 16:28 (and Mark 9:1) a statement of the Lord which may give us some light on the passage before us. There the Lord says that "some of them that stand here shall in nowise taste of death till they see the Son of Man coming in His Kingdom." This, as is generally admitted, refers to Christ's coming in judgment over His people, in the destruction of Jerusalem (in the year 70 A. D.). But more than this, as Bengel and Stier particularly have set forth in very forcible manner. The Lord came in a specific sense to His beloved disciple when He gave him that Book of Revelation, whose theme from beginning to end is: I come, behold, I come! John was reserved for the work of writing the last and crowning revelation of the Scriptures, and after finishing the Apocalypse he departed. "For Peter the cross, for John the Apocalypse! Behold what a distinction for the beloved disciple!" (Bengel: Petro crux. Joanni apocalypsis. Vide, quanta dignatio erga discipulum dilectum!).

4. Conclusion. The Gospel Attested (21:24, 25)

24–25. This is the disciple which beareth witness of these things, and wrote these things; and we know that his witness is true.

And there are also many other things which Jesus did, the which if they should be written every one, I suppose that even the world itself would not contain the books that should be written.

Thus far this supplementary chapter (21:1–23) has pictured the future lifework of the Apostles, its labor and toil, its fruit and blessings, its joys and trials, culminating in bloody martyrdom for the one and in quiet, silent waiting for the coming of the Lord, for the other. With this picture the author's work is finished.

What we have here in these last two verses, is written by another hand than that of the author. The last verse is omitted from the text of the

---

[1] This then would practically be the ancient tradition, which is distinctly rejected by John himself. And yet, even a man like Lavater is said to have actually believed this.

Gospel by Tischendorf, Gebhardt and others on the testimony of the Sinaitic Codex, which, however on this point is not supported by any other manuscript. But it was probably added, together with the 24th verse at the time of the publication of the Gospel.

Three distinct statements are made in this addition: 1. That the disciple whom Jesus loved, that is John, is the writer of this Gospel. 2. That his witness is, attested as absolutely reliable. 3. That it is utterly impossible that all the things which Jesus did, could ever be fully written out. This testimony is given by a circle of men, who were in a position to know about these things and who speak with the assurance that their testimony will have weight and authority with the church at large. One of their number is singled out in the 25th verse in that peculiar statement "I suppose" (οἶμαι), which certainly could never have been John's mode of expressing himself.

There can hardly be any doubt as to the circle from which this final addition and attestation of the Gospel comes. It is the church in Ephesus, where John spent the latter part of his life, which through her elders gave this testimony to the authenticity not only of this supplementary chapter, but thereby also of the whole Gospel of St. John. Into their hands the author had probably first given his Gospel, together with the supplement 21:1–23. And it was probably during the lifetime of the Apostle that this testimony of the church in Ephesus was added.

The legend that the disciple whom Jesus loved, the disciple who witnessed and wrote these things, would never die, is, as John himself declared, without historical reality. But there is a beautiful significance in it for the very Gospel which John wrote. It has been declared dead again and again by the enemies of our Christian faith. They have buried it and locked and sealed its tomb. But the message goes forth again and again among the brethren, that that Gospel should not die. And this is not a saying but a fact, attested by impregnable witness. It lives and shall live forever.

VI. Appendix. The Appearance of Christ at the Lake of Galilee (21)

SYNOPSIS OF THE GOSPEL OF JOHN

FIRST PART.—CHAPTERS 1–4
the beginning of faith in the incarnate word as the absolute revelation of god

    I. Opening Section ["The Prologue"] 1:1–18.
1. *Beginning and Theme of the Gospel.*
2. *The Word ("Logos").*
3. *The Eternal and Creative Word* (1:1–3).
4. *The Word of Salvation* (1:4–9).
5. *The Word Rejected by the World* (1:10, 11).
6. *The Word Received by the Children of God* (1:12, 13).
7. *The Word Incarnate* (1:14).
8. *The Incarnate Word Dwelling among Us* (1:14).
9. *Receiving out of His Fulness* (1:15–18).

    II. The Testimony of John the Baptist (1:19–34).
1. *First Testimony before the Jewish Delegation* (1:19–28).
2. *Second Testimony of John the Baptist Addressed to his Disciples* (1:29–34).

    III. The First Disciples of the Lord (1:35–51).
    IV. The First Sign (2:1–11).
    V. The First Prophecy of the Lord Concerning His Death and Resurrection (2:12–25).
    VI. The Conversation with Nicodemus (3:1–21).
1. *Character of Nicodemus and his Motives in Coming to Jesus* (3:1, 2).
2. *The Necessity of a New Birth* (3:3).
3. *The Nature and Means of the New Birth* (3:4–8).
4. *The Heavenly Witness* (3:9–13).
5. *The Serpent in the Wilderness* (3:14, 15).

6. *The Father's Love the Headspring of Salvation* (3:16).
7. *Salvation, not Judgment, the Mission of the Son of God* (3:17).
8. *The Present Judgment Incurred by Unbelievers* (3:18, 19).
9. *The Climax and the Parting Word to Nicodemus* (3:20, 21).

VII. Jesus in Judæa and the Last Testimony of John the Baptist (3:22–36).

1. *Jesus in Judæa* (3:22–24).
2. *The Occasion for the Last Testimony of the Baptist* (3:25, 26).
3. *The Last Testimony of the Baptist* (3:27–36).
(a.) *Christ and the Baptist* (3:27–30).
(b.) *Christ and the World* (3:31–36).

VIII. Samaritan Faith (4:1–42).

1. *Historical Introduction* (4:1–6).
2. *The Conversation with the Samaritan Woman* (4:7–26).
(a.) *The Living Water* (4:7–15).
(b.) *The Prophet* (4:16–26).
3. *The Conversation with the Disciples* (4:27–38).
4. *Believing Samaritans* (4:39–42).

IX. Galilean Faith (4:43–54).

1. *Historical Introduction* (4:43–45).
2. *The Nobleman's Unbelief Rebuked* (4:46–48).
3. *The Nobleman's Faith Supported and Trained* (4:49, 50).
4. *The Nobleman's Faith Crowned with Experience* (4:51–54).
5. *The Nobleman's House Believing* (4:53).

SECOND PART.—CHAPTERS 5–12

THE HOSTILITY OF UNBELIEF THAT REJECTS THE INCARNATE WORD

I. The Beginning of the Conflict in Judæa (5:1–47).

1. *The Healing of the Sick Man at the Pool of Bethesda* (5:1–16).
2. *The Lord's Discourse following this Miracle* (5:17–47).
(a.) *The Personal Relation between the Father and the Son the Explanation of the Latter's Work* (5:17–30).
(b.) *The Testimony of the Father* (5:31–40)
(c.) *Unbelief of the Jews Lamented and Explained* (5:41–47).

VI. Appendix. The Appearance of Christ at the Lake of Galilee (21)

    II.   The Crisis in Galilee (6:1–71).
    (A.)   The Miraculous Feeding (6:1–15).
    (B.)   The Meeting with His Disciples on the Water (6:16–21).
    (C.)   The Discourses Following these Miracles in Capernaum (6:22–59).
    1.   Historical Introduction (6:22–24).
    2.   The Jews Asking Questions (6:25–40).
    3.   The Jews Murmuring (6:41–51).
    4.   The Jews Striving One with Another (6:52–59).
    (D.)   The Wavering Disciples and the Crisis (6:60–71).
    1.   The Wavering Disciples (6:60–65).
    2.   The Decision of the Twelve (6:66–69).
    3.   The Devil among Them (6:70, 71).
    III.   The Conflict in Jerusalem again Taken up (7:1–8:59).
    (A.)   Historical Introduction (7:1–13).
    (B.)   Three Discourses during the Feast of Tabernacles (7:14–36).
    1.   Christ's Authority for Teaching (7:14–24).
    2.   Whence is Christ? (7:25–32).
    3.   His Approaching Departure (7:33–36).
    (C.)   The Discourses on the Last Day of the Feast (7:37–8:59).
    1.   Jesus the Fountain of Life (7:37–52.)
    (a.)   The Words of the Lord (7:37–39).
    (b.)   The Division in the Multitude (7:40–44).
    (c.)   The Chief Priests and Pharisees (7:45–52).
    2.   Jesus the Light of the World (8:12–20).
    3.   The Lifting up of the Son of Man (8:21–30).
    4.   Last Words on and after the Feast of Tabernacles (8:31–59).
    (a.)   Whose Servants are the Jews? (8:31–36).
    (b.)   Whose Children are the Jews? (8:37–47).

(c.) *The Eternal Majesty of Christ* (8:48–59).

IV. **The Conflict with the Unbelieving Jews Reaching its Climax (9:1–12:50).**

(A.) *The Healing of the Man Born Blind* (9:1–41).
1. *The Fact itself* (9:1–12).
2. *Investigation by the Pharisees* (9:13–34).
(a.) *First Appearance of the Man before the Pharisees* (9:13–17).
(b.) *Questioning his Parents* (9:18–23).
(c.) *Second Appearance and Expulsion of the Man Born Blind* (9:24–34).
3. *Jesus the Saviour of the Blind and the Judge of the Seeing* (9:35–41).

(B.) *The Discourses Following the Healing of the Man Born Blind* (10:1–42).
1. *First Discourse* (10:1–21).
(a.) *Christ the Shepherd* (10:1–6).
(b.) *Christ the Door* (10:7–10).
(c.) *One Flock and one Shepherd* (10:11–18).
(d.) *Impression Made by these Words on the Jews* (10:19–21).
2. *Second Discourse on the Feast of the Dedication* (10:22–42).
(a.) *Historical Introduction* (10:22–24).
(b.) *First Section of the Discourse: I and the Father are One* (10:25–31).
(c.) *Second Part of the Discourse. Christ's Defence against the Charge of Blasphemy* (10:32–39).
(d.) *Christ's Retreat to Percea* (10:40–42).

(C.) *The Raising of Lazarus. The Crisis in Judæa* (11:1–57).
1. *Sickness and Death of Lazarut, and Message to Jesus* (11:1–16).
2. *The Miracle of the Raising of Lazarus* (11:17–44).
(a.) *Arrival of Jesus and Conversation with Martha* (11:17–27).
(b.) *Meeting with Mary* (11:28–37).
(c.) *Jesus at the Tomb* (11:38–44).
3. *The Effect of the Miracle* (11:45–57).

VI. Appendix. The Appearance of Christ at the Lake of Galilee (21)

- (a.) On those Present at the Tomb (11:45, 46).
- (b.) On the Chief Priests (11:47, 53).
- (c.) The Lord's Retreat into Ephraim (11:54–57).
  - (D.) The End of the Public Ministry of Christ (12:1–50).
    1. The Supper at Bethany (12:1–8).
    2. Excitement among the Common People and Counsel of the Chief Priests to Put Lazarus to Death (12:9–11).
    3. Entrance into Jerusalem (12:12–19).
    4. The Greeks Knocking at the Door of the Kingdom (12:20–36).
      - (a.) The Historical Fact (12:20–22).
      - (b.) Significance of this Fact (12:23–36).
        1. For the Lord Himself (12:23–30).
        2. For the World (12:31–33).
        3. For Israel (12:34–36).
    5. Final Review of the Unbelief of the Jews (12:37–43).
      - (a.) Their Unbelief Prophesied by Isaiah (12:37–41).
      - (b.) Cowardly Fear of the Pharisees (12:42, 43).
    6. Summing up of the Lord's Testimony (12:44–50).

THIRD PART.—CHAPTERS 13–21

the triumph of faith—the incarnate word glorified among his own

section first: the parting discourses of the lord (13:1–17:26)

I. Historical Introduction (13:1–30).
1. Jesus Washing the Disciples' Feet (13:1–17).
2. Judas Iscariot Forced to Withdraw (13:18–30).

II. First Parting Words Addressed to the Eleven (13:31–14:4).
1. The Son of Man Glorified (13:31, 32).
2. The Imminent Departure (13:33).
3. The New Commandment (13:34, 35).
4. Peter's Interruption Answered by the Lord (13:36–38).
5. The Disciples Comforted Concerning the Lord's Departure (14:1–4).

III. Further Interruptions of the Disciples Answered by the Lord (14:5–11).
1. Thomas (14:5–7).
2. Philip (14:8–11).

IV. The Parting Words Continued (14:12–31).
1. The Disciples Doing the Works of Jesus (14:12–14).
2. Praying for Another Comforter (14:15–17).
3. The Lord Coming with the Father (14:18–21).
4. To Whom will He Manifest Himself t (14:22–24).
5. The Teaching of the Holy Spirit (14:25, 26).
6. The Peace of Jesus (14:27).
7. The Believers' Joy in Christ's Departure (14:28, 29).
8. Jesus and the Prince of the World (14:30, 31).

V. New Parting Discourse (15:1–16:33).
1. The Vine and the Branches (15:1–8).
2. Abiding in His Love by Keeping His Commandments (15:9–17).
3. The World's Hatred against the Disciples (15:18–25).
4. Jesus Sending the Spirit (15:26–16:15).
5. Last Words to the Disciples (16:16–33).

VI. The High Priest's Prayer (17:1–26).
1. Introductory Remarks
2. The High Priest Praying for Himself (17:1–5).
3. The High Priest Praying for the Disciples (17:6–19).
4. The High Priest Praying for All Believers (17:20–24).
5. Conclusion of the High Priest's Prayer (17:25, 26).

section second: the history of the passion and resurrection of the lord (18:1–21:25)

I. The Capture of Jesus (18:1–11).
1. Arrival of the Band (18:1–3).
2. Jesus Meeting the Band (18:4–9).
3. Peter Striking with the Sword (18:10, 11).

II. Jesus before the High Priest (18:12–27).
1. Jesus Taken to Annas (18:12–14.)

VI. Appendix. The Appearance of Christ at the Lake of Galilee (21)

2. *First Denial of Peter (18:15–18).*
3. *Hearing of Jesus before Annas (18:19–24).*
4. *Second and Third Denial of Peter (18:25–27).*
   III. Jesus before the Governor Pilate (18:28–19:16).
1. *First Charge of the Jews (18:28–32).*
2. *Jesus the King (18:33–38¹).*
3. *Jesus and Barabbas (18:38²–40).*
4. *Scourging and Mocking of the King of the Jews (19:1–3).*
5. *Behold the Man (19:4–6).*
6. *Jesus the Son of God (19:7–11).*
7. *Cæasar's Friendship. The Governor Yields (19:12–16).*
   IV. The Execution (19:17–42).
1. *The Crucifixion (19:17, 18).*
2. *The Inscription on the Cross (19:19–22).*
3. *Dividing His Garments (19:23, 24).*
4. *Last Will of Mary's Son (19:25–27).*
5. *Death of Jesus (19:28–30).*
6. *Piercing His Side (19:31–37).*
7. *The Burial of Christ (19:38–42).*
   V. The Resurrection of Jesus (20:1–31).
1. *Peter and John at the Tomb (20:1–10).*
2. *Mary Magdalene (20:11–18).*
3. *First Appearance before the Disciples (20:19–23).*
4. *Second Appearance before the Disciples, including Thomas (20:24–29).*
5. *Conclusion (20:30, 31).*
   VI. Appendix. The Appearance of Christ at the Lake of Galilee (21:1–25)

www.ingramcontent.com/pod-product-compliance
Lightning Source LLC
Chambersburg PA
CBHW050852160426
43194CB00011B/2129